Festival and Events Management

An international arts and culture perspective

Festival and Events Management

An international arts and culture perspective

Edited by

Ian Yeoman

Martin Robertson

Jane Ali-Knight

Siobhan Drummond

Una McMahon-Beattie

Routledge
Taylor & Francis Group

LONDON AND NEW YORK

First published by Butterworth-Heinemann

This edition published 2011 by Routledge
2 Park Square, Milton Park, Abingdon, Oxon OX14 4RN
711 Third Avenue, New York, NY 10017, USA

Routledge is an imprint of the Taylor & Francis Group, an informa business

British Library Cataloguing in Publication Data
A catalogue record for this book is available from the British Library

Library of Congress Cataloguing in Publication Data
Higgins, Jonathan.
  An introduction to SNG and ENG microwave/Jonathan Higgins.
  p.cm – (Media manual)
  1. Direct broadcast satellite television. 2. Microwave communication systems.
  3. Electronic news gathering.
  I. Title. II. Media manuals

  TK6677.H54 2003
  621.382-dc22

ISBN: 978-0-7506-5872-0

Contents

Contents

Foreword

As Director of *Unique Events*, a company at the forefront of the cultural and creative festival and event industry, I am always heartened when real interest; real passion; real ideas; and a real sense of professionalism is given to the running of any festival or large cultural event. There are some things that come from the gut, from a sense of what will work and what won't. Ensuring that an experience is one of amazing spectacle, or emotional enthralment, or perhaps just out-and-out inspiration, takes something special. Believe me, I know.

Nevertheless, there are also a lot of things which can make festivals and events not work, things that no amount of amour and unbridled hard work can repair. The need for professionalism cannot go unanswered. The cultural, artistic and fun experiences of people are becoming more wide-ranging as the world becomes an ever smaller stage in which to set up and view a performance. Whether staged in a village, a town, in the city or in the countryside, the people that come to enjoy, to watch or to perform all know what has quality and what does not. Professionalism means knowledge and understanding. A book which is placed to offer that, and which prepares to view all management aspects of it, and to do so in various international contexts, has to be a good thing.

Enjoy the read. Remember, events don't just happen, they are made to happen!

Peter Irvine
Director of Unique Events
Edinburgh

Foreword

In Scotland, Festivals and Events are seen as an important part of the country's strategy for economic development. The Scottish Executive's approach is designed to link in to the tourism and cultural strategies and to encourage more people to visit Scotland to experience sporting cultural and business events.

Within the overall brand for Scotland there are five main themes which reflect what visitors are looking for in Scotland.

Freedom of Scotland including touring, island hopping and the natural environment.

Active Scotland including winter sports, walking, golf, cycling, fishing, adventure activities and indoor and outdoor pursuits.

City breaks including shopping, nightlife, food and drink.

Culture and Heritage including the performing arts, the visual arts, historic attractions, museums, galleries and genealogy.

Business tourism including conferences, exhibitions and incentives.

The interesting and important realisation is how festivals and events cut through all five themes and are critical to the reputation, confidence and success of a nation. This book encompasses all of these themes very effectively.

Peter Lederer
Chairman, VisitScotland

Contributors

Jane Ali-Knight is currently Programme Leader for the new Leisure and Festival Management programme at Napier University, Edinburgh. She has presented at major international and national conferences and has published in the areas of wine tourism, tourism marketing and management. Current research interests include tourist motivation and experiences in wine regions; wine festivals and regional transformation; and the role and impacts of festivals to the Edinburgh economy. She has extensive experience in conference organization in Australia and was also conference convenor for the 'Running Events in Scotland: International, National and Local Perspectives' conference (2003).

Heather Anderson is a lecturer in tourism, University of Paisley; previous experience includes hospitality management and positions in the arts and entertainment industries: Front of House Manager, Crucible Theatre, Sheffield; Artistic Director of Le Meridien hotel entertainment programme, Phuket, Thailand; Box Office Manager, Scottish Opera Theatre Royal, Glasgow; Front of House and Customer Care Training Services Manager at The Glasgow Royal Concert Hall. She was a participant in 'The Disney Approach to Quality Service', Disneyworld, Florida. She is a qualified trainer, experienced lecturer and consultant. Specialist research interests include: quality service and marketing in the arts, events, leisure and tourism industries, the development of alternative tourism, the ethics of tourism, quality assurance and evaluation of the tourist experience.

John Beaumont-Kerridge is a Principal Teaching Fellow (special projects) at the University of Luton Business School. In addition to teaching internet marketing management and research methods, he has a primary role with regard to developing online learning systems for the Business School. Current research interests include marketing policy and planning applied to the public sector (combined with online issues), multivariate marketing research techniques and service delivery and quality. His PhD thesis (2001) was entitled 'Market Orientation and Service Quality of Public Sector Sport and Recreation Providers: a case study approach'.

Zuleika Beaven is a researcher in arts management at the University of Greenwich Business School and has developed the BA Events Management programme. She has worked on a range of arts projects and festivals and has a research interest in management practice in music organizations.

Steve Brown is one of Australia's most respected event designers, producers and marketers. He began in the event industry at the Adelaide Festival Centre in 1975 and, with the Adelaide Festival of Arts, worked on every Adelaide Festival from 1975 until 1997. He moved to Canberra in 1984 to take up an appointment as Director of the Arts Council of the Australian Capital Territory and late in 1985 formed his own event design and management company, Visible Management. In 2001 he was appointed an Honorary Visiting Scholar at Flinders University and – with the endorsement of the South Australian Tourism Commission and Australian Major Events – was instrumental in the development and delivery of the undergraduate and graduate programmes in festival and event management there. In 2003 Steve continues to lecture at Flinders University and has commenced work on his PhD on the event industry. He continues to design and oversee the management of a wide variety of corporate and cultural events.

Jack Carlsen is the Malayan United Industries (MUI) Chair in Tourism and Hospitality Studies within the Curtin Business School, Curtin University of Technology, Western Australia. He is also Co-Director of the Curtin Sustainable Tourism Centre, which provides leadership in teaching, research, policy and consulting in sustainable tourism. At the national level, Jack provides a leadership and coordination role in the Cooperative Research Centre for Sustainable Tourism. He is currently co-authoring a book on family firms in tourism and hospitality and conducts research into many aspects of tourism management, including events management.

Ros Derrett is on the academic staff of the School of Tourism and Hospitality Management at Southern Cross University, Lismore, NSW, Australia. She delivers programmes in event planning and management, special interest tourism, and tourism planning and the environment at undergraduate and postgraduate level. Her particular research interests include cultural and heritage tourism, community consultation, regional development and festivals and special events. Her doctoral investigation demonstrates how community cultural festivals reflect and determine a community's sense of itself and place. Ros is Project Manager at the Centre for Regional Tourism Research at Southern Cross University, part of the national CRC in sustainable tourism.

Stephen A. Doyle is a lecturer in marketing in the School of Marketing and Tourism at Napier University, Edinburgh. Key areas of research and teaching are situated in retailing and retail marketing with a particular focus on research in retail design.

Siobhan Drummond is a senior lecturer in tourism at the University of Paisley, Scotland. Siobhan has worked in a managerial capacity in a range of tourism posts in both the private and public sector from hotel companies to national tourist organizations. An experienced lecturer and consultant, her research interests centre on the management of service quality in tourism, development of small businesses and the relationship between culture and tourism. Siobhan has authored a range of articles in the field of quality and edited a text on quality and heritage.

Kevin Fields has been teaching at the Birmingham College of Food, Tourism and Creative Studies since 1991. He is subject leader for both events planning and convention management, and also teaches food and beverage management. Prior to entering education, he worked as a catering consultant and also spent time in the convention and exhibition Industry.

C. Michael Hall is Head of the Department of Tourism at the University of Otago, New Zealand and Honorary Professor in the Department of Marketing, University of Stirling, Scotland. He is Co-editor of *Current Issues in Tourism* and has published widely in the tourism, leisure and environmental history fields. Current research interests include temporary mobility, SME tourism entrepreneurship and regional development, gastronomy and cool climate wine.

Lee Harrison is Managing Director of Fairdene Productions, which he established in 1993. Fairdene Productions organizes events ranging from conferences to multimedia spectaculars, fashion extravaganzas, film premieres, cocktail parties, large dinners and product launches. Lee has also hosted numerous internationally acclaimed film directors, producers and actors. Lee's background ranges from being a community worker and nightclub manager to film and TV production.

Jane James is Associate Professor and Head of Cultural Tourism at Flinders University in South Australia, where she coordinates the award-winning Bachelor of Cultural Tourism degree and the graduate programme in festival and event management. She has developed curricula for expanding areas in tourism education, including festival and event management, in partnership with industry, both in Australia and overseas. Jane has also taught in graduate programmes in heritage and cultural resource management in the UK and Canada. Her research interests lie in the areas of evaluation of visitor experiences at heritage sites, and at festivals and events, and in the effective and sustainable management of natural and cultural resources. She has been involved with the evaluation of the cultural, environmental and economic impact of numerous festivals and events and in the subsequent development of professional development workshops and university courses in this field.

Eleri Jones is Head of the Welsh School of Hospitality, Tourism and Leisure Management. Eleri project manages a portfolio of European Structural funded projects aimed at destination, business and employee development, as well as supervising a number of PhD students. She has a Masters degree from the University of London and a PhD from the University of Wales.

Karl Knox is senior lecturer in information management at Nottingham Trent University. Prior to joining NTU, Karl has worked at a number of universities gaining a wide variety of experience both culturally and academically. Karl has been on staff at The Robert Gordon University, in Aberdeen, Scotland, Leeds Metropolitan University, Dubai Polytechnic, UAE and Southern Cross University, in Australia. His industrial experience has been gained in a variety of five-star establishments worldwide, including: Inter Continental Hotels, Hilton International Hotels, the Dorchester Hotel and the Laneborough Hotel. His research interests are in the field of information management and information strategy and the process of information strategy development within organizations.

Chantal Laws is a lecturer in heritage management at the University of Greenwich Business School. She has worked as Operations Manager in a large London music venue and teaches on the BA Events Management programme at Greenwich.

Phyllis Laybourn is a senior lecturer in psychology and a Teaching Fellow at Napier University, Edinburgh. She completed her degree and PhD at the University of Dundee and thereafter took up postdoctoral research at the University of Oxford. She currently balances research interests in cognitive psychology (the areas of decision making and critical thinking) with an active interest in innovations in teaching and learning in higher education.

Kenneth MacMillan Wardrop is a tourism professional with nearly 20 years of experience in the development and implementation of tourism strategy and policy, the provision of tourism infrastructure, visitor facilities and attractions, and the delivery of high-profile events primarily in the City of Stirling and most recently in the City of Edinburgh, Scotland. Major projects have included the refurbishment of the National Wallace Monument and other historic properties in Stirling's old town, the Rob Roy and Trossachs Visitor Centre in Callander, the 700th Anniversary Celebrations for the Battle of Stirling Bridge in 1997, the Edinburgh Capital Christmas Programme, the Edinburgh International Science Festival and International Festival of the Sea 2003. He is also a Winston Churchill Travelling Fellow investigating tourism led urban regeneration projects in North America.

Peter Mason is Professor of Tourism Managment and Head of the Tourism, Leisure and Sport Management Department, University of Luton. He worked previously at Massey University, New Zealand and the University of Plymouth, UK. He is the author of over forty refereed publications and three books. The main focus of his research is tourism impacts, planning and management issues.

Guy Masterman is a senior lecturer and the MSc Events Mangement course leader at the UK Centre for Events Management at Leeds Metropolitan University. For 12 years he was an independent consultant working in sports marketing and licensing, sports and music events and business development. His clients have included Coca-Cola, Pepsi, Nabisco, Capital Radio Group, Chelsea FC, Team Scotland and international sports governing bodies: the ATP Tour, IYRU and the World Wheelchair Sports Federation. He has also worked extensively with the charities Scope, Muscular Dystrophy and Sparks, and sports stars Seb Coe, Steve Backley and Lennox Lewis. His events include the Coca-Cola Music Festival, Pepsi Extravaganza, Nabisco Masters Doubles, Nigel Benn fights, World Games, and concerts at major venues with diverse acts such as Ray Charles, B.B. King, Take That and orchestras at Kenwood.

Lester D. Matthews is a lecturer in strategic management, events planning, research methods, marketing and outdoor adventurous activities at Birmingham College of Food, Tourism and Creative Studies. He initially practised as an architect, designing and administering projects worth over

£14m, including new-build, conversions and alterations, before running his own business as an outdoor activities consultant and instructor. He is currently conducting consultancy and marketing research in the UK and Finland and has coaching and marketing development interests in Finland.

Fiona McDonald joined Fairdene Productions as Event Coordinator in January 2002 bringing with her a Wellington Polytechnic and PRINZ (Public Relations Institute of New Zealand) Certificate in Public Relations, a Bachelors Degree in Education and a Diploma of Teaching. She is set to begin a Postgraduate Diploma in Business Administration endorsed in Communications.

Una McMahon-Beattie is a lecturer, researcher and consultant at the University of Ulster. Her research interests focus on the areas of revenue management, variable pricing and consumer trust. She has published widely as an author and book editor in the UK and internationally. Una is Practice Editor for the *Journal of Revenue and Pricing Management*.

Nigel Morgan is a University of Wales reader in tourism based at the Welsh School of Hospitality, Tourism and Leisure Management. He has worked in tourism, marketing, public relations and leisure policy in local authorities in South Wales and at the Sports Council for Wales. He has a PhD from Exeter University and has written a number of papers and books on resort promotion and tourism and leisure advertising and branding.

Marina Novelli is senior lecturer in tourism studies at the Centre for Tourism Policy Studies, University of Brighton, UK. Italian by origin, she completed a PhD entitled 'Rural and Farm Tourism: a comparative study of Apulia (Italy) and the West Country (UK)'. Her main research interests include rural development and tourism, niche tourism markets such as wine and food, festivals and events, and ecotourism, as well as tourism planning and management in the international context. Her most recent research activity focuses on wine and gourmet tourism, tourism clusters and the local economy, integrated quality management and tourism, consumers' behaviour in the rural environment and other niche tourism forms of consumption. She has been involved in a variety of European planning and management consulting projects focusing on regional development and tourism. She is also part of an Italian research team sponsored by the Ministry of Universities and led by Prof. A. Celant at Universitá La Sapienza (Rome), on 'Tourism and Economic

Growth: Local Factors and Territorial Competitiveness'. She is visiting lecturer at the University of Bari (Italy) and at the MIB School of Management in Trieste (Italy).

Razaq Raj is a senior lecturer in events management at Leeds Metropolitan University. His research interests include community events, outdoor events, impacts and risks, and financial management for events. He has published work and delivered papers at international conferences on special events, financial management in events, information technology and events sponsorship.

Martin Robertson is programme leader for the undergraduate tourism management programmes at Napier University, Edinburgh. He has published and presented papers in the areas of event management, leisure marketing and urban tourism. He has co-edited a book on the policy and practice of managing tourism in cities. His specialist research areas include event management and destination marketing, the socio-economics of urban tourism and the social science of leisure management. He has extensive public and private sector work experience in the tourism, travel and conference management industries, both in the UK and overseas.

Kristy Rusher is a graduate student in the Department of Tourism, University of Otago, Dunedin, New Zealand. Kristy was formerly also an assistant lecturer in the Department of Tourism but moved to a position with a regional tourism organization in the South Island of New Zealand at the end of 2002.

Galal Salem is a lecturer at Helwan University, Egypt, seconded to undertake PhD research at the Welsh School of Hospitality, Tourism and Leisure Management sponsored by the Egyptian Ministry of Tourism. Holding a Masters degree from Helwan University, Galal has extensive experience of events management in an Egyptian context.

Paul Stansbie has been teaching at the Birmingham College of Food, Tourism and Creative Studies since 1994. He teaches operations, food and beverage, and finance management, at graduate and undergraduate level. Prior to his career in education, Paul had spent a number of years working in food and beverage for Marriott Hotels, the theme restaurant development division for Six Continents, as well as holding management positions in a full service four-star hotel.

Gordon Waitt teaches human geography in the School of Geosciences at the University of Wollongong, Australia. He is co-author of *Introducing Human Geography* (Sydney: Pearson, 2000). His research centres on tourism geographies, particularly the relationship between tourism activities and place-making processes.

Paul Walters has an employment history that spans 14 years within the area of music management, exhibition design and project management, touring theatre management, film production, marketing/sponsorship and public relations. This wealth of knowledge and experience has enabled him to undertake a senior lecturer position within the area of Events management at the UK Centre for Events Management at Leeds Metropolitan University. Paul's area of proficiency over the past 4 years at the UK centre covers law and licensing, technical production for indoor and outdoor events and communication through multi-media platforms. His areas of research and professional activities include: festivals and cultural events; planning and operational management of large-scale outdoor events linked directly to the deployment of an Event Manual; strategic development for outdoor events through the unitary development plans for cities and rural areas. Papers directly related to the aforementioned areas have been written and presented at the EuroCHIRE conference 2002 and IFEA conference 2003.

Emma Wood is senior lecturer in events marketing within the UK Centre for Event Management based at Leeds Metropolitan University. Emma has substantial experience in a number of industries undertaking marketing management and marketing research roles and has worked overseas in Australia and South East Asia. She has considerable experience of quantitative research relating principally to small business and public sector marketing, and has been part of numerous research teams. Recently, she acted as Project Director for an events-based impact study in Blackburn and is currently Director of the most comprehensive postal questionnaire survey of small firms in the UK events sector. She is invited regularly to present at national and international conferences and has a good track record of dissemination via journals.

Ian Yeoman is the editor of a range of publications, including *Journal of Revenue and Pricing Management, Yield Management: Strategies for the Service Industries*, and a new book, *Revenue Management and Pricing*. Ian has taught revenue management on a number of university courses and is presently the Scenario Planning Manager with Scotland's National Tourist Organization, VisitScotland.

Introduction

Defining the management of festivals and events

An entire global industry of festivals and events has evolved and developed since the early 1990s. The phenomenal growth, coupled with increased consumer awareness and choice, requires the industry to manage the sector effectively and efficiently to ensure sustained development and growth in the future. Many of the products and services on offer are entering the mature stage of their lifecycle, while others are at the embryonic stage. The need for management and education has become more important as people make life-long careers in this area. The purpose of this book is to highlight and understand the management of festivals and events and provide guidance for those in the industry or embarking on entering the sector. The approach is holistic in nature, from the evolution of festivals and events, through the stages of policy development, to operational issues and strategic management. Examples are used throughout the book to cover the key management functions and these range from local to international cases from around the world.

On a global basis there is unprecedented interest in festivals and events – at international and national level, in cities and towns, villages and hamlets, and in rural and coastal areas. Everyone wants to celebrate their particular form of culture, tradition, difference or similarity with others. Festivals and events can help promote their destination and attract tourists – they can be viewed as a new form of tourism in which to anchor economic prosperity and development. A new industry has grown up around this emerging sector, and politicians and entrepreneurs have also grasped the value of this worldwide interest. The image of a destination, product or service can be enhanced or damaged by the success or failure of a festival or event.

The characteristics of festivals and events are unique and as such, no one standard model of management fits all. These characteristics include intangibility, production often taking place at the same time as consumption and perishability. Festivals and events have different levels of operating costs and they fall into both the not-for-profit and profit-making categories. Their purpose varies – some have an entertainment and educational remit and can be used to bring different communities together, others can be used for business promotion. The role of sponsorship is often an important one in defining their objectives. Some festivals and events can be arts related, while others can focus on other forms of culture such as sport. They can range from small-scale, locally based events, to large international festivals.

No matter what the reason is for hosting a festival or event, there is a wide range of customers, each with different expectations, and this will impact on the management processes considered for each individual festival or event. The management model adopted needs to match the requirements of all those involved in each stage of the individual festival or event, and tools such as those employed in managing projects and quality are useful.

Although festivals and events vary enormously in type and form, the management issues relating to this wide range are often surprisingly similar and include working within an increasingly competitive environment with decreasing resources and more discerning and sophisticated consumers.

This book addresses the wide-ranging operational and management issues of such a diverse sector, allowing the reader to understand how festivals and events are developed, why they are hosted and how we manage them. It also illustrates best practice through a variety of international case studies and offers guidance and professional advice.

Part A is an overview of the festivals, events and cultural experience, highlighting the definitions, concepts and internationalism of such a subject.

Part B focuses on the management process of design and creation, allowing the reader to explore the concepts of design, visitor management, service quality, and information and communication technology.

Part C considers key operational areas such as marketing and retail operations and illustrates how festivals and events can be used as a strategic marketing opportunity. It includes an overview of revenue generation as well as discussion on merchandising, catering, ticketing and pricing operations that are needed in today's competitive environment.

Part D analyses the roles of politics and policy in festivals and events. It examines the world of public sector strategic management in which local and national politics prevail, as well as economic evaluation, decision making, sponsorship and risk.

Finally, *Part E* reflects on international practice in festival and event management through a range of case studies from wine tourism in Italy to considerations on the Olympic Games in Sydney.

Experience the variety of insights and enjoy the book's examination into a rapidly growing management area – *Festival and Events Management: An International Arts and Culture Perspective.*

The Editorial Team

Ian Yeoman, VisitScotland

Martin Robertson, Napier University

Jane Ali-Knight, Napier University

Siobhan Drummond, Paisley University

Una McMahon-Beattie, University of Ulster

Festivals, events and the cultural experience

Introduction to arts, culture and leisure

Jane Ali-Knight and Martin Robertson

Introduction

This chapter introduces and defines art, culture and leisure. It will examine the development of these concepts, particularly in relation to the cultural economy and evolution of festivals and events. The issue of participation and government involvement in arts, culture and leisure is explored.

A case study examining cultural policy and the Edinburgh Festivals is included to show the interface of the above concepts, particularly in relation to festivals and events.

Arts for arts' sake

The term 'arts' is often closely linked to festivals and events (the Adelaide *Arts* Festival, Perth International *Arts* Festival, Harrogate

Arts Festival) and the arts are seen to be an integral part of any celebration of a country's history and culture. Traditionally, the arts were seen to incorporate works and activities such as classical music, opera, theatre, ballet, painting (fine art) and sculpture (Hughes, 2000). However, the arts today include a wider collection of activities such as contemporary dance, film, popular music and the various components of the visual arts. Indeed, the programme of any international arts festival reflects the diversity of the contemporary arts and its audience base. For example, the 2003 programme for the Perth International Arts Festival included traditional arts such as theatre, opera, dance and classical music along with contemporary arts such as the Lotteries Film Season (an outdoor world film festival), International Writers Festival, Visual Arts Festival, Johnnie Walker Watershed (outdoor live alternative music stage), C.Y.O. Connor Bush Fleadh (folk festival held out in the hills in Perth) and an Indigenous Arts Showcase.

There is a generally held view that people who are involved in or participate in the arts (artists, performers) often are involved because of a 'love of the arts' and not for any financial gain, although once people reach the top of their profession they are certainly no longer struggling actors or performers and will often subsidize younger performers in their particular artform. LIPA (the Liverpool Institute of Performing Arts), a forum for the integration of popular and academic culture, partly funded by Paul McCartney (of 'The Beatles' fame), is a good example of this. The centre is dedicated to providing the best teaching and learning for people who want to pursue and maintain a lasting career in the popular performing arts economy.

What is leisure?

Grainger-Jones (1999) defines leisure as the 'application of disposable time to an activity which is perceived by the individual as either beneficial or enjoyable'. Actually, defining leisure is surprisingly difficult; there is no precise meaning, as individuals and groups interpret leisure differently. To one person, leisure time may be best spent watching soaps on the TV, while to another, running a marathon may be a wise way to engage in leisure activities. Torkildsen (2000) further breaks down this definition to say that leisure has four constituent parts:

■ Leisure as time
■ Leisure as expenditure

- Leisure as a state of being
- Leisure as antithesis – something which is not work or enforced.

The leisure industry is one of the largest in the UK, worth more than £1.7 billion a week (Family Expenditure Survey 2000–2001) and responsible for 25–38% of consumer spending. Leisure supply is often facilitated by central and/or local government directly, which often leads to issues such as finance constraint, lack of shareholder collateral and the difficult role and place of quangos such as the Arts and Sports Councils. It is seen as one of the leisure functions of local authorities to directly promote and in some cases fund festival and events programmes, and this is again reflected in the case studies in this text.

Festivals and events are therefore a significant and integral segment of the leisure industry. This is examined further in the Edinburgh Festivals Case Study in this chapter.

Culture and events

Culture is the mechanism through which individuals, communities and nations define themselves (*A Cultural Policy for the City of Edinburgh*, 1999).

Meanings of culture have grown and developed but universally accepted definitions are still lacking. Tomlinson (1991) notes that hundreds of definitions exist, indicating a level of confusion, or that this area is so diverse that it can accommodate all these definitions. The solution proposed by Tomlinson is to concentrate on the way that it is used. As a process it is derived from anthropology and sociology (Richards, 1996) and the term may refer to a process of intellectual, spiritual and aesthetic development. Culture is very much seen as a *process* or a *product* and, if so, the product of individual or group activities. For example, culture can range from 'high' culture such as the arts to 'popular' and 'contemporary' culture which can include such diverse activities as football, music and television.

In the field of tourism, culture is seen very much as a product and a process. Bonink and Richards (1992) identified two approaches: the 'sites and monuments approach' which focuses on the type of attraction, and the 'conceptual approach' which attempts to describe the motives and meaning attached to cultural tourism.

Extending the definition to include cultural festivals and events it can be seen that cultural events have benefits to both the arts world and the tourism destination. Many cultural events are now even competing with major events in terms of economic and sociocultural impacts. Paul Gudgin, Director of the Edinburgh Fringe Festival, cites how the 2002 Fringe Festival sold more tickets and brought in more revenue than the 2002 Commonwealth Games held in Manchester. As can be seen in further case studies in this text, cultural events are growing internationally and are significant economic and cultural drivers for communities and host destinations.

Cultural economy

French sociologist Pierre Bourdieu championed the concept of cultural capital in the 1970s, and the economic significance of the arts and cultural sector has long been overlooked. Cultural organizations have traditionally been seen as of little economic significance and an underlying resource for education or business. As well as being sources of learning and knowledge, the cultural and creative industries are now increasingly recognized as an economic sector in their own right. According to research undertaken by the European Commission, around 7.2 million people are employed in the cultural sector. Between 1995 and 1999, employment in the sector grew by an average of 2.1% a year, making it one of the fastest growing areas of the European economy.

It can be seen therefore that there is a new relationship emerging between culture and economy. In policy terms the problem has been the language difficulties between economics and culture and the struggle with the increasingly central role of cultural value within economic production (O'Connor, 2003).

Culture is central to promoting the continued renaissance of the city and has a role to play in creating a more inclusive and sustainable community. Culture creates jobs, attracts investment and enriches the lives of people who live and work in and visit the city. Culture brings distinction to the image and profile of the city; it enriches the experience of the city centre and makes each community unique in its history or sense of place. Culture is an essential creative force in the new knowledge-based economy and helps to build skills and confidence in people. Cities are finally realizing the economic potential of their cultural products and are looking strategically at positioning and supporting them. Manchester City

Council in their cultural strategy acknowledge the importance of the cultural economy and aim 'to maximise the direct and indirect benefits of the City's cultural economy, its contribution to Manchester's distinctive identity and to innovation in business and education' (Manchester City Council, 2002).

Case study

Edinburgh, festival city

Edinburgh's Festivals are a vital part of city life – both for local residents and for the hundreds of visitors who come to Edinburgh each year (Steve Cardownie, 2001, Festivals Champion, Edinburgh City Council).

Edinburgh is host to fifteen diverse national and international festivals annually (see Table 1.1), as well as several community and participative festivals. These range from the prominent and internationally known Hogmanay and the Edinburgh International Festival (EIF) to lesser-known but equally important festivals such as the Harp Festival and the Scottish International Storytelling Festival. The festivals are a vital part of Edinburgh's life, with principal impacts lying in the area of cultural, social and economic benefits and civic pride.

A study by the Scottish Tourist Board (now VisitScotland) in 1990 measured the economic impact of the festivals. Results showed that in Edinburgh and the Lothians, £44 million of direct expenditure, £9 million local income and 1300 full-time equivalent jobs would not exist if the festivals did not take place. In Scotland as a whole, direct expenditure measured £72 million, resulting in over 3000 full-time equivalent jobs (Scottish Tourist Board, 1991). The multiplier effect on tourism businesses in the city is also significant with hotel occupancy rates typically soaring to 80–90% in the capital during the festival period. Research in 2002 shows that the city's festivals generate more than £120 million for the city. Edinburgh City Council claim to be making £150 million yearly from the festivals, making Edinburgh one of the fastest growing cities in the UK (The Guardian, 2002).

Compared with their peers in the UK and internationally, the festivals provide extremely good value to the city. Festivals with the turnover of Edinburgh's would, on a national average, expect to receive about £300k more in local subsidy, while internationally public support accounts for approximately 42% of major European festivals' budget (against EIF 35.4%). Smaller festivals receive about 35% (Edinburgh 28%) and fringe festivals 11% (Edinburgh 7%). Australian and even American festivals also enjoy a greater proportion of public support. For example, the Perth International Arts Festival (PIAF), Australia's oldest and largest multi-arts festival and the only statewide multi-arts festival in the country, also known as the 'Edinburgh of the South', has received a $1 million donation from Japanese businessman Haruhisa Handa. This donation is the largest single philanthropic donation ever given to an Australian festival (Perth International Arts Festival, 2003).

The overall economic impact of PIAF is estimated to be $22.4m. (The Australian Bureau of Statistics estimates that for every dollar invested in the arts industry an additional $2.80 is generated through direct and indirect involvement with the industry. Applying this multiplier effect to the total expenditure of the 2001 Festival results in $22.4m.)

Table 1.1 Edinburgh's key festivals

Festival	Date
Edinburgh's Hogmanay	December/January
Puppet Animation Festival	March–April
Edinburgh International Science Festival	April
Harp Festival	April
Scottish International Children's Festival	May–June
Edinburgh International Jazz and Blues Festival	July–August
Edinburgh Tattoo	August
Edinburgh Festival Fringe	August
Edinburgh International Book Festival	August
Edinburgh International Film Festival	August
Edinburgh International Festival	August
Edinburgh International Television Festival	August
Edinburgh Mela	August–September
Scottish International Storytelling Festival	October–November
Fiddle Festival	November
Capital Christmas	December

Cultural policy: the Edinburgh Festivals Strategy

The Edinburgh Festivals Strategy was launched in 2001; it followed the Cultural Policy (1999) for the city and was commissioned and funded by the City of Edinburgh Council with financial support from the Scottish Arts Council and Scottish Enterprise Edinburgh and Lothian (Graham Devlin and Associates, 2001). It was developed in tandem with an Events Strategy for the city, which was launched in December 2002. Both strategies are evidence of Edinburgh's commitment to position itself as the 'festival city' and their realization of the importance of festival and events to the cultural and economic viability of Edinburgh.

The Festivals Strategy was a result of personal interviews with key stakeholders in the festivals and tourism industry, discussion with core groups (i.e. Joint Festivals Working Group) and extensive desk research, which included benchmarking Edinburgh festivals against other cities.

The strategy recognized the need for a shared vision which the City of Edinburgh Council (CEC), the various festivals and other interested parties could sign up to with a common plan of action. The key aims the strategy hoped to achieve are summarized and highlighted below:

- A year-round programme of cultural festivals and events
- A range of independent festivals, satisfactorily balancing the demands of creative ambition, social objectives and commercial viability
- Maintenance of a summer programme which continues to be recognized as the pre-eminent international festival in the world, complemented by a programme of festivals and events at other times of the year which achieves an equally high level of quality and diversity
- The involvement of a broad range of Edinburgh's citizens and encouragement of festival initiatives which address social inclusion goals for the city
- A learning culture around the festivals
- Interconnectedness between the festivals, enabling cooperation, joint initiatives and the sharing of resources, stimulating a positive sense of creative competition
- A healthy relationship between CEC and the festivals
- An explicit recognition of the festivals' worth which is reflected in appropriate funding
- An effective advocacy and marketing campaign based on the above and involving CEC, Scottish and Area tourism boards, Special Area of Conservation (SAC), The Audience Business, Scottish Enterprise Edinburgh and Lothian, festivals and other cultural institutions, intended to develop Edinburgh's reputation as the festival city and as a city of culture, both nationally and internationally.

If the above aims are to be achieved they need to be grounded in strategic objectives, which will help to realize the city's vision. The Strategy Implementation Group holds responsibility for the implementation and monitoring of the Festivals Strategy Action Plan. The Action Plan is critical as it addresses recommendations, implementation partners, timescale and resource implications. Paul Gudgin, Director of the Edinburgh Festival Fringe, comments that 'it is helping to foster closer working relationships across many of their departments, and between all the festivals and a number of other key agencies' (Edinburgh Festival Fringe: Annual Report 2002, http://www.edfringe.com/). Edinburgh's Festival Strategy is another clear indication of the importance and direction of Edinburgh as the festival city.

Culture, arts and the public sector: a brief history

As indicated in the section 'Culture and Events', the use of culture and cultural events has become an ever more important economic and culture drive factor for towns and cities. Moreover, the economic phenomena of cultural and cultural-driven festival and event strategies are global phenomena. The international contexts shown in this text are testimony to that. It is also true to say that the economic role of these phenomena have changed over the time as both the contributory significance of them has been realized and as shifts in economic structures have necessitated it. Nowhere else is this more clear than in cities and medium to large town conurbations. Not always by design but certainly by witness to other such developments, many cities have been searching out ways in which to secure advantage over others. Consequently, investment and development of appropriate attractions, events and concomitant infrastructure have occurred rapidly. Many cities are doing so in the belief that culture, in its various forms, is sustainable and has the potential for long-term synergy with other forms of development (Russo and van der Borg, 2002; O'Sullivan and Jackson, 2002).

The 1980s saw a proliferation of municipal government-backed arts and cultural-based projects (Bianchini and Parkinson, 1993). However, this process began throughout the western world from the 1960s onward, and can be seen as indicative of a shift from the manufacturing to the service industry as part and parcel of the emergence of a *post-industrial* western world. As the 1980s saw central government take many powers of the local government away (Voase, 1994), most certainly within Europe, the concept of cultural regeneration was born into an increasingly large array of cash-strapped local public sector *families*. Faced with a new form of living, in an environment with less commercial activity (at least for those places with a history of strong reliance on the manufacturing industry and with a population with reduced spending potential), the apparent opportunity of cultural tourism has been, for many, irresistible. Grand *cultural* product-based events emerged in Paris, in Birmingham (predominantly through the building of the conference and convention centre, the ICC), and then through South London and throughout many other conurbations in the UK as it entered the 1990s.

The record of change in the 1990s is most clearly visible. Blazing examples of these are Glasgow's *City of Culture* in 1990; Madrid's *Year of Culture* and Seville's *Exposition*, both in Spain, in 1992; and Toronto's *Arts Week* and *International Film Festival* in Canada throughout the decade. In the case of Toronto the drive in the 1990s has established the city as the capital of culture in Canada, with many now believing its strength in North America is only surpassed by New York. While each place in Europe had specific requirements, desires and hopes during this time, in all the development of culture has arisen through a reaction by the respective local government and its agencies to the needs of its people. It may be the case that, as Voase (1994) states, for the UK the encouragement of and investment in cultural events and cultural attractions in the UK was a direct reaction to a society in need of something to fill the vacuum left by the descendent manufacturing sector and the search for a new *quality of life*. This would certainly reiterate and verify the thoughts and writings of Pierre Bourdieu (1984). Or it may be that, as Hughes (1987, in Hall, 1992) infers, this new form was in fact a compensatory reaction to the otherwise deficient normal life people lived. This aside, it is most apparent that councils increased their capital investment and their applications for European Union *Structural Funds* for a great range of cultural arts and leisure-centred projects during this time (Voase, 1994; Law, 1994). In the late 1990s, and as now, festival- and event-based tourism has become of increasing importance to the public sector, with the notion of place promotion, image regeneration and the economic and social *multiplier effect* ever more central in the policy and strategy pronouncements leading to, or in the retention of, festival and event hosting and management. Further explanation of this relationship and more recent developments can be found in Chapters 3, 8 and 14.

While the character of culture itself is diffuse, the growth of theoretical approaches to it in relation to festival and events has been less so.

O'Sullivan and Jackson (2002) comment that *festival tourism* literature has tended to include all elements of events and festivals, of all sizes and organizational purpose. They further opine that the growth of literature in these areas has not been commensurate with the growth of the industry itself, although the diffuse nature of the study perspectives has. Nonetheless they are able to categorize four broad perspectives taken, namely sociological, leisure participation, community development, and tourism industry (2002: 326). Interestingly, and reflecting the increasing complexity attributed to the emerging theories on cultural events, Waterman (1998) sees the study of arts and cultural festivals as reflecting a real 'tension between festival as art and economics' and 'between culture and cultural politics'. A reflection on the predominance of tourism or business management text on large-scale festivals and events does perhaps give credence to this conjecture. It is good then that this text looks at many types and sizes of event and, it is believed by the editors, will help to form the specific and holistic management attributes and applications for as many of these as possible.

Bibliography

City of Edinburgh (1999). *Towards the New Enlightenment: A Cultural Policy for the City of Edinburgh*, UK.

Bianchini, F. and Parkinson, M. (eds) (1993). *Cultural Policy and Urban Regeneration: The West European Experience*. Manchester: Manchester University Press.

Bonink, C. and Richards, G. (1992). *Cultural Tourism in Europe*. Centre for Leisure and Tourism Studies, University of North London.

Bourdieu, P. (1984). *Distinction*. Cambridge, MA: Harvard University Press.

Cardownie, S. (2001). Fresh plans to improve Edinburgh as festival city. *The Scotsman*, 15 June.

Graham Devlin and Associates (2001). *Festivals and the City; The Edinburgh Festivals Strategy*.

Grainger-Jones, B. (1999). *Managing Leisure*. Oxford: ILAM/Butterworth-Heinemann.

Guardian, The (2002). *Show me the Money*, B. Logan, 26 August.

Hall, C.M. (1992). *Hallmark Tourist Events – Impacts, Management and Planning*. London: Belhaven Press.

Hughes, H. (2000). *Arts, Entertainment and Tourism*. Oxford: Butterworth-Heinemann.

Law, C.M. (1994). *Urban Tourism: Attracting Visitors to Large Cities*. London: Mansell.

Liverpool Institute of Performing Arts (2003). Website: http://www.lipa.ac.uk/ex/place/whatislipa/index.htm, 15 March.

Manchester City Council (2002). *Manchester's Cultural Strategy*.

O'Connor, J. (2003). *The Definition of Cultural Economies*. MIPC Paper, Manchester Metropolitan University.

O'Sullivan, D. and Jackson, M.J. (2002). Festival Tourism: a contributor to sustainable local economic development? *Journal of Sustainable Tourism*, **10(4)**, 325–342.

Perth International Arts Festival (2003). Website: http://www.perthfestival.com.au/festival/index.cfm/fuseaction/home.home, 15 March.

Richards, G. (1996). *Cultural Tourism in Europe*. CAB International, UK.

Scottish Tourist Board (1991). *Edinburgh's Festivals Study 1990–1991: Visitor Survey and Economic Impact Assessment Summary Report Festival Management and Event Tourism*, Vol. 1, pp. 71–78.

Tomlinson, J. (1991). *Cultural Imperialism: A Critical Introduction*. London: Pinter.

Torkildsen, G. (2000). *Leisure and Recreation Management*, 4th edn. Spon.

Voase, R.N. (1994). Strategy or chance? A perspective on the cultural regeneration of our cities. *Regional Review* **4(4)**. Leeds: Yorkshire and Humberside Regional Research Observatory.

Waterman, S. (1998). Carnivals for elites? The cultural politics of arts festivals. *Progress in Human Geography*, **22(1)**, 55–74.

Questions

1 Describe what is meant by the terms 'arts', 'culture' and 'leisure'. Why might there be problems in reaching a precise meaning for these terms?

2 Give examples of festivals and events which might be classed as 'high' culture and some that may be viewed as 'popular' culture. Justify your choice.

3 Why is the development of strategic cultural policy important to a tourist destination?

An overview of events management

Galal Salem, Eleri Jones and Nigel Morgan

Introduction

This chapter provides an overview of event management practice applicable to festivals and cultural events, borrowing a performance management model as a framework for the systematic identification and deconstruction of four major stages of event development, namely: decision; detailed planning; implementation; evaluation (see Figure 2.1). The relative importance of each stage in the practice of any individual event can be very different, and the balance and order of activities change according to the nature and purpose of the event, e.g. for recurrent events with a standing organizing group, or one-off events.

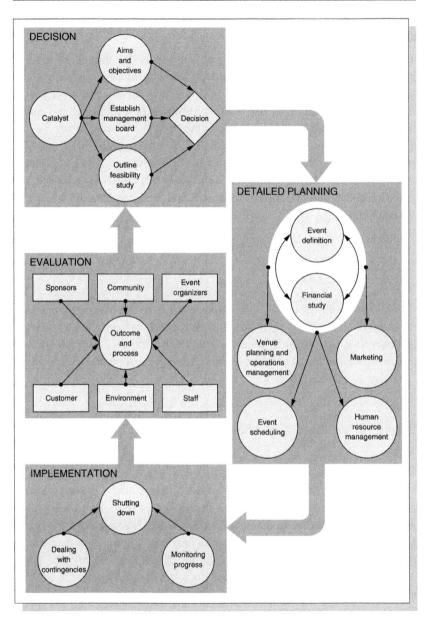

Figure 2.1 A unified model of special events management.

Decision

The decision phase initiates the process and determines ultimately whether the event goes ahead or not. It can be relatively simple for a small recurrent event or where previous experience is used as a judgemental tool to justify decision making and may be concluded in a meeting of key members of the organizing board. It can, however, be complex, multifaceted and iterative. At its most complex the decision phase comprises five distinct activities: catalysis; specifying the event aims and objectives; establishing the management board; outline feasibility study including market research and an initial financial study; decision making.

Catalysis

The person(s) who provide the original idea for the development of an event – the event catalyst(s) – are not necessarily event experts and may emanate from the public (government, local authority or agency), private (corporation, firm or individual) or voluntary sector. The organizational affiliation of the event catalyst is likely to impact on access to resources for event implementation.

Specifying the event aims and objectives

Aims and objectives are crucial and must be resolved early as they impact on many aspects of the event, including marketing and sponsorship. The aim of the event, *per se*, may be identical to those of the event organizer but at least will be complementary, 'fitting' with the organization's aims and having a key role in achieving them (Watt, 1998). Event aims may fall into one of three main categories: economic, social and cultural, political. Most events, even not-for-profit events, have economic aims, although these might not be the overriding priority and at most may be to achieve break-even. Economic aims may be direct or indirect, e.g. marketing a particular product, area or even an entire country. They may be short term, relating to making a profit or attracting new sponsors, or longer term, e.g. encouraging long-term investment; creating new permanent and/or temporary jobs; generating direct economic benefits for the host community through increasing visits, improving levels of visitor expenditure or minimizing 'leakage of resident money from the economy' (Long and Perdue, 1990: 10).

Cultural and social aims may focus on encouraging local participation to: increase awareness of a venue, occasion, tradition or sociocultural value, increase 'civic' pride, heighten an area's profile, satisfy the needs of special interest groups or conserve local heritage. Events may galvanize particular segments of society strengthening volunteerism, cooperation and intercultural interaction (Getz, 1997). Events can be used at 'both the macro- and micro-political level' (Hall, 1992: 88) to enhance image and ideology or strengthen the position of elites within local or regional power structures (Hall, 1992). Macropolitically, events create or enhance international images of a country or regime (Hall, 1992). Micropolitically, events can be 'policy tools' (Getz, 1997: 34) – arts and music festivals promoting cultural development, ethnic and multicultural events reducing social or racial tensions, fostering intergroup understanding, and preserving traditions. In Egypt, the Nile Bounty Festival was re-established in 1992 when the Ministry of Tourism restored the old celebration of the Nile flood to offer free entertainment to Egyptian citizens and enhance civic pride, as well as to enrich the international tourist programme and enhance the image of Egypt as a tourism destination.

Event aims are usefully broken down into specific objectives – the steps required to achieve each aim. Objectives ideally should be 'SMART', i.e. *Specific* to the event, *Measurable* quantitatively, *Agreed* (or achievable) by those involved, *Realistic* (or relevant) to the resources available, *Timed* around the event schedule. SMART objectives help identify performance targets for the event which facilitate the later evaluation of the event, e.g. by specifying volumes of income or profit, ticket sales, advertising revenue, merchandising sales, sponsorship, donations, subsidies or cash flow, number of local or international visitors, or levels of investment (e.g. for building a new stadium).

Establishing the management board

A management board usually plans, implements and evaluates the event. For complex events, specific tasks may be delegated to subgroups. The board needs to reflect a diverse range of skills and expertise, which may be vested in one or more individuals, covering all aspects of event management, marketing, financial management and the law, although 'titles are often used loosely' (Getz, 1997: 12). Specialist consultants may be invited to undertake work as required. A board operating as a team is likely to be more effective.

17

Outline feasibility study

An outline feasibility study checks that the event 'stacks up' and does not need detailed answers – a broad indication of likely success or failure is sufficient. For a small event the feasibility study may be relatively informal and may just involve a 'chat with a colleague' (Watt, 1998: 8). For larger events with more risk associated with event failure, more detailed research may be required to enable a decision to be made. The initial feasibility study tends to focus on market research and an initial financial study.

Market research can facilitate decision making, providing useful evidence of potential financial success, ensuring it fulfils its aims by providing information about potential customer characteristics, motivations, preferences, promotional tools. Market research may influence sponsorship decisions, marketing, venue selection and dates for launching the event. Defining the data required from market research, in primary or secondary terms, is a key issue. If secondary data is sufficient then appropriate data sources need identification. Primary data collection is very costly and event managers must be convinced of its necessity, although it can be a vital part of implementing an event, facilitating later evaluation.

Financial implications can lead to major or minor modifications to event features, notably the range of activities included, the choice of venue and, most commonly, ticket price. Early determination of financial non-feasibility can minimize wasted time and effort. A significant proportion of the data used in an outline financial study (e.g. anticipated number of attendees, venue costs) is likely to be secondary data from other, similar, events.

Decision making

Decision making is the last substage in the decision phase and the stage at which the board needs to have collected enough information to decide whether the event should go ahead to the detailed planning stage. Perhaps there need to be some modifications to the original idea, e.g. scale, location, ticket price? If the answer is negative then a detailed report should be prepared to identify the issues which prevented continuation so that information is available should a similar idea be progressed later.

Detailed planning

Following a positive outcome from the decision phase, the event moves into a detailed planning stage, which is the essence of managing the event. Detailed planning includes event product definition and development of a detailed financial study, before moving on to development of strategies relating to human resource management, marketing, venue planning/operations management and event scheduling.

Event product definition

The event product is a unique blend of activities, which are the tools for achieving the overall event aims and satisfying customer needs. Event design should be customer oriented, and event organizers should create a mix that satisfies the largest number of potential customers – Getz (1997: 251) points out that 'many events suffer from a "product orientation" – that is, they try to sell their event with little or no regard for what potential customers need, want, and will pay for'. Core activities are determined by event nature and overall budget to reflect the event theme and may be supplemented by secondary attractions to give the event its overall shape. For some attendees, the benefit and importance of secondary attractions exceeds that of the core. Some events are described as multicore, e.g. a festival of culture may include a street parade, a firework show, a concert, etc. The earlier the features are specified the better, although 'events are organic and will evolve all the way through the event itself' (Armstrong, 2001: 49). For a mega-event, product definition may take place over a period of several years leading up to the event.

Theme

The theme is an umbrella to unify the final event image – it should be complementary and synergistic to the event aims. Historical and ethnic themes are common and 'once the theme is established, the elements of the event must be designed to fit in' (McDonnell et al., 1999: 246), including the event name, logo, venue décor, staff uniforms, performers' costumes, activities, entertainment, lights, music, special effects, food and beverage, mascots and merchandise.

Location and venue

An event location differs from an event venue. The term 'location' describes where the event will take place, e.g. a desert or open-air, whereas the venue denotes a specific place, e.g. the Luxor Temple, the Millennium Stadium or the Royal Albert Hall. 'Location is everything' (Allen, 2000: 37). Choosing an event location and venue goes beyond just finding an arena that will hold the crowd. An appropriate venue is of primary significance to the overall success or failure of the event and should complement the theme of the event, e.g. alongside the Pyramids to communicate an Egyptian theme, e.g. for the Aida Concert 2000. The venue can help the event command prestige ticket prices – tickets for front-row seats at the pyramid-side Aida concert cost $1500 in contrast to tickets for front-row seats for the same concert held at the Egyptian Opera House which cost $120.

Some events have permanent venues, e.g. the International Musical Eisteddfod at Llangollen or the Royal Welsh Show at Builth Wells; others do not and need to select a venue. There are considerable advantages in selecting an established venue for an event, since it will provide some, if not all, the infrastructure required for the event (e.g. power supply, water and drains system). In selecting the specific venue there are a number of specific issues for consideration:

- *Size and capacity* – space considerations must include the needs of staff, performers, equipment, stores, administration and other services as well as the seating capacity of the venue.
- *Facilities* – the services and facilities are vital to an evaluation of suitability. Requisite technical facilities may include information and communication technology connectivity, power supply and sound/audiovisual systems, as well as toilets, food and beverage facilities and first aid services.
- *Visibility, centrality and clustering* – these play an integral role in the process of selecting the event venue (Getz, 1997). Visibility is especially important when financial constraints preclude a major promotional campaign. Centrality relates to the proximity of services and other facilities, e.g. airport, bus or train station. Clustering is 'the association of events with other attractions and services' (Getz, 1997: 84) (e.g. natural landmarks, historical sites, entertainment or shopping centres) to form a stronger package, even if there is no cooperation between the event and the co-located attractions. Clustering is important for events

seeking to attract medium- and long-distance travellers who need stronger motives to travel.
- *Venue cost* – this is a major factor for most events, especially those with limited budgets.
- *History* – this can impact positively or negatively on the reputation of a venue and needs careful consideration. Tian'anmen Square, Beijing, for example, has no history of hosting events but its association with bloody clashes between the Chinese civilian students and police led to severe resistance from human rights groups to it hosting the Olympic Games 2008. Some venues are not equipped for events but have a strong appeal due to their distinctive history (e.g. the Pyramids).
- *Other considerations* – examples are crime rates and perceptions of safety or prevailing political situation (especially for international events), prevailing weather conditions (especially for outdoor events) and environmental considerations.
- *Personal preference* – however unscientific, it must be recognized that organizers' personal preference is a major factor influencing venue selection. Event organizers can be 'passionately in love with inappropriate venues' (Armstrong, 2001: 51).

In selecting an appropriate event location/venue, event organizers should draw up a list of inclusion criteria as well as exclusion criteria, which can be further categorized as essential and desirable. A venue may meet some criteria and not others, which might make it difficult to evaluate overall. A venue clearly must meet all the essential criteria for consideration. Desirable criteria can be weighted in terms of their importance, e.g. 1 = not important, 2 = important and 3 = very important. Rating the 'desirable' criteria for each venue and multiplying this rating by the 'importance' weightings can result in an overall score for the venue in terms of overall suitability for the event.

Timing

Event timing, down to the hour, is critical to success and needs extremely careful consideration. Target audience, event activities, venue availability and event organizers' preferences help define suitable dates, e.g. if the market segment targeted is families with young children then school time must be avoided. An event should avoid clashing with competitor/major events, e.g. World Cup football, as this would 'be destructive for all involved' (Watt, 1998: 6). The final date must include enough lead-time to allow the proper event organization and marketing.

Ticket price

Ticket price may cover entry alone or may include in-site services, e.g. parking or transportation. Ticket pricing has major implications for customer decision making and participation (Weaver and Oppermann, 2000) and usually involves collaboration between the financial and marketing managers. Backward pricing, setting the price regardless of costs (Getz, 1997), cannot be used unless sufficient funds are available to cover potential losses or the event is sufficiently established to give organizers confidence. Backward pricing is often used for events, which focus on achieving social or political goals.

If backward pricing is not used then there are three important stages in setting a price: costing; selecting a pricing strategy; determining a pricing structure.

Firstly, costing provides a basis for a pricing decision through consideration of fixed costs (costs that do not change with the volume of customers, e.g. capital costs, staff salaries, equipment rental) and variable costs (costs which change according to the volume of customers). Costings must be coupled with estimates of the likely minimum number of customers to determine an appropriate price for tickets to break even, i.e. to cover event costs without profit.

Secondly, pricing involves four considerations: event objectives, i.e. whether the event is not-for-profit or for-profit; competition – few events have no competition and whilst some events 'apparently have no price-resistance (e.g. one-off mega events) ... most others do have a point where price turns the crowd away' (Ernst & Young *et al.*, 1992: 136); customer characteristics and propensity to pay which can be determined by market research; product characteristics, e.g. quality, image and history. There are a plethora of different pricing strategies; however, those suitable for events include:

- Cost-oriented pricing, which bases 'pricing structures on the actual cost of providing the goods or services' (Weaver and Oppermann, 2000: 231). Full-cost recovery aims to cover all costs with a margin for profit. Grants may offset capital costs so ticket prices may aim to recover operating costs (Getz, 1997). Most mega-events cannot hope to recover all their costs from admissions, given the enormous capital investment, and will probably set a revenue target that will guide a pricing strategy.
- Competition-oriented pricing (follow the leader), where 'The emphasis here is on competitor behaviour as the major criterion for setting

prices' (Weaver and Oppermann, 2000: 231). The risk is that whilst prices are similar, costs, objectives, quality and customers may be very different. The advantage is that the price will always compare favourably and is good for new events competing with mature events.

- Prestige pricing, where 'the price is deliberately set higher than the competitors for positioning reasons – usually to suggest quality and attract higher-spending visitors' (Getz, 1997: 215), although this may be a difficult message to deliver. Events 'with guaranteed high demand can sometimes get away with charging high prices' (Getz, 1997: 216) and maximizing profits, although event organizers need to consider 'consumer backlash' (Getz, 1997: 216).
- Yield management recognizes that an event usually deals with multiple market segments and, for example, ringside seats can be sold at a premium. Yield management relates service quality to price and enables the event to deal with different economic segments – 'the number of tickets available in each price category should be managed to yield the best revenue picture' (Getz, 1997: 216).

The third and final phase involves selecting a pricing structure. Getz (1997: 213) suggests a range of potential pricing structures: a single admission price; different admission prices based on age, time, group, etc.; multivisit tickets or season tickets; free admission with charges for specific attractions or extras (parking, reserved seats, programmes, etc.); admission price plus charges for specific attractions.

Financial study

The financial analysis usually focuses on three issues: anticipated income and expenditure, budgeting and cash flow. Potential income sources vary extensively from one event to another and include grants or subsidies, donations, fund-raising and sponsorship. Income may be generated before, during and after an event, e.g. back-end income from selling off equipment after the event. The budget is 'a quantified statement of plans' (McDonnell et al., 1999: 172) and a key tool in financial control. The written budget is presented when asking for grant aid or sponsorship. Walsh-Heron and Stevens (1990) recommend widespread participation of senior staff in budget preparation to get corporate understanding of implications and impacts of the work of various sections. Overall profit is not sufficient – income and expenditure must be accurately scheduled to ensure appropriate cash flow (Getz, 1997). Most costs are incurred pre-event and most revenue is generated during the event. Negotiating delayed payments to suppliers and getting sponsorship and grants 'up front' can help cash flow.

Grants or subsidies from governmental and non-governmental organizations (e.g. Tourist Boards) can 'guarantee against loss' (Waters, 1994: 46) and are favoured funding sources placing limited responsibility on event organizers. However, they may be difficult to obtain and increasingly have 'strict accountability criteria' (Getz, 1997: 207). Generally to be eligible for a grant the event must demonstrate social, political, or economical benefit for the host community. Donations are more difficult to predict and some patrons like to remain anonymous (Waters, 1994). Fund-raising may involve a range of activities before, during or after the event, e.g. auctions, award ceremonies, banquets, galas, raffles, or competitions. Sponsorship is widely considered by the event literature, although it is not appropriate for all events (Geldard and Sinclair, 1996), since the investment of time and money required to get sponsorship may outweigh the benefits. The right sponsor enhances the event image through association with a positive corporate image (Getz, 1997) and thus attracts better participants, customers and media coverage.

Broadcasting rights (as a result of the phenomenal growth in the number of broadcasting channels) are an important income source for some events, which may generate enormous sums from media coverage both from the broadcasting of the live event and as back-end income from selling the right to broadcast tapes of the event. Advertising revenue (e.g. on the venue, tickets or pamphlets) may be linked to media coverage.

Catering is an important element of the event experience from a customer perspective and can provide a lucrative income stream. Alternatively, income may come from renting ready-equipped catering facilities either as a flat fee, as a percentage of sales or a combination of the two or from selling permits for merchandising food and beverage inside the event venue. Market research and feedback from similar events can provide useful information of the potential expenditure of customers on food and beverage and facilitate decision making on this issue.

Merchandising is a major income stream for major events – 'events are naturally merchandising marts, and many events have retailing as their primary purpose' (Getz, 1997: 207). Merchandising is an important promotional tool to brand an event as well as providing souvenirs (Weaver and Oppermann, 2000). However, organizers should be reasonable when estimating merchandising income – Getz (1997: 207) suggests: 'Event managers cannot assume that everything with the event logo or design on it will sell.' The sale of licences for the production and sale of merchandise may be a safer option and reduce financial risk.

Marketing

Hall (1992: 136) identifies three important objectives of event marketing: 'read their customer needs and motivations, develop products that meet these needs, and build a communication programme which expresses the event's purpose and objectives'. Market research, although not always utilized, can help understand customer motivations. 'You may have the best quality event product, but unless you have a strategic plan for promoting this product it will remain the best-kept secret in the world' (Goldblatt, 1997: 230).

Promotional techniques include advertising, publicity ('securing ... free space in printed media or free time in broadcast media' (Davidoff and Davidoff, 1994: 197)), public relations and merchandising. Advertising is the most common, recognizable and visible promotional technique and may use, either singly or in combination, print media (e.g. magazines, newspapers), broadcast media (radio and television), speciality products (e.g. calendars, key rings) or mobile platforms (buses or taxis). Testing the effectiveness of different advertising media is not really feasible for events due to their temporary nature.

The marketing budget, characteristics of the target market, the event aims, methods selected by competing events and cross-promotional contracts with sponsors inform the marketing mix. Three approaches can be used to determine the marketing budget:

- An arbitrary judgemental approach (what was spent the previous year or by a similar event) or a percentage of sales (previous sales or anticipated sales (McDonnell *et al.*, 1999))
- A competitive approach defining the budget in terms of equalling or exceeding what the main competitors are spending
- An objectives and strategy approach that defines marketing and communication objectives and develops strategies to achieve them.

Human resource management

Human resources are a key element of the event experience contributing to customer satisfaction. Human resource management for events is more complex than for other leisure organizations and differs between one-off events, events with a permanent home and peripatetic events. Clearly the strategy will flow from the initial analysis of which elements are to be delivered by the event organizers and which are to be subcontracted to other organizations and will result in a staffing structure and a plan for event delivery.

Several different categories of staff are likely to be involved – a professional core comprising full-time and part-time permanent and/or temporary staff supplemented by specialist consultants, and hourly paid staff employed directly by the event or indirectly through contracts and unpaid volunteers. Assessment of requirements for the various categories of staff – labour demand – is complex, requiring analysis of the requirements of each event element. Two techniques are used for forecasting the labour demand: managerial judgement, which depends on the personal experience of managers, and work study, which is more scientific (Pratt and Bennett, 1985; Getz, 1997). Having decided on staff numbers for each event element, detailed job descriptions can be drawn up:

■ Job title to 'reflect ... position in the organization and ... functional areas' (Getz, 1997: 187), an important tool for coordinating event staff
■ Duties and responsibilities divided into 'most frequent ... and ... occasional duties' (Torrington and Hall, 1995: 215)
■ Reporting arrangements, i.e. 'to whom the person reports, and who reports to the person' (Getz, 1997: 187), are especially important with volunteers unaccustomed to organizational working
■ Working conditions and circumstances including location (e.g. office, tent, open air), hours (e.g. full time, part time, fixed hours), remuneration details, special physical requirements, holidays
■ Performance standards against which performance will be evaluated
■ Recruitment criteria, i.e. the type and level of skills, knowledge and experience required to perform the job satisfactorily.

Volunteers, i.e. 'those who enlist or offer their services to an organization of their own free will, and without expecting remuneration' (Getz, 1997: 198), are particularly important in the implementation of festivals and cultural events and can work in most roles, including the organizing committees. A major issue for events is that there is no precise tool for forecasting productivity rates of volunteers, so an overestimation of volunteer numbers is required. Understanding volunteer motivations is key to designing an acceptable reward package to fit those motivations. Two interacting dimensions dominate volunteering – 'personal enrichment and helping others' (Gibbins, 1986 cited in Getz, 1997: 200). Depending on the nature of the event, sources of volunteers for consideration include: sponsors; universities, schools and colleges; service, social and sport clubs; special interest groups; previous volunteers; religious groups; professional organizations and unions. A volunteer recruitment plan should be developed, although Ernst & Young *et al.* (1992) optimistically argue that once news of the event is out, people will volunteer immediately, which may be true for mega-events where to have 'been there' is an important motivation.

Venue planning and operations management

Armstrong (2001) and McDonnell *et al.* (1999) suggest that a map of the venue, list of facilities, frequent visits and conversations with the venue staff are good tools to start the venue planning process. Allen (2000: 11) suggests supplementing these through visualization – 'a step-by-step process that walks organizers through an event and allows them to see the areas that could pose potential problems in advance'. Using these techniques the organizers can plan how the event will fit into the venue and how facilities, staff, equipment services, etc., will be distributed.

Signage external to the event requires consideration of the flow of customers to the event and the different potential modes of transport. Careful consideration needs to be made of where people are likely to come from to facilitate routes to car parks and minimize traffic problems. Established venues are likely to be clearly signposted with appropriate car parking and event entrance arrangements in place and probably printed on the back of tickets.

The venue, the nature of activities and the characteristics of potential customers can help define risks, e.g. crowd control issues. For some events 'mobbing the stage, screaming and yelling' are not part of the 'crowd's psyche' (Ernst & Young *et al.*, 1992: 81). Crowd control involves constraining a disorderly crowd, e.g. fighting due to hooliganism or drunkenness or confusion following a bomb threat, and is normally the job of police or professional security. Event organizers must plan for quickly clearing the venue in an orderly fashion, and effective coordination of crowd control from one central point using mobile communication devices is critical. Crowd management aims to distribute the crowd as evenly as possible, preventing congestion, enhancing customer experience and minimizing queuing (McDonnell *et al.*, 1999). Queuing may form a significant part of the event experience, making people frustrated and tired (Getz, 1997). Volunteers can be used to manage queues and training of volunteers for this is important and needs careful consideration.

Event scheduling

An event schedule describes the timing of the different elements of the event in minute detail. Event schedules are designed to help monitor event progress and as an evaluation tool. They usually identify date, time, action, location, responsibility and explanatory notes. For complex events a master schedule may coordinate the major elements, with each manager producing a separate schedule for his/her crew. Getz (1997: 147) suggests 'Gantt graphs' as a simple, visual way to schedule event planning.

Implementation

Despite the fact that implementation is what the event is all about, there is little systematic discussion in the literature. This chapter will consider three issues under implementation: monitoring event progress, dealing with contingencies and shutting down activities.

Monitoring event progress

Youell (1994: 111) suggests holding 'an eve of event briefing session to go over the final details, iron out any last minute hitches and confirm any alterations to schedules'. Thus, the event opens with a confirmed management plan identifying key activities. Activities can be monitored to ensure that the event is going to plan and, where necessary, corrective actions taken. Where the plan is modified it must be communicated effectively to all staff.

Dealing with contingencies

Unexpected happenings, leading to event cancellation, postponement or confusion (e.g. fire, flood, power failures, bomb scares), are generally out of the control of the event organizers. Insurance transfers part of the risk from the event organization and provides two benefits: specialist advice on risk management and guaranteeing financial recompense (McDonnell *et al.*, 1999). Event organizers need to ask 'What if...?' and rehearse solutions. Armstrong (2001: 152) suggests 'two good defences against most problems: well-prepared leadership and a strong set of contingency plans', although they 'cannot possibly cover every conceivable occurrence'. Well-trained staff members able to deal with most expected contingencies are vital, although staff must also know what to do in the case of unexpected contingencies.

Shutting down activities

Shutting down post-event ensures that everything is put back in place after the event and includes two tasks: dismantling and removing the equipment, and cleaning up. A timetable for suppliers to dismantle and remove hired equipment (e.g. sound and lighting systems; mobile toilets; temporary stages) should be identified in the hire contract. Selling off equipment after the event may generate additional back-end income. Cleaning up should not be confined just to the cleaning of the venue but should extend beyond the event and include the removal, and ideally recycling, of promotional materials and special signage.

Evaluation

The purpose of evaluation is to learn from experience how the event could have been done better. Evaluation can be divided into outcome and process evaluation. Six different perspectives are important in evaluation – the event organization, volunteers and other staff, event sponsors, customers, the host community and environmental considerations. Performance indicators for evaluating outcomes for the event organizer and the sponsors are likely to be derived from the original SMART objectives set for the event in the decision phase. The data for the evaluation, e.g. final profit, numbers of tickets sold, will emerge after the event.

Process evaluation requires feedback from event staff and customers. Staff debriefing sessions, e.g. in focus groups, are useful for collecting data. Timing is critical as volunteers are likely to disperse quickly after the event. Staff can be asked to reflect on the event – Youell (1994: 112) suggests using records, 'such as ... video footage, ... photographs, and media coverage', as tools for reflection and discussion.

Customer feedback can be obtained in various ways. Informal feedback through customer comments, complaints and suggestions is useful. Formal feedback may involve questionnaire surveys providing data on customer profiles (e.g. age, gender, income, social and education level), motives for attending and spending patterns. Other tools, such as interviews and focus groups, can also be used for covering specific areas in more detail.

29

After data collation and analysis a formal evaluation session is invaluable so that event managers can 'constantly learn, and improve management' (Getz, 1997: 331). In this session all stages of the process must be reviewed including the initial objectives, e.g. for ticket sales or profit, which may not have been achieved because they were not feasible or other reasons, e.g. the promotional campaign running late. However, evaluation can also be used to enhance activities that went well during the event.

Summary

The chapter has used a performance management cycle as a framework to build a systematic phased model of event management comprising: decision, detailed planning, implementation and evaluation. In practice the model is not necessarily linear and may be iterative, e.g. redefining the event product in the light of a detailed financial study or market research. Activities do not take place in series but are broken down to facilitate parallelism and the involvement of different groups, whether employed directly by the event or subcontracted. The model was developed as part of a larger research project to facilitate discussions with event managers. What is clear from initial discussions with managers is that the model reflects practice but that not many managers use an explicit model to guide actions.

Bibliography

Allen, J. (2000). *Event Planning: The Ultimate Guide to Successful Meetings, Corporate Events, Fundraising Galas, Conferences, Conventions, Incentives and Other Special Events.* Toronto: John Wiley and Sons.

Armstrong, J. (2001). *Planning Special Events.* San Francisco: Jossey-Bass.

Davidoff, P.G. and Davidoff, D.S. (1994). *Sales and Marketing for Travel and Tourism*, 2nd edn. Englewood Cliffs: Prentice-Hall.

Ernst & Young, Catherwood, D.W. and Van Kirk, R.L. (1992). *The Complete Guide to Special Event Management: Business Insights, Financial Advice, and Successful Strategies from Ernst & Young, Advisors to the Olympics, the Emmy Awards and the PGA Tour.* New York: John Wiley and Sons.

Geldard, E. and Sinclair, L. (1996). *The Sponsorship Manual.* Victoria: The Sponsorship Unit.

Getz, D. (1997). *Event Management and Event Tourism*. New York: Cognizant Communication Corporation.

Gibbins, R. (1986). *How Volunteers View Volunteerism*. Calgary: Research Unit for Public Policy Studies, University of Calgary.

Goldblatt, J.J. (1997). *Best Practices in Modern Event Management*, 2nd edn. New York: John Wiley and Sons.

Hall, C.M. (1992). *Hallmark Tourist Events – Impacts, Management and Planning*. London: Belhaven Press.

Long, P.T. and Perdue, R.R. (1990). The economic impact of rural festivals and special events: assessing the spatial distribution of expenditure. *Journal of Travel Research*, **28(4)**, 10–14.

McDonnell, I., Allen, J. and O'Toole, W. (1999). *Festival and Special Event Management*. Brisbane: John Wiley and Sons.

Pratt, K.J. and Bennett, S.G. (1985). *Elements of Personnel Management*, 2nd edn. London: Gee.

Torrington, D. and Hall, L. (1995). *Personnel Management: HRM in Action*, 3rd edn. London: Prentice-Hall.

Walsh-Heron, J. and Stevens, T. (1990). *The Management of Visitor Attractions and Events*. London: Prentice-Hall.

Waters, I. (1994). *Entertainment, Arts and Cultural Services*. Harlow: Longman.

Watt, D.C. (1998). *Event Management in Leisure and Tourism*. Harlow: Longman.

Weaver, D.B. and Oppermann, M. (2000). *Tourism Management*. Brisbane: John Wiley and Sons.

Youell, R. (1994). *Leisure and Tourism: Advanced GNVQ*. London: Longman.

Questions

1 Explain why both process evaluation and outcome evaluation are important in the evaluation of an event.

2 How would you design a package to motivate volunteers?

3 How would human resource management issues differ for a peripatetic event from a static event?

Festivals, events and the destination

Ros Derrett

Introduction

The chapter explores the relationship between festivals and events and a destination's prosperity, identity, tourism image and marketing strategies. It explains the roles festivals and events play as attractions and markers in the tourism system. It identifies qualities that make festivals special. It explores the links between event management and host communities, government at all levels, media, community cultural development and specific interest sectors.

There is growing interest in what Getz (1997: 326–327) highlights as 'unique leisure and cultural experiences, powerful travel motivators and facilitators of community pride and development'. Festivals and events provide *authenticity and uniqueness*, especially with events based on inherent indigenous values;

convenient *hospitality* and *affordability*; *theming* and *symbols for partici-pants and spectators.*

Festivals play a number of significant roles in a town or region. Getz (1997) identifies these as 'attractions, image-makers, animators of static attractions and catalysts for further development. They can be seen to minimise negative impacts of mass visitation and foster better host–guest relations. Festivals can lengthen tourist seasons, extend peak season or introduce a "new season" into the life of a community'. The community development perspective on event tourism acknowledges the elements of community spirit and pride, cooperation, leadership, enhancement of cultural traditions, capacity to control development, improvements to social and health amenities and environmental quality.

The defining characteristic of a special event or festival is its *transience* (Gilbert and Lizotte, 1998: 73). This suggests that it would be difficult to induce and sustain the same sense of occasion and excitement if such an event was to be held more frequently. Goldblatt (1997) defines an event as 'a special event recognises a unique moment in time with ceremony and ritual to satisfy specific needs'. The word festival derives from *feast* and implies *a time of celebration.*

Festivals link landscape to lifestyle in simple and complex ways by introducing the human dimension to static spaces that become animated. They encourage further use of that space at the end of the festival. The provision of amenities of a lasting nature is an attractive aspect of com-munity investment in events. Events require physical settings in urban or rural areas, in forests, by rivers, in open fields and purpose-built amenities. Events entertain locals and provide recreational activity in and out of season for visitors. Media coverage generated by events helps destinations build confidence and a positive image in the tourism marketplace.

Festivals are attractive to communities looking to address issues of civic design, local pride and identity, heritage, conservation, urban renewal, employment generation, investment and economic development. The more an event is seen by its host community as emerging from within rather than being imposed on them, the greater that community's accep-tance of the event will be. There is growing interest in the notion that festivals and events represent the host community's sense of itself and sense of place. This requires a close reading of the host–guest relationship and the options chosen by residents who initiate, plan, manage and mar-ket festivals and events to be shared with visitors.

33

The arts and cultural industries, especially through festivals and special events, can offer something for the tourism sector to exploit – experience (Reiss, 1993). Arts administrators seek to compensate for falling investment from government and recognize their products can add glamour and a unique travel experience that is otherwise unavailable at a reasonable price.

Some destinations are precisely in the public psyche because they host spectacular public festivals and events. The Carnivale in Rio de Janiero, the Calgary Stampede in Canada, Mardi Gras in New Orleans, Oktoberfest in Munich, the Country Music Festival in Tamworth, Australia, the Edinburgh Festivals in Scotland, and London's Thames Festival all now define the destination in terms of a festive brand. Some of these festivals have been sustained over long periods of time and seek to satisfy the needs of residents as well as visitors. Oktoberfest started in 1810 to allow residents to celebrate a royal marriage and with the subsequent additions of horse races, funfair amusements and now corporate promotional opportunities, it attracts seven million visitors each September to Munich.

Festival and event management

It is important to understand where festivals and special events originate. Initiatives to stage a festival can come from the public sector where authorities invest in celebrations of a national nature, to honour national heroes or past events. Management can be centralized with investment coming from the public purse, or decentralized with local committees responding to a national holiday with distinctive local responses. Generally a feasibility study will establish the best 'fit' between the event and venue, host destination and organizational track record.

Festivals and events can be generated by the private or corporate sectors. Entrepreneurs, companies and special interest groups can deliver ticketed arts, sport or fundraising promotional events. Events can be 'mega', affecting the whole community; national or have worldwide implications like the Olympic Games or Soccer World Cup; or 'hallmark', which are large in scale, have limited duration and are regularly used by authorities to enhance awareness of the destination and position it in a specific marketplace. The annual Sapporo Snow Festival in Hokkaido is the most famous winter festival in Japan. It attracts people from all over the world. It lasts about a week, showcasing more than 300 large snow statues, which are illuminated at night.

Decisions about the staging of an event essentially come from a special interest group eager to educate a wider audience, showcase cultural practice and maybe preserve and enhance its acceptance. A celebration of a community's way of life and identity can be initiated by numerous agencies, business, government, by individuals and by community groups. Local government is engaged with community events. The non-profit community sector and charities are generally managed by volunteers.

Organizational structures may vary, but the outcomes are similar for destinations. Whether the structure is simple, functional, network, task-force or committee based (McDonnell *et al.*, 1999) each host organization has responsibility to the host community and other stakeholders for effective event management whether they are government agencies, participants and spectators, sponsors, the wider business community, employees and volunteers, suppliers or media. Whatever structure is utilized, the host organization needs to deal with the complexity of risk (e.g. poor weather conditions) and financial management, public accountability, human resource management and marketing professionally.

Destination management

For destinations to use festivals and special events effectively, a strategic, integrated and systematic model will deliver superior outcomes for all stakeholders. Spatial and resource management are significant elements of understanding how destinations can capture the 'magic' of the place. Through effective leadership and management of public and private spaces that magic can be turned into something that can be maintained and sustained. The importance of community consultation, with all stakeholders, is important, particularly if government is the agency required to manage the area for the common good. An audit of existing events, resources, spatial and temporal needs will allow for gaps in annual calendars to be examined and choices made in terms of when and where to site particular events.

Choices to stage a festival may assist a destination deal with the peaks and troughs associated with seasonality in visitation. By determining the target market for the festival and event, destination managers seek to minimize adverse impacts of events and enhance the benefits. They need to ensure that sustainability is built into the planning and management of each event to allow for benefits across the host community. This can be informed by ongoing monitoring and evaluation before, during and after the event.

The strategic approach will identify the portfolio of events, with differing scale, size, themes, activities, needs, organizational structures and audiences to be catered for. Festivals can be designed to contribute to a destination's attractiveness, to create dynamic ambience, services and entertainment. Some destination managers encourage a cluster of festivals as with the annual Edinburgh International Festival. Each August the city hosts a Fringe Festival, a Jazz Festival, the Military Tattoo, a Film Festival and in alternate years a Writers' Festival. It broadens the portfolio of activities for locals and visitors and may encourage greater spending and longer stays.

Event stakeholders

It is evident that festival and event host organizations cannot deliver attractive programmes without acknowledging the context within which they occur. Organizers need to be mindful of the political, environmental, technological, economic and community environments. There can be tensions between the various stakeholders for particular recreational activities and the organizers need to identify ways to minimize conflict and manage the competing interests. This is particularly evident when crowd control, traffic congestions, noise concerns, litter, and access to natural and built amenities by locals are challenged by the pressure of an influx of visitors.

Greater emphasis is being placed on the role of partnerships between major players in event management. Economies of scale can benefit not only the organizers; the sharing of resources can enhance the amenity of the destination for residents and visitors. A more successful event can eventuate when the needs of each stakeholder are understood and a satisfactory investment can be made by each. It is not always about money, but can be about public acknowledgement, 'in kind' support, shared expertise, human resources or logistical support. Ongoing consultation with all stakeholders through regular briefings, awareness raising and promotion can minimize negative impacts and encourage useful collaboration.

Many individuals and groups have buy-in for an event. Attendees at the successful, long running Woodford Folk Festival in Australia camp at the site for the duration of the six-day, six-night event in a lush sub-tropical landscape in the hinterland of the Sunshine Coast. It presents more than 2000 performers and 400 events with concerts, dances, work-shops, forums, street theatre, writers' competitions, film festival, comedy sessions, acoustic jams, history forums, an entire children's festival, art and craft workshops. This creates a community within a community and serves as a draw for repeat visitation as attendees renew acquaintances on annual basis with others and play with local and international artists. A spectacular finale allows thousands to actively participate in an unforget-table feast of sound and light and movement. The Woodford Folk Festival is organized by the Queensland Folk Federation Incorporated, a community-based non-profit organization whose object is to foster the folk movement.

Policy and planning

Governments at all levels can ground policy in an exploration and expan-sion of the destination's character, tradition, values and context to gen-erate significant tangible and intangible benefits in the interests of the long-term development of the city, town, village or region. Politicians can use festivals and events to improve image and raise profiles of destina-tions (McDonnell et al., 1999). Some festivities and events are under-pinned by political ideologies and can be used to introduce different perspectives and challenge attitudes (Dimmock and Tiyce, 2001), like the Sydney Gay and Lesbian Mardi Gras and Nimbin's Mardi Grass held to promote the end to prohibition of marijuana.

Choices made through thorough strategic planning can endow the destination with a vibrant and vigorous artistic texture, and make the place a stimulating and enjoyable location to live and work in and to visit. Local governments' involvement in cultural policy making for example can highlight its statutory or discretionary involvement through partnerships emphasizing what unites rather than what divides a com-munity and generate mutual confidence and respect with positive atti-tudes backed up with practical support by demystifying processes and practices. This can be through joint training options and recognizing that the culture and sports sectors constitute a series of industries that can create employment and enjoyment.

Government authorities can provide partnerships between local government, community interests, the private sector and individuals.

This can protect the essentially unpredictable quality of festivals and provide enabling support, rather than formulaic frameworks that can restrict rather than enhance distinctive festivals, and can encourage an open attitude to cross-disciplinary work. In the case of community-based non-profit event organizations, it can assist with the provision of professional administration. Volunteer work is indispensable but professional help greatly enhances the festival's development aims. It can have a dedicated event strategy that includes investment in the promotion of events.

Visitor management

Like consumers of many experiences, individuals participating as audience at a festival or special event wish to satisfy their curiosity about place and people. Often they want to 'do what locals do' and hope the festival experience will give them entrée to the ways of life of a particular place. Festivals rooted in specific destinations provide opportunities for the appreciation and exploration of sights of beauty and spirit of place. Attendees like to collect things endemic to the place as souvenirs that remind them of their celebratory experience. Attendees can improve themselves in terms of accessing knowledge and expertise new to them, express their personalities through dress, food and beverage consumption in the company of like-minded people and be respected or even receive approval from others.

Participants wish to emerge from the event with stories and experiences to talk about back home. This word-of-mouth promotion becomes an important tool for destination promoters. These people want to avoid unsafe situations, discomfort, doubts, worries, embarrassment, making too many complex decisions, or being treated as a computer number and being made to feel a nuisance. It is a marketing truism that people do not buy products or services, they buy the expectation of benefits that satisfy a need. Identification of needs is often the basis for developing a successful events programme and fitting that into specific locations.

Festivals and events in the tourism system

Festivals are identified as one of the fastest growing forms of leisure- and tourism-related phenomena (Dimmock and Tiyce, 2001; Gunn, 1994).

Festivals are a significant element of the attractions sector of tourism. 'Event tourism is concerned with the roles that festivals and special events can play in destination development and the maximisation of an event's attractiveness to tourists' (Getz, 1997). Getz and Frisby (1988) and Hall (1992) suggest that events may not only serve to attract tourists, but also assist in the development or maintenance of community or regional identity.

Tourism and culture are not strangers. Cultural tourism may appear a new term, but the phenomenon is not new. As elements of culture are converted into the market system, existing cultural institutions and patterns need to be preserved. Festival and event tourism may change the characteristics of the destination community (Craik, 1995: 89; Urry, 1990: 57–59; Leiper, 1995: 233). Issues identified include the threat to host communities experiencing tourists as invaders; the loss of privacy; destruction of the culture that attracts visitors as attractions are transformed into a 'museum'; hostility at perceived exploitation, commoditization and lack of consultation.

From the residents' perspective there are several reasons for the strains to the hospitality offered to visitors. One stranger may be acceptable, but in mass a threat exists and implies many of the concerns represented in the growing literature on negative impacts of tourism. Locals seek to retain their sense of the territorial imperative, particularly at a time of influx generated by festivals (Leiper, 1995: 240).

The number of tourists visiting a place compared with the size of the host population and scale of the destination, the character of the attraction and the degree to which it can be packaged for tourist consumption, the organization of the industry servicing tourists (small or large scale, locally or foreign owned), and the economic and social differences between hosts and tourists all need to be considered by destination and event management (Urry, 1990: 57–59). How well the host community anticipates and plans for these is crucial.

Festivals offer the potential, too, to foster local organizational development, leadership and networking, all of which are critical underpinnings of community-based tourism development. It is suggested that the consequence of this process would be tourism development more in keeping with community wishes, more authentic, thus more satisfying to residents and visitors and more sustainable over the long term (Getz, 1997).

Host community relationships

Values and beliefs held by individuals in a community are inextricably linked and shape people's attitudes and the way they act in specific situations. Notice how the values, interests and aspirations of individuals are influenced by their natural environment (space and place) and how this leads to a sense of community that influences how the community celebrates; that affects the community's wellbeing, which is shared with visitors who in turn interact with host community; they now have a shared image and identity to reflect and determine their values and beliefs. A cyclical process is in train.

Festivals and events provide an opportunity for community cultural development, which, like a sense of place, is nearly an invisible phenomenon. People know when it is not there. The complex relationships that festivals provide for individual members of a community, as each exchanges information and energy, offers the stability and protection that community can provide and that isolation cannot. They provide a 'now' and offer opportunities to speculate on a future. Community events can use place to demonstrate confidence in how they have kept order and developed interpretation so that others can do likewise when they visit.

A sense of community which visitors can feel when they participate in a festival is an intangible amalgam of services and experiences. While such festivals allow local people to satisfy their leisure needs, residents are able to work as volunteers at large and small events. That is another way for visitors to get a sense of local values and interests. The Sydney 2000 Olympic Games engaged thousands of volunteers in the management of the massive logistical exercise. Visitors have commented favourably on how happy they were to meet locals in formal and less formal ways, breaking down the host–guest gulf that can exist when large numbers of visitors descend on a destination.

How communities share their culture through festivals

A particular phenomenon, the community cultural festival, appears to be generated for 'the common good'. Community cultural festivals that share their 'culture', which in turn becomes the 'content' of the tourism experience for visitors, demonstrate how regional and local distinctiveness can influence festivals. Wood (1993) suggests that 'community, the custodians of the content of Australian tourism, must be enabled to participate in tourism by forming its content. Only if Australians are involved in tourism will it survive'. This sentiment can be applied globally.

To better explain the phenomenon it is useful to map the major elements, processes and relationships. These are presented in Figure 3.1. Festivals can emerge from the congruence of three major elements: the destination (place) in which they are held, the people who reside in that location (and within the region) and the visitors who are attracted to the festival. All of these are underpinned by the physical landscape in which they collaborate. The specific features of the local landscape and the lifestyle choices of residents are under scrutiny because they provide the region's 'identity'.

What can be observed is the importance of place and its impact on residents' lifestyle choices. The landscape changes, settlement patterns

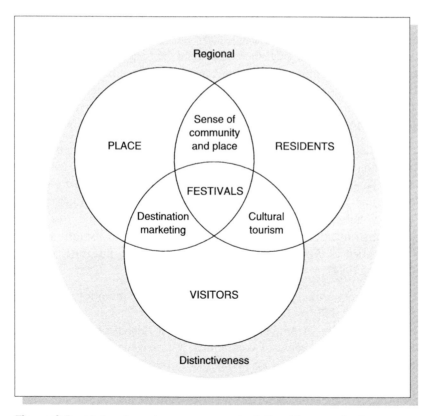

Figure 3.1 Major elements, processes and relationships contributing to festivals.

evolve and visitor segments vary over time. Destination marketing, cultural tourism, and a sense of community and of place essentially manifest themselves when festivals are turned into commodities in the tourism marketplace. The commodification of a way of life has become a concern for residents as a proliferation of festivals fills the annual community entertainment and recreational calendars.

Once festivals become part of a destination's marketing messages there is a shared image and identity. Thus a 'brand' representing core community values becomes a brand that can be used by both the community and tourism sectors. It is evident that destinations can be branded by festivals, e.g. the very old cultural landscape of Oberammergau in Bavaria for the Passion Play staged every 10 years.

Simply, this is about hosts and guests. Where outdoor dining has become *de rigueur*, patrons of local cafes and restaurants demand produce that is locally grown. A natural extension of this interest in regional produce and cuisine is the proliferation of specialist food-related events. While agricultural shows, harvest festivals and fishing competitions are stood to one side, there is a trend for 'experiencing' local food and wine in public places. Gilroy in California started hosting the Garlic Food Festival in the early 1980s. In the first year, 20 000 people joined in the celebration. In 2002, more than 125 000 people came to enjoy gourmet food, fine wines, quality arts and crafts and entertainment.

Dunstan (1994) suggests festivals can be used to build communities. Organizing a major festival takes a lot of individual and collective effort. To get the job done the organizers have to be able to give a lot of time personally and be able to call in a lot of favours and/or inspire volunteerism. Celebration can bind a community and it can also be the instrument that keeps community a fresh and constantly renewing experience. Celebration is the way humans integrate change (Dunstan, 1994).

Community cultural festivals help create communities of values (Ulrich, 1998: 157) by forging strong and distinct identities. One mechanism that assists in establishing whether festivals effectively represent their constituency's sense of community is to engage with a 'wellbeing model'. *Community wellbeing* (Wills, 2001) demonstrates clear rules of inclusion, sharing information across boundaries, creating social reciprocity, using symbols, myths and stories to create and sustain values and managing enough similarity so that the community feels familiar with clear building blocks.

Community wellbeing identified by the Local Government Community Services Association of Australia (Wills, 2001) incorporates qualities for developing healthy and sustainable communities. These seven elements provide an opportunity to sensitively assess how communities see themselves and measure themselves against a set of criteria that can meaningfully underpin how a sense of community and place contributes to cultural festivals (Table 3.1).

Table 3.1 Community wellbeing

Community wellbeing dimensions	Community wellbeing outcomes
Social and cultural	Conviviality, equity, vitality
Economic	Adequate prosperity
Environmental and built	Livability, sustainability and viability

Source: Wills (2001: 22).

These results are linked to wellbeing building blocks (Wills, 2001: 34) that include democratic governance, active citizenship, social justice and social capital (Table 3.2). These assist in clarifying how a sense of community and place contribute to regional cultural festivals.

Communities seek to enhance the livability quotient for their constituencies. There is increasing recognition of the economic value of natural and human capital. Festivals and events offer an integrated approach to creating the vibrant communities to which people aspire (Getz, 1997; Hall, 1992; Dunstan, 1994). Festivals serve the needs of

Table 3.2 Wellbeing building blocks

Wellbeing building blocks	Components/features
Democratic governance	Visions, goals, leadership, policies
Active citizenship	Equal political, civil and civic rights
Social justice	Human rights, social supports, empowerment
Social capital	Interpersonal and organizational trust, reciprocity and collective action

Source: Wills (2001: 34).

residents. They can protect the natural environment, increase social equity and provide a vision for participants. By providing a local focus they can satisfy specific industry niches (e.g. the Casino Beef Week celebrations or the Northern Rivers Herb Festival, both in NSW).

Festivals and place

Place is said to have spirit or personality. It seems that a sense of place can vary from person to person and time to time. There can be a distinction between the characteristics of place for residents and of those of visitors. Can visitors ever develop an appreciation and commitment to the same extent as locals? Does the contact with place and space allow visitors to go beyond just appreciation and understanding to conservation of sites or experiences based on access to particular location and natural forms?

Tourism, for example, is typified in some respects as the experience and consumption of place (Meethan, 1996). For places to achieve distinctiveness and status as places to go, to be seen in, they have to be created. Festivals and events also provide a medium for interpretation of place. That is why some popular events are sited in spectacular locations. This can be through the naming of the event, through a visual identification with the landscape so that appearance makes the location immediately identifiable for locals and visitors, or as a reflection of the local consciousness where the mood of a place is integrated into the content of the programme.

Festivals and events can place pressure on natural environments. It is important that organizers encourage a responsible approach to each individual's relationship with the space in which the event occurs, but also provide adequate waste management resources, information, interpretation and signage, and hardened surfaces, and minimize the harm that can come to water, vegetation and fauna in specific locations. Increasing attention to details of livability in more fragile event environments has provided opportunities for increased awareness and education in sustainable practices.

Authorities responsible for public environments like town squares, harbour and river foreshores, parklands and zoos and coastal zones are also addressing issues of maintaining quality landscapes for event practitioners and visitors. While holding events in such environments could encourage vandalism, litter and noise, major urban recreational areas have been redeveloped from slums or run-down business precincts and now provide revitalized access, improved amenities, interesting design, seating, lighting and public art elements for the public.

Image and identity

The publicity that festivals and events can generate for a community can have not only a cumulative impact on the destination but also feed into the image and identity of the community and assist with creating an appealing authenticity. The imagery generated by people having a good time attending a festival or special event can position a destination in the marketplace and attract others to visit in the future, stay longer than the event, and explore the tourist attractions.

Festivals can shape the image of the host community and its physical location in the mind of potential visitors. Technology now readily matches growing global curiosity with the capacity to beam images of ways of life around the world. Nimbin's Mardi Grass Cannabis Law Reform Rally held annually in a village of 600 residents in NSW has images of the mood, tone and street action of the festival parade or Hemp Olympix shared with a global audience through digital-camera- and web-based technology.

The proliferation of television lifestyle programmes emphasizes 'the what to do on holidays' elements of the travel experience and such pro-grammes regularly focus on the local leisure pursuits as attractors for visitors. Whether the events are of short or extended duration, highlight authentic traditions, showcase cultural practice or afford visitors to mix at play, the dynamics of such events are caught in a tourist space, often constructed by the industry. The packaging of festivals and events in tourism terms, with entry to event, accommodation, transport and food and beverage, creates an image of a comprehensive service being available to visitors.

Infrastructure and amenities

A destination will get value from a substantive festival or event if close attention is paid to the adequate supply of all goods and services required for its effective staging. Organizers' requirements include access to power, security, water, waste management, good communication, media contact, state-of-the-art technology, ticket distribution and marketing expertise and emergency procedures (McDonnell *et al.*, 1999). Those supplying the product or content of the event will require such amenities as transport, accommodation, hospitality and materials for their specific arts practice. Some of this will be supplied from the agency convening the event, some will be outsourced locally, some may be part of a package of support elements contracted with the venue manager.

Access to venues, efficient transport, well-signed directions and cost-friendly events will be attractive to audiences. Tickets may be purchased online, with early-bird discounts, with group incentives, as part of packages of accommodation, transport and other tourism services. Queuing, whether to enter the town, site, toilets or seats, can generate negative responses from the audience. Maps and information updates should be readily accessible. Secure parking, pathways, access to amenities like automatic teller machines, phones, first-aid and emergency services, water, food and beverage outlets, shade, seating, exits and roads should be known to all those on the festival or event site, as well as outside agencies connected with security and emergency services.

Some destinations have invested in purpose-built venues that provide outstanding amenities for participants and spectators. These venues, in fact, can be the attraction for visitors. As a legacy of hosting mega- (or other) events, communities often appreciate improved facilities in going about their everyday life. However, they are also alert to what is known as the opportunity cost of such investments; when dazzling structures are built, other amenities considered important to the host community are forgone.

Sociocultural impacts of festivals on residents

Positive legacies of festivals and events in destinations include the estab-lishment or the strengthening of traditions and values held by residents. Much is written on the growth in pride and spirit when communities host successful events. The delivery of successful events can encourage greater participation in sports or arts practice or other recreational activity. This combined with the adoption of new social patterns and exposure to new cultural forms can stimulate an increase in volunteerism, community involvement and intercultural interaction and cooperation. The Asia Pacific Triennial of Contemporary Art held at the Brisbane Art Gallery encourages a diverse audience to a series of associated activities that in turn encourages cultural contact during the intervening years.

Not every event is well received by host communities. Doxey's (1975) index of irritation is the most regularly cited framework demonstrating the impact on communities of visitors:

- *Euphoria* is the initial phase of development, when visitors and investors are welcome. Locals are enthusiastic and there is a feeling of mutual satisfaction.
- *Apathy* is evident as visitors are taken for granted.
- The *irritation/annoyance* phase indicates the saturation point is reached as residents have misgivings about the tourist industry.
- *Antagonism* demonstrates irritation openly expressed with visitors seen as the cause of all problems; planning becomes remedial but promotion is increased to offset the deteriorating reputation of the destination.
- The final level indicates that the host community has forgotten what they cherished in the first place or what originally drew the tourists and so the environment in which it is operating has now changed.

This list provides an introduction to the complexity of the changes that may take place over time in the resident community, but it also suggests that all members of the community have the same attitude. It fails to recognize the various opinions that may exist simultaneously in any community and how each adapts to the impacts of visitation. Each destination and community resident in it develops a series of boundaries through their habits, daily routines, beliefs, values and social lives.

Destination and festival and event marketing

Destinations and festivals and events need to establish a point of difference in order to attract an audience. The themes chosen by each need to be symbiotic and readily translated into the marketing and promotional mix undertaken to place both 'on the map'. The name and theme of an event needs to be translated effectively into a logo, signage, media, advertising, merchandising, civic design, banners and billboards. A strategic promotional strategy will involve contact with internal and external markets; that is, within organizations and established markets, within the host community and in the outside world. The use of e-media and technology allows for a simultaneously dispersed and targeted message to be distributed.

By encouraging journalists to familiarize themselves with the event and the destinations, editorial will find its way into the marketplace. Packages with other elements of the tourism system will increase awareness of the event; refining the product to include an attractive programme at a date and time that appeals to the target market and when the destination looks at its best will ensure ongoing attention.

Economic implications of festivals for destinations

Festivals can be big business for a destination. Festivals become part of destination tourism strategies because they can bring in new money to the local economy. There needs to be a businesslike approach by all stakeholders to embracing the more substantive festivals in a destination's portfolio. There is the distribution of income and expenditure to consider firstly. There is the generation of jobs not only within the events and tourism sectors but beyond. There is accounting for the investment in infrastructure, amenities, marketing, government grants, box office and sponsorship.

There needs to be consideration of the business community's involvement in festivals. The commercial sector's response, as a significant stakeholder in the host community, may be critical to the success of an event. Businesses provide a variety of support mechanisms, cash, in-kind sponsorship, influence and reflection of community attitudes. Business activity is impacted upon during the staging of community events.

Festivals can be a cost-effective means of developing tourism attractions and leisure activities for a destination. The contribution of volunteers rather than paid staff has become a feature of many cultural and sporting events like the Masters Games. Local income multipliers are seen as an advantage, and while mega-events are costly, some urban and regional destination managers seek out such events as blockbuster art shows or large-scale musicals as a catalyst for growth and as image-makers.

Conclusion

Differing forms of tourism, including festivals and special events, vary in nature from place to place. As a form of tourism, festivals can be examined in relation to their social and cultural contexts. A better understanding of the cultural identities of host communities in tourist destinations shows festivals holding a significant position in three areas of the human condition. They celebrate a sense of place through organizing inclusive activities in specific safe environments. They provide a vehicle for communities to host visitors and share such activities as representations of communally agreed values, interests and aspirations. Thirdly, they are the outward manifestation of the identity of the community and provide a distinctive identifier of place and people.

Bibliography

Asia Pacific Triennial of Contemporary Art, Queensland Art Gallery, Brisbane, Australia. www.qag.qld.gov.au.

Cotter, M.M., Boyd, W.E. and Gardiner, J.E. (eds) (2001). *Heritage Landscapes: Understanding Place and Communities*. Lismore, NSW: Southern Cross University Press.

Craik, J. (1995). Are there cultural limits to tourism? *Journal of Sustainable Tourism*, **3(2)**, 87–98.

Crompton, J.L. and McKay, S.L. (1997). Motives of visitors attending festival events. *Annals of Tourism Research*, **24**, 425–439.

Derrett, R. (2002). Making sense of how festivals demonstrate a community's sense of place. Conference paper, *Events and Place Making: Building Destinations and Communities through Events*, UTS, Sydney, July.

Dimmock, K. and Tiyce, M. (2001). Festivals and events: celebrating Special Interest Tourism. Chapter 15 in *Special Interest Tourism* (N. Douglas, N. Douglas and R. Derrett, eds), pp. 355–383. Brisbane: John Wiley and Sons.

Doxey, G.V. (1975). A causation theory of visitor–resident irritants, methodology and research inferences. *The Impacts of Tourism, Sixth Annual Conference Proceedings of the Travel Research Association*, San Diego.

Dunstan, G. (1994). Becoming coastwise, the path of festivals and cultural tourism. In *Landscape and Lifestyle Choices for the Northern Rivers of NSW*. Lismore, NSW: Southern Cross University.

Edinburgh International Festival, Scotland. www.eif.co.uk.

Ferris, W.R. (1996). *A Sense of Place*. National Endowment for the Humanities, Commonwealth Club of San Francisco. www.neh.fed.us/news/humanities/1998-01/ferris.html.

Getz, D. (1997). *Event Management and Event Tourism*. New York: Cognizant Communication Corporation.

Getz, D. and Frisby, W. (1988). Evaluating management effectiveness in community run festivals, *Journal of Travel Research*, Summer, 22–27.

Gilbert, D. and Lizotte, M. (1998). *Tourism and the Performing Arts*. Travel and Tourism Analyst, p. 73.

Gilroy Garlic Festival. www.gilroygarlicfestival.com (22 October 2002).

Goldblatt, J.J. (1997). *Special Events: Best Practices in Event Management*, 2nd edn. New York: VNR.

Greene, T. (1996). Cognition and the management of place. In *Nature and the Human Spirit: Toward an Expanded Land Management Ethic*. Venture Publishing.

Gunn, C. (1994). *Tourism Planning*, 3rd edn. London: Taylor and Francis.

Hall, C.M. (1992). *Hallmark Tourist Events: Impacts, Management and Planning*. London: Belhaven Press.

HSE (2000). *Managing Crowds Safely*. HSE Information Centre, Broad Lane, Sheffield. www.hsebooks.co.uk.

Leiper, N. (1995). *Tourism Management*. Melbourne: RMIT Press.

McDonnell, I., Allen, J. and O'Toole, W. (1999). *Festival and Special Event Management*. Brisbane: John Wiley and Sons.

Meethan, K. (1996). Place, image and power, Brighton as a resort. In *The Tourist Imagination*. John Wiley.

Nimbin Mardi Grass, NSW, Australia. www.nimbinmardigrass.com.

Oberammergau Passion Play. www.oberammergau.de (22 October 2002).

Reiss, A. (1993). Arts ties to tourism offer new support opportunities. *Fundraising Management*, August, p. 47.

Richins, H. and Pearce, P. (2000). Influences on tourism development decision making: coastal local government areas in eastern Australia. *Journal of Sustainable Tourism*, **8(3)**, 207–231.

Sapporo Snow Festival, Hokkaido, Japan. www.snowfes.com/english.

Ulrich, D. (1998). Six practices for creating communities of value, not proximity. In *The Community of the Future* (F. Hesselbein, M. Goldsmith, R. Beckhard and R.F. Schubert, eds), pp. 155–166. San Francisco: Jossey-Bass Publishers.

Urry, J. (1990). *The Tourist Gaze: Leisure and Travel in Contemporary Societies*. London: Sage Publications.

Wills, J. (2001) *Just, Vibrant and Sustainable Communities, A Framework for Progressing and Measuring Community Wellbeing*, Local Government Community Services of Australia, Townsville.

Wood, C. (1993). Package tourism and new tourism compared, *Proceedings from National Conference, Community Culture and Tourism*, July 1993, Melbourne, p. 11.

Woodford Folk Festival, Queensland, Australia. www.woodfordfolkfestival.com.

Questions

1 Why do communities host festivals and events?

2 How can festival managers work in partnership with others in the tourism system?

3 How can a destination maximize benefits from staging an event attractive to domestic and international visitors?

Part B

Managing the arts, culture and leisure experience

Event design and management: ritual sacrifice?

Steve Brown and Jane James

Introduction

In their rush to become part of the industry, and in their rush to satisfy and mould their events to meet the demands of their 'stakeholders' (e.g. sponsors, media partners, government agencies) and, indeed, in their rush to create an event 'industry', event managers have sacrificed the ritual element and the 'from the ground up' development of events. They have put aside, ignored or failed to consider the conceptual development and design of their events – the very heart and soul, the *raison d'être* of any truly great event – in favour of artificially manufacturing events that try to meet the needs of clients and stakeholders. Such events alienate the very community that makes up part of their target market, and from which many events have evolved.

Definitions

What are events? There are as many definitions as there are event texts. Getz (1993) talks of 'themed public celebrations' and Douglas *et al.* (2001) refer to festivals and events 'for people to come together to celebrate, to demonstrate, to worship, to honour, to remember, to socialise...'. To McDonnell *et al.* (1999) they are 'specific rituals ... or celebrations that are consciously planned and created to mark special occasions', and that it is 'impossible to provide a definition that includes all varieties [of events]'. To Goldblatt (1997) an event is 'a unique moment in time celebrated with ceremony and ritual to satisfy specific needs' and Van Der Wagen (2001) acknowledges that 'the most common events are community related'. This concept is supported by Douglas *et al.* (2001) who identify that 'community-based festivals and events originate ... within a sector of the community that has a need or desire to celebrate features of its way of life or history'. A dictionary (Brown, 1993) definition of a festival is as 'a joyful or honorific celebration'.

Common to most of these definitions is that events were originally a celebration of ceremony and ritual – and were a reflection of a culture and a community. Most events come from a good idea that is linked to the culture of the community and are underpinned by a reflection of place and a reflection of that culture, as evidenced by the IFEA Code of Professional Conduct and Ethics, which states that 'Festivals, events and civic celebrations are at the foundation of characteristics that distinguish human communities and interaction. The future development of our communities and world depend in part on the existence of these celebratory events' (International Festivals and Events Association, 2002).

Event management is simply, but essentially, the design and management of an event. Unfortunately the structure of the typical event management organization, and the job description for the typical event manager, fail to include the 'design' component. 'Design' is excluded even from the descriptive title 'event manager'.

Yet McDonnell *et al.* (1999) refer to an industry survey where over one hundred respondents stated that 'vision' was the essential attribute for a successful event manager. '[A] passion for helping people celebrate runs deep among serious event managers. Some even see their work as part ministry rather than solely as a commercial profession.' Goldblatt (2002) acknowledges that 'an event manager is a person responsible for researching, designing, planning, coordinating and evaluating events'.

Yet the design component is often missing. Why have contemporary event managers involved themselves so heavily in ritual sacrifice – 'constituting a social or psychological ritual, conventional, habitual' – and the 'loss incurred in underselling an item to get rid of it; the surrender of something valued or desired' (Brown, 1993)?

Under pressure

Goldblatt (1997) defines a special event as 'a unique moment in time celebrated with ceremony and ritual to satisfy specific needs', and celebration as observing 'with ceremony and ritual'. Sponsors, government and other funding agencies are, however, increasingly defining events as successful only in terms of ever-increasing attendance and in terms of the event's ability to return a profit, or at the very least to break even financially. It is these 'performance indicators' that pressure many an event manager to abandon the meaningful or authentic, in favour of the 'successful', and to make pronouncements about attendances with more than a little hyperbole – often with consequences for successive event managers trying to increase already artificially inflated figures.

Classification of events, too, is based on their audience (often an electronic-media – mainly television – audience) and their success in attracting large numbers of interstate and international visitors, rather than anything meaningful.

Dimmock and Tiyce (2001) state that 'the potential economic benefits of festivals and events are often emphasised over other impacts, particularly by local authorities and investors. Indeed, the success of a festival or event is commonly measured in terms of its economic contribution to event stakeholders, the community and the region.'

Since the mid-1990s, much of the focus of festivals and events has been on attracting tourists for the additional economic benefits they bring to the community. In Australia, some state governments even called for an 'event-led recovery' from their economic woes, and an intense bidding war developed between the states for those events seen to deliver these real or hoped for – and in some cases, imagined – economic benefits. In Australia, Melbourne, the state capital of Victoria, successfully lured the Australasian Formula One Grand Prix away from Adelaide, after eleven successful award-winning years in South Australia.

As a consequence, the economic impact of an event has become more important for the event managers than the ritual itself. 'Commoditisation occurs when community activities are altered to meet the needs and expectations of tourists, thus eroding the integrity, authenticity and traditional value of the culture', and 'Cultural integrity must take priority over economic gain or satisfying tourists' needs' (Dimmock and Tiyce, 2001: 368).

In the beginning

The emergence of an event industry in Australia has really only occurred since the mid-1990s. In South Australia the title 'event management' was first used as late as 1986 and at that time there was only one person with that title. In 1996, at an industry seminar in Adelaide, 316 people attended and listed themselves as practising event managers. They finally had a category in their own right – 'Event Management' – in the telephone business directory. Previously, event managers were listed either under 'Entertainment Agents' or with no heading alongside 'Escort Agencies'!

Their role is diverse. Van Der Wagen (2001) lists thirteen tasks in their job description, including developing the event 'concept, purpose and objective' and including aspects of marketing, budgeting, risk assessment and management, but with little emphasis on design. McDonnell *et al.* (1999) refer to 'vision' as being the single most important attribute for event managers.

Concurrent with the growth in the numbers of event managers has been a proliferation of events and the development of a wide range of training and accreditation programmes at tertiary institutions and universities, which include both professional development and award programmes. Many have been developed in partnership with relevant industry bodies such as the programmes at Flinders University in South Australia and the University of Technology in Sydney. However, the rapid growth in the number of events and 'event managers' still exceeds the number of appropriate training programmes that provide the key competencies, or 'core values' as outlined below.

Australian Major Events still has a requirement that any event it supports must have strong national and international visitation – bringing 'new money' to the state. Events that are widely supported only by the local community are not necessarily discriminated against if they have a 'heritage' focus or are a traditional part of the state's event calendar (e.g. the Christmas Pageant), but new events that fail to meet the economic criteria are unlikely to be supported. McDonnell *et al.* (1999) testify to the potential of events to 'increase[d] profile and economic benefits to a city and to an entire country', and the Economic Impact Study of the 1996 Adelaide Festival has as its opening remarks that 'It is now well recognised that cultural events ... are not only a significant promoter of a destination for interstate and international tourism, but also provide a significant injection to the local economy' (Market Equity, 1996).

Other training programmes across Australia concentrate on the management alone of events, rather than their design and management. This concept is also reflected in the many textbooks published since the late 1990s, which give scant attention to the creative development and design of events. Indeed, there are very few event texts internationally that have more than a passing mention of the equal importance of the ritual and cultural component and design of events, exceptions being Goldblatt (1997), Malouf (1999) and Van Der Wagen (2001).

Case study

The festival experience of the Adelaide Festival and Fringe

The Adelaide Festival of Arts commenced in 1960 at the instigation of the 'city fathers' and quickly became established as the pre-eminent arts and cultural festival in Australia ('The role that the Adelaide Festival plays in the cultural life of Australia is immense', *Newsweek*, noted in Whitelock, 1980), and it progressively established an international reputation akin to that enjoyed by the Edinburgh and Avignon Arts Festivals.

The impact of the festival on the city and the people of Adelaide was as important as the impact of the city and the people on the festival itself. 'It seems there is a "psychical and chemical" connection between the Adelaide community and its landscape; a deep affinity between this landscape and the Festival. The social and physical environment engendered that cultural activity which encouraged [the founders] to make their foray into the demanding sphere of international arts festivals' (Whitelock, 1980). Andrew Porter, the *New York Times* art critic, wrote: 'When you put everything together – and that elusive quality, the "feel" of the whole place – well, then, Adelaide comes out on top. I simply can't fault it' (Porter, 1996, noted in Whitelock, 1980).

As the success of the Adelaide Festival grew, along with its audiences, another, complementary festival evolved on the margins, following Edinburgh's successful model – the Fringe Festival – which ran concurrently with the Adelaide Arts Festival, and enjoyed community support. Both were examples of events that reflected the culture of the community, flourished in the harsh economic and increasingly competitive environment and were sustainable.

In 1984, with Orwell's novel in mind, the festival named its mainstream cabaret venue and programme 'Big Brother's'. The Fringe that same year created an alternative cabaret venue called 'Little Sister's'. The success of Little Sister's, the hit of the Fringe that year, was too great a temptation for the Fringe, and, over the next 12 years, the alternative became more and more mainstream commercial.

In 1996, Barrie Kosky, the Artistic Director of the Adelaide Festival, sensing that the Fringe was drifting away from its core values – had committed ritual sacrifice – lured that audience to the mainstream festival by creating 'Red Square', a giant, outdoor, performance venue, in the heart of the city, programmed for the very audience that had originally spawned the Fringe. It was a huge success and 'out-Fringed' the Fringe.

In 1998 the Fringe attempted to regain its lost audience by creating a giant outdoor alternative cabaret performance venue in the heart of the city called 'Big Red'. It failed to attract significant audiences away from the Adelaide Festival.

The Fringe started with success at the community level and was a platform for emerging and local artists not given that opportunity within the curated mainstream Festival. Now it was heading to the mainstream and, with limited resources compared to the Festival, was unable to capture the mainstream audience as its own, whilst alienating and marginalizing its community base.

In 2002, ignoring the fate of the Fringe, the new Artistic Director of the Adelaide Festival, Peter Sellers, proposed a programme that rejected the Festival's traditional base. The perception was that the

Adelaide Festival had moved away from the expectations of its community and lost focus and support. Sellars resigned amongst much acrimony and even more terrible press.

Productions that were refused a place in the 'mainstream' Festival were welcomed back by the 'alternative' Fringe, which in 2002 was a huge success both with audiences and economically (James, 2002). The Adelaide Festival suffered a financial loss and had marginalized its traditional audiences.

Aspirations are local, national and international for both Fringe and Festival and it is likely that the seesawing will continue until the Festival and the Fringe come to terms with the 'Why?' of their events.

Contemporary research into regionally based festivals suggests that a common goal or vision – the 'Why?' – is the single most important factor for the success of an event (Brown and McIlvena, 2001).

Core values

Design is essential to an event's success because it leads to improvement of the event on every level. An event can be 10 per cent better than a 'competitor' without necessarily needing additional resources – financial or otherwise.

Event management encompasses financial and risk management; proposals and bidding; marketing, publicity and protocol; legal, environmental and access issues; production and site management; staging; income generation, sponsorship and VIP servicing; evaluation; planning and event management methodologies. However, event design is the critical component, underpinning every other aspect of the event, and central to event design are the core values of the event.

Goldblatt (1997) suggests that there are five questions that must be posed and answered before any event is attempted: Why? Who? When? Where? What? The core values, which are mission critical to the success and sustainability of any event, can be established by asking: Why? Who? What? and Want?

- *Why?* Goldblatt and Nelson (2001) ask what is 'the compelling reason for this event? Why must this event be held?' If there is no compelling reason, if you do not know why you are proposing to do – or are already doing – the event, stop now!

■ *Who?* Who is the event for? Who is the target market? This would include stakeholders, participants and the event management team, as well as the audience. Contrary to Goldblatt and Nelson (2001), who next determines the 'When?' and 'Where?' of the event, the present authors would maintain that making these decisions, at this point in the planning and design of the event, is too soon.

■ *What?* This determines the 'event product' (Goldblatt and Nelson, 2001) or the broad parameters (not the finest details) of what the event will be, e.g. a launch, festival, carnival, dinner, award ceremony, or a fair.

■ *Want?* What is it that you want to achieve with this event? McIlvena and Brown (2001) talk about 'Establishing measurable ... objectives and projected outcomes', and the importance of evaluation of those outcomes prior to, during and after the event. As someone once said, if you aim at nothing you will hit it with monotonous regularity!

Almost certainly at this stage, the passionate event manager wants to embark on the detailed planning of all aspects of the operation, the logistics and the programming of the event. Again there are reasons to pause, to consider the design principles.

Design principles

There are five design principles – scale, shape, focus, timing and build – that can be identified and applied prior to the logistics and operational aspects of any event.

■ *Scale* – matching the scale of the activity to the venue and ensuring that, regardless of the distance from the activity to the audience, the audience can clearly see and understand what is being presented. This may involve using elements that are visual rather than aural, three-dimensional rather than two-dimensional, multiple rather than single. It allows for the psychological impact of the space on the audience and the audience's need for a sense of enclosure, but not restriction.

■ *Shape* – simple, clean lines. The removal of any visual clutter and/or distractions is essential. Understanding audience psychology – which way will they want to walk or turn and how will they respond to site layout – is crucial. Visitor observation surveys or tracking will provide invaluable information. Ensuring clear sight lines for every seat in the house is vital.

■ *Focus* – ensuring that the audience is focused on what you want. Utilizing blocking techniques from theatre and film direction to 'force' attention to specific locations will prove useful, as will understanding the physiological response of the human eye to colours, movement and changes in intensity when lighting an event, and the psychological response of audiences to shape and structure.

■ *Timing* – accurate timing throughout the event will go a long way towards maintaining the contract established with the audience. Allowing sufficient time for each and every programme element and programming tightly (to the second) creates a feeling of spontaneity, and relaxed 'flow' to events. Understanding an audience's likely attention span and response to programme elements, and being able to programme to maximize their attention, is also critical. 'Event time' is different from real time and audiences respond differently to it. Event design needs to incorporate local social, cultural and environmental conditions when scheduling activity, and allow for a 'time contingency' in the schedule.

■ *Build* – understanding the 'event curve' (McIlvena and Brown, 2001) and how to apply it to the programme to 'build' the event over its duration, including the ebbs and peaks, so as to maximize its impact with the audience, is vital. So is how to maximize limited event and programme resources to create high impact.

The event design process is not time consuming. The overwhelmingly positive effects of this level of planning, prior to any detailed logistical or operational planning commencement, can be quite dramatic.

Understanding and embracing the core design principles of an event gives that event a clear direction that is easily marketed and easily understood by all those involved, whether internal or external to the organization. It is clearly understood by the event management team that every decision made must relate back to, and be in accord with, the core values for the event.

Everything is different, everything stays the same

As the pressure on event managers to respond to the demands of financial stakeholders increases, almost exponentially, events are in danger of straying from core values and of becoming increasingly generic. The event calendar in each Australian state is littered with generic events that if not dead, are certainly in danger of dying.

Once the success of an event is noted multiple copies arise, not from any demand or need, but because it is often perceived as safer than investigating ritual, celebration and community aspirations to develop an appropriate, but possibly different event, that reflects the 'sense of place' (Carter, 1997) or cultural authenticity (Douglas *et al.*, 2001) of a particular community. Governments, commercial sponsors, states, local councils, and committees, however, are also much happier playing it safe – especially so in the increasingly frustrating litigiousness of Australian society and the rapaciousness of event insurers at this time. Great events, whether major, minor or hallmark (Getz, 1993), need to be not safe. They can stretch and challenge event managers and audiences alike. They can introduce the new, whilst celebrating the old and the traditional.

Vast numbers of generic events around the world have disappeared almost as quickly as they are created. This puzzling lack of sustainability is linked to their very generic nature. In marketing terms, generic events are doomed before they are launched. Every event offers food, drink, entertainment and free fun for all the family. What makes someone attend one event over another? What is, in marketing terms, the point of differ-ence, the unique selling point for this event? Community ownership, integ-rity and authenticity make a difference. Developing an event based on an understanding of the rituals and celebrations of a specific community makes a difference and gives an event a head start over its competitors. Marketing tricks can be used to convince an audience to attend – once. A great visual, a great name or logo may attract them, but if they do attend and the promise is not delivered they are lost, and so is the event.

Playing it safe is often a part of the event manager's need to be viewed as a professional working in a professional industry. The terminologies and methodologies of project management, financial management and marketing have been adopted to give credence to the position. The event industry has developed its own industry associations, holds its own conventions and conferences, and has established credentials and levels of accreditation. These are not to be decried, and it is important that these professionals continually re-educate themselves and develop as festival and event managers – but not with just one focus. Goldblatt and Nelson (1997) argue that 'special events require people with the ability to move easily between the left (logic, order, systems, planning) and right (creative, spontaneous thinking) quadrants of the cerebellum'. Therein lies not only the challenge, but also the excitement!

Conclusion

It is easier to dwell solely within the confines of the logistics and operational side of an event. It requires common sense, a systematic approach, attention to detail, and a good data management system. Committees, authorities and insurers will be happy with such a manager. Nothing will be overlooked. The event will run on time and as scheduled. Problems encountered will be systematically dealt with and resolved. There will be a stack of strategic plans, SWOT (strengths, weaknesses, opportunities and threats) analyses, emergency response plans, risk management appraisals, and colour-coded files on shelves or on a laptop. There will also be, quite possibly, a one-dimensional event that lacks the inspired 'something' that makes an event truly great. And it probably won't last.

When you are asked to participate in an event – in whatever capacity – seek out the community, look for the ritual elements, find the celebration, know the 'why' and the 'who' and the 'what' and the 'want'. Seek to design, as well as to manage – and you will discover a whole new meaning and a whole new and inspirational event. Your ministry is to create that event for and with your audience, and to prevent the ritual sacrifice that is often the consequence of events designed primarily for economic gain alone.

Bibliography

Brown, L. (ed.) (1993). *The New Shorter Oxford English Dictionary*. Oxford University Press.

Brown, S. and McIlvena, M. (2001). Festival feasibility reports. Unpublished commercial in-confidence reports.

Carter, J. (ed.) (1997). *Sense of Place*. Tourism and Environment Initiative, Scotland.

Dimmock, K. and Tiyce, M. (2001). Festivals and events: celebrating special interest tourism. In *Special Interest Tourism* (N. Douglas, N. Douglas and R. Derrett, eds), p. 364. John Wiley and Sons.

Douglas, N., Douglas, N. and Derrett, R. (eds) (2001). *Special Interest Tourism*, p. 356. John Wiley and Sons.

Getz, D. (1993). Corporate culture in not-for-profit festival organisations: concepts and potential applications. *Festival Management and Event Tourism*, 1, 11–17.

Goldblatt, J. (1997). *Special Events – Best Practices in Modern Event Management*. John Wiley and Sons.

Goldblatt, J. (2002). *Special Events – Twenty First Century Global Event Management*, 3rd edn. John Wiley and Sons.

Goldblatt, J. and Nelson, K. (eds) (2001). *The International Dictionary of Event Management*, 2nd edn. John Wiley and Sons.

International Festivals and Events Association (2002). Code of professional conduct and ethics. *IE – The Business of International Events, International Festivals and Events Association (IFEA)*, **13(3)**.

James, J.A. (2002). Economic impact and visitor survey of the Adelaide Fringe 2002. Unpublished report.

Malouf, L. (1999). *Behind the Scenes at Special Events – Flowers, Props and Design*. John Wiley and Sons.

Market Equity Pty Ltd (1996). *1996 Adelaide Festival – An Economic Impact Study*. Prepared for the South Australian Tourism Commission, Department for the Arts and Cultural Development and the Australia Council.

McDonnell, I., Allen, J. and O'Toole, W. (1999). *Festival and Special Event Management*. John Wiley and Sons.

McIlvena, M. and Brown, S. (2001). *The Next Big Thing*. Visible Management and Flinders University Press.

Van Der Wagen, L. (2001). *Event Management for Tourism, Cultural, Business and Sporting Events*. Melbourne: Hospitality Press.

Whitelock, D. (1980). *Festival! The Story of the Adelaide Festival of Arts*, Newsweek, 29 March 1976.

Questions

1 Where do the festivals and events that you have attended or managed come from? What role do they play in the community within which they take place?

2 Identify the core values for festivals or events that you have attended or managed. How have these been balanced against the often-competing demands of the stakeholders?

3 In what ways can the design of an event contribute to its success and sustainability?

Visitor management for festivals and events

Ian Yeoman, Martin Robertson and Una McMahon-Beattie

Introduction

There are few texts that endeavour to cover the requirements of managing visitors at a festival or event. This is strange when one considers how the satisfaction of this intangible product, more than any other, is so dependent on the collective experience of people who spend an extended period of time in close proximity to each other: in the immediate run-up to the event, for either part or all of the time of the central event experience, and then again as they exit from the event.

Research has pointed, however, to the fact that crowding or periods of what this chapter goes on to describe as queues and bottlenecks are less of a motivational influence in outdoor, natural or backcountry festival settings. In these situations, while crowd management is still a vital element in both safety and the customers' sense of wellbeing – and satisfaction – studies reflect that they are not as significant a determining factor in the experience goals of the event audience as they are in the urban or *frontcountry* environment in which the customer has lower tolerance levels (Shelby *et al.*, 1989; Lee and Graefe, 2003). Accordingly this chapter focuses on festival venues which are either purpose built for public performance or which are in some other way constrained by the (largely) urban environment in which they are set.

The chapter draws on a number of models to animate the need for a visitor manager to balance the requirements of demand forecasting and managing capacity with appropriate levels of service quality and cost.

Inventories of festivals and events

The ability to manage inventories in anticipation of demand is easier in the manufacturing sector (Schmenner, 1995) than it is in preparation for the management of visitors. In visitor management, demand is an uncertain science in which the visitor manager – however well prepared – has to, in effect, guess demand and define capacity. If demand falls below forecast, the event suffers from underutilization of resources. If demand exceeds capacity, potential revenues are lost. It is the nature of the experience of events and festivals that differentiates the management of visitors from manufacturing operations. This difference is based upon the following core elements: the perishability of the product; the predominantly inflexible scope of capacity; the difficulty in predicting demand; the variability of the visitors' perception and enjoyment of the experience, and the relationship of all these elements with the venue location. In summary, visitor management for any large service encounter or experience is a decision-making process of:

- Designing a pattern of visitor flow
- Balancing tasks, equipment, space and time
- Incorporating different visitors' operational needs
- Scheduling demand in a way that is manageable and most suitable for visitors
- Determining appropriate capacity thresholds
- Managing queues and bottlenecks.

Shackley (1999) pronounces visitor management in terms of the control of visitor demand in relationship to a festival or attraction's relatively fixed capacity. This process employs methods to shift demand from peak periods to those that are off-peak, as well as creating temporal capacity or the offer of ancillary services to further encourage optimum shifts of audience consumption and thus affect positively the experience they have. The delivery of this experience is bound up in what is referred to by Jan Carlzon (Schmenner, 1995) as the *moment of truth*, a moment when the visitor comes face to face with the service process. This is known as the visitor service encounter and within this, the role of the visitor manager at any event is to schedule the service experience so as to manage visitor flows, minimize bottlenecks of people and ensure queues are well managed.

The nature of capacity and demand

The movement of visitors through a festival or attraction can sometimes incur a capacity ceiling, where demand equals or exceeds capacity. When this is the case a capacity constraint emerges, resulting in queues and bottlenecks. To explain the particular nature of *capacity* it is useful here to mention that commonly the word explains the static, physical, fixed volume of a container or the space in a building. While, similarly, capacity can be measured by the terms of an inventory – for example by the number of seats in a theatre – the essential difference for a festival or attraction is that this physical measurement does not reflect the *processing capacities* of operations. The capacity of most events and festivals is relative to the immeasurable elements of visitor duration. Thus the visitor service encounter is a perishable experience, something that cannot be touched or stored as inventory. As an example, the experience of the internationally recognized Glastonbury Festival is music, the people and the atmosphere that emerges from the combination of both. Accordingly it is not a physical product. It is these intangible elements that visitors value rather than the physical or ancillary products (although these are synonymous with the overall experience). So, unlike manufacturing, the consumption of the visitor service encounter is simultaneous with its production and cannot be inventoried, stored or resold for later consumption (it should be noted in support of this that while income is generated from the packaging of alternative forms of the experience, in the forms of aural or visual recordings or publications, the experience offered cannot be the same as that consumed at the event). Therefore, the unit of inventory becomes the time slot that is available, i.e. the specific date or time of day of the event, whether this be a festival, pop concert, theatre production or any other form of intangible consumption.

Capacity in manufacturing can be increased in the short term through practices such as overtime or additional shifts. Similarly, there are festivals and events that can increase maximum capacity through extending hours of operation. However, not all festival service encounters can do that. It is particularly difficult to increase capacity, for example, where theatres have a fixed capacity. In the case of performances – as part of the Edinburgh Festival – in Traverse Theatre 1 at the Traverse Theatre Festival Theatre (a permanent theatre venue) the audience (at the time of writing) is restricted to a maximum capacity of 350. So even where a particular performance has additional demand, the Traverse Theatre Festival cannot create extra capacity for it. This is the case in most built venues. This is complicated further by the fact that predicting demand is also an uncertain science: demand variations are typically severe and subject to many uncontrollable influences, not least of which in the UK is weather. Purchasing decisions can occur over shorter time periods and may be emotive spur-of-the-moment decisions induced by circumstances of that day or week. Again, this is another dynamic for decisions about capacity.

The nature of the visitor service encounter is such that there is also variability in the service time. This may be dependent on the variety of services and products offered at an event, or the degree of customization required for the service experience, or – where the service encounter allows – the variability of each customer's needs and requirements. In the last of these variables one can use as an example the difference in time required to serve a child, or a visitor with special needs, e.g. someone with visual or hearing impairments, or a whole family.

It is rare that the visitor service encounter can be transported and thus many festivals and events are unequivocally bound to the venue. Capacity is thus set by the venue capacity and the appropriate time period (Haksever et al., 2000). Where festivals and events offer a range of products, e.g. various forms of performing art, including, for example, comedy or drama, utilizing any number of stages within or outwith one building, shifting demand from one part of the venue to another is very difficult. Correspondingly, it is of vital importance that a balance is kept between the performance areas. Where one venue area is oversubscribed and another unpopular it is exceptionally rare to be able to transfer one audience from one area to the other. In the case of the Edinburgh

International Festival or the Fringe Festival, demand may shift on a daily basis consequent on a good (or bad) newspaper review.

One of the means to control demand in capacity constrained venues is through *revenue management and pricing*. The objective of revenue management is to maximize revenue and control availability for specific time periods. Revenue management is a suitable approach (Kimes, 2000) when the venue has the following attributes:

■ A relatively fixed capacity
■ Demand can be segmented
■ The inventory is perishable
■ The product is sold in advance
■ Demand is varied
■ Fixed costs are high
■ Variable costs are low.

The basic idea of revenue management is to partition the inventory for any good or service and to sell its parts to different visitors – taking on board the needs of income maximization. Thus, for a theatre venue, it is possible, for example, to offer seats at different prices, at different times of the day. For a comprehensive overview of revenue management and pricing, please refer to Chapter 13.

Managing capacity and demand

Visitor management is the combined process of delivering the elements that form the experience in the right order, at the right time, at the right speed, and at the right price – all in a way which will best satisfy the visitor. As mentioned in the introduction, this requires the visitor manager to forecast demand and define capacity in such a way as to avoid, on the one hand, underutilization of facilities, labour and equipment and, on the other, to ensure that demand does not exceed capacity. In the latter scenario, revenue is likely to be lost, complaints will be incurred and often queues and bottlenecks will form.

Accordingly, *capacity management* is a vital link in the management of visitors and entails determining the appropriate capacity for any given festival or event venue and making decisions appropriate to this. For instance, the preparation for peak period of demand involves having capacity to cope with it. At this point it would be normal that the revenue generated will justify holding off excess capacity. Such cases classically can be seen in theatres, concert halls and one-off events. Full capacity can only be maintained when there is appropriate management of the service delivery system. This involves scheduling of:

■ Labour and equipment
■ Maintenance
■ Visitor movement.

This equation can be further complicated when venues have multiple uses. In this situation, proceeds from an off-peak time may contribute towards the venue's fixed costs. For example, the Albert Hall, London, is known as a venue for a series of classical music concerts called the *Proms*. However, the venue also doubles as an indoor tennis centre for the Davis Cup tournament (amongst a great many other events) outside the traditional concert music season. For the Albert Hall's income, one is complementary to the other and helps maximize the overall potential income.

Demand management, on the other hand, 'is about shifting the timing of demand so that the peak is "shaved" and the off-peak times, with their excess capacities, are fed more' (Schmenner, 1995: 136). Examples of this include the use of ticketing and reservation systems for theatre performance. Here, when capacity is constrained, events can be managed by introducing a system of scheduling to control demand. Reservations obviously guarantee the certainty of demand, making the scheduling and allocation easier for the visitor manager. Importantly, reservations help ensure that more revenue can be gained out of customers who are themselves satisfied by the opportunity to pay a higher price for a better seat. Complementary to this, by focusing on pricing and service policies, demand can be managed in an indirect manner and can aid the shifting of customers from peak period to non-peak times.

Understanding demand and capacity means considering strategies of managing fluctuations. The methods associated with this include *level capacity, chase demand* and *change demand*. To look at each in turn: a *level capacity plan* is about forecasting capacity without any fluctuations for alternations in demand. A level capacity plan is suitable where capacity is fixed and high margins are earned at the peak, resulting in holding excess capacity. This is the desired position. A *chase demand plan*, on the other hand, attempts to match capacity close to varying levels of forecast demand. This is more difficult to achieve, as flexible scheduling is required in which there is a need to respond quickly to change. This may simply mean the ability to enable – possibly at great speed – any number of skilled staff, or casual staff, or equipment. Or it may require a greatly more complicated scenario of quick action. A *chase demand strategy* is more readily ascribable to festivals and events as the experience cannot be inventoried; it is service rather than product based and involves the processing of visitors (Slack *et al.*, 2001). This strategy uses a variable cost based structure rather than incurring high-fixed costs. This is important, as the wasteful provision of excess labour, materials and equipment, as needs to be maintained in a level capacity strategy, is eliminated. A chase demand strategy has the drawback of giving a visitor manager the difficult task of managing and maintaining the variables of the visitor service encounter, such as service quality, safety procedures, service specifications, cost and delivery. Finally, a *change demand strategy* means deploying a strategy that changes demand. This would normally require the transference of visitor demand from peak periods to off-peak periods. In order to do this, alternative products or services can be altered or price changes used as control mechanisms.

Visitor flows: bottlenecks and queues

One of the best ways to manage demand in an environment of constrained capacity is to map out the visitor flow within a venue. This involves a range of tools, perhaps the most vital of which are visitor flow process charts.

Visitor flow process charts are a depiction of the movement of visitors in a venue. According to Schmenner (1995) they are a sequential identification of the steps of visitor flow, and how things happen relative to this. The development of such diagrams helps the visitor manager alter and manage visitor flows at festivals and venues through decisions relating to space allocation, visitor throughput and utilization of time. Significantly, they show the service delivery system and identify bottlenecks and queues within this.

In summary, visitor flow process charts enable the visitor manager to:

- Calculate capacity constraints at a range of points along the visitor flow
- Balance demand and capacity, in order to reduce or eliminate potential bottlenecks and queues
- Make decisions in the design of visitor flow and process delivery for events and festivals.

By using such charts, information is generated which will allow management to examine flows as well as question how things happen within and during that flow. By questioning the sequence of visitor (audience) flows, alternative suggestions can be generated which will allow the visitor manager to make improvements and eliminate waste.

Process and information flow diagrams show the movement in a visitor service encounter that is sequential and parallel to different processes. A range of symbols are used to depict different meanings; examples are shown in Figure 5.1.

Bottlenecks occur where demand either becomes close to or exceeds capacity. The closer demand is to capacity, the longer the queue and the more serious the bottleneck. Shackley (1999) and Schmenner (1995) identify two types of bottleneck: chronic and episodic. Episodic bottlenecks are concerned with equipment breakdowns, material shortages and

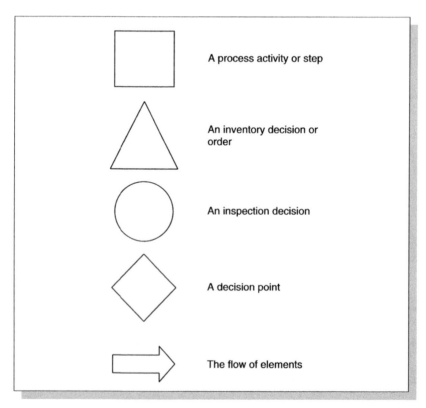

Figure 5.1 Process and information flow diagram symbols.

labour shortages. Chronic bottlenecks are more serious, and fall into the categories of *material* and *process* problems. Material problems are associated with either ordering the wrong, or else not enough, materials. Process problems are more strategic, one example being where there is insufficient information suggesting utility of the wrong kind of process and incorrect demand forecasting. Quality problems, which are fundamentally episodic, if not remedied can turn into chronic problems.

The address of layout and service design can sometimes precipitate a process problem in which the visitor service delivery will not match the process design. The problem here is that these two elements are treated as separate despite the fact that the slightest change to either specification has a profound implication on the visitor flow. In many cases, the visitor is part of the visitor service encounter rather than a product of it. Accordingly this understanding cannot be separated in layout design. Visitor service processes have to be designed in such a way as to create all of the processes that are needed to deliver the experience in an effective manner. This means the balancing and utility of quality, speed, dependability, flexibility and cost as design performance indicators (Slack *et al.*, 2001).

Service processes should influence how the visitor manager designs a layout to deliver the visitor service encounter. The visitor manager is concerned with the specifications and process of the visitor service encounter. Schmenner (1995) proposed a model which categorized service delivery systems into four main categories, namely: *service factory*, *service shop*, *mass service* and *professional service* (Figure 5.2).

The grouping takes account of the degree of labour intensity and the degree of customization and interaction. The majority of events fit quite

		DEGREE OF INTERACTION & CUSTOMIZATION	
		LOW	HIGH
DEGREE OF LABOUR INTENSITY	LOW	Service factory *e.g. hotels, restaurants, resorts, recreation*	Service shop *e.g. hospitals, car repair*
	HIGH	Mass service *e.g. retailing, schools*	Professional service *e.g. doctors, lawyers*

Figure 5.2 The Schmenner service process matrix.

easily into the category of service factory in that labour intensity is fairly low and they rarely offer a *one-to-one* professional service. For the visitor manager at any live performance a decision will have to be made as to the number of stewards and venue staff to engage. The same decision will have to be made for the operation of the ticket booth, for marshalling visitors around the venue and in the organization of refreshment provision. Personal contact will very much be about directing and ensuring safety and catering provision. In many events the user is expected to gather his or her own information from any signage, programme or electronic source provision. Where there is little contact with the venue staff, appropriate standards of service to ensure customer satisfaction (as well as ensure vital factors such as safety) is dependent on great depth in planning.

As part of the process towards planning, Schmenner's matrix (Figure 5.2) provides a simple way of categorizing different types of service organization. It is important to recognize in this that within each quadrant there is the capacity for considerable variation.

Layout types are a physical manifestation of a service process type in which the characteristics of the visitor service encounter determine the process type. These depend on the service process, which in turn determines how the service is delivered to the visitor. According to Schmenner (1995) this relationship is dependent on the degree of customization, interaction and labour intensity in the service scenario. Basic layout types include: fixed position layout, process layout, and product layout. *Fixed position layouts* are concerned with the visitor being in a fixed position or where the product is too large to move. This may be the case when performances are given on a stage and audiences are sat at tables at its edge. *Process layout* is concerned with the need and convenience of transforming resources which constitute a large part of the layout decision (Slack *et al.*, 2001). Here it is convenient for the visitors to flow through the operation. So, for example, it may be that the audience of a festival or event move between different sections of an event such as sideshows, catering facilities or displays. *Product layout* involves the location of the transforming resources entirely for the convenience of consuming the transformed resources.

Visitors have a propensity to follow a determined sequential flow or line layout. This facilitates the efforts of the visitor manager to control the flow of visitors. However, the challenge is to avoid bottlenecks in a rigid process as this results in long queues and often counter congestion for those who may be wishing to exit. It is to queues and their management that this chapter now turns. While the focus of this chapter is on events and festivals housed in either permanent or semipermanent structures, it is important to observe that some of the same traits are displayed in more structured outdoor events. As the organizer of the cultural programmes for the Glasgow Garden Festival in 1988, Michael Dale, now Director of Glasgow's West End Festival, observed (March 2003) that visitor pathways and routes were changed a great many times in the first month of the five-month festival before they got it right. Dealing with anything between 12 000 and 108 000 visitors a day meant that the night-time deliberations in rerouting paths were undertaken without hesitation.

Queues

The role of the visitor manager in managing queues relates to the tradeoff of the cost of providing good service and the cost of the visitors waiting. Ideally it is preferred that queues are short enough that visitors will not leave without purchasing a ticket (or going on to enjoy the festival experience if they are required to queue again after payment) nor purchase the ticket but be so put off by the waiting experience that they do not return. These service encounters can be classified in terms of the number of channels (i.e. number of servers) and number of phases (i.e. the number of service stops that must be made). This may be a product layout *single line channel*, with one ticket vendor and one single queue. Alternatively, if an event has several ticket vendors and one single queue, then it would be a *multichannel* queuing system (Haksever *et al.*, 2000).

One of the problems with uncertain demand is the statistical uncertainty or variability of arrivals. These can cause bottlenecks and the formation of unanticipated queues. Obviously this situation affects the visitor service encounter. The core management factors to control are the timing of arrivals and how the operation deals with the ensuing variety of speed, capacity, quality and capability of the process. It is this variety and uncertainty that causes the visitor service encounter process to lose some of its ability to generate satisfaction for the festival or event visitor. Crucially for the manager, the greater the variety of the management in the process, the greater the potential for bottleneck occurrences.

Queuing models help visitor managers balance desirable capacity costs with waiting-line costs. These models are based on the following range of decision points:

- The average time each visitor spends in a queue
- The average queue time at peak period
- Queuing and service time per transaction point
- The probability that the event facility will be idle (during or between performances)
- Utilization factors
- The probability of visitor distribution and arrivals.

There are a range of mathematical and simulation models that deal with single and multiple channels. For further details of these please refer to Render and Stair (2000).

The understanding of the *psychology of queuing* provides visitor managers insights and understanding of waiting line and time phenomena in the service encounter. From this understanding, Maister (1985) provides a range of propositions about people and how they interpret and react to queues:

- Unoccupied time feels longer than occupied time
- Preprocess waits seem longer
- Uncertain waits seem longer
- Uncertain waits are longer than known, finite waits
- Unexplained waits are longer than explained waits
- The more valuable the service, the longer the visitor will wait
- Solo waits feel longer than group waits.

Each of these psychological aspects can and should guide the event manager in deciding how to best create and attempt to manage queues at those points where the visitor is likely to experience queues.

Forecasting

Forecasting is a natural starting point for event managers when matching demand and capacity. As stated previously, the ability to predict demand is the foundation for the development of an appropriate strategy to manage the service encounter. Barlow (1999) highlights a number of factors that must be considered when selecting an appropriate forecasting method. These include:

1 Time
- Span of the forecast
- Urgency with which the forecast is needed
- Frequency that the updates must be made.

2 Resource requirements
- Mathematical requirements
- Computer resources
- Financial resources.
3 Input characteristics
- Antecedent data available
- Variability of fluctuation range and frequency
- External stability.
4 Output characteristics
- Detail or degree of desegregation
- Accuracy.

Taking into consideration the above factors, the visitor manager must then select an appropriate forecasting method that is classified on *judgements, counting, time series* and *causal effect*. For a comprehensive overview of forecasting methodologies, readers are referred to Georgoff and Murdick (1986).

Conclusion – balancing operations

The event manager is concerned with the need to balance operations. This is to say that it is important that the service encounter ensures that the needs of the visitor are balanced with the need for a smooth, efficient and cost-effective operation. To prepare for this the role of the visitor manager is to forecast the demand for the actual capacity, and then to take appropriate decisions to ensure that the service offers the best possible experience to the right visitor, at the right time, with the right service level and at the right cost. Further decisions should then be made to maintain the balance. Importantly, appropriate management has a key influence on the event participants' satisfaction. Equally, where the physical layout of the venue allows, visitor management can also offer the potential for added income generation.

Bibliography

Barlow, G. (1999). In *Heritage Visitor Attractions: An Operations Management Perspective* (A. Leask and I. Yeoman, eds). London: Cassell Publications.

Georgoff, D.M. and Murdick, R.G. (1986). Managers' guide to forecasting. *Harvard Business Review*, **64(1)**, 110–120.

Haksever, C., Render, B., Russell, R. and Murdick, R.G. (2000). *Service Management and Operations*. Englewood Cliffs, NJ: Prentice-Hall.

Kimes, S. (2000). A strategic approach to yield management. In *Yield Management: Strategies for the Service Industries* (A. Ingold, U. McMahon-Beattie and I. Yeoman, eds). London: Continuum Press.

Lee, H. and Graefe, A.R. (2003). Crowding at an arts festival: extending crowding models to the frontcountry. *Tourism Management*, **14**, 1–11.

Maister, D.H. (1985). The psychology of waiting times. In *The Service Encounter* (J.A. Czepiel, M.R. Solomon, and C.F. Surprenant, eds). Lexington: Heath and Co.

Render, B. and Stair, R. (2000). *Quantitative Analysis for Management*. London: Prentice-Hall.

Schmenner, R. (1995). *Service Operations Management*. London: Prentice-Hall.

Schmenner, R. (1999). Foreword. In *Heritage Visitor Attractions: An Operations Management Perspective* (A. Leask and I. Yeoman, eds). London: Cassell Publications.

Shackley, M. (1999). Visitor management. In *Heritage Visitor Attractions: An Operations Management Perspective* (A. Leask and I. Yeoman, eds). London: Cassell Publications.

Shelby, B., Vaske, J.J. and Heberlein, T.A. (1989). Comparative analysis of crowding in multiple locations: results from fifteen years of research. *Leisure Sciences*, **11**, 269–291.

Slack, N., Chambers, S. and Johnston, R. (2001). *Operations Management*. London: Prentice-Hall.

Yeoman, I. and Leask, A. (1999). Yield management. In *Heritage Visitor Attractions: An Operations Management Perspective* (A. Leask and I. Yeoman, eds). London: Cassell Publications.

Questions

1 What are the factors that may lead to extended queues and bottlenecks of people in the following (skeleton) event scenario? Winter dance festival in UK city: set in council building with two main entrances, one with single outward opening door and one wide inward opening door at the top of a ramp for wheelchair access. Ticket desk is near to the second of these doors. Council chambers have a capacity for 100 people. The entrance area is 5 m in depth and 20 m in width.

2 How can potential bottleneck situations be alleviated in such a way as to both induce further spending from audiences and to maximize their satisfaction?

3 What elements of the visitor management sequence at a festival are reliant on an understanding of the psychology of the visitor?

6

Service quality and managing your people

Siobhan Drummond and Heather Anderson

Introduction

Can you remember the last time you received good service at a festival or event? What was it about that occasion that set it apart from other events or festivals that you have attended? The level of quality service received relates to the enjoyment of the experience and when an organization delivers good service quality it can reap many benefits from increased profits to satisfied internal and external customers.

This chapter will define what service quality means in the field of arts festivals and events and examine the characteristics of service in this area. It will then provide a guide to managing your people and suggest ways of improvement for those involved in the planning, operation and management of this growth sector of tourism.

Defining service quality

According to Drummond and Yeoman (2000), quality as a concept has been with us for millennia but it is only comparatively recently that a quality movement has emerged with professional bodies devoted to the development of a specialist literature and a technology of the subject. In the twentieth century the three principal theatres for the development of quality have been in Europe, America and Japan. Initially this was in the manufacturing sector and the Japanese progress in quality after the Second World War was spectacular, helped along by gurus W.E. Deming and J.M. Juran.

Quality has been defined in a variety of ways including:

- 'Quality should be aimed at the needs of the consumer, present and future' (Deming, 1982)
- 'Quality is conformance to requirements' (Crosby, 1979)
- 'Quality is in its essence a way of managing the organisation' (Feigenbaum, 1993).

These definitions of quality integrate the needs of the customer with the way in which an organization and its systems are managed. The focus is on satisfying the customer and changing the organization to achieve that objective.

Service quality is concerned with the delivery of customer needs and expectations. Different customers will expect, want and/or need different things from essentially similar offerings. Festivals and events can be packaged for many different markets, from the mass market to the tailored group and individual. When similar price and delivery mechanisms are adopted by the provider it is the focus on quality that can often provide the competitive edge, ensuring that growth continues and can be sustained.

Quality in service has been the subject of research since the early 1980s. Academics such as Gronroos (1990), Berry (1980) and Bateson (1979) have undertaken extensive investigations into the issues surrounding service quality. Kotler (1982) defines service as 'any activity or benefit that one party can offer to another which is essentially intangible and does not result in the ownership of anything. Its production may or may not be tied to a physical product'.

The intangible aspect of a service was seen as its most distinctive feature in those early days but other key characteristics have emerged as well and they can be additionally defined:

- *Intangibility*. This means that the service cannot be directly seen, tasted, felt or heard prior to their purchase and consumption. Furthermore, customers usually only have a receipt, a souvenir or a photograph to show that they actually had that experience.
- *Inseparability*. Production and consumption of the service occur simultaneously. This is demonstrated by the audience at a theatre performance (i.e. the play is being 'produced' while the audience is 'consuming' it). It also illustrates that all parts of the event 'package' are inextricably linked, e.g. the experience of viewing an old master painting in a gallery is influenced not only by the quality of the art form, but by other factors including the lighting, surroundings and access to facilities such as toilets.
- *Heterogeneity*. There is a high level of variability in services in that each encounter is a unique experience influenced by a number of 'human element' factors. These include the mood and expectations of each participant at a particular moment. For example, two members of the audience at an opera performance may experience different levels of satisfaction as a result of their seating and viewing arrangements.
- *Perishability*. A seat at the theatre or an entry ticket for an event cannot be produced and stored today for some future point in time. This characteristic can help explain why potential customers can be offered last-minute sales at reduced rates.

A major challenge for any manager involved with festivals and events is to effectively reconcile all of these characteristics with offering a high level of service quality and, at the same time, matching demand with supply.

These characteristics will now be examined in relation to the people involved in the service encounter.

Experience of service in festivals and events

The service experience of customers at events and festivals is as unique as the individual people involved. Certain events and festivals evoke extreme emotional responses from customers. In the arts and in sporting events, for example, for many people, there is a passion about the art form or event – positive or negative. There is a sense in which if a customer hates the event, does not understand the art work, or their team did not score, there is little can be done to convince them they have had a quality service experience anyway. The product and the service experience in many events are inextricably linked. When customers engage in performance, promotional or sporting events there is always an interpretation of what is presented and this individual perception and understanding enables the customer to evaluate, sometimes at an unconscious level, the quality of the experience for them.

The service experience is complex and the contributing elements of the festival or event offering come together in a way that satisfies each individual customer to a greater or lesser degree. How can the essential nature of service be defined, in this context? Firstly, the contributing elements of the experience, from a timescale perspective, can be considered as the stages in the service journey:

■ *Pre-event.* Awareness and interest is generated by promotional material and information produced in advance of the event. The quality of information, accuracy of details, tone of language and the image created will influence customers' expectations. If motivated to book a ticket or reserve a ticket, the anticipation of the event will be influenced by the experience of the booking process. Box office and sales staff, technical systems and the availability and efficiency of online and e-booking facilities can have a great influence on visitor perceptions of the organization. Providing accurate information regarding facilities, parking, welfare services and transport arrangements can often lessen customer fear or anxiety. Well-informed and appropriately trained sales staff can make or break the quality of service experience in this important first stage of the service journey.

■ *Arrival at the venue.* First impressions matter – whether it is a torn poster advertising the event or graffiti on the outside of the venue or newly painted exteriors, fresh flowers and smart staff, customer perceptions of the event itself are influenced by their perceptions of the ancillary services and surroundings. Is there someone to welcome and assist customers? How clear are the signs? Are all facilities in good working order? Is a first-time customer put at their ease? A professional attitude of front-of-house staff will make both the first-time customer and the seasoned regular feel equally at home.

■ *Engaging in the event.* This is the time when impressions of the event itself filter into the customer evaluation process. It is at this stage that the complex nature of service quality in events becomes obvious. Is the experience that of a service or a product on offer? What is the product? In the case of performance events it might be said that the product is the performance and the service is simply that which enables the customer to experience the product – i.e. the management of the venue: technical staging, booking processes, programme sales, merchandising and facilities management. Quality in service at events is more than just responding to customer requests or dealing with complaints. Every interaction between event attendees and staff presents an opportunity to influence the perceived impression of the organization and the event. In other words we create a 'moment of truth' where the behaviour of the staff member is crucial in influencing the quality of the visitor experience. In other events such as new product promotional events it is very much the new product that is the focus. How customers enjoy a promotional event is very much integrated with an expression of a desire to purchase or an interest to find out more. Conferences and exhibitions fall somewhere in the middle where the whole experience of the event can be a service experience, the individual elements being essential to form the complete event.

■ *Post-event.* This is often the time when some organizers of events or festivals lose interest in the visitor and yet this is the time when the groundwork is laid for future customer relationships. Evaluation of events is crucial in identifying opportunities for improvement and critical success factors. Customer feedback forms, evaluation sheets and informal conversations can all reveal a great deal about how the event was received. It is also the time when last impressions can be made and a 'thank you' to visitors for actually attending can go a long way in influencing an appreciative attitude towards the quality of service received.

In summary, quality service in all events comes about through a complex interaction of all the contributory aspects of the overall experience; in general this will include systems or procedures quality, technical quality, professional quality and customer communication quality.

Measurement of service quality and customer satisfaction

Customer satisfaction measurement can significantly help managers and employees to focus more attention on improving service quality. Satisfying the customer is the first stage in getting recommendations, developing customer loyalty and resulting in a profitable enterprise.

The relationship between service quality and customer satisfaction is a key one for any manager but in the field of festivals and events, where there are such close service encounters, it becomes crucial. Customer satisfaction is directly connected to the quality of service that an event offers.

It is important to establish that quality perceptions do not require prior experience of the particular service. Many events are perceived as high quality by customers who have never experienced them because of the images projected by the producers or promoters – for example, Ascot Races, opera performances at La Scala, the Edinburgh International Festival. An appropriate sponsor can influence the quality of the image, e.g. many opera events are sponsored by top corporate organizations perceived to be in the 'quality' end of the product and service markets they offer, from telecommunications to legal services.

Satisfaction, on the other hand, is experiential. Over a period of time, positive and negative service encounters lead to an overall high or low level of satisfaction. The two elements – quality and satisfaction – are so intertwined that measurement needs to be viewed and managed as one process. Deming (1986) developed a simple model that can be used to help managers deal with measurement in a systematic fashion, as illustrated in his PDCA cycle (Figure 6.1). This can be adapted to processes and projects, including events.

After operational plans have been made for an event (*Plan*) and the activities for each stage of the event have been put into practice (*Do*), measurement and control of the event can take place (*Check*) and lead to a review and changes (*Act*) necessary to improve each stage of the event, from design to evaluation, and this can feed into the first stage again. This simple model can be applied to each process involved in the service delivery at an event.

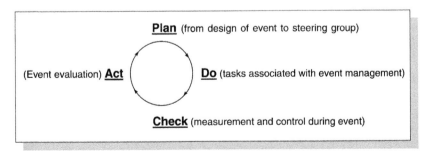

Figure 6.1 Deming's PDCA cycle.

Methods of measurement

There are a number of measurement methods used from critical incident techniques using comment cards to direct survey methods and attribution-based measurement that focuses on quality dimensions. These include personal interviews with customers and performers at each stage of an event and can focus on quality aspects from customer care before and during the event, the fabric of the surroundings and facilities provided, to the qualitative aspects of the 'performers' at the event.

According to Fivars (1975), critical incidents describe customers' attitudes as a result of experiences that have created a lasting positive or negative impression. Customers can provide their own comments under headings such as 'Positive Statements' and 'Negative Statements'.

Direct survey methods can make use of focus groups who provide feedback and ideas for service improvement, e.g. groups made up of regular subscribers to a theatre are in a position to comment on service changes over time and variation of standard. This feedback enables management and staff to review standards and operational practice and they can then address the areas where the level of service delivery has slipped.

Customers seem to use different standards for their comparisons on quality depending on the product, service, situation and experience they have had and attribute-based measurement can help organizations to quantify the situation. The method mathematically calculates the gap or difference between the customers' expectations and the actual performance received.

The widely cited model SERVQUAL was developed in the late 1980s by Parasuraman *et al.* (1988) to measure the gaps in perceptions and expectations across the following five dimensions:

- *Tangibles* – physical facilities, equipment, and appearance of personnel
- *Reliability* – ability to perform the promised service dependably and accurately
- *Responsiveness* – willingness to help customers and provide prompt service
- *Assurance* – knowledge and courtesy of employees and their ability to convey trust and confidence
- *Empathy* – caring, individualized attention the organization provides to its customers.

The above methods provide a link between customers and organizations and can provide valuable information upon which organizations can act to improve service quality, but measurement has its limitations and it is preferable to use more than one method. According to Lewis and Pizam (1981), comment cards, for example, can attract as low a response rate as 1 per cent but incentives for people can raise the response level significantly.

Some of the most useful feedback can come from staff via observation checklists and end-of-duty reports. Employees can experience a dip in operational quality service that is often not discernible to the customer, e.g. staff are aware of the timing and sequences of tasks and they are able to see when processes take longer than they should. They are often aware of the factors causing barriers to efficiency and a high level of service quality.

A review of competitive performance in key elements of the service experience can also form an integral part of measurement. Processes including queuing, ticketing, food and beverage services, emergency procedures and follow-up communication with customers can be measured in both competing event organizations and best-in-class to assist with improvement techniques.

Data collection and analysis is vital to undertake measurement; without measurement it is difficult to set targets, improve performance and gain competitive advantage. Monitoring and evaluation form a key part of this checking process.

Setting operational procedures and targets are ways of making measurement an easier task, but checking on whether these have been followed and achieved is an area that is often left too late in the cycle of operational management. When procedures are not followed and targets are not met it follows that standards slip and the quality of service falls. Management must be trained and developed to comprehend the importance of measurement and be competent in its undertaking.

The results from measurement are used in a number of ways to:

■ Identify customer and competition trends
■ Highlight service delivery weaknesses
■ Feed in to a review of operations
■ Assist with the development of an overall training and management development programme
■ Develop a blueprint for future events
■ Establish a basis for strategic planning.

For example, when customer surveys and questionnaires include the question 'Please tell us if there is any aspect of your experience at this event which disappointed you or could be improved?' this invites customers to identify aspects of the event experience that were important to them rather than those aspects considered important to the organizers. In the Glasgow Royal Concert Hall, in 1991, shortly after the hall opened, at some events, there was a perception by some customers that the queue for coffee was too long. This was a comment made on the comment cards available and made verbally to staff on duty. This gave greater understanding of the issues which were important to customers and it led to a detailed programme of measurement involving recording actual waiting times, reviewing the operation of the coffee service, training staff in queue management and was built in to the management of every event where coffee was served. It also meant that strategically, coffee service was important and efforts were made to improve efficiency by improving staff techniques, reviewing equipment and operational systems. In reality the speed of service did not change greatly but the waiting time was perceived to be better by customers.

The results from measurement enable the service provider to accurately target areas of poor service to enhance the customer experience. Ultimately this requires investment in the people providing each element of service quality.

Managing your people

Quality in the operational environment of events and festivals is directly related to the people delivering the service. There are particular problems in the events industry as a whole because of the project-based and short-term contractual nature of most of the key jobs. Many positions are seasonal and the members of staff are already doing at least one other job, which may, or may not, be their main source of income. The costs involved in training, coaching and briefing staff have to be weighed against the improvement of service quality that can be achieved. For example, front-of-house staff used in many of the temporary venues during the Edinburgh International Festival have to be paid to attend refresher training and briefing sessions as the jobs only last for the duration of the festival.

Effective job analysis and design are crucial, but training, enabling and mentoring staff means the chances of successful customer encounters are greatly increased.

The importance of managing your people

The interface or point of delivery of the event service experience could be said to be while watching a performance, viewing an exhibition or participating in an event. The relationship between the service provider and the customer, however, is much more complex. The service provider could be considered to be the performer or the promoter or the venue or the event organizer, but their representative on the ground is usually the front-of-house staff at an event. They might be stewards more interested in safety and security rather than the quality of the performer's singing, they might be point-of-sale staff more concerned with booking procedures or on commission for maximizing programme sales. In most events, however, there will be staff whose job it is to look after the customer and these are the people that the customer has direct relationship with. The communication and professional skills of these people influence the whole understanding of the organization in the visitor's mind.

The public visitor, however, is not the only customer in the event and festival industry; equally important are the internal customers and they are essential links in the supplier–customer chain. If an event is organized by a commercial event management company then the main customer would in fact be the event organizer or producer who has contracted this company. The connections with subsidiary service providers, such as sound and public address suppliers, outdoor catering and security companies, will be the other 'links' in the quality process. The overall quality of an event will only be as good as the weakest link in the service connections 'chain'. Here the relationships between performers, artists, their managers, promoters, the event organizers, technical staff, the media and the relationship of the events organizers and the paying public all have to be taken in to account. All of these relationships are part of the supplier–customer interface throughout the complex nature of event realization.

From planning to operations management, the relationship between the organization and its front-line staff is crucial in determining the quality of relationship these people will be able to have with the visitor or external customer. It will influence the level of communication, management, training and development available to the staff and will ultimately affect the quality of service they are able to offer.

Illustrative example: Celtic Connections Festival, held every January in Glasgow

Festivals are excellent examples of the importance of service provider and customer relationships. In Glasgow, in January 2003, the tenth annual festival celebrating Celtic culture in words, music, art and performance was held. Celtic Connections began in 1993 just three years after the Glasgow Royal Concert Hall opened – it was a brave and exciting move – a festival in Scotland in the darkest, coldest month and in the first few weeks of January when the nation was recovering from the excesses of the traditional New Year celebrations. It was, and is, a resounding success and one of the contributing factors has been the quality of the relationship built up over the years between the event organizers and the performers, the host venues, their staff, the media and the public. If just one of these vital connections were to be strained or broken the success of the festival would indeed be threatened.

Key factors in successful service relationships

For successful service relationships we have to remember that they are all about people, rather than inanimate objects; in the arts and cultural industries – as in many special interest areas – there are sensitivities and passionate views held which require careful management, just like any relationship really. Here are five key factors for successful service relationships:

- *Communication* – this needs to be open, honest, regular and using more than just written media. Individuals need to be trained to give and receive effective messages.
- *Information* – accurate and timely provision of information is essential to maintaining a good relationship, as is efficient record keeping and data retrieval systems.
- *Understanding* – real empathy is needed not just for the external customers' situations but the employees' circumstances. There is also a need to completely understand the expectations and vision of the final outcome.
- *Behaviour* – all human behaviour has the power to significantly change communication encounters and interactions. Here all staff need to feel able to respond appropriately to customer and colleague behaviour.
- *Action* – all the other factors fade away if all we have is a knowledge or understanding of what is required; the real professional knows how

to translate these factors into effective action for the benefit of the customer, the event and the organization.

Opportunities to enhance service relationships

By considering the factors outlined above we can use staff development in the form of training and management development to enhance the personal effectiveness of all customer contact staff and to support event managers in achieving professional results.

Comparing competitors' performance in the main business areas in a benchmarking exercise can be one of the most useful ways of improving the management of events. This might involve reviewing promotional material issued for similar events, identifying ticket and information outlets and examining facilities management first-hand while actually attending an event.

It is important to use all experience effectively – good and bad – keeping management reports, staff and customer feedback records accessible, ready to learn from and adapt to new ideas for service improvement.

Experiment with new ways of dealing with old customers – tell them you are experimenting and ask for feedback – internal and external. This might be simply designing new booking forms or asking for more information at point of sale. Sometimes we need to alter the running order or location of events to try to attract new customers but existing attendees can often be disappointed if we do not give them the courtesy of an explanation and an opportunity to give feedback.

Illustrative example: First Nights Festival, Glasgow 2002

This was a pilot project run in October 2002 with the assistance of the Scottish Arts Council, Glasgow City Council, the Scottish Media Group (*The Herald* newspaper) and participating venues throughout the city. The main focus of the festival was audience development and in particular, enhancing the relationship that arts venues and events organizers have with their varying customers. The initiative offered a limited number of reduced-price tickets (usually £2 or less) for certain performances and events in the city's main arts venues, including exhibitions, dance, opera, film, drama, music and comedy. Some of the events were indeed 'first nights' but the main objective was to encourage people to experience different art forms for the first time – to experience their own 'first nights'.

91

The Herald produced a comprehensive guide to the arts for first timers and promoted the festival in community outlets.

One interesting aspect of the festival was the opportunity for the collaboration of the different independent and city run arts venues. The City of Glasgow Cultural and Leisure Services Department spearheaded the city's involvement and initiated a staff development programme which was offered to the managers and staff of the participating venues. The training enabled front-of-house staff and venue managers to explore the issues of engaging with first-time or lapsed attendees. It also dealt with the anticipated special needs of new audience members including, for example, people with disabilities, asylum seekers, people from varying multicultural backgrounds, differing religious and social groups. Part of the programme was to agree some specific customer service standards which were to be offered during the First Nights project and beyond and to develop customer service guidelines to be issued to all venue staff to enable service to be consistent and reliable. The success of the initiative is currently being evaluated but initial feedback suggests a considerable uptake of tickets, and feedback from staff who participated in the training suggests that it enabled them to better deal with the needs of first-time visitors.

Operational issues of service quality

The customer's overall evaluation of the quality of an event takes in to account several factors:

■ Systems or procedures quality
■ Technical quality
■ Professional quality
■ Customer communication quality.

What is needed in each area to truly achieve excellence in the event service experience?

Systems or procedures quality

The 'how' of event management; this is the culmination of the planning, training, organizing and delegating of essential tasks to key personnel. It is here that the quality of the systems involved in registration, ticket checking, ticket sales, merchandise sales and queuing is scrutinized. An important aspect of queuing theory is the 'perceived waiting time' that customers have to endure and Bowdin *et al.* (2001) illustrate that this can be improved by distractions and good operations management.

Technical quality

It is here that the techniques of lighting designers, sound technicians and image makers can create the opportunity to dazzle, to impress and to entertain. It is also the point where training in the use of technical equipment is most important and the use of experienced and well-qualified technicians can make all the difference. According to Bowdin *et al.* (2001) they can provide valuable input into the creation and design of the staging of the event.

Professional quality

There might be a need to bring in additional contracted staff to provide professional services in the fields of information technology, safety and risk management. Professional quality is equally evident by the attitude and behaviour of staff towards customers in distress and of the responses to customer difficulties, complaints or indeed emergency situations. This quality reflects the vision, ethos and image of the whole organization.

Customer communication quality

This is not so much to do with personality or individual differences as it is to do with staff being appropriately trained, informed and encouraged to behave in a highly communicative and enabling way with customers and colleagues alike. Yes, it is about using appropriate language, tone and non-verbal communication techniques, but it is also about a professional attitude and a sense of knowing the importance of the job that each individual member of staff is required to do. Whatever the chosen methods or processes, efficient lines of communication must be established within an organization and they must be flexible enough to respond to changes because changes are almost inevitable (Watt, 1998).

Illustrative example: Edinburgh International Festival box office/ hub tickets

Edinburgh International Festival brings to Edinburgh some of the best in international performers, artists, musicians and the quality of the productions is second to none (Bowdin *et al.*, 2001). However, one of the early stages in the visitor journey has to be the communication with the ticketing service – the box office staff or hub tickets staff as they are now known. Many of the staff that deal with ticket requests are employed only for a few months of the year and while some come back again and again, there are new faces every year. Human resource management in the events industry is notoriously difficult, dealing with a predominance of part-time and seasonal staff. How then, can quality of customer service be preserved? In the years from 1993 to 2000 a staff development package was offered to box office staff which evolved over the years not only to develop customer service techniques, but also to identify the real training needs of these staff to be developed as individuals over the years. The very first programme simply looked at customer service and communication skills, the next year, dealing with people with disabilities, then dealing with conflict and aggression was added and in the final programmes the objectives were about maximizing personal resources, developing the customer service team and enhancing personal effectiveness. So a progressive training package enabled new staff to cover the basics but for continuing staff there were opportunities for real personal development.

Strategy and service quality

The environment in which events are staged and managed is increasingly volatile and complex. Customers have changed a great deal since the early 1990s. They demand more value for the price they pay and tend to substitute products for services – thus the role of service quality is ever more important.

In order to survive, organizations need to differentiate themselves by re-emphasizing quality in service so as to establish a viable competitive position. To achieve this they need to pay more attention to operational details and to offer what the customer perceives as value. Heskett and Hart (1990) in their research identified some organizations in the hospitality field as 'break-through' service providers, providing evidence that service excellence pays off in relation to profitability. Many elements in hospitality management are similar to event management and present opportunities for benchmarking.

The globalization of economic activity and the resultant intensive competition means that the service industry has to restructure and reposition to survive and be sustainable. Many event managers are finding that the usual way of running their business is no guarantee for success. Strategic planning and the development of competitive strategy are now playing a more important role. There is a need to link service quality and the strategic management process. Providing customers with what they demand requires a strategy for managing our people effectively in order to attract and retain customers and achieve profitability at the same time.

The event manager needs to know what customers to attract, what they want and the standards to set for service. Research is one of the keys to achieving this objective and our people can help in gathering information about our current customers as well as directing us to potential new segments. Database marketing is successfully used in helping develop marketing strategies in other sectors, namely retail, and event managers could also make use of this strategic tool.

The event manager also needs to provide the level of service quality demanded by the customer. The internal customer can play an important role in this process as it is the attention to detail in operations coupled with meeting the customer expectations that results in satisfied customers.

Strategic management in relation to quality takes into account the environment as well as the customer. This requires the events manager to monitor the environment, and provides the opportunity to keep track of customer changes and gain valuable feedback to improve the level of service quality.

Change in the external environment often leads to a need for change internally. This can be effectively managed by recognition of the need for a culture change, good leadership and establishing a shared vision, implementation of change by empowering staff to make decisions and evaluation of the strategy by means of a bottom-up approach.

There is no single strategy for competing on service but a number of strategies in different functional areas. Those people charged with managing events need to view the value of service in a different way and understand the role created by service employees. The importance of managing your people effectively and the effect on service quality is crucial to survival, profitability and competitive advantage.

Bibliography

Bateson, J. (1979). Why we need service marketing. In *Conceptual and Theoretical Developments in Marketing* (O. Ferrell, S. Brown and C. Lamb, eds). American Association of Marketing.

Berry, L.L. (1980). Services marketing is different. *Business*, **30(3)**, 24–29.

Bowdin, G.A.J., McDonnell, I., Allen, J. and O'Toole, W. (2001). *Events Management*. Butterworth-Heinemann.

Crosby, P.B. (1979). *Quality is Free*. McGraw-Hill.

Deming, W.E. (1982). *Quality, Productivity and Competitiveness Position*. MIT Press.

Deming, W.E. (1986). *Out of the Crisis*. Cambridge University Press.

Drummond, S. and Yeoman, I. (2000). *Quality Issues in Heritage Visitor Attractions*. Butterworth-Heinemann.

Feigenbaum, A.V. (1993). *Total Quality Control*. McGraw-Hill.

Fivars, G. (1975). The critical incident technique: a bibliography. *JSAS Catalog of Selected Documents in Psychology*.

Gronroos, C. (1990). *Service Management and Marketing, Managing the Moments of Truth in Service Competition*. Lexington Books.

Heskett, J.L. and Hart, C.W.L. (1990). *Service Breakthroughs: Changing the Rules of the Game*. The Free Press.

Kotler, P. (1982). *Marketing for Non Profit Organisations*, 2nd edn. Prentice-Hall.

Lewis, R.C. and Pizam, A. (1981). Guest Surveys: a missed opportunity. *Cornell Hotel and Restaurant Administration Quarterly*, 22.

Parasuraman, A., Zeithaml, V.A. and Berry, L.L. (1988). SERVQUAL: a multiple-item scale for measuring consumer perceptions of service quality. *Journal of Retailing*, **64**, 12–40.

Watt, D.C. (1998). *Event Management in Leisure and Tourism*. Longman.

Websites

Edinburgh International Festival. www.eif.co.uk.
First Nights Festival, Glasgow. www.firstnights.org.

Questions

1 How do you define service quality and what are the key characteristics that need to be managed in relation to events?
2 Outline the ways in which you can improve service quality by managing your people.
3 Discuss the importance of measurement in effective event management.

Implications and use of information technology within events

Karl Knox

Introduction

The use of computerization within the business arena has dramatically changed how we do business; relatively little of our work can be done without the use of information technology (IT) in some shape or form. The events environment is no different, yet very little IT has, formally, been incorporated into the working practices of event managers. This is changing and will continue to do so as technology becomes more and more present in our working lives.

Events can vary in size and intensity but whatever they support, be it corporate, sport or promotional activities, they have one thing in common; that is, they need to be organized, controlled, promoted, coordinated and in many instances financially viable. Therefore these issues are addressed in terms of how IT can be used within:

- Organizing an event
- Planning the event process
- Coordinating an event
- Promoting the event
- Controlling the event
- Financial implications of the event process
- Evaluation of the event.

Technology is playing an increasingly important role within the events arena. Innovation and software developments are providing vast improvements both in terms of speed and capabilities, which is then infiltrating into management and the operational aspects of business. This technological advancement was highlighted extremely well in 1999, with the Net Aid fundraising concerts. Modern technology allowed the concerts to be broadcast simultaneously in different parts of the world, a feat that was not comprehensible in 1985 when the forerunner 'Live Aid' took place.

Bowdin *et al.* (2001: 73) identify that 'changes in equipment and machines have revolutionised the way people undertake tasks'. Specifically they go on to state how the internet has become a medium for promoting all aspects of special events and highlight the use of the internet as a medium to inform all participants from organizers, promoters and consumers through to students and academics (go to http://www.worldofevents.net).

Organizing an event

The role of organizing and managing an event has only become formalized since the late 1970s. This is seen both in the increase of event management companies and the formalization of event-focused education programmes.

In the past the role of events has been viewed under the 'hospitality' umbrella and its related activities, i.e. dinners, promotions, launches or award ceremonies. In many organizations the responsibility of organizing a lunch, dinner or the annual general meeting tended to be dealt with by, for example, the secretary to the managing director, or a member of the marketing team, or in extreme circumstances someone from the personnel department. Now, as the event industry may be seen to exist in its own right, a new profession has arisen, that of the 'professional event manager', who arranges, manages, organizes, coordinates all aspects of the proposed event and in essence acts as a 'middle person' between the suppliers and the commercial organization.

The ability to use and implement new technology within the role could be seen as imperative, given the increase and diversity in activities and the specialist services on offer. The fundamental process here is one of distributing information regarding the event.

Allen *et al.* (2002: 301) identify that a 'fundamental use of the web in today's configuration is for the distribution of information to participants, potential attendees, sponsors, organisers and suppliers'.

This highlights the all-encompassing nature of the World Wide Web (WWW) as a distribution medium. The ability to connect and inform all aspects of the supply chain quickly and efficiently is a phenomenon of IT. This is further enhanced by the ability to keep this process updated on a regular, almost hourly basis. Previously this could have been carried out by e-mail, if one still wanted to use some form of electronic medium, but this assumes the ability of e-mail to ensure that the relevant details or information have been received by the intended recipients and acted upon. The WWW and intranets have allowed a 'pull' process to the distribution of data as opposed to a 'push' approach. That is, interested parties have the ability to select what is relevant and pertinent to them, making the whole process more efficient. This is a huge step forward in that computer literacy does not become an issue. As in the past the ability to open (i.e. compatible software), manipulate and respond to electronic distribution and its attachments was imperative; now recipients need only log on to a website to access relevant information. This could be used, for example, to provide maps of the venue, transportation details, and more specific details such as delivery schedules, traffic information or weather conditions. This has a knock-on effect in that what is often an expensive process is now shared by others involved.

Planning the event process

Events and other large 'happenings' take a great deal of time, care, energy and understanding; that is to say if the event is to have some chance of being successful for both the manager and the delegate it requires 'planning'. Even if one takes a small event the planning required to bring this together can take up to 3–4 months; therefore when one considers a larger, more internationally focused event the planning stage could take years and involve a substantial number of participants. In fact planning will have already begun for the 2006 Commonwealth Games, to be held in Melbourne, Australia. Also the announcement by Federation Internationale de Football Association (FIFA) that the 2014 World Cup will be held in South America offers the chosen host nation an 11-year opportunity (from the time of writing) in terms of planning. Given the magnitude of the World Cup and the logistics involved in such an event the chosen host nation (Brazil) may need every bit of the 11 years to promote, plan, and coordinate the activities for a successful event.

It therefore cannot be overstressed that the way to achieve a successful event will inevitably involve some planning, which requires time, effort and skill for it to work seamlessly. Maintaining a handle on this process is where IT can be of unquestionable assistance, from informing individuals and companies of their roles through to reminding and prompting one to confirm the caterers. It is in fact a further element to that of the organizing stage.

Often due to the size or complexity of events there will be a number of people involved, at different stages, required at different times and needing different levels of information and instruction. Obviously this will and does vary from event to event, hence the view that all events are in some way unique and therefore require different levels of involvement. The participants involved may vary from the actual event organizer, or company, through to the client, the venue centre, the suppliers and the delegates attending. Do they all require the same information or need to be supplying their particular element of the event at the same time? In general no; therefore the need to plan these inputs is extremely important, if the event is to be successful.

How does the professional event manager bring all of this together? Essentially the event manager is the 'glue' that holds all of these activities and interactions together. As mentioned earlier, they are often the 'middle-person', the only one who knows the whole story, therefore ensuring that all processes, participants, and products:

- Are available at the right time
- Are from the right source
- Meet the required quality
- Are in the correct numbers – quantity.

Ensuring that this occurs is not an easy or straightforward task; but it can be made easier with precision planning and understanding of support mechanisms. Information technology may assist in the overall process. Managers need to identify its benefits, its relevance and its role; they must identify a need for it and only then will it be successfully implemented and used within the planning process.

Whenever an event is undertaken or any large activity for that matter, it will involve a sequence of choices and decisions, which must be acted upon by various people. These activities may involve the commitment of resources, people, and capital; essentially, however, they all have one thing in common – that is, they will all occur over a set time period. In order for this to be successful a number of factors need to be in place:

■ Remember who and what is involved at various stages, and their various inputs; this becomes more difficult as the event increases in size and complexity
■ Ensure that timings and any changes are communicated to all participants and agreements reached
■ Ensure that all resources are used effectively and efficiently.

Obviously, due to the volatility of the event function, with many participants, resources, services and activities being involved at any one time, there is a requirement for all of the activities to be up-to-date, communicated and available. For example:

■ Have any ancillary services changed regarding timing, equipment or numbers?
■ Have any dates altered (end date or start date)?
■ Has a supplier or resource run over time or failed to materialize?
■ What are the critical activities for this event in terms of differing perspectives (i.e. those involved)?

Given the above, it is important that when planning an event it is essential, if not imperative, to identify activities or jobs and in what potential order they need to occur for the event to run smoothly and for successfully meeting all of the aims and objectives identified at the outset of the event.

This level of planning could take a number of forms from a 'progress calendar', charting events and activities over a yearly time period, to the use of some form of project management tool (e.g. CA Superproject, Microsoft Project, often used in the construction or engineering arena). Alternatively, a fully dedicated events management tool could be used (e.g. EVENTS, which includes various activities from demographics database, marketing systems and project organization through to a basic diary and an analysis package).

Software for project planning has a number of main functions; initially, it may be the production of some form of flow chart, which identifies activities, resources, timings, and relationships. Secondly, it could be the allocation of resources to actual individuals, through to preparing individual schedules. Specifically, two techniques are evident: *critical path analysis* (network analysis, CPA) and *Gantt charts*.

- *Critical path analysis.* Specifically, the critical path (CP) 'is the series of tasks that push out the project's end date if they are delayed' (Chatfield *et al.*, 2001). However, the majority of individuals when referring to the CP are in fact referring to the network diagram, where they identify and examine the whole interconnectiveness of the resources, activities and timings. The word 'critical' is not referring to the importance of the task, in terms of the overall project. In fact once the task has been completed, and it is no longer critical, it cannot affect the overall project. Therefore, over the whole life of the project, or in our case the event, the CP is likely to change from time to time, emphasizing how imperative this type of planning is to the success of the event. Keeping all participants informed and up-to-date is a huge task; therefore by breaking down an event into its constituent parts, for example a banquet, conference or fund-raiser, and showing these parts separately but also highlighting their interrelationship in the form of a network diagram, assists in the planning process, and in turn reducing risk and uncertainty. In reality, CPA is mainly used to sequence activities, which in turn determines the shortest time needed to complete the project. Within the events industry one would normally have a given date upon which the event must occur, and that date cannot be extended, therefore managers and organizers are working back from that date. However, CPA allows the manager to consider times and resources required to complete each of the tasks. It allows one to identify the critical path and so create a workable time frame in which to complete all tasks and operate a successful event.
- *Gantt charts.* Gantt charts or progress charts are created from the same initial process as the network diagram. They are useful for smaller, less complex events; and most software allows one to switch between different views, which will show both the Gantt chart and the critical path or network diagram.

It is important to note that the use of such tools has been highlighted due to their availability; in most cases they are easily obtainable. Most will be already in use and are fully integrated with other software in the Microsoft range. However, the tools are not specifically designed for the events industry and its individual needs; nevertheless they are still important and widely used both in industry and in academia as a medium to bring IT and events planning together. All in all, CPA is a useful tool that allows event managers to reduce risk, communicate roles and responsibilities and plan activities.

Exercise

Think of an activity or event that you may be involved in or have participated in, e.g. a wedding, a special birthday (18th, 21st), an anniversary or graduation ball. Identify the tasks involved and relationship between activities and length of activities, then place them into a grid (Table 7.1). A small conference has been used as an example to assist in developing an understanding of the planning process. (A detailed answer can be found in the Answer Book, obtainable from the Publishers at www.bh.com.)

Table 7.1   Event tasks

Task	Preceding task	Duration of task (days)
A. Arrange the presentation system	C	3
B. Arrange food	E	7
C. Arrange speaker	E	12
D. Set up room	A	5
E. Detailed planning	G	8
F. Stage conference	B, D, H	4
G. Initial visit	–	2
H. Set up PA system	A	9

Coordinating an event

Although there may be some similarities between the concepts of organizing, planning and coordinating, within this section the author has identified coordinating as dealing with the operational aspects of the event; that is, the 'running' of the event. This will be heavily reliant upon the planning stage as a blueprint of what is supposed to happen and in what order, but goes that one stage further in actually looking at the event operation.

This will rely on good communication throughout the event, constant involvement, updating and rechecking of activities both prior to them occurring and during their operation. Often meetings late into the evening will be necessary to bring the 'team' up-to-date on the day's events and what is scheduled for the coming twenty-four hours. Obviously, given a shorter time frame there may be requirement to schedule meetings at certain crucial points throughout the day. Information technology within this arena may be as simple as walkie-talkies or mobile telephones, through to portable digital assistants (PDAs), which allow data to be collected, transmitted and even analysed in some instances then and there.

This process is all about keeping the event running smoothly and according to schedule. It is putting all of the 'planning' into operation and making adjustments when and where needed. It is also an opportunity to collect data about the event for analysis, which can be used at a future date.

Promoting the event

'One of the certainties about the future of technology in the events environment ... is that it will change – the technology will change and so will the way events are managed and marketed' (Allen *et al.*, 2002: 292).

Information technology and its related activities are here to stay. As events become larger and more global the promotion of these events will change. Competition from other events or activities will become more intense, requiring event managers to find better and more sophisticated ways of attracting potential customers to their specific event.

Promotion of an event may involve the use of the WWW, but this may not necessarily be enough. Allen *et al.* (2002: 301) identify that 'the web as a major promotional tool quickly dissipated when it did not return the expected results'. Murray and Summer (2001) argue that the 'goal of the internet should be to provide rapid and easy access to the products and services the organisation offers'. But customers want more as all organizations are in essence able to provide easy access to their products and services.

However, what organizers and others have identified is that one must bring added value to the promotional tool. That is to say, what benefit will individuals receive by using this promotional tool? One can identify the discounts offered to shoppers on the web; this logic has followed through within the events industry. For example prizes, competitions, discounts are all offered, even selection of specific seating can be chosen from the virtual seating plan located on the web page. In this relationship, potential customers can identify for themselves quickly and easily the benefits they receive over other, more traditional methods.

Given this, IT will change the way managers promote their event. The ability to market and promote one's product or event nationally, internationally and globally in an effective, efficient and financially viable way is a 'spin-off' from the use of IT. Previously, the cost of doing this nationally or even internationally has been prohibitive to many firms, particularly many smaller firms within the events industry.

'The major barrier costs to market entry are usually advertising and business promotion' (Benson and Standing, 2002: 12). Therefore the use of IT has in some way negated the high costs involved, both in terms of promotion via the web and sales through virtual and graphical representation of the event to clients and stakeholders involved in the process.

Technology assists in maintaining continuity, again reducing costs; if event documents are created using templates or require some form of theme, this becomes cost-effective as it is created once and applied to all literature, promotion material or merchandising with regard to the particular event and can be used again and again with minor alterations. The fact that customers are able to 'pull' information from a website reduces the burden placed on the organization.

Sophisticated software, for example computer-aided design (CAD), allows managers to offer a real-world visualization of the event for prospective clients, customers, suppliers and delegates, giving the potential recipient a better and more informed idea of how the end product will look, and offering, at the beginning, a very cost-effective way to 'test out' ideas and themes before more expensive and hard-to-change work is carried out. This concept also acts as a huge promotional tool for event managers as it gives them the ability, in a transportable format, to show new clients what is possible and what work they, the organizer, have been involved in, i.e. the type, level, numbers involved, and the professionalism of their work.

Evaluation of the event and IT

'Think of information as an asset or a strategic resource. The more up-to-date and accurate your information is, the greater the advantage you possess' (Benson and Standing, 2002). This link with information is vital for event managers as it is this process of reflection that encourages managers to 'stand back' and contemplate what has occurred and what their involvement was in the success of the event. Information can be collected prior, during and after the event; all of these aspects are important to the success and continuity of the event process.

It is important for event managers, and for that matter all managers, to be aware of the role of IT. One way of achieving this is through the consideration of efficiency and effectiveness. Efficiency is the ability to use the available resources (i.e. resources in terms of tools, methods, techniques, skills and for the manager innovation and initiative) to achieve the desired results as quickly as possible without wasting time, money and effort. This in essence can be interpreted as being the completion of the task in the most cost-efficient manner. Effectiveness is concerned with the correct selection and utilization of resources in relation to the task at hand. This is all part of the evaluation of a particular event.

Data can be collected electronically and with the assistance of IT manipulated easily and quickly so as to provide information regarding certain activities, for example the numbers of delegates per day, the average spend in different outlets per day or per session, through to revenue from programmes or car parking.

It is the ability to collect, manipulate and analyse data that is a skill event managers must be able to achieve. Prior to this occurring, the event manager must be thinking about what data is relevant to their activities but also what data would be useful and pertinent to their customers, how this data will be collected and how the data will be presented in the most informative way.

The collection and analysis of data can be, in some instances, extremely difficult. Using a dedicated package to do this can be helpful. In the past this has not been easy due to the scale, type of clients and variety of events. However, there are a number of packages available that allow both traditional and electronic collection, manipulation and analysis of data in one bundle, i.e. that does not require managers to transfer data between different applications, which in the past has been somewhat problematical. SNAP questionnaire software is one such package and one that the author has used on numerous occasions with great success.

Financial implications of the event process

Finally, when all of the activities of an event have been taken into account, the overriding issue is that of feasibility and financial success. This may also be referred to as the controlling and monitoring of the event. It is also an area that in many cases is poorly addressed, due to lack of experience or professional qualifications. Recognizing that the professional event manager will require skills in the area of budgeting and financial management is not something students, for example, are keen to acknowledge. But in reality, without sound financial skills the event is not going to get off the ground.

One initial venture into this area is that of 'what-if' or scenario analysis. This can be done with a simple spreadsheet package and offers great insight and control of the financial aspects of an event.

Exercise

Most events or situations will incorporate either/or questions, such as how much to change, or how much must be sold to cover costs. This becomes the starting point for most decisions on viability of events. Therefore you are asked to investigate the process of 'break-even' analysis based on the data shown in Table 7.2. Using MS Excel, produce a worksheet that will allow your manager to change various items to see what happens if x sales are changed, or what happens if y costs are changed.

■ Is this the best way to show the data? Is there a more flexible way, which highlights relevant information and is more suitable to 'what-if' analysis?
■ Fill in all of the cells which are marked with an asterisk (remember to use formulae).
■ What is the variable cost, in a figure amount?
■ What is the profit for each level of sales? Can you identify the break-even point in units sold? (*Hint:* use the goal-seek facility within Excel.)

- Use formulae for each of the costs and sales, therefore assisting in 'what-if' scenario analysis.
- Produce a chart that shows all of this data diagrammatically and links into your spreadsheet, i.e. it changes as your figures change.

(A detailed answer can be found in the Answer Book, obtainable from the Publishers at www.bh.com.)

Table 7.2 Break-even analysis data

Units sold	0	500	1000	1500	2000	2750	4000	5000	6000
Sales	£15ea.	*	*	*	*	*	*	*	*
Fixed costs	18000	18000	18000	18000	18000	18000	18000	18000	18000
Variable costs	*	*	*	*	*	*	*	*	54000
Total costs	18000	*	*	*	*	*	*	*	72000

Reality check

Although throughout this chapter the author has indicated and high-lighted many potential benefits of using IT within the events industry, it would be prudent also to indicate that there is also an alternative side, one which event managers should be aware of that is, what happens if the whole thing falls apart? For example – the system crashes, all of the data on delegates is lost, a theft takes place, the seamless integration does not work or a virus is introduced or downloaded.

The ability to assess the potential risk and cost to the event is one which managers should be aware of and have some sort of 'back-up' plan. The emphasis here is that IT is only a tool – it is not the panacea. But the ability to use, manipulate, integrate, disseminate and interrogate information is a requirement of the event industry for the twenty-first century.

	One-day tickets sales	Two-day tickets sales	Discounted tickets sales
November	650	940	180
December	1200	2450	350
January	1150	1500	560
February	2350	2175	60
March	760	0	450

	Expenses					
	Oct.	Nov.	Dec.	Jan.	Feb.	Mar.
Office	1000	600	800	800	1175	1850
Security	5000	1500	1500	2000	12500	26500
Printing	2500	450	690		1280	
Advertising	375	1275	1275	6700	7200	1375
Staging						6500
Wages	1800	1800	1800	6700	13700	42000
Equipment hire	1500	2350			1000	2450
Artist fee				15000		15000

The use of 'back-ups' is an unavoidable cost but one which with today's technology can be restricted. The ability to store data cheaply and effectively and transport this with the event manager should not cause too much of an issue.

Conclusion

Technology certainly seems to be the central focus of the business community. Orlikowski and Barley (2001) identify that 'micro-electronically based information technologies are substantially altering the way ... people live, work, communicate and organise activities'.

Upon reflection, what needs to be stressed is that the whole is more than the sum of its parts. The success of an event operation is not totally down to one particular thing, item or person but to a seamless integration of all parts of the operation. It is the ability for delegates to have the correct information when it is needed, for the caterers to be there on time with their equipment and resources, for the 'show', to allow speakers, products or presentations to fulfil their contribution. It is the ability to bring all of this together that identifies the success (or failure) of the event; the author feels and has hopefully shown that IT is an important tool that can assist in this process, one that can be incorporated in every aspect of the event manager's role, including:

- Organizing the event
- Planning the event
- Coordinating the event
- Promoting the event
- Controlling the event.

The use of IT within the events industry is only limited by the innovation and creativity of the event managers themselves.

Bibliography

Allen, J., O'Toole, W., McDonnell, I. and Harris, R. (2002). *Festival and Special Event Management*, 2nd edn. Sydney: John Wiley and Sons Australia.

Benson, S. and Standing, C. (2002). *Information Systems: A Business Approach*. Sydney: John Wiley and Sons Australia.

Bowdin, G., McDonnell, I., Allen, J. and O'Toole, W. (2001). *Events Management*. Oxford: Butterworth-Heinemann.

Chatfield, C., Johnson, T. and Chatfield, R. (2001). *Step-by-Step Courseware Microsoft Project 2000*. Washington: Microsoft Press.

Murray, J. and Summer, D. (2001). Adding value to the Information Technology function. *Information Systems Management*, **18(3)**, 58–59.

Orlikowski, W.J. and Barley, R.S. (2001). Technology and Institutions: What can research on Information Technology and research on organisations learn from each other? *MIS Quarterly*, **25(3)**, 146.

Questions

1 What are some of the benefits of using critical path analysis within the planning stages of an event?

2 Is information technology a benefit or hindrance for the events industry, given that the industry is people oriented?

3 Your immediate supervisor has given you the task of costing out the following event. It is your first opportunity to show your supervisor your IT skills and ability to handle data. An event is taking place in March 2004, with ticket sales starting in November 2003. Ticket prices are:

One-day tickets £18.00

Two-day tickets £26.00

Discounted tickets £22.00 for concessionary card holders

With the use of a spreadsheet, determine a format and presentation style that would allow your supervisor to easily identify:

■ Total sales for each month
■ Opening balances month on month
■ Expenses for each month
■ Overall profit
■ If extra funds may be needed during this process.

Marketing, revenue and retail operations

Events and the destination dynamic: Edinburgh festivals, entrepreneurship and strategic marketing

Martin Robertson and Kenneth MacMillan Wardrop

Edinburgh: a background

The need for an events strategy and framework emerged from Edinburgh's growing reputation and increased profile as a host for large-scale events. The re-establishment and physical presence of Scotland's Parliament in Edinburgh in 1999, alongside its role as capital city and official residence of the Queen in Scotland at Holyrood Palace, together increased the number of new events and civic occasions taking place in the city.

Although the city is best known for its summer festivals, inclusive of the Edinburgh International and Fringe Festivals, a strategic approach has been adopted by the City Council and public agency partners to maximize usage of the tourism and event infrastructure of the city, and to develop a year-round calendar of events activity. By and large the city is operating in a close to full situation in August and effort has been applied to spread the pressures throughout the year in a bid to ensure sustainability.

Since the late 1990s the city economy has also experienced a period of rapid growth and dynamic change, spurred on in 1999 by the re-establishment of Scotland's Parliament. Driven (at the time of writing) by tremendous growth in financial, professional, and knowledge-based services current economic indicators show it to be the fastest growing UK city economy. In August of every year, when the population of the city can swell up to three times above its norm, and the combined forces of the Edinburgh International Festival, the Festival Fringe, alongside the Jazz, Book, Television, and International Film Festivals, are at their peak, Edinburgh is seen by many as the cultural capital of the world. One-and-a-quarter million tickets (Edinburgh International Festival Annual Report) were sold in 2001. From a study in 2000 it was estimated that £23.3 million was generated from the Edinburgh International Festival alone with an estimated £125.3 million generated annually in the city economy from all the city's festivals. Moreover, there are an increasing number of additional events either wishing, or being planned, to come to Edinburgh. This desire by event promoters to be associated with the high brand values of the city – with a world class image – does increasingly, however, require strategic direction and management.

This chapter addresses the role of image, marketing, brand awareness, commercial partnerships (sponsorship) and stakeholder legitimacy as part of that strategic direction. (It is advised that it be read in conjunction with Chapter 22, the case study 'Edinburgh's Winter Festival'.)

Events, cities and economics: an introduction

Cities, or, rather, their leading public and private partners, have to give an event, or series of events, cognitive value understandable to all its potential stakeholders. Without this the event will not gain the wider support – financial or social – it needs to operate effectively. Consequently it is normal to espouse the economic benefits that it is believed the event will engender. Most often these economic benefits will be denoted as additional expenditure by visitors; direct local expenditure on services and supplies by organizers and event participants; the positive effects of direct promotion campaigns for the event, and indirect media activity within and about the city itself. Most recognizably described as multiplier analysis, the event-related expenditure – external to factors such as initial and ongoing infrastructure costs – is then translated into the most readily identifiable measurements of additional local income amassed and jobs generated. On this basis Edinburgh's tourism activity can be characterized as (*Capital Review*, 2002):

- Annual contribution to the Edinburgh economy: £2.2 billion
- Annual visitors: 4.6 million (overnight) and 91.6 million (day)
- Edinburgh City region workforce employed by the sector: 33 348 (8%)
- Annual room occupancy of hotels, 66%; of guest houses, 56%.

Based on this evaluation of the economic contribution of tourism and event-based tourism these figures represent a sense of success for Edinburgh. However, the value of events cannot be appraised in the above terms alone. It is of immense importance that it is also evaluated on the capacity of the investment in events to cognitively effect changes in the image of the city (Paddison, 1993). Evidently, it has not gone unnoticed by either the public or private sector that Edinburgh is a place – with an image – worth investing in. Furthermore, the fact that Edinburgh is increasingly viewed as a gateway to the rest of Scotland, and has been positioning itself as one of Europe's 'must-see' short-break city destinations, corroborates an awareness and motivation by public and private sector investors that goes well beyond the 'here and now' desires that can prevail in attempts to use visitor attractions or events for short-term image boosting of cities (Hall, 1992; Robertson and Guerrier, 1998). As further evidence of this, in 1999/2000, Edinburgh City Council invested £5.5 million in supporting over 50 major events in addition to the normal festival activity. Simultaneously, the newly approved strategic framework for events gave equal emphasis – for the public and private sector – to the cultural and celebrity nature of many of the events taking place in the city, as well as focusing on their tangible economic factors. The raising of the profile of the city through festival and events clearly became a key focus for the city. Significantly then, though the City of Edinburgh Council asserts that this £5.5m investment has an estimated economic impact of some £119m (City of Edinburgh Council, 2002), this investment was (and is) not just focused on the short- to medium-term economic gain, but also on the long-term change of the image and the market positioning of the city.

Image and cities

The concept of marketing cities has grown from the process of economic restructuring required in the post-industrial period. In this a city in pursuit of internal investment will compete with other cities for investment through urban entrepreneurial displays (Paddison, 1993: 339). This competitive display requires cities to redefine or re-image themselves. Events and festivals as well as other forms of 'entrepreneurial display' (Robertson and Guerrier, 1998: 224) offered by the city are seen as playing a vital part in the acquisition of that investment needed for restructuring. Indeed, as Robertson and Guerrier state, 'Image creation is not incidental to overall development, it is a catalyst for other changes' (1998: 221), which is to say that it is vital for a city to create an attractive civic image not only for the aesthetic pride of its residents but also as the necessary milieu for public and corporate investment and activity.

Image and place marketing and the destination lifecycle

Importantly, it must be remembered that image creation is not only part of a strategic process to change the perception of a place so as to receive appropriate interest – from visitors and business – but it is also a way of appropriating the best potential for the place to continue to succeed in the future, i.e. to facilitate both city and regional long-term development. Thus it is part of a strategic marketing plan in which the destination's public and private partnership can be seen as an organization involved in a 'process of developing and maintaining a strategic fit between the orga-nisation goals and capabilities and its changing marketing opportunities' (Kotler and Armstrong, 1991: 29). In this the city – the place – must be seen as the product consumed. The city (the destination) is after all the place where the consumer experiences the product, where the organiza-tion (the public and private partnership) sees the experience enjoyed by the consumer as part of the destination development process, and the individual providers (non-public sector) see their success within the des-tination (Ashworth, 1991; Buhalis, 2000; Godfrey and Clark, 2000; Opperham, 2000; Morgan et al., 2002). The difference here is that, unlike the usual perspective of the marketing goal being profit, place marketing has (or should have) longer-term, specialized marketing goals (Buhalis, 2000) in which profit has more social, economic and often cultural values than it is usually ascribed.

Events as significant, often vital parts of that place-marketing strategy, in which the image of a place, in this case Edinburgh, can be changed for long-term objectives, have to be used, as Hall (1992) states, strategically. The management of marketing of an event and the image it is attempting to stimulate have to be understood within the context of the marketing of the place, and, significantly, with awareness of their respective position in the history of the product and the environment in which it is both consumed and promoted. Referred to most commonly as the destination lifecycle (Butler, 1980; Hall, 1992; Buhalis, 2000) and derived from the four stages of development attributed to tangible products that have not undertaken appropriate strategic action, i.e. introduction, growth, maturity and decline, this model assimilates the basic assumptions that a product without appropriate marketing action will decline or decay (Ritchie and Smith, 1991) through a combined process of market saturation and market competition. In the case of destinations, keen not to descend into this latter prognosis, this should mean, as Buhalis (2000: 104) states, that initially marketing strategies should generate awareness and develop promotion in the early stages of the cycle and concentrate on 'image alteration and re-design and re-launch' in the latter. Essentially, all those involved in the organization, promotion, marketing and strategic management of an event – and the destination it signifies – must be attentive to how their event and the place (city or otherwise) may fall into a product or destination lifecycle (Hall, 1992). Without this attention it is quite possible that the overall development objectives, of which the event is to play a part, will either be undermined or else unaffected by its activity. Moreover, this understanding of the significance of the destination lifecycle to the short-term and strategic long-term success of an event has to encompass an understanding of the perception of the market (the viewers or participants) to whom it is aimed. While there is long-standing evidence to suggest that the image of a destination affects the destination choice of a tourist as well as their behaviour within it (Etchner and Ritchie, 1991; Stabler, 1988) the process of its application for many destinations has been based on an illusory belief that potential visitors are latent recipients of information (Page, 1995), failing to realize that the reception and interpretation of place-product images can have a great many demographic as well as media determinants (Figure 8.1).

Destination image cannot change instantly other than in the formation of short-term spectacle. Long-term strategies require long-term and systematic image and product change.

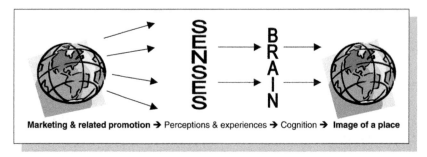

Marketing & related promotion → Perceptions & experiences → Cognition → **Image of a place**

Figure 8.1 From image projection through to the filters of reception. (Adapted from Page, 1995: 224.)

Accordingly, the developments of new events within the context of Edinburgh's Event Strategy, and with particular reference to the Winter Festival (comprising Edinburgh's Hogmanay and Capital Christmas), are evidence of a systematic approach to the stimulation and targeting of other key target markets. The added market penetration animated by the development of the Winter Festival programme has extended the visitor product. This extension of the initial Hogmanay one-day event to the current five-week Winter Festival is also evidence of a proactive assimilation of the requirements of the event product life-cycle to those of the destination lifecycle plans. Significantly, then, the other aspects of the visitor product – visitor attractions, retail, restaurants and the accommodation sector – have also kept up with the evolving needs of the visitor. This synergy is vital for long-term success.

Competitive advantage versus audience/spectator advantage

Thus maximum economic advantage is gained when, through strategic marketing-based development, the destination – in this case Edinburgh – has secured recognition for being the place to see and to consume a particular product. It has endeavoured, through marketing forms, to ensure that the direction of the destination is guided through status (brand value) rather than one of short-term value (commodity). This is to say that Edinburgh has established a competitive advantage. Thus, in reference to the destination product lifecycle previously referred to, Edinburgh has established a stage in which the image of its main event, the Edinburgh Festival and Fringe, does what is strategically imperative:

consistently ensuring the continued loyalty from, as well as attracting new, market segments appropriate to its stage of growth.

However, for Edinburgh, much of its past success may have been reached not through long-term strategic foresight, but, instead, firstly, through the guidance of the post Second World War objective of shaking off the austerity of that time and, secondly, through the effective management of the physical environment. However, given the increasingly competitive intranational and international environment for all destinations, Edinburgh has, in common with a great many other cities, had to think more strategically about the use of events as a marketing tool and as part of the destination marketing mix. So while it is recognized that the market favours some cities (as with all destinations) because of factors already established, most notably previous investment and a long-standing recognition factor by the global market (Harding, 1994; Robertson and Guerrier, 1998), even in these the often non-participatory nature of arts organizations and independent representative groups and venues still have the potential to restrict development and, given time, undermine attempts to ensure that festivals are seen as legitimate (to host residents and visitors) and composed of quality and clearly market-defined event products.

For many cities, particularly those on the initial stages of the event product lifecycle, the alternative is preparation for a battle of market endurance dependent on events of, as Robertson and Guerrier (1998: 224) state, 'originality and short term spectacle'. This is to say that development through a display of entrepreneurial vigour is always a risk. Events are chosen to redefine the city, to create a new image and, thus, it is believed, new avenues for economic and social development. However, in the absence of a formed image they are competing for interest through spectacle. Bearing in mind that spectacle can have more to do with entertainment than the perception of the event being part of the place, such events risk a mere ephemeral interest in the city, based entirely on their entertainment value. Given that interest in spectacle is dependent on each spectacle being better than the last, it is quite possible for a city to repeatedly invest in short-term competitive bouts with other cities without an awareness of the limited scope for external investment. Large-scale events have a history of requiring public investment, often ongoing and only achieving payback through wider economic benefits in the long term (if at all). Ritchie and Smith (1991), Getz (1991) and Hall (1992) all make clear that long-term views are the only appropriate vantage from which to judge the value of event-based development.

Edinburgh tourism: a collaborative approach

In 1999 a revisiting of the Edinburgh Tourism Review of the early 1990s led to the drafting of the Edinburgh Tourism Action Plan (ETAP) and, finally, to its publication in October 2000. ETAP has as its mission statement the 'aim to make Edinburgh one of Europe's premier capital city destinations with an outstanding built heritage and quality of visitor experience that is second to none'. The action plan was drafted by the key public sector agencies of the City of Edinburgh Council, Scottish Enterprise Edinburgh and Lothians, and the Edinburgh and Lothians Tourist Board in conjunction with the private sector. In respect of events and festivals the action plan states: 'Edinburgh is world famous for its festivals and events. We will work to ensure that they continue to be world class. We will create new events and develop and improve venues which attract our target markets and stimulate new visitors to the city, particularly outwith the main tourist season' (Edinburgh Tourism Action Group, 2000).

As Buhalis (2000) and Godfrey and Clark (2000) state, the marketing of the products which together form the tourist experience for visitors in any one destination is a mechanism to facilitate regional development and rationalize tourism to ensure the strategic objectives of that particular place. Significantly, both in these texts and in Spilling (1996), the emphasis is on synergy, collaboration and entrepreneurship, whereby 'economic development is a result of complex entrepreneurial processes ... [in which] ... many ventures develop in close interaction with each other and with environmental factors' (Spilling, 1996: 91). An important characteristic of the ETAP model is the collaborative nature and breadth of the partnership it represents. As champions of ETAP the Edinburgh Tourism Action Group (ETAG) represent a coming-together of mutual interests of the public and private sector.

Entrepreneurship, the market and marketing activity

According to Spilling (1996: 94), 'entrepreneurship takes place within the framework of existing economic and sociocultural structures, and the entrepreneurial activity is based on knowledge, competence, and role models embedded in these structures'. Vitally, the significance of the individual is incomparable to the magnitude ascribed to stakeholder involvement (Buhalis, 2000; Spilling, 1996; Godfrey and Clark, 2000). The multifaceted and multistakeholder history of the tourism action plan and the festival and events strategy in Edinburgh – although not without incumbent difficulties – has, it would appear, ensured the city's continued competitive market position and can be viewed as being consequent on that very same process of entrepreneurship. The essentials of entrepreneurship as outlined by Bruno and Teybjee (1982: 293, in Spilling, 1996: 94) are:

- Venture capital availability
- Presence of experienced entrepreneurs
- Technically skilled labour force
- Accessibility of suppliers
- Accessibility of customers or new markets
- Favourable governmental policies
- Proximity of universities
- Availability of land or facilities
- Accessibility of supporting services
- Attractive living conditions.

All of these are corroborated in the strategic policy statements adopted by the partners in the city, i.e. within the Edinburgh Festivals Strategy (Graham Devlin Associates, 2001), ETAP (2000), and the tandem and integrated plans of Edinburgh Events Strategy and Events in Edinburgh (City of Edinburgh Council, 2002).

Marketing, product lifecycle and event branding

Tourism development has a vital part in the economies of many cities. As stated previously, for Edinburgh it has been a key economic driver. It should be orated here, however, that while the festival and events have been largely successful and indeed exhibit all the hallmarks of a series of events running concomitantly and in juxtaposition to the product lifecycle and destination lifecycle, the entrepreneurship that brought this about was not born of a strategic framework for its planning or management. In fact this has only emerged in the last three years (Events Strategy for Edinburgh, 2001) and it is important to remember that the rationale for many of the events prior to this, particularly the summer festivals, was never based on tourism. It has only been with the growth of tourism and its evolving significance for the city that it has become a core component of the operation and characteristic of festivals and events. Indeed it is fair to say that there has been a historical body of belief – amidst some involved in festivals and events – that strategic frameworks serve only to stifle entrepreneurship and creativity. However, the mutuality that has grown regarding audience generation and provision for visitors, i.e. between tourism and festivals and events, has precipitated the need for a more strategic approach. Concomitantly, the increasing ease of world travel and thus visitor comparison of destinations and events throughout the world has made partners aware that failure to strategically manage the image and quality of the Edinburgh event product for these potential visitors would likely have led the events and the city either to an impasse of market saturation and experiential decline or else a shifting and lost market. The decision in Edinburgh to capitalize on infrastructure development, coupled with the collective mobilization of industry through ETAG, is increasingly addressing the vital issues of seasonality and maintenance of market share. The packaging of event tourism products as a device for the retention of market share in the competitive global market is impacting positively on the vital issue of sustainability and the destination product lifecycle. Entrepreneurship here is thus a process – as Spilling (1996) suggested – taking place within the existing framework of economic and sociocultural structures, and is equally based on the knowledge, competence, and role models embedded in these structures. The ETAG has been influential in facilitating these mechanisms.

Edinburgh and brand image

Very much reflecting the national strategic objectives articulated by VisitScotland in *A New Strategy for Scottish Tourism* (Scottish Executive, 2000), ETAP highlights the importance of promoting culture as a key niche market. A culmination of many years of action by organizers, performers and visitors alike, the summer festivals (primarily the Edinburgh International and Fringe Festivals) and the Winter Festival, in particular, have aided a brand recognition of Edinburgh which many other international destinations envy. This recognition carries with it many of the qualities, as opined by Morgan *et al.* (2002: 12), of a brand, i.e. 'a unique combination of product characteristics and added values' whereby the meanings of these added values have culminated in 'an overall impression of a superior brand'. Edinburgh is the suprabrand, which is to say that Edinburgh is recognized first and foremost as a quality place (destination). This suprabrand strives not only to attract visitors but also private investors. Its sub-brands include Edinburgh the festival city; Edinburgh the world heritage city; and Edinburgh the city of contemporary culture. So although it may be the case that the Edinburgh International Festival and Fringe Festival and Hogmanay will be the first-mentioned attributes when thinking of Edinburgh, this does not diminish from the fact that they are sub-brands and that, given time, any number of sub-brands can be introduced, developed and utilized to sustain the destination brand. Each of these has a strategic function. They have the potential to be repositioned in the marketplace within their own lifecycle, and thus extend the longevity of their (sub-)brand. Arguably the cultural product has this facility more than any other, for its very nature often serves to affect and ultimately define culture norms and values. This makes them exceptionally well placed to (re)invigorate brand values. It is the conjecture here that there is a strong symbiotic relationship between tourism and culture which plays a portentous part in explaining the rapid evolution of tourism itself. While this is a dynamic for Edinburgh, it is has also been important that this evolution has not gone unchecked. The longevity of a sub-brand is consequent on both the desires of all stake-holders to support it and its appropriateness to the stage of development for the destination. In the case of Edinburgh, then, it remains vital that the sub-brand does not diminish or undermine the brand awareness of Edinburgh. In Edinburgh the message of the suprabrand is updated and communicated regularly and new sub-brands and product lines are added systematically.

Commercial partnerships

Highly developed commercial partnerships are a vital ingredient of a developed and sustainable festival and events product. This is particularly so for cultural events where events have a community – host resident – responsibility. This often comes in the form of either free or highly sub-sidized events or services, for it is often the case that the long-term legitimate function of festivals and events can be sustained only through subsidy to ensure competitive pricing levels. Again, this is often dependent on the position of the festival or event product in the event/destination product lifecycle and the relationship of this to the perceived opportunity cost of the event visitor.

Indirectly, commercial partnership with sponsors can also serve to either improve or legitimize the value of an event. This may take the form of direct image association, e.g. the association of a quality product or sponsor name with the event; or it may be a more long-term liaison in which the sponsor may grow in line with the establishment of the festival brand with consequent niche market sales and evolving recognition opportunities.

Commercial partnerships for events should facilitate a mutually beneficial business affiliation where both the event promoters and commercial partner achieve their agreed objectives (Head, 1981, in Hall, 1992). These objectives can be financial or social.

Striking the balance between the needs of the commercial partners and those of the festival and events can bring with it a challenging set of compromises. Moreover, the availability of commercial support and sponsors is often tied to the economic cycle in a way that creates an exigent instability. With this there are also significant sensitivities around such commercial relationships that do prevail to ensure that the integrity of both the city's and event's image and brand values – as well as those of the commercial partner – are protected (Hall, 1992; Morgan et al., 2002). For Edinburgh there are also potential conflicts over the promotional requirements of the partners. These have involved testing negotiations in relation to both the city's world heritage status and its planning rules and the new set of guidelines on advertising and promotion in public spaces associated with commercial partners adopted by the city in 2002. The protracted disputes that have arisen from these and other matters have shown that Edinburgh is not always able to fully accommodate the interests of all.

Event management legitimacy and conclusion

With regard to retaining legitimacy and the facilitation of stakeholder involvement, the Events Strategy (2000) stated that the City of Edinburgh Council in implementing the festival strategy must avoid the temptation to view the outcomes of the festival purely in economic terms. It argued instead that while every festival must have identified cultural outcomes and associated criteria, some will offer only marginal economic benefit and others may have less obvious social impact. The Millennium Hogmanay festival, in particular, with funding from the Millennium Lottery Fund, represented a clear, conscious effort to target and support the local audience (see Chapter 22 for further information).

For Edinburgh, seeking additional financial support and greater income generation is becoming ever more important as the costs of staging a world-class event product – and the objectives of raising quality and the number of product sub-brands – escalate. In the case of the summer

International Festival, one-third of total funding comes from grant aid from the City of Edinburgh Council, Scottish Arts Council and Millennium Lottery Fund collectively. Funding sources are, however, finite and securing and managing commercial partners is an increasing challenge. It is hoped by many that the new national events organization, Event Scotland – a joint public sector venture between the Scottish Executive and the tourist board, VisitScotland – and the opportunity this offers to seek core grant funding for landmark events may assist in this matter.

The introduction in January 2003 of the anthem 'Edinburgh's Eventful year' and new website (www.eventful-edinburgh.com) add a new marketing tool to the process of image change, product development and supra- and sub-brand awareness. The internet is an increasingly important marketing and management tool in which markets can be effectively targeted, opportunities for niche product packages created, and consumer spending and consumer perception of value-added products generated (Buhalis, 2003). With clear links to participating accommodation and other visitor service providers in Edinburgh, the aim of Eventful Edinburgh is to develop a joint marketing partnership approach in which Edinburgh's festival and event products can articulate and offer product packages to the visitors to the site. Clearly allowing individual providers to augment the core events and festival products, the Eventful Edinburgh marketing initiative also seeks to encourage intrasector partnership and product packaging through utility of the generic Eventful Edinburgh platform. Taking a seasonal approach, rotating around Edinburgh's annual spread of events and festivals, it is believed that this will encourage the short-break domestic and European market all year round and take advantage of the increasing numbers of budget flights to Edinburgh Airport. Whether Eventful Edinburgh's new online mascot, Eventful Ed, described as 'cool, contemporary and cheeky' (*The Scotsman*, 15 November 2002), will aid this process remains to be seen.

However, the fact remains that the management of image and matching product creation to ensure brand recognition alongside market retention and development is expensive. Public funding is finite and private sector support initiatives are dependent, in large, on the economic environment. This is a worry for all cities competing on the UK cultural and tourism stage. Edinburgh has many advantages over its neighbours but must continue to work hard to maintain its strong brand and the associated benefits that come with it.

Bibliography

Ashworth, G.J. (1991). Products, places and promotion: destination image in the analysis of the tourism industry. In *The Tourism Industry: An International Perspective* (Sinclair Stables, pp. 121–141. Cab International.

Buhalis, D. (2000). Marketing the competitive destination of the future. *Tourism Management*, **21**, 97–116.

Buhalis, D. (2003). eTourism – Information technology for strategic tourism management. Prentice-Hall.

Butler, R.W. (1980). The concept of a tourist area cycle of evolution implications for the management of resources. *Canadian Geographer*, **24(1)**, 5–12.

Capital Review (2002). Research Section, City Development, City of Edinburgh Council, January.

City of Edinburgh Council (2002). *Events in Edinburgh*, April.

Echtner, C.M. and Ritchie, J.R.B. (1991). The meaning and measurement of destination image. *Tourism Studies*, **2(2)**, 2–12.

Edinburgh Tourism Action Group (2000). *Edinburgh Tourism Action Plan*, October.

Getz, D. (1991). Assessing the economic impacts of festivals and events: research issues. *Journal of Applied Recreation Research*, **16(1)**, 61–77.

Godfrey, K. and Clark, J. (2000). *The Tourism Development Handbook: A Practical Approach to Planning and Marketing*. Cassell.

Graham Devlin Associates (2001). *The Edinburgh Festivals Strategy*.

Hall, C.M. (1992). *Hallmark Tourist Events: Impacts, Management and Planning*. Belhaven Press.

Harding, A. (1994). Conclusion: towards the entrepreneurial European city? In *European Cities Towards 2000: Profiles, Policies and Prospects* (A. Harding, J. Dawson, R. Evans and M. Parkinson, eds.), Manchester University Press, pp. 195–206.

Kotler, P. and Armstrong, G. (1991). *Principles of Marketing Practice*. Prentice-Hall.

Morgan, N., Pritchard, A. and Pride, R. (2002). *Destination Branding: Creating the Unique Destination Proposition*, Chapters 2 and 11. Butterworth-Heinemann.

Opperham, M. (2000). Tourism destination loyalty. *Journal of Travel Research*, **39**, 78–84.

Paddison, M. (1993). City marketing, image reconstruction and urban regeneration. *Urban Studies*, **30(2)**, 339–350.

Page, S. (1995). *Urban Tourism*. Routledge.

Ritchie, J.R.B. (1984). Assessing the impact of hallmark events: conceptual and research issues. *Journal of Travel Research*, **23(1)**, 2–11.

Ritchie, J.R.B. and Smith, B.H. (1991). The impact of a mega-event on a host region awareness: a longitudinal study. *Journal of Travel Research*, **30(1)**, 3–10.

Robertson, M. and Guerrier, Y. (1998). Events as entrepreneurial displays: Seville, Barcelona and Madrid. In *Managing Tourism Destinations: Policy, Process and Practice* (D. Tyler, Y. Guerrier and M. Robertson, eds). John Wiley and Sons.

Scottish Executive (2000). *A New Strategy for Scottish Tourism 2000*.

Spilling, O.R. (1996). The entrepreneurial system: on entrepreneurship in the context of a mega-event. *Journal of Business Research*, **36**, 91–103.

Stabler, M.J. (1988). The Image of Destination Regions: Theoretical and Empirical Aspects. In *Marketing in the Tourism Industry: The Promotion of Destination Regions* (B. Goodall and G. Ashworth, eds.), London: Croom Helm, pp. 133–161.

Questions

1 What are the advantages and disadvantages for destinations in the holding of major art or cultural events?

2 Why do destinations – more particularly cities – wish to change their image and what are the core factors in ensuring image change is successful for the destination?

3 What is, and what is the purpose of, event branding?

9

Marketing information for the events industry

Emma Wood

Introduction

There is, undoubtedly, a need for an increased use of marketing information within the events industry in order to improve all aspects of decision making and marketing activity planning. This chapter details why the information is needed, how it can be obtained and how it should be used in a practical and realistic way. Examples and short case studies from the events industry are used throughout to emphasize the practical use of the techniques being discussed.

Information for marketing decisions

In order to gain and sustain competitive advantage, all organizations need to gather, analyse and use information from a variety of sources. At the very least a knowledge of existing and potential markets, business trends, competitors, and the effectiveness of marketing programmes is critical to the success of any organization. This requires a focused, continuous gathering and use of information against which to measure the achievement of objectives.

The relationship between information use and the marketing value chain is illustrated in Figure 9.1.

Because of the failure to focus on information issues, few organizations know what information they have or need. In high customer contact services and hence the events industry, a firm's ability to deliver quality service depends largely on its ability to collect, process and distribute information. Berkley and Gupta's (1995) list of what they suggest as areas of prime importance in a service-based industry highlight the complexity and variety of information needs within events organizations. These are: demands and capacities; service specifications; service history; market trends; service standards; customer instructions; process information; knowledge; job status; security; quality control; internal quality measures; external quality measures; complaints and compliments; service recovery; customer defections.

Much of the information generated in the service industry results from personal interaction: employee–customer, customer–customer and employee–employee. This type of qualitative data is highly valuable but more difficult to systematically collect, analyse and use and this may be one of the reasons that these organizations have not initiated systematic efforts in realizing the benefits of formal marketing information systems (Sisodia, 1992).

Event managers are often preoccupied with delivering a high-quality programme (Getz, 1998) which provides for the visitor experience but can lead to neglect in other areas such as service quality, visitor satisfaction, and evaluation before, during and after the event. Indeed, a survey by the Meetings Industry Association (MIA) found that only 40% of venues solicited the event organizers' opinions on their service and fewer than 15% of organizers and venues thought to ask the delegates or attendees (The Right Solution, 2002; Tum, 2002).

As well as this lack of evaluation of the attendee's experience or satisfaction there is also a paucity of information gathered in other areas. For instance, there is very little comprehensive empirical investigation into the sponsorship phenomenon (Lee et al., 1997), particularly from the consumer's perspective, i.e. the event attendee's attitude towards the sponsor,

Marketing value chain	Market Understanding →	Strategy Formulation →	Detailed Planning →	Marketing Operations →
Evaluation and Adjustment				
Information needed	Monitoring data: Environment Markets Customers Competitors	Objective setting Strategic choices Segmentation Product portfolio	Resources Programmes Processes Systems	Positioning & image Pricing structures NPD & product mix Service & quality Promotion Channels
Information use	Awareness of market needs Alertness to opportunities & threats	Quantifiable objectives Identified critical success factors Effective & efficient targeting	Priorities in resource allocation Detailed plans with alternative actions Creative strategies	Implementation Budgeting Control Evaluation Adjustment Identification of information needs
Outcome	Insight	Vision	Creativity	Drive

Figure 9.1 Information and the marketing value chain. (Based on Skyrme, 1989.)

its influence on their attitude to the event and on their subsequent behavioural intent.

Although the main uses for marketing information are for continuous improvement of all marketing activities, to gain competitive advantage, build customer loyalty etc., within the events industry there are additional benefits to be gained from having access to valid and reliable data. This data will often provide the evidence required to secure continued political and financial support from a number of important stakeholder groups which may include host cities, regions, countries, arts councils, local government, corporate sponsors etc. Indeed this type of information can provide the basis for successful bids for hosting major events, and post-event evaluation data is often a condition required by sponsors and other funding bodies.

Glazer (1997) argues that information itself is the key strategic asset to be maximized as well as the guiding principle around which corporate structures or departments are organized and that the focus of this information should be the customer who becomes central to everything the firm undertakes. The value of pertinent, reliable, timely information in providing competitive advantage has grown with increasing competition and improvements in information-based technologies. The many advantages of applying information technology in these areas are illustrated in Figure 9.2 and it becomes clear that events organizations can no longer afford to neglect this valuable resource. 'Companies with deep knowledge about their customers, competitors and operations will be the winners of this age' (Sisodia, 1992: 63).

Marketing decision making in the events industry has traditionally relied on creativity, and intuition sometimes supplemented by attendance figures, as opposed to the systematic use of a range of information sources. Yet there is a variety of information available to events organizations ranging from detailed economic impact analysis (Dwyer et al., 2000) to eavesdropping on subject-specific internet chat rooms (Poria and Harmen, 2002) that can inform decisions in all areas of marketing from initial target market selection and competitor analysis, through to future product ideas or improvements and more effective marketing communications.

The following sections take the reader through these sources of information, how they can be accessed, generated, applied and managed, in the context of the events environment.

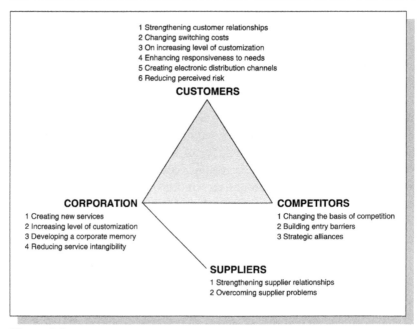

1 Strengthening customer relationships
2 Changing switching costs
3 On increasing level of customization
4 Enhancing responsiveness to needs
5 Creating electronic distribution channels
6 Reducing perceived risk

CUSTOMERS

CORPORATION
1 Creating new services
2 Increasing level of customization
3 Developing a corporate memory
4 Reducing service intangibility

COMPETITORS
1 Changing the basis of competition
2 Building entry barriers
3 Strategic alliances

SUPPLIERS
1 Strengthening supplier relationships
2 Overcoming supplier problems

Figure 9.2 Information technology and the extended strategic triangle (Sisodia, 1992: 58).

The information required – event marketing research objectives

Before beginning any data-gathering exercise it is necessary to have clearly defined objectives. This is as important for recurrent monitoring of data gathered from continuous scanning of the environment as it is for one-off market research projects, and there is a need to detail why the information is needed and how it will be used. Once these objectives have been set it is then possible to determine the information required in order to make each marketing decision.

For many types of events the event objectives are stated in terms of 'the triple bottom line' (Kenyon *et al.*, 2002). This refers to the economic, social and environmental benefits resulting from the holding of the event. These varied benefits (and/or costs), therefore, need to be measured to ensure that objectives are being met and will require a range of information sources and data-gathering techniques.

The first stage in any research exercise is to check if the information required already exists and is in some usable form. If not, it is necessary to ascertain whether or not the information can be obtained in time, at an acceptable cost, and whether the likely benefits of its use will outweigh the resource requirements of producing it. For all organizations, however, there will always be a minimum amount of primary research that needs to be undertaken on a regular basis in order to provide sufficient information on which to base decisions.

Research of a programme of events run by a venue, event organizer, local authority, charity or promotions department etc. needs to be both formative and summative, therefore creating a continuous process which rolls from one event into the next. Although information generated within the organization is a good starting point it is important not to rely on this to the neglect of external data. Xu and Kaye (1995) argue that 80% of information should be generated from outside the organization rather than the current practice of 80% from internal sources.

Marketing information needs in the events industry

The four event-marketing research areas of market analysis, consumer research, promotion studies and performance evaluation suggested in Bowdin *et al.* (2001) can be expanded upon to provide a more comprehensive checklist of information needs:

- Setting event objectives
- Macro-environment analysis
- Customer analysis, segmentation and targeting strategy
- Customer satisfaction
- Customer expectations
- Competitor analysis and positioning
- Tactical marketing decisions
- Wider impacts
- Long-term planning.

Setting event objectives

Realistic objective setting requires hard, quantifiable data which can be largely historically based using the experience of previous events and the events of other organizations, but also requires a knowledge of the current financial and other organizational resource constraints along with an understanding of current market conditions.

Macro-environment analysis

The economic, social, political, legal, technological, demographic and political environment requires monitoring on a continuous basis. The regular scanning of a number of key sources of information to build up a market intelligence database is a relatively cost-effective way to gain useful insights and a precursor to an accurate forecasting system.

Customer analysis, segmentation and targeting strategy

A detailed knowledge of customers and markets is the most valuable resource an organization can have. In events organizations, customers are likely to include a whole range of stakeholder groups including the event attendees, the sponsors, the local community, the participants etc. The complexity of these customer groups means that a detailed knowledge of their preferences and behaviours is of greater importance if their various needs are to be met. Only once the characteristics within these groups have been identified can the market be usefully segmented and only when those segments have been quantified and assessed can a targeting strategy be developed. The more detailed the knowledge of each customer the closer the organization can get to a customized offering creating greater satisfaction and long-term customer relationships.

Glazer (1997) argues that an organization's information system should be based around a central customer information file (CIF) which contains information on customer characteristics, customer responses to firm decisions and customer purchase history. This needs to be built upon continually and becomes a vital part of the organization's memory, utilizing past, present and likely future actions of customers, potential customers and lost customers.

Customer satisfaction measurement

This requires primary research during and after each event as well as the monitoring of repeat business levels, customer complaints, front-line staff comments etc. Quantitative measures are needed for meaningful comparison with other events and qualitative data to provide insight into areas for improvement. Care must be taken in ensuring that the methods employed will produce useful information which can be used to improve the offering rather than a 'didn't-we-do-well happy sheet' to boost the organizer's image.

Measures of satisfaction also need to include an analysis of other stakeholders' needs which may include sponsors, community, employees, volunteers etc. These groups are often overlooked but are as valuable to the process as the end customers. An evaluation of 'the event experience' through on-the-day research using all stakeholder groups, in order to build up a complete picture, is recommended.

Customer expectations

It is imperative to ascertain these before the event as expectations have a great effect on levels of satisfaction and future purchase behaviour. High expectations may sell more tickets for one event but if those expectations are not met then future business will be lost. The expectations of the event need to be gleaned from those who did not attend as well as those who did, as these market perceptions create the event organization's relative competitive position.

Competitor analysis and positioning

An understanding of the industry structure coupled with regular competitor intelligence can be used in a number of ways. Market share can be estimated from financial data and used to inform generic strategies. An understanding of competitor reactions to strategic moves can inform future plans, and recognition of best practice through benchmarking can enable the organization to learn from others in the industry. A thorough understanding of competitive offerings provides an insight into the decision-making process of the prospective customer and can suggest which benefits to emphasize in promotional material.

Tactical marketing decisions

As many event products have relatively short lifecycles, regular innovation and improvement in all aspects of the event (or programme of events) is needed. Information from a variety of sources, such as monitoring the events of others, using expert panels, customer feedback etc., can be used to inspire idea generation, aid portfolio planning, and maintain product innovation for competitive advantage.

As part of this process, research is needed to ascertain the market perceptions of related brand images (event brand, organizer brand, venue brand, sponsor brand, host city brand etc.) prior to creating new brands, developing brand extensions or re-imaging existing brands.

In order to set customer-value-based pricing strategies and structures, information is also needed on the perceived benefits received and costs incurred for each market segment and stakeholder group. An understanding of the price elasticity of each event using supply and demand estimates is vital if price is to be used effectively in yield management, and a competitive distribution strategy can only be initiated once customer preferences for the 'where, when and how' of the event purchase have been identified.

A large proportion of the marketing budget of event organizations is spent on marketing communications. In order to monitor the effectiveness of this, spend information is needed on the reach, impact, and short and long-term effects on attitude and purchase behaviour of each promotional component and on the integrated communications strategy as a whole. This requires pre-campaign testing as well as monitoring of post-campaign results.

Wider impacts

Monitoring the wider economic and social impacts of the event is required as these impacts are often clearly identified as event objectives. This information also helps to ensure that the interests of other stakeholders are catered for, e.g. local businesses, local community and local government, and can help to give leverage for future funding and support. The measurement of social impacts is often omitted from post-event research due to their intangibility and long-term nature; however, quantitative methods have been developed which provide a framework for evaluating the event's effect on areas such as civic pride, sense of belonging, healthier lifestyles, community involvement etc. (Wood, 2002a).

Long-term planning

A strategic rather than operational use of information is required in the long term in order to provide the basis for planning several years ahead rather than one event ahead. This strategic orientation requires the development of a 'learning organization' making use of historical information, learning from mistakes and successes and forecasting ahead.

The development of appropriate long-term objectives and clear strategic paths to achieve them can only be achieved by the effective use of the information gathered from all the above activities in marketing decision making.

The availability and location of information – types and sources of data

In order to provide management decision makers with relevant, timely and reliable information it is important to utilize a variety of types and sources of data. However, it needs to be borne in mind that the exact data required will always be determined by the objectives of the research, which in turn are determined by the needs of the decision maker, for example to ascertain why ticket sales have fallen this year, to justify continued investment in the event or to identify new target markets etc.

The cheapest and most easily accessible type of data is that which is generated by the day-to-day running of the organization. The usefulness of this type of data can be greatly enhanced by systematic and consistent report generation using database and query software. This internal data is often the starting point of a developing marketing information system; however, caution is required as it is easy to become over-reliant on internal data to the neglect of vital external sources.

Quantitative internal data includes information on ticket sales, accounts, customer records, costings, merchandise sales, bar sales etc. Internally generated qualitative data might include sales staff reports, sponsorship bids/feedback, minutes of meetings, feedback from customer service staff, customer complaints/compliments etc.

Data gathered from outside the organization is vital for decision making in a market-focused competitive firm. External data in the form of market intelligence, continuous market scanning and recurrent stakeholder surveys should be the priority of the event organization's information-gathering activities.

The starting point for external data is to make use of information which already exists in some form. This secondary data can be quantitative, such as government statistics, online data, industry surveys, published market research reports, trade or association data, published financial data etc., or qualitative, including news reports/articles, trade journals, other media, competitor sales literature, trade directories, CD-ROMs, websites etc. For major events an important source of qualitative secondary data are previous bid documents which are increasingly being made public. The continuous monitoring of identified key external sources creates longitudinal data, which can be used to anticipate customer trends, competitor reactions, economic fluctuations etc., and is vital for forecasting and hence long-term planning decisions.

To complement these existing sources and to provide a richer picture of the organization's proximate macro-environment (customers, competitors, suppliers, publics) it is necessary to generate first-hand data. As this process will be comparatively costly and time-consuming it is important to have clear objectives for the research and to ensure that it can be carried out reliably (in-house or outsourced) within the given budget and time constraints. Again this primary information can be either quantitative or qualitative or preferably a combination of the two. Quantitative data tends to result from larger-scale surveys, resident panels, visitor profiles etc. and requires the application of correct sampling procedures to ensure validity and reliability. Qualitative data is normally smaller scale but gives more depth of information and is useful for ascertaining opinions, feelings and attitudes and for identifying initial problem areas for further investigation. This richer information can be gathered using observation, focus groups, in-depth interviews with attendees, participants, sponsors etc., recording staff and volunteer feedback, and utilizing management notes and commentary.

Any successful marketing information system needs to combine internal and external sources and use both quantitative and qualitative data in order to provide statistical reliability plus in-depth insights in a meaningful and usable manner. Most organizations will start with internal and secondary information as this is quick and cheap to obtain. The scanning of external data regularly to build up market intelligence begins to give a market focus but the core research activity should always centre on gathering customer information and it is not sufficient for this to come from internal systems. The gathering of external primary data is vital for event organizations who tend to have a variety of stakeholders with changing needs and who operate in a highly competitive environment. It is this information that will enable the anticipation of future needs, the development of innovative offerings and hence a sustainable competitive advantage.

The type of information gathered may also be dependent on the audience of the report. For example, quantitative data, traditionally viewed as more tangible and providing 'hard facts', tends to be preferred by supporting organizations, i.e. sponsors, government, arts councils etc. The challenge may therefore be to either measure intangibles such as social impacts in a quantifiable manner or to make qualitative 'soft data' easier to interpret and use.

Methods for obtaining first-hand information – generating data

In determining the parameters of primary research the focus throughout should again be on 'fitness for purpose'. How will the final report be used? Who will read it and what decisions will be based on it? Starting at the end helps to focus on the objectives and not get carried away with an 'it would be nice to know' research agenda.

For all research projects there will be a range of tools and techniques which can be applied and need to be evaluated and selected. The quantitative/qualitative mix needs to be considered, as does the sampling methods and sample size. These again will depend upon the depth of information required and the levels of reliability and accuracy expected. Even if the research is to be outsourced to an agency the initial decisions of methods and size should be considered.

A useful technique suggested by Smith and Fletcher (2001) is to start by detailing the ideal research design and then to trade down from this based on constraints of time, budget, expertise etc. These constraints lead to what they call a 'five-way tradeoff' consisting of precision, depth of understanding, credibility, practicality and cost. Once the practical design has been achieved it is necessary to assess what sources of error have been introduced and whether these are acceptable.

Main techniques for gathering first-hand data

Surveys
The use of questionnaires to generate largely quantitative data are often used to gain customer opinions post-event (Figures 9.3–9.5). These can be administered in a number of ways to meet the needs of the research undertaken either using a trained interview (face-to-face or telephone) or self-completion by the respondent (hard copy, e-mail or online).

Online surveys are growing in popularity and are often used in the business-to-business market where customer access to the internet is close to 100%. Research has shown that 80% of event organizers would be happy to complete an online survey after each event (The Right Solution,

---

THE INTERNATIONAL TRADE CONFERENCE 2002
SEMINAR EVALUATION QUESTIONNAIRE

Name: ....

Organisation: ....

Please rate each category on a scale of 1-5:
  1 = Poor   2 = Average   3 = Good   4 = Very Good   5 = Excellent

Name of seminar: ....

A) How did you rate the overall presentation?

  ☐ 1   ☐ 2   ☐ 3   ☐ 4   ☐ 5

Please comment: ....

B) How did you rate the speakers?

  Name of speaker: ....

  ☐ 1   ☐ 2   ☐ 3   ☐ 4   ☐ 5

Please comment: ....

  Name of speaker: ....

  ☐ 1   ☐ 2   ☐ 3   ☐ 4   ☐ 5

Please comment: ....

  Name of speaker: ....

  ☐ 1   ☐ 2   ☐ 3   ☐ 4   ☐ 5

Please comment: ....

C) How did you rate the subject matter?

  ☐ 1   ☐ 2   ☐ 3   ☐ 4   ☐ 5

Please comment: ....

D) How did you rate the registration procedure?

  ☐ 1   ☐ 2   ☐ 3   ☐ 4   ☐ 5

Please comment: ....

Figure 9.3 Example of an e-mailed questionnaire.

Your thoughts about this conference

Please can you indicate your strength of agreement or disagreement with the following statements about this conference.
(please tick one box only for each statement)

	Strongly agree	Agree	Neither agree nor disagree	Disagree	Strongly disagree
The conference was conveniently located					
The venue was well equipped					
The conference ran to time					
The conference was well organised					
The staff/organisers were helpful					
The staff/organisers were available when needed					
The conference was run professionally					
The staff were courteous					
Individual needs were catered for					
The staff were attentive OR There was a caring environment					

Figure 9.4   Example of self-completion survey question.

2002). An example of this trend is the MIA Tracker system developed by the Meetings Industry Association. Event venues subscribe to an online software system which automatically solicits the opinions of event organizers on the venue shortly after each event. A further benefit is that as a syndicated research tool it can also provide each subscribing organization with information for competitive benchmarking (Meetings Industry Association/Catlow Consulting, 2002).

A variation on the one-off survey is one that is repeated at regular intervals to provide longitudinal data. These surveys usually recruit a panel of consumers, businesses, residents etc. who are used each time a survey is conducted. This type of research is very useful for tracking changes over time and often give far better response rates. One disadvantage, however, is that the respondents' reported behaviour and attitudes may be influenced by their knowledge that they are regularly questioned and this variation on the 'Hawthorne effect' can be very difficult to recognize and quantify.

Any quantitative survey requires robust sampling procedures and a recognition of any error or bias inherent in the process. These errors can be created by the number and type of non-response, by the interviewer technique, by initial sample size and selection, by data entry and analysis

Attendees and Participants

Please can you estimate how much your group/family spent on the following items during your outing to 'Arts in the Park'
(*include all expenditure related to attending the event, eg staying in Blackburn for a meal/drink afterwards etc*)

Items	Spent on Sat £	Spent on Sun £
A. Food (restaurants, take-aways, snacks etc)		
B. Drink (soft drinks, alcohol, tea/coffee etc)		
C. Transport (bus fare, taxi, train, petrol, parking etc)		
D. Gifts/Souvenirs (toys, crafts, programmes etc)		
E. Other items (please specify)		
F. Estimated total cost of day out		

Please can you estimate how much your group/family would spend in Blackburn on a *normal weekend.*

Saturday	£
Sunday	£

Local businesses

How did 'Arts in the Park' affect your turnover on the days of the event?
(*Tick one box only*)

Saturday	Large increase	5	Increase	4	No change	3	Decrease	2	Large decrease	1

Sunday	Large increase	5	Increase	4	No change	3	Decrease	2	Large decrease	1

How do you foresee the longer term effects of 'Arts in the Park' on your turnover?

Large increase	5	Increase	4	No change	3	Decrease	2	Large decrease	1

Non-attendees

Did the 'Arts in the Park' festival have any effect on how you spent your weekend?

Yes	1	No	2

If yes please explain why.

Figure 9.5   Excerpts from a telephone-administered questionnaire.

procedures etc. The subsequent use of the data for decision making must always allow for levels of reliability and validity and can be improved by making use of a number of sources of information rather than be reliant on the results of a single quantitative survey.

Focus groups/interviews

When information is required on attitudes, opinions or motivations it is often difficult or inappropriate to use quantitative techniques. Prompted but not controlled expression direct from the respondent can provide very rich insightful data which can lead to further areas for study or provide substance to the findings of parallel quantitative research. The depth of data generated from group discussions or in-depth interviews with attendees, participants, local residents etc. often provides the key to problem areas which would otherwise not have been anticipated by the researchers (Figure 9.6). Although guided in discussion areas, the respondents are not forced into making choices from preselected responses as with quantitative research, so there is no second guessing of the outcomes. However, the richness and unstructured nature of the data generated leads to problems in analysis and interpretation and requires skilled and experienced researchers if the findings are to be reliable and objective.

Event attendees' attitudes to the event sponsorship

1. Warm-up/Explanation of focus group rules
2. Attendees' opinions on the event itself
   Why they attended, level of enjoyment/satisfaction
3. Knowledge of who sponsored the event
   Unprompted response initially. Where they saw the sponsorship/What was remembered about it?
4. Discussion of sponsors' products
   Attitudes, perceptions, image, knowledge, changes in attitude
5. Their purchase behaviour and sponsors' products
   Previous use, competitors' products purchased, future use
6. Opinions of relationship between event and sponsors
   Was the sponsorship appropriate to the event? Did sponsorship affect attitude to the event?

Figure 9.6   Example of an interview schedule.

Internet chat rooms and discussion groups can be set up as virtual focus groups with either an overt facilitator whose role is recognized by the participants or with a covert facilitator who poses as an ordinary participant. These e-groups can provide the opportunity to monitor attitude changes over time in a longitudinal study.

A useful variation on focus groups is in soliciting expert opinion. Here the members of the discussion group are chosen based on their experience and knowledge of the topic rather than on the basis of being representative of a larger segment or population. The soliciting of expert opinion can be used in idea generation and product innovation as well as in recognizing the causes of previously identified problems. Experts can be drawn from any of the event stakeholder groups and often involve suppliers and distributors. For example a post-event mixed expert focus group may consist of the event organizers, representatives from the venues involved, local government tourism/event managers and local community representatives. The diversity of views expressed and the differing objectives of each group help to generate innovative ideas and solutions. In some situations it is possible to create discussion groups consisting of direct competitors if the topic is of mutual benefit and the findings are to be shared.

Observation

Observing attendees' behaviour at events can provide detailed information on how the product is used by the attendee and give clues to the benefits gained as well as helping to gauge levels of enjoyment or satisfaction (Figure 9.7). Observing behaviour as it happens provides very reliable information as it does not depend upon the respondent's memory or desire to be seen in a certain light; however, the recording and interpretation of that behaviour requires a high level of skill and objectivity.

Participant observation has been used to investigate young people's social behaviour as a precursor to developing products such as club nights and promotional events. The observer joins the group being

Observation date: _____ Please record your observations in the appropriate cells.			
Attendance	10am	12noon	2pm
Record number of males, females and total in your observation area	M F Total	M F Total	M F Total
Age groups (Number in each age group)	0-14 15-24 25-34 35+	0-14 15-24 25-34 35+	0-14 15-24 25-34 35+
Visitor types	Family Family and friends Friends Individual Other	Family Family and friends Friends Individual Other	Family Family and friends Friends Individual Other
Involvement *Tick one 'A' scale variable to indicate crowd involvement level*	Anticipation Arousal Action Aggression	Anticipation Arousal Action Aggression	Anticipation Arousal Action Aggression
Expenditure *Any evidence of spending on sponsors' products or other products? If yes, which ones? Tick boxes. If other items, note below other*	Coca-Cola Sol Beer Emu Bitter Food T-shirts Caps Other (if yes, what?)	Coca-Cola Sol Beer Emu Bitter Food T-shirts Caps Other (if yes, what?)	Coca-Cola Sol Beer Emu Bitter Food T-shirts Caps Other (if yes, what?)
Environment *Any evidence of environmental impacts? If yes, what type?*	Litter Food waste Plastics Cans Other Vegetation trampling Other	Litter Food waste Plastics Cans Other Vegetation trampling Other	Litter Food waste Plastics Cans Other Vegetation trampling Other

Figure 9.7   Example of observation tool checklist. (Adapted from O'Neill *et al.*, 1999.)

observed on a social occasion and records their movements, purchases and conversation. The information is then combined with other sources to provide a detailed picture of prospective customer characteristics and their preferences.

Covert observation of the event experience is a variation on the 'mystery shopper' technique pioneered in the retail industry. Here a trained researcher experiences the event and records the positive and negative aspects of it. This technique can be combined with experimentation by the observer setting up certain situations. For example they may play the role of a dissatisfied customer and record how they are dealt with by customer service staff or they may stipulate particular dietary or mobility needs when booking and experience how these are implemented etc.

Estimating attendance

An important aspect of event evaluation is generating accurate estimates of attendance. This is fairly straightforward at ticketed events or at events with restricted entrance and exit points but can become complicated for non-ticketed open or semi-open access events. Objective and reliable methods are needed to overcome the tendency to massage attendance figures for different ends and to provide meaningful data on which to base future decisions.

Raybould *et al.*'s (2000) summary of the various methods available for estimating attendance at open events is given in Table 9.1.

In order to undertake a thorough evaluation of an event, to gain a deeper understanding of potential markets or to generate new ideas it is important to use a combination of the techniques discussed in this section. This holistic use of sources of information provides triangulation of findings and therefore improves reliability while giving a much greater depth of understanding of the issue being researched. For example, O'Neill *et al.* (1999) combined skilled participant observation with a self-completion survey plus management, staff and visitor input in their evaluation of the 1998 Coca-Cola Masters Surfing event, and Shone (2001) suggests that several sources are needed for a complete event evaluation (Figure 9.8).

The two case studies outlined below demonstrate the use of a variety of information sources and primary research methods to provide a comprehensive evaluation of events.

Table 9.1   Comparison of methods used in attendance estimates at open events

Method	Applicable situation	Labour needs	Limitations and concerns
Tag-and-recapture[a]	Single venue; limited duration	High	Need large samples to achieve acceptable levels of confidence
Parade counts	Where crowds line a route; crowds largely static	High	Count time needs to be coordinated carefully; problems with parade followers
Entrance and exit counts (people and/or vehicles)	Single venue; small number of entry points	High	Need to identify and survey all entry points; problems identifying multiple entry and exit points
Aerial photography	Open air, daylight	Low	Need to predict peak attendance times; may need estimates for undercover areas

[a]Need turnover rate from survey data. *Source:* Raybould *et al.* (2000: 30).

Case study 1

International Boat Show

A combination of quantitative and qualitative methods was used to evaluate whether the International Boat Show was meeting the needs of exhibitors, visitors and the general public. Visitors and exhibitors were interviewed as they attended the show and then again a few weeks later once they had reflected on the show and once the exhibitors had chance to assess the orders resulting from the show. Key members of the media were interviewed at the event and a detailed audit of press coverage generated by the show was collated and analysed to check against key criteria and improvement on previous years. The evaluation of the show was compared to other boat shows around the world as well as to previous years. This holistic analysis of an eclectic array of evidence generated both robust quantitative data on overall levels of satisfaction and also in a qualitative fashion pinpointed specific improvement action points for the organizers. (*Source:* Smith and Fletcher, 2001: 149.)

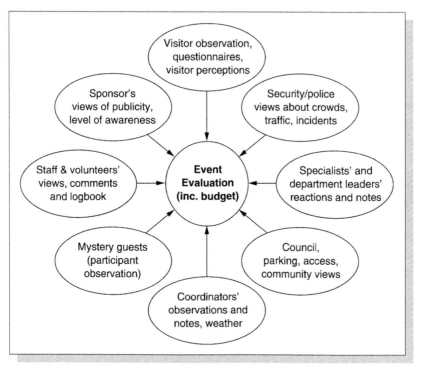

Figure 9.8 Sources of information for evaluation (Shone, 2001: 263).

Case study 2

Blackburn Fiesta

Blackburn with Darwen Borough Council used a combination of focus groups and expert panels to develop a bank of questionnaires to assess the impacts of the Fiesta on attendees, non-attendees, participants, sponsors, local businesses and community groups. The mainly quantitative results generated by the questionnaires were combined with in-depth interviews using a residents' panel to provide an overview of the economic and social impacts of the event and an assessment of its success from the various stakeholders' perspectives. The methods used were to be repeated at other local authority events and at the same events in following years to provide comparable data to be used in benchmarking, identifying trends and in service improvement. (*Source*: Wood, 2002b.)

'Effectively executed market research is a key vehicle for understanding spectator perceptions of event quality and success. It is critical therefore that event organizers use both formal and informal methods of data collection to ascertain clearly visitor perceptions of the quality of events and that this information be communicated fully post-event so that subsequent events may be consistently improved upon' (O'Neill *et al.*, 1999: 164).

Interpreting the information – analysing, managing and using the data

The importance of bringing information from a number of sources together in order to provide substantiated, reliable evidence on which to base future decisions has been highlighted above. This process will require the application of a number of techniques for analysing qualitative and quantitative data and the use of information technology for analysis, storage, manipulation and retrieval.

The data analysis process for complex information from a variety of sources requires an initial clarification of the decision maker's goals. This sets the objectives for the analysis and presentation of results. It is then necessary to check and clearly acknowledge the data validity and reliability. Once this is done the data can be reduced through the use of statistical methods for quantitative data or through techniques such as content analysis for qualitative data. The reduced data can then be investigated to identify trends, shapes and patterns and these can in turn be used to develop and build models to explain behaviours. The final stage is to present the findings in an objective and usable manner to those who will be using it to inform strategic marketing decisions.

Although the procedure outlined above is valid for each project being undertaken, there also needs to be a system in place to manage the continual flow of information from market intelligence, internal records, *ad hoc* projects etc. The complexity, competitiveness and volatility of the events industry creates a greater need for marketing information to be managed within a bespoke system and this system development is a key stage in the development of an information-based decision-making culture within events organizations.

As we have seen, the information needs of events companies are great and cannot afford to be overlooked as they will be faced with the need to control an ever larger and rapidly changing marketing environment. To handle the increasing external and internal information flow and to improve its quality companies have to take advantage of the opportunities offered by information technology (IT) and information systems. Managing marketing information by IT has become one of the most vital elements of effective marketing (Talvinen and Saarinen, 1995).

The marketing information system must ensure a continuous flow of pertinent information to the decision maker without restricting the creativity and freedom needed within the events industry. A semi-informal system, similar to that suggested by Wright and Ashill (1998) for the smaller firm, is needed which takes into account the distinct nature of the events industry. This system needs to incorporate the 80% external data suggested by Xu and Kaye (1995), the accessing of online information and the sharing of information within industry groups (Wood, 2001), be centred around Glazer's (1997) 'customer interface file', make use of Talvinen's strategic partnerships and cross-functional networks and incorporate the informal creative insights that abound in the events industry.

Figure 9.9 illustrates the key areas that an event marketing information system should incorporate, although it is recognized that the needs of each organization will differ and that the system needs to remain flexible and fluid.

What can go wrong – pitfalls to avoid

Although, generally, the benefits of collecting, managing and using marketing information far outweigh the costs and inconveniences involved, there are a number of issues which can affect the effectiveness of its use and the acceptance of its importance within the organization:

- Information overload
- Stifling creativity
- Information cost versus effectiveness gains
- Skills, training and personnel shortages
- Privacy and data protection issues.

Information overload

In the present information age a scarcity of information is rarely the problem. It is the sheer abundance of information which can have a detrimental effect as information consumes attention and decision

151

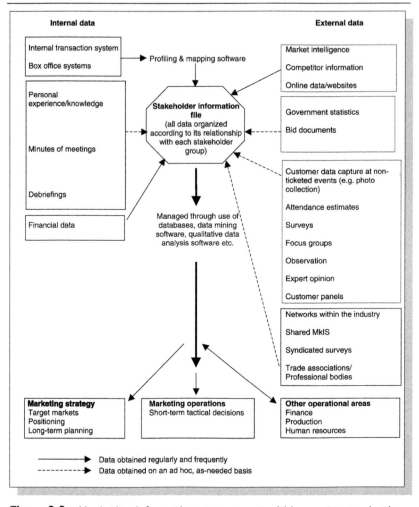

Figure 9.9 Marketing information management within events organizations.

makers have many demands upon their time. One way to overcome this is to recognize the short shelf life of information and to focus on becoming a 'market-driven learning organization'. This requires acceptance of the idea that what is known at any time is always less important than the ability to learn (Glazer, 1997).

Stifling creativity

Many of the arguments against information systems, formalized research and planning stem from the fear that they will in some way prevent artistic flair, intuition and creativity and therefore innovation or compromise artistic integrity.

Information cost versus effectiveness gains

In setting up a marketing information system it is possible for its 'champions' to become carried away with the importance of the system while losing sight of the needs of the decision makers it serves. It is imperative that the users control the inputs to the system and this is achieved by designing information around end use and fitness for purpose rather than being driven by 'the machine'.

Skills, training and personnel

An efficient and effective marketing information system is dependent upon those who manage and use it. This will inevitably mean that existing staff will need to be informed of its benefits and should be given ownership through being involved in the design and set-up stages. This requires a certain amount of internal marketing and is undoubtedly helped if there is a 'champion of the system' to move it forward. Once initiated, the system requires staff with skills in data gathering, data input, analysis and interpretation and in report preparation and presentation, and this may require some investment in training.

Privacy and data protection

In collecting and using information on individuals the organization needs to be aware of the legislation that governs its use to ensure that they are not infringing the far-ranging data protection laws. The key principles of the 1998 Data Protection Act are given in the appendix. Although there are legislative requirements the ethical use of information goes beyond these. For example, these might include issues around unsolicited direct marketing material, the use of photographs taken at events or 'small print' opt-out clauses. One way to help ensure that the use of information does not alienate customers is to use the principles of 'permission marketing' (Godin, 1999). The basic premise of permission marketing is that customers are only marketed to if they have asked to be and in doing so their information is only being used with their express permission.

Conclusion

In order to succeed through strategic competitive advantage, events organizations need to make use of marketing information. To do this it is necessary to firstly identify clearly and precisely their information needs in terms of the marketing decisions to be taken. Once the needs have been identified, the sources of information can be investigated and if necessary, primary data collected. The information collected on a continuous and on an *ad hoc* basis then needs to be organized within a marketing information system. This system needs to be organized so that decision makers can access a broad range of information, creating an holistic view of specific marketing problems.

Bibliography

Berkley, B.J. and Gupta, A. (1995). Identifying the information requirements needed to deliver quality service. *International Journal of Service Industry Management*, **6(5)**, 15–31.

Bowdin, G., McDonnell, I., Allen, J. and O'Toole, W. (2001). *Events Management*. Oxford: Butterworth-Heinemann.

Dwyer, L., Mellor, R., Mistilis, N. and Mules, T. (2000). Forecasting the economic impacts of events and conventions. *Event Management*, **6**, 191–204.

Getz, D. (1998). Information sharing among festival managers. *Festival Management and Event Tourism: An International Journal*, **5(1/2)**, 71–83.

Glazer, R. (1997). Strategy and structure in information-intensive markets: The relationship between marketing and IT. *Journal of Market Focused Management*, **2**, 65–81.

Godin, S. (1999). *Permission Marketing: Turning Strangers into Friends, and Friends into Customers*. New York: Simon and Schuster.

Her Majesty's Statistical Office (1998). http://www.hmso.gov.uk/acts/acts1998/19980029.htm. Updated 24 July 1998, accessed October 2002.

Kenyon, P., Aitken, J., Goldblatt, J.J. and Derrett, R. (2002). Building community futures – the triple bottom line. *Events and Place Making Research Conference*, 15–16 July, UTS, Sydney, Australia.

Lee, M-S., Sandler, D.M. and Shani, D. (1997). Attitudinal constructs towards sponsorship: Scale development using three global sporting events. *International Marketing Review*, **14(3)**, 159–169.

Meetings Industry Association/Catlow Consulting (2002). http://www.miatracker.org/. Accessed 25 October 2002.

O'Neill, M., Getz, D. and Carlsen, J. (1999). Evaluation of service quality at events: the 1998 Coca-Cola Masters Surfing event at Margaret River, Western Australia. *Managing Service Quality*, **9(3)**, 158–166.

Poria, Y. and Harmen, O. (2002). Exploring possible uses of multi-user domains in tourism research. *Tourism Today*, **2**, 15–33.

Raybould, M., Mules, T., Fredline, E. and Tomljenovic, R. (2000). Counting the herd. Using aerial photography to estimate attendance at open events. *Event Management*, **6**, 25–32.

Richards, B. (1992). *How to Market Tourist Attractions, Festivals and Special Events*, pp. 61–62. Harlow: Longman.

Shone, A. (2001). *Successful Event Management: A Practical Handbook*. London: Continuum.

Sisodia, R.S. (1992). Marketing information and decision support systems for services. *The Journal of Services Marketing*, **6(1)**, 51–64.

Skyrme, D.J. (1989). The planning and marketing of the market intelligence function. *Marketing Intelligence and Planning*, **7(1/2)**, 5–10.

Smith, D.V.L. and Fletcher, J.H. (2001). *Inside Information: Making Sense of Marketing Data*. Chichester: John Wiley.

Talvinen, J.M. (1995). Information systems in marketing. Identifying opportunities for new applications. *European Journal of Marketing*, **29(1)**, 8–25.

Talvinen, J.M. and Saarinen, T. (1995). MkIS support for the marketing management process: Perceived improvements for marketing management. *Marketing Intelligence and Planning*, **13(1)**, 18–27.

The Right Solution Ltd (2002). *UK Conference Market Survey*. Broadway: Meetings Industry Association.

Tum, J. (2002). Measuring the satisfaction of conference delegates. Discussion paper. School of Tourism and Hospitality, Leeds Metropolitan University.

Wood, E. (2001). Marketing information systems in tourism and hospitality SMEs: A study of internet use for market intelligence. *International Journal of Tourism Research*, **3**, 283–299.

Wood, E. (2002a). Events, civic pride and attitude change in a post-industrial town: Evaluating the effect of local authority events on residents' attitudes to the Blackburn region. *Events and Place Making Research Conference*, 15–16 July, UTS, Sydney, Australia.

Wood, E. (2002b). Measuring event economic and social impacts: A case study of Blackburn with Darwen Borough Council. Discussion Paper. School of Tourism and Hospitality Management, Leeds Metropolitan University.

Wright, M. and Ashill, N. (1998). A contingency model of marketing information. *European Journal of Marketing*, **32(1/2)**, 125–144.

Xu, X. and Kaye, R.G. (1995). Building market intelligence systems for environment scanning. *Logistics Information Management*, **8(2)**, 22–29.

Questions

1 Develop a self-administered questionnaire to assess theatregoers' satisfaction with the community theatre's programme of events.

  ■ Specify survey objectives
  ■ Sample size and method
  ■ Draft questionnaire

2 What other methods should be used to complement this survey in order to evaluate the success of the community theatre?

3 What sources of secondary information could be used to gather competitor intelligence on other entertainment providers? How could this information be used?

Appendix. Extract from the 1998 Data Protection Act

THE DATA PROTECTION PRINCIPLES PART I. THE PRINCIPLES

1. Personal data shall be processed fairly and lawfully and, in particular, shall not be processed unless –

   (a) at least one of the conditions in Schedule 2 is met, and
   (b) in the case of sensitive personal data, at least one of the conditions in Schedule 3 is also met.

2. Personal data shall be obtained only for one or more specified and lawful purposes, and shall not be further processed in any manner incompatible with that purpose or those purposes.

3. Personal data shall be adequate, relevant and not excessive in relation to the purpose or purposes for which they are processed.

4. Personal data shall be accurate and, where necessary, kept up to date.

5. Personal data processed for any purpose or purposes shall not be kept for longer than is necessary for that purpose or those purposes.

6. Personal data shall be processed in accordance with the rights of data subjects under this Act.

7. Appropriate technical and organisational measures shall be taken against unauthorised or unlawful processing of personal data and against accidental loss or destruction of, or damage to, personal data.

8. Personal data shall not be transferred to a country or territory outside the European Economic Area unless that country or territory ensures an adequate level of protection for the rights and freedoms of data subjects in relation to the processing of personal data.

Source: Her Majesty's Statistical Office (1998).

10

Merchandising and retail

Stephen A. Doyle

Introduction

It should be clear by this stage in the book what is meant by 'event'. However, since a chronological reading may be presumptuous, it may be worthwhile establishing the context in which merchandise and merchandise management is about to be discussed. In this context, events are not naturally occurring phenomena (although by definition these are indeed events); instead, the term refers to a special event that is instigated for a particular purpose. In effect, the term 'event' might be seen as a linguistic contraction of the term 'special event'. However, further clarification is required as this does not eliminate all those natural events that may be infrequent, memorable or personally significant (and therefore personally special). Thus, what in fact is encompassed by the term 'event' is an event that has been identified and managed for a specific purpose. The type of event that this book concerns itself with is not therefore the result of happenstance, but is instead 'a one-off happening designed to meet special needs at any given time' (Wilkinson, 1988).

The other aspect of events that is worthwhile bringing to the fore at this stage is that they vary based upon their purpose. They vary in scale, in location, in purpose, in context and in duration and as such, the management issues that are associated with them must take into cognizance the nature and purpose of the event. Given that the focus of this chapter is merchandising, it is therefore essential that the individual responsible for the merchandise (its selection, sourcing etc.) is aware of the event's purpose in order that the merchandise is appropriate to that purpose.

Merchandise in context

Before exploring the role of merchandise in detail, it may be worthwhile exploring a variety of events and the merchandise that may be associated with them. Perhaps, to begin with, consider the professional wedding organizer. What merchandise might be associated with the organizing of a wedding? The organizer may be asked to provide a selection of invitations and then buy, print and send them: these are part of the merchandise offered to the client. It is unlikely that there will be a 'one size fits all' invitation, so a selection will be needed to show what is available to suit differing customer needs, possibly also a 'tailor made' service so that the client can select a design that reflects their self-image or the image that they want to portray. It is unlikely that the organizer will carry a stock of these cards, ready to be printed with names and other details, so a reliable supplier will be required. If these need to be made to order then a lead time needs to be established. What at the outset may have seemed a simple piece of the 'wedding kit' has become a substantial management issue, and in the context of a wedding, a crucial one.

In addition, arrangements may be needed for the cake and in so doing, that becomes part of the merchandise range of a wedding organizer, as does the bride and groom that sit on top; also the place names, the wedding album, the favours to be dispersed to the guests as they leave. All of these components can be viewed as products integral to the wedding experience and whether these are managed successfully or unsuccessfully can have considerable implications for the quality of that experience for the wedding party and its guests.

159

This example demonstrates that certain aspects of the merchandise may be consumed *in situ*, whereas others, such as the favours and the album, may serve as remote reminders of that experience. Favours and other transportable merchandise represent a 'tangible memory' of the wedding in the same way that a holiday souvenir provides a 'tangible memory' of another place. This is a theme that shall be returned to later, but what is important to note is that some event merchandise may be transient, while other elements of it may be intended to provide a long-lasting reminder of the event itself. Furthermore, what is also highlighted in this example is that there are a number of players with an interest in the merchandise. There is the wedding organizer, there is the wedding party (both as clients and as participants in the event) and there are the guests; the interaction that each player has with the merchandise will vary according to their roles.

A distinctly different exemplar can be found in one-off gallery exhibitions. In the winter months of 2001/2002 the National Gallery in London organized an exhibition of an Italian artist of the renaissance period, Pisanello. The event was recognized as being of international significance, bringing together as it did a number of his key works along with some smaller examples of the artist's work and preparatory sketches. However, while the critical aspect of the event was the art itself, associated with it was a merchandise range that sought to capitalize upon the significance of the event as well as prolong the attendees' experiences of it. The merchandise range for an exhibition of this nature may include an accompanying textbook (hardback and/or paperback), CD-ROM, mouse mat, poster, postcards, prints (framed and/or unframed), pens and pencils and other artefacts and objects derived from or associated with the paintings. All of these items of merchandise have to coexist with the merchandise that forms the core/ongoing merchandise offer of the National Gallery and so, while distinct from it in terms of its 'short-termness', it must relate to it in terms of market position, range association and customer expectation.

Significantly, although the event differs considerably from the first example, the role of the merchandise is remarkably similar. From the customers' perspective we can see elements of 'tangible memory' and, particularly in the case of the text book and CD-ROM, experience prolonging. This is akin to the wedding album and the favours. However, we can also see that, from the perspective of the organizers, the merchandise provides an opportunity to generate revenue and in this respect it is no different from the merchandise of the wedding organizer.

What is also brought to the fore in these examples is the need to have an offer that is commensurate with the customer's needs and expectations. It is unlikely that the wedding organizer will have only one type of customer who all share identical needs and expectations for their wedding day and so a range of merchandise is appropriate to enable the offer to be adapted or customized in respect of each customer's specific demands. However, it is also unlikely that the wedding organizer would want to carry an infinite merchandise range, one that incorporated an infinite range of options, because of the management and cost related to such. Similarly, the National Gallery (and this applies equally to its core offer as much as its event offer) seeks to identify and develop a range that is commensurate with the various visitors' requirements, from small inexpensive mementoes to academically informed texts that further develop the reader's understanding of the event focus.

Given that this chapter has commenced by exploring the idea of merchandise through the use of exemplars, it is perhaps appropriate at this stage to introduce yet another. In 2002 the MOBO (Music of Black Origin) Awards demonstrated an innovative way in which to reimburse the performers who participated in the award ceremony. Rather than paying presenters and performers, they were given a 'goodie-bag' containing the various sponsors' products. On the basis of cost alone, this method of payments was an innovative and effective mechanism as the costs of the organizers were reduced, as were those of the sponsors and the recipients of the gifts in terms of taxable income. Thus merchandise in this case is a reward for participation. However, the innovation did not stop there. During the weeks following the award ceremony, photographers were commissioned to follow the celebrity recipients of the bags and record them wearing or using the bags' contents. In effect, the goodie-bag was a component of a highly sophisticated publicity campaign that enabled payment to be made, costs to be minimized and, importantly for the donors, it enabled them to develop brand/product awareness through celebrity endorsement. The event and the event merchandise then became part of a wider campaign. This example thus raises another pertinent point: merchandise communicates; that is to suggest that the merchandise, and the merchandising thereof, says something about the company it keeps, from the organizer to the buyer/user. Developing that theme further, this example reveals the importance, if donating merchandise to an organization or individual, of whether there is a mutuality of image.

The roles of merchandise

The examples given in the previous section have already identified some of the roles of merchandise within the context of an event. However, the consideration of such was conducted in a manner that sought to situate an understanding of both merchandise and event. Before reviewing the role of merchandise in, perhaps, a more abstract approach, it may be useful to think about what we actually are referring to when we discuss merchandise. It may also be useful to highlight that the primary sources on the subject are embedded in the retailing and retail marketing literature (e.g. Varley, 2001). This is not surprising, since it is within the retailing arena that the role of merchandise is most eminent – without a merchandise offer there would be no retailer, since merchandise is at the core of retailing (Varley, 2001).

When referring to merchandise, it is generally the tangible product that is a part of the event that is being referred to. In the situation of events, this may include product for sale, product for reward, product for sample or any combination thereof. Brassington and Pettitt (2000) suggest that a product is a 'physical good, service, idea, person or place that is capable of offering tangible and intangible attributes that individuals or organizations regard as so necessary, worthwhile or satisfying that they are prepared to exchange money, patronage or some other unit of value in order to acquire it' (p. 262). In this definition is seen all of the components of the earlier examples summarized and as such, this definition is a potent and pertinent one for the purpose of exploring the merchandise role.

It is possible to break down the definition offered by Brassington and Pettitt in order that we establish a clearer understanding. It is no coincidence that in their list of characteristics of a product they cite the tangible good first and foremost as this is the primary nature of merchandise; nevertheless, it is useful to recognize that there may be some inter-relationships among the factors. Hence, the physical merchandise may constitute an important element of the service product (as in the example of the wedding organizer) as perhaps does the organizer's access to appropriate locations; thus the location, and all that is associated with it, becomes part of the merchandise offer. Consider the concept of tangible and intangible attributes; what is meant by this? In essence, any merchandise, if it is to be valid and valuable, must actually satisfy the customers or recipients of it. This leads to the following part of the definition, that the customer or recipient must perceive it to be so if they are to exchange some predefined unit of value for it. Thus if the merchandise is undesirable, the customer will be unlikely to want to purchase it nor, if it is donated, will the recipient be willing to use it. In referring to the MOBO example, what would have been the value to the donors of the 'goodie-bag' contents if the recipients had not considered the products worthwhile having? Would the celebrities be seen wearing the products? Unlikely. Instead, the organizers would have had unhappy participants (and possibly unwilling ones in terms of future participation) and the donors would have wasted their efforts and investment on a publicity failure.

From the Brassington and Pettitt (2000) definition and the examples, it is now possible to summarize that merchandise may serve the following purposes:

■ *Income generation*. Merchandise may constitute part of the event offer as a means of increasing the income generated from the event for the organizers. In this respect, products sold are generally identified, through branding devices, as being associated with the event. Examples of this include arts festivals (e.g. the Edinburgh Festival) and concerts (including the sale of programmes). It is also worthwhile noting that, at events such as commercial exhibitions, there may be generic merchandise that is offered by the exhibition organizers and merchandise that is offered by the participating organizations. In respect of the latter, the merchandise may take the form of a sample with the purpose of encouraging future, long-term income generation.

■ *Reward*. Merchandise may be given to participants as a gesture of thanks. This is not the preserve of ceremonies such as the MOBO awards, but occurs at, for example, academic conferences where delegates may be given bags, pens, books, partly as the essential tools of conference participation, but also as a token or reward for attendance. Similarly, organizations may invite key customers or attractive prospects to an event with the intention of rewarding their custom or rewarding their consideration; part of that reward event may be a meal or a memento of the event itself. In this case, the event and merchandise may become part of a relationship-building strategy.

■ *Brand/product awareness*. Events and the merchandise that is a part of them may exist primarily to promote awareness of brands and/or products. This phenomenon is not new, with examples being found in the Great Exhibition of 1851 at the Crystal Palace, a showcase event that presented a platform to demonstrate all that was good about the British manufacturing, technology and idea generation of the period. In so doing, exhibitors were brought to the attention of a consumer public through the ability of those consumers to interact with the merchandise. Later, the Empire Exhibitions attempted to do something similar, but on an international basis (rather like 'Expo'). What is also noteworthy about these examples is that the merchandise was not restricted to the participating organizations, but dedicated merchandise was developed for sale as a memento of the event, highlighting the social and recreational significance of these events.

■ *Integral component.* In certain situations, the merchandise may be an essential aspect of the event, as identified in the case of the wedding organizer. However, it extends beyond that one scenario. Consider events such as the Ideal Homes shows or the various motor shows that are used to platform new products and keep existing ones in the customer's mind. Without the merchandise there would be no event as the event or show is wholly predicated upon product. In such situations, the merchandise is an integral part of the event. The key difference between the wedding example and the motor show is that the marriage could take place without the products that augment the service, whereby the merchandise is integral to the subsequent celebration rather than the ceremony. However, to the event organizer, the product is an essential element of both.

■ *Experience enhancement.* In many respects this merchandise function has already been touched upon in as much as the merchandise adds something to the event experience. However, it is worthwhile isolating it as a role in its own right to ensure that event organizers afford it the consideration that is its due. Appropriate merchandise, and the ability to leave an event with something tangible, is an important aspect of participation in many events. Garden festivals and horticultural shows are a blend of showcases, in terms of design, skills or new products, and shopping centres where attendees can buy the plants and products that they have just seen or that are not locally available. The quality of the merchandise can impact upon the quality of the experience.

■ *Experience memory.* It is often the product or merchandise that remains long after the event has passed and as such, the merchandise should represent a positive tangible memory of the event. In marking her return to live performance in April 2002 at the Royal Albert Hall, Liza Minnelli included in her tour merchandise offer limited edition, signed posters commemorating the event. Here can be evidenced the juxtaposition of income generation with the desire of the audience to acquire some souvenir of the event, emphasizing an element of exchange stressed in the definition of product (Brassington and Pettitt, 2000). The concert has passed, but the posters and the programmes will remain significant to the audience, and may indeed become significant to a new audience through their desirability, appearing at collectors' fairs in the future whereby the experience memory of one person becomes part of a new event experience memory of another.

Merchandise management

Having reviewed the nature and role of merchandise, it is apposite to dedicate the final section of this chapter to the issue of merchandise management. It was established at the outset that the events that are the concern of this chapter are not natural but are managed. Part of that management function is to manage the event merchandise strategically and operationally.

The strategic role of merchandise management

Varley (2001) stresses the need for merchandise to be based upon a knowledge of the customer and his or her expectations and whether those expectations have changed over time. McGoldrick (2002) suggests that 'Buying represents the strategic positioning statement into the overall assortment and the specific products to support that statement' (p. 279). In this declaration, McGoldrick is emphasizing that the buying function (i.e. the part of the organization that is responsible for product sourcing and selecting) must select merchandise that is in keeping with the transmitted image and identity of the organization or the event that is being organized, a declaration that is supported by Aufreiter et al. (1993) who described the correct product assortment as the engine of success. It could be argued that, for the buyer to be able to translate the organization's positioning strategy into tangible terms through merchandise selection, it is necessary to have, as Varley (2001) suggests, a knowledge of the customer.

However, what is also implied is that the selection of merchandise, and for the purposes of this section we shall assume that this is carried out by the organizational 'buyer', is dependent upon a knowledge of the strategic rationale behind the merchandise. In effect, which of the roles (individually or in combination), as described in the previous section, does the merchandise seek to perform? There must be thus an understanding of the organization(s) involved, of the event itself and of the event attendees to determine the nature of the merchandise. Strategically, therefore, the merchandise offer should be linked to the event's objectives and to the merchandise objectives, thereby revealing two interrelated strategies – the event strategy and the merchandise strategy. The key issue is to understand that there is not a standard merchandise package that suits all events, but that cognizance must be taken of the purpose of the event, the nature of the attendees and the desired role of the merchandise itself before decisions are taken with respect to the actual products that constitute the merchandise offer.

Operationalizing the merchandise strategy

While it is important that consideration is given to the roles of merchandise and how it is related to the organizational/event strategy, it is also important to think about the various stages and activities that are necessary to ensure that the merchandise strategy is actualized. Newman and Cullen (2002) identify a number of key issues that relate to the development of a merchandise range. These include budget definition, sourcing, layout planning and price, quality and quantity decisions. To this list Varley (2001) would also add deciding upon who was responsible for the merchandise. Even without expanding upon the details of the list, it can be seen that as a single component of the event (regardless of its eminence as part of the event), merchandise management can be complex and time-consuming. This would suggest, correctly, that if not managed appropriately, that there are many areas where error can be made and the merchandise offer may fail. Given the importance of effective and efficient management, it is appropriate to review each aspect in some detail now in order that fuller understanding can be reached.

Budget definition

Before any steps are taken to decide upon the nature of the merchandise, to engage suppliers and to develop promotional materials, the event organizers must define the merchandise budget. Even if the purpose is to sell the merchandise for income generation, there will be an initial outlay necessary to secure stock for sale. The budget may be influenced by the event itself, the importance of merchandise to the success or failure of the event, levels of support and sponsorship, access to finance, previous experience, risk and other associated costs. Merchandise is only one part of event management and therefore the budget for that part must respect limited resources and multiple demands. Defining the budget will have implications for the following factors.

Sourcing

Having established the budget, a decision has to be taken in respect of who will supply the merchandise. This will be influenced by the budget and the strictures that may ensue in terms of contract. As well as straight supply to order, McGoldrick (2002) highlights that there are alternative supplier arrangements that may result in shared costs and shared risks, although the supplier will generally seek some form of added value for assuming risk and cost. If the supplier benefits from association with the event, then this may be sufficient to offset the risks. Prior to such negotiations, it is essential to identify the organizations that are able to supply (whether they are willing or not is a separate matter). Included in this search for product sources, the buyer must have defined the product specifications, the quantity, delivery details and price (to organization). In addition, consideration must also be given to merchandise distribution and payment terms, whereby, all other factors being satisfactory, the feasibility of a supplier may hinge upon the terms demanded.

Layout planning

Having secured a satisfactory source, the location of the merchandise needs to be planned to ensure that it is visible and accessible to its target customer. If organizing a trade fair, this may result in certain locations being more attractive than others and therefore more expensive to secure. If offering merchandise that has been developed specifically for the event, then it is wise to ensure that the merchandise is located so that it is within view of the largest footfall. There is also the layout of the merchandise in respect of its immediate surroundings. Consideration may need to be given to whether the customer is to be able to handle the products before purchase and if so, how this can be achieved while minimizing the risk of theft. Is it appropriate to provide samples, with the purchase stock held discreetly, notwithstanding the fact that this becomes slow and labour intensive? If adopting a 'show then sell' policy, projections will need to establish which products are likely to be the best sellers in order that these are easiest for staff to locate. Inefficiency may result in customer disillusionment and a loss of sales.

Price decisions

Even if the merchandise is free to the recipient, this is still a pricing decision. Where there will be a cost to the customer, consideration must be given to the cost to the organization, the sales and profit targets and the customer's personal involvement with the event and its associated merchandise. Where there is a high level of involvement, there may be greater price elasticity and thus an opportunity for premium pricing. An example of such practice may be found at rock and pop concerts, whereby the nature of 'fandom' overcomes price sensitivity. In addition, while market pricing, i.e. pricing based upon a knowledge of customer thresholds, is attractive and generally more valid, an element of accounting-based pricing must be introduced into the decision to ensure that merchandise is not sold below cost.

Quality

Merchandise quality is strongly linked to merchandise cost and more importantly, from the customer's perspective, price. It should also relate to the market position of the event itself, to ensure that there is compatibility across all components of the event. It may be that, where there is a degree of dedication associated with the event customers, such as a concert, prices reflect affiliation to the performer rather than the tangible elements of the product and so the merchandise has an intangible quality that allows for premium pricing. Where such relationships do not exist, then the merchandise quality will be adjudged on its own merits and on the basis of price and alternatives available.

Quantity

Decisions on quantity may affect the product costing and thus, generally, the larger the quantity, the lower the price. However, caution must be exercised no matter how tempting the bulk offer may be. Large quantities may incur storage or insurance costs that had not been budgeted for or may result in unsold merchandise that is redundant when distinct from the event. Quantity decisions should be based upon minimum, maximum and optimal levels to allow for margins in the predicted levels of consumption. Such an approach may incorporate a sliding cost per unit scale, whereby the supply costs decline as the quantity increases and vice versa. The buyer, based upon predictions using such figures as previous attendances, prebooking and/or comparative events, will attempt to estimate the demand for merchandise with the joint purpose of ensuring that supply meets demand, but does not exceed it. This exercise is repeated for all of the merchandise range, taking into consideration variations in demand for the individual range components. Thus, quantity decisions are not simply about the overall quantity of merchandise, but the balance of the individual merchandise elements.

Who manages?

Finally, consideration must be afforded the person who is responsible for selecting, sourcing and scheduling the merchandise range, as well as perhaps negotiating costs and establishing quality levels. This person is generally referred to as the 'merchandise buyer'. Varley (2001) emphasizes that the management of the merchandise through its various stages is dependent partly upon the scale of the operation and the experience of the individual(s). Where the event is a one-off, then management of the merchandise may assume an *ad hoc* approach, whereas for those agencies that exist to organize events, it is likely that there will be a dedicated staff whose function is partly, if not wholly, to manage the merchandise offer. However, consistent in all of the considerations of the issues relating to the who and what of merchandise management is the irrefutable fact that it must be managed.

Summary

The purpose of this chapter was threefold: firstly, to introduce merchandise in the context of events; secondly, to explore the roles of merchandise; and finally, to consider issues relating to merchandise management. At the outset three different event scenarios were examined and a number of key issues identified relating to the merchandise, its significance to the various parties involved in the event and, critically, the need to manage the merchandise. Throughout this chapter the theme of management has loomed large. The situated examples stressed the fact that merchandise may represent an important component of an event and as such should not be left to chance. Reference to the literature served to emphasize this further, by stressing that merchandise management should be an integral aspect of event management. In addition, it served to delineate the strategic roles and operational elements associated with merchandise and its management. Furthermore, while the examples were based upon substantively distinct event types, on reflection of them and the literature, we can summarize that there are common factors relating to events and merchandise and as such, a schema for its effective incorporation into events can be developed. However, central to the consideration of merchandise is that, like events, it does not simply happen; good, effective merchandise and merchandising is made to happen.

Bibliography

Aufreiter, N., Karch, N. and Smith Shi, C. (1993). The engine of success in retailing. *McKinsey Quarterly*, **3**, 101–116.

Brassington, F. and Pettitt, S. (2000). *Principles of Marketing*. Harlow: Pearson Education.

McGoldrick, P. (2002). *Retail Marketing*. London: McGraw-Hill.

Newman, A.J. and Cullen, P. (2002). *Retailing: Environment and Operations*. London: Thomson Learning.

Varley, R. (2001). *Retail Product Management: Buying and Merchandising*. London: Routledge.

Watt, D.C. (1998). *Event Management in Leisure and Tourism*. Harlow: Addison Wesley Longman.

Wilkinson, D. (1988). *The Event Management and Marketing Institute, 1*. Ontario: IBD.

Questions

1 Event merchandise may be described as multifunctional, serving as it does a variety of purposes. Using examples, identify the various roles of merchandise from the perspective of multiple stakeholders.

2 The 'merchandise buyer' has responsibility for managing merchandise; what are the key issues that the buyer must address? What might be the implications of not managing events merchandise effectively and efficiently?

3 In what respect may customer characteristics influence the event merchandise characteristics? Use examples to illustrate your answer.

Festival and event catering operations

Kevin Fields and Paul Stansbie

Introduction

The issues that will be addressed in this chapter affect the operation and management of food and beverage services at events. There are a number of key questions that need to be answered at the planning stage to ensure that the appropriate requirements of all the stakeholders are met. There is a need to establish whether food and beverage (F&B) provision will be a peripheral service, doing little more than covering costs and providing basic sustenance, or if it will be a significant income stream. There is also the consideration of whether F&B provision should be managed in-house or contracted out and if the catering provision should be themed to match and enrich the actual event, or be based upon standard and traditional F&B services. These issues and questions will be considered consecutively but their interdependence requires each to be explored as a whole and not in isolation of the others.

The development of food and beverage services at events

Historically, events have been associated with food & beverage (Goldblatt, 2002: 195).

It could be argued that the first ever event in the history of the world took place in the Garden of Eden. The meeting, involving Adam and Eve, had been running very smoothly until it was ruined by the catering. The consumption of that 'forbidden fruit' led to a less than satisfactory outcome and the rest is biblical history.

In more recent times, the growth of the hospitality industry and specifically the F&B provision at festivals and events has changed radically. In some cases, the driving forces behind this change have been the advent of better-educated guests and clients. Their knowledge, and insistence on a quality product, has led to more innovation and creativity in the way F&B is produced and delivered. That is not to say that fast food, in its various guises, is not the most suitable type of provision at certain types of event.

The market for delivering these services is a multimillion dollar industry, characterized by fierce competition with diverse, fragmented operations whose provision could range from full-service fine-dining restaurants to hotdog and beer vendors at sports and music events. Irrespective of the size and scale of the F&B provision, this competition to gain contracts inevitably has driven businesses to focus more on the synergies that exist between the type of event and the nature of the F&B offered.

Food, beverage, and celebration are inextricably connected. From social lifecycle events to giant hallmark events such as the Olympic Games or Super Bowl, the relationship between food and frivolity has been a close one. This is not to suggest that it is not serious business as well (Goldblatt, 1997: 153).

Peripheral service or income stream?

The extent to which visitors may avail themselves of F&B provision must be determined. The timescale of an event will influence the visitors' propensity to purchase food and drink. The shorter the visit, the less the need – snacks may be sufficient. However, if an event traverses one or more 'traditional' meal times, the greater the provision will need to be. The time of day will also be an issue, determining the type of foodstuffs most suitable.

The type of event will also affect the required provision. For corporate and association events, a banquet may be the highlight of the proceedings. In this case, a high-quality service must be provided – often delivered by an outsourced catering company. It may be the case that the entire event is managed by the same company that provides the catering and peripheral services. 'The future of event management may include both good food & beverage as well as equally excellent services managed by the caterer' (Goldblatt, 2002: 167).

When one company is delivering the majority of the services required for an event, the communication process should be less problematic. This should lead to the seamless integration of all aspects of the event. Good communication systems should provide a seamless event regardless of how many different service providers are involved, but mistakes do happen.

Case illustration 1

A food and beverage team was providing catering for a banquet for 1300 guests. The dining area was a circus tent that, together with a full-scale funfair, had been erected within a major exhibition hall. As the guests were seated, the catering manager gave the go-ahead for 130 silver-service staff to enter the tent carrying the first course. At the opposite side of the tent, an event manager gave the go-ahead for teams of jugglers, jesters and unicyclists to enter and circulate around the tables. The fact that a catastrophe did not ensue was sheer good luck. The guests thoroughly enjoyed the food and the entertainment, though the nerves of many staff were considerably frayed. (*Source:* Chapter authors.)

Case illustration 2

Van Morrison was due to give a concert in Seville in the early 1980s. It was to be in the open air, in a park. The stage was erected and the sound systems installed, with much of the cabling running under the stage. One thing had been overlooked. The park had automatic sprinklers that came on in the late afternoon. Some of the sprinklers were actually situated where the stage had been erected. Fortunately, nobody was hurt – though all the electrics had quite a soaking. (*Source:* Chapter authors.)

Event managers must work on a need-to-know basis. Each service provider, including F&B managers, must know what the other service providers' intentions are. Details of the site/venue should be exactly that – detailed. This is the only way to prevent conflict of actions.

Where F&B is less of a focus at events, considerations such as whether food and drink can be consumed whilst engaging in the event must be made. If so a number of questions need to be answered:

■ Do spectators have to leave their seat or position in order to obtain food and drink, or can it be made available via roving vendors?
■ Is there an interval or lull during which spectators can leave their position? If the interval is short, provision must be geared up to deliver quickly, thereby maximizing sales opportunities.
■ To what extent are spectators able to bring their own food and drink? At some venues this is discouraged, if not actively forbidden. This is particularly true at sports events were food and drink items may be utilized as missiles to pelt other spectators, players or officials. At events where the bringing in of food and drink is permissible, organized provision may have to be scaled back to prevent wastage.

Case illustration 3

The City of Birmingham (UK) ran a Super Prix road race for several years from 1986. One of the first lessons learnt was that catering vendors would not benefit to any significant extent because once spectators had managed to acquire a suitable vantage point, they were unlikely to move until the race was over. As a result of this pattern most spectators had brought their own F&B requirements with them. (*Source:* Chapter authors and Sara Binns, Head of Business Development, Admirable Crichton.)

The type of event will also determine the types of visitor. Determining the profile of visitor types is important as valuable information about levels of disposable income, and the propensity to spend on food and drink, may be apparent. Champagne bars and strawberries-and-cream stalls are perfectly suitable during the Wimbledon championships (and have become something of an institution at this event), but are hardly apt at a pigeon-showing event!

To summarize this section it is suggested that in order to determine the required scale of F&B provision at an event, one must first determine whether it will be a central focus or a peripheral service. This is done by considering the time of day, the purpose of the event, the duration of the event, and the profile of likely attendees.

Should food and beverage services be provided in-house or be outsourced?

This decision can be a complex one, particularly within purpose-built venues. Some event venues run their own F&B operations and others utilize the services of one of the many, often international, catering organizations such as Aramark, Compass Group and Sodexho. According to the type of event, and the anticipated role that F&B will play, different priorities will be given to F&B providers. Although these services may be outsourced, the seamless integration of the event and its delivery are seen by the visitor as one and the same.

Therefore, both good and bad F&B experiences will reflect on the event organizer and will underpin the perception visitors formulate when evaluating its success. It is paramount that, irrespective of priority, F&B providers focus on meeting and ultimately exceeding the expectations of guests and visitors.

If provision is going to be arranged in-house then the required level of expertise, staff and equipment needs to be considered. For basic provision of snacks and drinks this is usually relatively straightforward but for extensive catering provision it can be immensely complicated. In-house provision does offer certain benefits: 'The advantage of in-house catering is the knowledge of the venue' (McDonnell et al., 1999: 260).

The key factor which may decide this issue is the frequency with which large-scale catering provision is required. If it is only a few times a month, or even less, then the money required to equip and staff a catering department is likely to be an investment with a very poor return. The dedicated catering organizations have levels of expertise and can achieve economies of scale that individual operations can seldom hope to match.

Additionally, they may be able to offer employees career progression, attracting better staff than static, single-venture catering operations.

The outsourcing of catering services does not relieve the event organizer of responsibility for the service delivered. As previously mentioned, the customer will attribute every service experience to the event company or organizer. It is therefore their reputation that is at risk if problems occur. Legal responsibility is also a consideration and this will vary depending upon the country in which the event is held.

The fact that an outsourcing initiative can easily bring problems rather than benefits demonstrates that it is no good for an organization simply to embark on the initiative and hope that everything will turn out as planned (Gay and Essinger, 2000: 15). Further: 'Unfortunately, most people, companies, committees, and groups that are getting ready to hold an event think that by renting a space, and selecting a menu for the day they want the event, guarantees success' (O'Toole and Mikolaitis, 2002).

The old adage that those who fail to plan, plan to fail, is never more true than in the events industry. Selecting the providers of the various services required is not the end of the story – control and management of the event is still the organizers' primary concern. Selecting and monitoring the service providers, ensuring that the actual delivery matches the initial promise, should pay dividends. The selection of the proper professionals is paramount and can avoid negative occurrences: '... outsourcing is the most potent management tool ever invented for driving efficiency into an organisation' (Gay and Essinger, 2000: 17). The inference is that the hiring in of specialist knowledge and skills can deliver increased efficiency.

A particular area that requires attention, especially when bringing service providers in from outside, is that of food safety. Ensuring that your own staff are trained and qualified is relatively simple. Not so with the staff of others. There are few days when a food scare of one sort or another fails to appear in the media. This has raised public awareness to an unprecedented level. This is particularly true in relation to events and festivals: '... food served at outdoor fairs and festivals is perceived as significantly less healthful and less safe than food at other food preparation sites' (Boo et al., 2000: 91).

Whether the catering provision is in-house or outsourced, an event organizer must determine that the knowledge and skill of those delivering the service is of an acceptable standard. The primary concern used to be food hygiene. Though this is still paramount, many other dangers have entered the equation: '... ingredients can be highly allergenic to some people and can cause illness or even death' (Tarlow, 2002: 153).

This means that food service staff must not only be trained in hygienic practices but also have complete awareness of the ingredients of the dishes they are serving. For example, if a nut-based oil has been used for frying, or as a dressing, a potentially fatal incident could result if a customer has a severe nut allergy. Customers in this category are aware enough to ask questions, but will staff know the answers? 'Make certain that all ingredients are known and that food servers can answer questions, or know who to turn to' (Tarlow, 2002: 153).

Fatalities or illness at events attracts media attention on a grand scale, damaging the reputation of the event organizer and threatening future viability – not to mention the moral and ethical issues that surround this whole subject.

To summarize this section it is clear that decisions concerning in-house or outsourced F&B provision should consider the variables of scale and frequency of events; the existing, or lack, of in-house catering expertise; the scale of F&B provision required; and the financial viability of investing in staff and equipment to the required level.

Should food and beverage provision be themed at events?

As with all other aspects of events there are many variables to be considered. A themed provision does not necessarily have to match the theme of the event; it may have a separate and distinct theme of its own – something that will excite, or at least interest the customer – though the resultant increase in cost must not be overlooked. 'However, what event managers should always ask their clients is what they want to achieve – in a budget-driven world objectives are the name of the game' (Bowdin et al., 2001: 267).

If the objective is to enthral and impress, then a themed event is the obvious choice. Increasingly, catering companies are building the skills and expertise to deliver what is required.

Special events have become a significant area of the catering industry requiring special skills in design. Theme parties have evolved into 'entertainment happenings' involving guests in activities and interactive venues (Scanlon, 2000: xiii).

To that end, managers must initially understand the type of guest participating in an event and start by revisiting some of the very basic provision questions when formulating strategies that underpin the F&B decision-making process. It could be that these strategies now need to be reformulated to account for the way in which delivery can be enhanced: '... one issue which will certainly colour their view of the experience is the provision of food and drink' (Shone and Parry, 2001: 150).

The nature of the event or festival will determine whether a formal dinner or a themed 'extravaganza' is more suitable. Consumers are becoming increasingly experienced and sophisticated, and consequently harder to please and excite. A strong theme may achieve this. A set four-course dinner may not deliver the same level of enjoyment as an Arabian Nights' experience. In this case, F&B provision delivers all round entertainment – not just food and drink – and it should be developed and delivered effectively: 'They need not only to conceive of an illusion, but to plan, design, and organise in such a way that they bring illusion to reality for their guests' (Malouf, 1999: 79).

A theme that delivers an experience that exceeds, rather than just meets, expectations contributes additional bonuses in the way that guests/customers evaluate the event: 'According to expectancy value theory, consumers compare their expected level of performance with the perceived service performance in order to reach satisfaction or quality decision' (Ekinci et al., 2001: 322). The indication is therefore that an experience that exceeds expectations is more likely to deliver high levels of satisfaction.

There are many companies, of varying standards, which can deliver the themed event or extravaganza required. A notable one in the UK is introduced in the following case study.

Case study:
The Admirable Crichton Event Catering Company

An industrial trading estate in Camberwell, South London, may be an unusual place to track down a team of event caterers; but behind the rather undistinguished frontage lies an operation that is rapidly reinventing the benchmarks in F&B provision for events.

Since the business was founded in the early 1980s, by Johnny Roxburgh and Rolline Frewen, The Admirable Crichton has built a reputation that has placed it at the forefront of cutting-edge catering for events. Their list of clients accumulated along the way is itself admirable; within their portfolio are names from the world of film, media, politics and European royal families, and over 500 premium corporate brands.

The name 'The Admirable Crichton' is taken from the play by J.M. Barrie. The lead character, a loyal family butler, demonstrates a wealth of talents when his family become stranded on a remote, deserted island. His resourcefulness in providing high-quality service in the face of adversity, through imagination, initiative, creativity and innovation, underpins the ethos by which this organization promotes itself.

Like all event catering companies, The Admirable Crichton offers a range of services covering the whole spectrum of F&B delivery. However, it is the 'big name' functions that tend to grab the headlines as the publicity generated from catering for movie premieres, exclusive store openings and high-society weddings enhance their reputation for delivering high quality in some of the most demanding 'guest' environments.

The case study illustrates that as a preferred caterer to many prestigious venues throughout the country, the strategies considered about the role F&B has in the delivery of an event are at the forefront of all their management decisions. As a result, their approach to the event and the importance of being flexible with the requirements of clients are fundamental to the planning process.

The growing popularity and demand for their services is attributed to this high degree of flexibility and customization offered to their clients. Each new guest enquiry commences from a 'blank sheet of paper' approach. There is no reliance on promoting set menus, standardized glassware, flowers, china and table linen, and thus churning out the same product each night of the week. Each guest and their requirements is treated individually where menus are devised around themes, appropriate table designs are developed and fixtures and fittings are outsourced, when necessary, to complement the type of event required. The result creates events where canapés are served on motorized vacuum cleaners, staff are dressed like animals working amongst fossilized dinosaurs and table decorations represent a small section of the Chelsea flower show.

This emergence as a 'bespoke' caterer means the provision of food, beverage and innovative design can be placed within the context of the type of event and can be used as a feature or a peripheral service depending on the requirements of the client. This is vital when offering products and services to the more affluent, discerning sections of the market. Many inevitable challenges are present, particularly when trying to deliver a fine dining concept (which is required by their clients) through, in many cases, a banqueting style of service. Guests will approach business development managers seeking menus and dishes similar to those experienced at their favourite restaurant and expect them to be replicated for an event for 500 guests. Finding a balance between meeting the guest's expectations and being able to physically deliver the product at a specified outside venue compounds these challenges.

As the company operates primarily from its headquarters in Camberwell, agreements negotiated with clients are considered against limitations that prevail with various standards of facilities available at the desired venue. The team have to plan and expedite the delivery of the agreed product in a variety of locations, which could be as local as central London or as far away as a penthouse in New York. Therefore, efficient management of logistics, sourcing of supplies and collation of resources are critical in ensuring standards are maintained when the production and delivery of F&B at the event takes place. There would be nothing worse than turning up to cater for a celebrity's birthday party, at their home overseas, and forgetting some silverware, food or linen. Such an error would significantly tarnish the image of the event and hinder the delivery of a quality product.

Therefore, in achieving this goal and ensuring omissions do not occur, a design team will usually visit the location in advance and work with local suppliers to source the products required. This approach to planning allows time to ship appropriate commodities, fixtures or fittings to the location or venue and thus ensure standards are not compromised and everything is 'just perfect' on the day. An example of this was when they were asked to provide the catering for a wedding in Morocco. Having searched the area and failed to find a suitable venue that was available on the specified dates, the team had to resort to building its own venue in the middle of the desert. This entailed constructing kitchens and dining rooms for the creation and delivery of the product some distance from local amenities and facilities.

To summarize this section it is evident that the decision to theme or not, as with all other aspects of events, is dependent upon a range of variables including the meeting or exceeding expectations, constraints (or opportunities) imposed by the budget and the extent of the skills that can be developed in house or brought in. The Admirable Crichton case study illuminates the fact that anything is possible.

Conclusion

Not too long ago, if you did 75% of the things you did right, it was okay. Now, if you don't do 98% of those things right, some competitor will eat you for lunch (John Spoelhof, source unknown).

The reality of this in the event business has never been more apparent. The room for complacency and error is marginal as the competitive nature of the industry forces organizations to be more creative and innovative in the way they package, design and deliver the F&B product. The true beneficiaries of these competitive forces are not restricted to the guests or attendees at events but include the industry as a whole. If organizations are prepared to re-evaluate the product and how it can be delivered, this will only serve as an inspiration to others in raising service benchmarks in event catering.

Bibliography

Boo, H.C., Ghiselli, R. and Almanza, B.A. (2000). Consumer perceptions and concerns about the healthfulness and safety of food served at fairs and festivals. *Event Management*, **2(6)**, 85–92.

Bowdin, G., McDonnell, I., Allen, J. and O'Toole, W. (2001). *Events Management*. Oxford: Butterworth-Heinemann.

Ekinci, Y., Riley, M. and Chen, J.S. (2001). A review of comparison standards used in service quality and customer satisfaction studies: some emerging issues for hospitality and tourism research. In *Consumer Psychology of Tourism, Hospitality and Leisure* (J.A. Mazanec, G.I. Crouch, J.R. Brent Richie and A.G. Woodside, eds). Wallingford: Cabi.

Gay, C. and Essinger, J. (2000). *Inside Outsourcing*. London: Brealey.

Goldblatt, J.J. (1997). *Special Events: Best Practices in Modern Events Management*, 2nd Edn, New York, Wiley.

Goldblatt, J.J. (2002). *Special Events*, 3rd edn. New York: John Wiley.

Malouf, L. (1999). *Behind the Scenes at Special Events*. New York: John Wiley.

McDonnell, I., Allen, J. and O'Toole, W. (1999). *Festival and Special Event Management*. Milton: John Wiley.

O'Toole, W. and Mikolaitis, P. (2002). *Corporate Event Project Management*. New York: Wiley.

Scanlon, N.L. (2000). *Catering Management*. New York: John Wiley.

Shone, A. and Parry, B. (2001). *Successful Event Management*. London: Continuum.

Tarlow, P.E. (2002). *Event Risk Management and Safety*. New York: John Wiley.

Questions

1 Analyse the factors to consider when deciding whether food and beverage provision should be a peripheral service or income stream.

2 What are the key lessons to be learned from the case study on The Admirable Crichton Event Catering Company?

3 Discuss the key areas that events organizers should consider when outsourcing food and beverage operations.

Principles and applications in ticketing and reservations management

Zuleika Beaven and Chantal Laws

Introduction

The purpose of this chapter is to give an overview of the principles and application of ticketing for event and festival management. Consideration is given to changes in the role of the ticketing function as a result of technological developments, and the current capabilities of ticketing software are explored. The chapter presents a series of points for consideration when establishing a ticketing system and discusses the advantages and disadvantages of various methods of selling tickets and the integration of ticketing into wider functions, and concludes with a discussion of some of the debates and ethical issues developing in the field.

Definitions

For the organizer of a festival or event, successful ticketing is the operation of selling the right ticket, in the appropriate manner, for the maximum long-term benefit of the organization. In its simplest form, a ticket is a token allowing access to a service or entry to an event and tickets are often given as a form of receipt for payment. However, in modern event and festival management, an integrated ticketing system can be a highly complex operation involving not only box office sales but also marketing, sponsorship, operations and accounting.

The development of ticketing

Advances in computer technology in the 1980s had a revolutionary impact on the way in which organizations sold their tickets. Previously, tickets were generally sold over the counter or by post through a venue box office. Tomlinson (1993) explains that systems were paper-based and transactions were conducted manually. Because of the heavy reliance on cash sales, it was common to have to reserve a ticket by telephone and call at the box office to pay and collect, and security requirements meant that the box office was a forbidding place protected by security screens and grills. The rather cumbersome system also meant that little information about customers was collected.

The increase in popularity of the credit card increased the use of the telephone for sales and the gradual arrival of the computerized box office helped to liberate ticket sales from the confines of the box office and to develop the use of ticketing beyond sales. This process also saw a concurrent reduction in the need for reservations, so that this function has increasingly been used for facilitating complex or group bookings. The pioneering BOCS software system was developed between 1979 and 1981 (Prochak, 1996), but was soon surpassed technologically and conceptually. As more sophisticated box office software was developed in the 1990s, ticketing was integrated with marketing (Tomlinson, 1993) to support customer relationship management (CRM). The development of relationship marketing practice helped ticketing to play a role in development and fundraising, and in the early 2000s, software developers have begun to recognize the need to fully integrate operations software with marketing and box office software, producing overarching products (Figure 12.1) with a single database at their core that provide built-in functionality to homogenize box office and venue/event management operations.

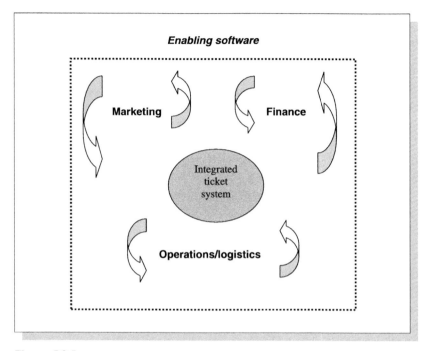

Figure 12.1 An integrated box office and venue/event management software system.

As information and communications technology products begin to fully link to communications networks, further developments in ticketing are now providing a powerful tool for event and festival organizers. The explosion in use of the internet has changed the way customers access information about events, and in some countries has become an accepted method of ticketing. The development of 3G and SMS mobile phone technology will transform late-availability ticket sales and marketing. Rapid developments in the communications field allow the presentation of audiovisual files promoting events, artists, performances and so forth, whilst increasingly sophisticated encryption provides a relatively secure environment for purchase of tickets via the internet so that by the early 2000s, online ticketing had become an essential tool for the festival manager.

The rationale for ticketing

For event and festival organizers, ticketing can represent a significant cost and an operational challenge. Therefore, when determining strategic aims to begin the planning process, it is necessary to consider the role the ticketing system will have.

Perhaps the most fundamental benefit a ticketing system affords is visitor management. By determining and enforcing a maximum ticket allocation, organizers can control capacity and promote safety of the audience and artists, and conservation of a building or environment. The change in approach by the Glastonbury Festival of Contemporary Performing Arts, Somerset, UK, at the end of the 1990s, in response to health and safety and licensing concerns, has positively impacted on the visitor experience. This appears to have secured the future of the festival, offering a model of good practice for other large-scale music festivals.

To fulfil this purpose it is not necessary for a ticket to be sold. At a VIP post-event party, for example, tickets may be given to guests for free. At a slightly more sophisticated level, it is possible to limit access to spaces, zones or specific seats, allowing differential charging or privileged access, and giving visitors choice. In certain circumstances additional tools may be required to realize this; for example at large-scale stadium events and open air festivals, it is common practice to issue coloured wrist bands to quickly and easily identify customers who may access an area. The use of timed ticketing at busy events or attractions such as Disneyland Paris can help to control capacity, manage queuing and therefore enhance the visitor experience.

For festivals, ticketing can be a valuable tool for facilitating collaborations with partners such as travel companies or hotels, and internal collaboration between different venues or performing companies in the same festival. The Melbourne International Comedy Festival, Victoria, Australia, facilitates a range of internal and external collaborations. The Laugh Pack is a multiple event season ticket that is managed centrally by the Festival coordinators rather than the promoters or venues. It is available through centralized ticket agencies or via the Festival's box office and audience members receive a discounted rate when they book at least three shows at the same time. The Festival also runs another scheme in conjunction with local train companies, the special Comedy Festival Train Ticket. This enables audience members to purchase an attractively designed travel ticket that can be used for reduced-price entry at the box office.

The sale of tickets is often essential for income generation as it is a mechanism to allow organizers to charge in advance for an event and to offer visitors a form of receipt for their payment. Allen *et al.* (2002) suggest this is the main function of ticketing and Thamnopoulos and Gargalianos (2002) note that ticketing is a major income source at festivals such as the Olympic Games. Advance sales are beneficial for the audience and organizer at popular events. For the audience member, this reassures them that they have the ticket they want for the event; for organizers it improves cashflow. Advance sales support timed releases favouring certain audience groups such as Friends to provide a customer relationship management benefit and helping customers to secure specific seats. The Glyndebourne Festival Opera, near Brighton, UK, is an exclusive event with high demand for tickets. Consequently applications are processed to give around 10 weeks' preference to members of the Glyndebourne Festival Society over the general public: general bookings are dealt with after Members, Waiting List and Mailing List applications.

In general, advance booking facilities may be beneficial for groups wanting to ensure they are seated together, for disabled visitors or those with children that have specific seating requirements, or for regular visitors who regard their usual seat as part of their relationship with a venue.

The capture of data about audience members and visitors can be invaluable for marketing planning and relationship marketing. However, a promoter using a venue's box office may not have automatic access to the details of their own audience. Ticket holders for the Rolling Stones World Tour 2002–2003 can send proof of purchase in exchange for free temporary membership of the Rolling Stones Fan Club. However, in order to receive this benefit they are required to supply personal information directly to the Fan Club. This enables independent control of audience data which may be used for CRM planning.

Tomlinson (2002) identifies data capture opportunities as a benefit of providing technology-based purchasing routes, such as the internet or SMS, as customers must provide contact details to receive their ticket. Where an event has a substantial walk-up audience, who purchase their tickets upon arrival, attendance may be affected by events outside the organizer's control, such as poor weather or transport problems. Tomlinson notes that data capture is weak from walk-up audiences, students, parents with children and pensioners. The Burning Man Festival, Nevada, USA, has adopted an innovative yield management strategy more usually associated with the low-cost airline industry. In order to dissuade the walk-up audience usually associated with this type of event, festival-goers may purchase tickets online or via outlets with prices increasing incrementally as the event approaches. Walk-up audiences can expect to pay substantially more than those purchasing when booking opens.

Putting tickets on sale in advance facilitates the highest profile for sell-outs, which Kotler and Scheff (1997) suggest are beneficial for organizers and performers, as they may gain in reputation from this demonstration of their popularity and show that they are engaging the public's interest. The Vienna Philharmonic's famous New Year's Day concerts are highly sought after and tickets are available exclusively by e-mail, on a single day a full year in advance of the performance. This incredibly restricted availability is integral to the reputation and success of the event.

Using ticket software to monitor take-up before and during an event allows marketers to review sales trends before an event and identify requirements for a modification to the marketing mix such as discounts and additional promotion. Monitoring can also allow the reduction in capacity for events that are selling badly, saving on overheads and providing a more comfortable experience for audience and performers (Kotler and Scheff, 1997). Summative evaluation of ticket sales may inform future marketing strategies, and is an important part of the financial reconciliation process. It also allows monitoring of behaviour patterns of audience segments or individuals to support customer relationship management.

The need to fulfil one or more of these roles makes the use of ticketing essential at many events and festivals. However, in certain circumstances, for example when an event is open-access, free and at a site where capacity is not a problem, ticketing may be inappropriate. An example would be any of the carnival and Mardi Gras events held around the world in public spaces such as beaches or parks. Ticketing these events could be inappropriate and completely impractical.

An understanding of the role of ticketing demonstrates that the choice of box office software is a strategic issue for event and festival managers. Selection of packages and design of box office systems should be made with reference to the aims of the ticketing operation.

The ticket

To fulfil its purposes the ticket itself must have an integrity that reassures the audience member and the organizers that it is genuine. For this to be effective, tickets must be difficult to forge, clearly linked to a specific organization or event, date, time and, if relevant, an area or seat. Counterfeit tickets may present a number of problems for an organizer and for audience members.

The fundamentals of a ticketing system

Whilst a relatively simple procedure from the customer's perspective, it is essential that the festival or event organizer has a ticketing strategy in place to fulfil their side of the transaction (Figure 12.2). The nature and complexity of this system will depend upon factors such as the size and type of the event and nature of the audience. In the following sections, some of the strategic decisions and operational issues that festival organizers must consider when designing a system are discussed.

Ticket distribution systems

The method in which tickets are offered and delivered is usually referred to as a ticket distribution system and it is part of the strategic planning of an event to determine what this will be. Bowdin *et al.* (2001) suggest that design of the ticket distribution system should be equated to place when designing the marketing mix for an event.

A range of ticket outlets are available when planning a ticket distribution system, incorporating various media and organizational forms. Tickets may be sold through a number of media, which may be offered in-house by the organizers or through an outside agency or partner. Each shares the characteristic of being an important interface between the customer and the organizers and for most methods, the first contact an audience member or visitor may have with a person representing the organization. This means that an efficient and effective service is essential.

Selling media include:

■ *Face-to-face*. A potential purchaser visits a venue or ticket outlet to reserve or purchase their tickets in person at a computerized or manual box office, or on the door.

189

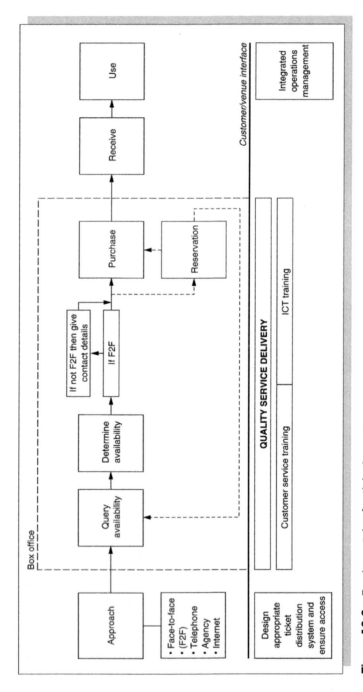

Figure 12.2 Fundamentals of a ticketing system.

■ *Telephone.* Calls are taken by box office staff, in a specialist phone room with dedicated staff or by an agency. Many venues have arrangements that route calls to agencies when their own box office is busy and large venues are introducing automated telephone booking systems to increase capacity.

■ *Post or fax.* Brochures publicizing events often have booking forms for posting or faxing to the box office. This tends to be the preferred method for organizing timed releases of tickets.

■ *Online.* Web-based interfaces and e-mail have revolutionized ticketing and have enhanced a range of benefits to the customer and promoter, including speed of booking, constant availability of booking facilities and streamlining of the management of festivals and events. The provision of online ticketing has become the norm in some markets, although this varies enormously internationally. However, even in countries where online booking remains relatively unpopular, it may be used at times of peak demand, for example on the day of release of tickets for a major event. It is also popular with tourists who do not feel comfortable talking to the box office because of language barriers. Peripheral benefits to the promoter can be derived from online ticketing systems, for example Tottenham Hotspur Football Club, London, UK, has used their web-based booking system to identify illegal sales and detect credit card fraud and ticket touts.

In-house or agency?

Event organizers must decide whether to run their own ticketing and reservations system or use an outside agency. Agencies may include other venues who usually sell the use of their box office at a fee or for a percentage of the takings; banks; retail outlets (a record shop might be a suitable outlet for a pop concert, a bookshop for a poetry festival); or specialist ticketing agencies.

Table 12.1 summarizes the advantages and disadvantages of outsourcing the ticketing operation to an agency. Festival and event organizers must weigh up these considerations before deciding whether to use an in-house box office, agency or a combination of the two. Kotler and Scheff (1997) argue that this strategic decision is an essential part of marketing planning as ease of access to tickets is central to the decision to purchase for some audience members and may greatly affect satisfaction with the process. The large-scale Grec Festival of Barcelona, which presents a diverse range of performing arts events at venues across the city each

Table 12.1   Advantages and disadvantages of outsourcing ticketing

Advantages	*Disadvantages*
■ Level of expertise and experience not available in-house	■ Additional direct costs reduce the yield per ticket to the organizers
■ Reducing up-front costs, e.g. purchasing equipment or hiring a suitable space to set up a box office	■ Increased cost to the customer due to booking fee
■ Avoiding the need to establish a system or employ staff for a small or time-limited event	■ A limit to control of customer service levels
■ Providing a more sophisticated service than is possible in-house, e.g. many agencies are able to offer a constantly available service or an impressive website with encryption technology for online sales	■ Limited knowledge of the venue or event by the agency staff
	■ Limited knowledge of the audience; may be problematic when relationship marketing is important to organizers
■ Increasing capacity by providing a back-up when the in-house box office is busy	■ Agencies may be unable to deal with complex transactions, e.g. ticket exchanges, subscription bookers, priority bookings, complex queries or complaints
■ Increasing the number and range of outlets facilitates ease of purchase and may reduce barriers to access	■ Loss of marketing data captured from purchasers

summer to locals and tourists, makes use of a range of outlets. As well as the traditional venue-based box offices, the festival organizers set up a booth in one of the main shopping streets, open daily and selling tickets for all events. There is a 24-hour telephone line and website, a dedicated box office at the tourist office and, from Monday to Friday, Caixa Catalunya Bank sells tickets over the counter and via 'Serviticket' machines in branches around the city. Table 12.2 summarizes the relationship between outlet and sales media.

Whichever choice organizers make, they must consider ticketing strategies to meet their aims and ensure that the box office system supports this. Table 12.3 outlines some of the software features that may be employed to support a coherent strategy.

Table 12.2 The relationship between outlet and sales media

	Face-to-face	Telephone	Post	Online
In-house	Own box office	Phone room	Own box office	Venue website
Out-of-house	Ticket booth/ another box office	Agency, e.g. Ticketmaster		Specialist ticket site, e.g. Ticketmaster

Table 12.3 Software features to support a ticketing strategy

Software feature	Strategic functions	Issues
Pricing/ differential pricing bands	Scaled price bands facilitate the sale of the ticket at the right price	The value of the ticket must match the value of the product so that marketing mix is congruous
Allocations to outlets	Allotment of appropriate number and range of tickets to appropriate outlets	Managing real-time booking
Release dates	Regulating demand, rewarding loyalty and/or generating hype	Planning capacity to meet peak demands at time of release
Holds (temporarily removing tickets from sale)	Introducing flexibility to allocation in order to support high-end CRM, reputation management and income generation (i.e. broadcast fees)	Managing potential conflicts between audience and management with respect to utilization of space
Reservations	Facilitating complex bookings, e.g. group bookings	It may be appropriate not to accept reservations for a very popular event expected to sell-out on release, or for the busiest night of the week

Continued

Software feature	Strategic functions	Issues
Comps (complimentary tickets)	Remuneration of performers and staff, and encouraging stakeholder participation	The number of tickets should be controlled and records kept
Group sales	Relationship management	Offer may need to be modified to reflect sales forecast
Special offers	Marketing promotions to encourage new sales to support audience development	Complexity of operation implementation may negate benefits
Batching and dispatching	Effectively managing workload whilst issuing the right ticket	Managing conflict of workload with customer expectations
Cobos (collection of tickets at the box office)	Facilitating late sales	Queue management of different types of ticket buyers and capacity control

These points relate primarily to organizers of medium and large events making use of computerized box office systems. For smaller events, or certain types of events, it is more usual to use a manual system where preprinted tickets are sold and manual records of sales kept. Whilst this is no longer the normal method of ticketing and may have some disadvantages, it is still fairly common for certain types of events such as comedy clubs, folk clubs and poetry readings.

So far, this chapter has set out how to use a box office system to sell tickets for an event or festival. The next section will consider the benefits of using the system for other functions and how to maximize the use derived from the box office.

Customer relationship management

The benefits of box office systems for CRM became truly obvious during the late 1980s, when developments in box office software began to focus on these functions.

Tomlinson (1993: 11) advocates twenty reasons for using box office data:

- Comparing venue audiences
- Defining the catchment area
- Evaluating responses to marketing
- Finding group bookers
- Focusing fund-raising efforts
- Identifying sales prospects
- Increasing ticket yield
- Measuring market penetration
- Monitoring campaigns
- Predicting sales
- Profiling audiences
- Reporting frequency of attendance
- Researching purchasing patterns
- Reviewing sales performance
- Seeking sponsorship contacts
- Selecting customers for direct mail
- Tailoring direct marketing packages
- Targeting potential customers
- Telemarketing campaigns
- Tracking customer purchases.

Increasingly sophisticated programmes allow a marketer to develop a picture of the audience and their patterns of attendance and to monitor promotional campaigns, audience development initiatives and the impact of programming. For a festival, this information can be aggregated or compared between outlets, venues and events. This information can then be fed into policies and campaigns based on facts about each audience, and can be overlaid with commercial data such as MOSAIC brought in from companies who specialize in data management to develop integrated campaigns.

A thorough knowledge of the behaviour of audience members will support the development of appropriate offers and services for customers, the design of individual donor schemes and corporate membership. Using box office software's marketing functions to monitoring booking and attendance patterns in relation to their RFM (recency, frequency and monetary value of purchases) can identify prospects who may develop into loyal customers and advocates for the organization.

195

Successful CRM activity within an organization should include the following features in the box office:

- Box office staff must be fully briefed about events and should understand their role within the organization: not just selling tickets, but building a potentially long-term relationship with the customer.
- A box office system must be set up to allow effective data capture while meeting the requirements of national data protection legislation. When advocating the CRM benefits of software, Morsman (2002: 1) suggests 'the more data you can squirt into your system, the more you can get out of it'.

A marketing department must effectively manage that data. A busy box office will quickly generate a large database of customers. As with any database, this requires regular attention to keep it up-to-date and accurate. Most software offers a function that removes duplicate records, and this 'cleaning' process should be built into the workload. In addition, regular back-ups should be kept, to guard valuable data against computer failure.

Facilities promotion and hire

It is easy when discussing ticketing to conceptualize an event in terms of audiences, and the volume of ticket sales to be generated. However, in the arts and cultural context, event management is as much concerned with the optimal use of space. Performance spaces in arts venues can be beautiful, spacious, unique and exciting environments that naturally lend themselves as backdrops to other types of events. Typically, these venues already possess the ancillary service areas of bar and catering that will make the opportunity to generate additional income a real possibility.

It should be noted that there is the potential to attract arts events on a purely commercial basis, where the risk is taken by the hirer, but the venue is ostensibly 'hosting' the event, which may or may not include the provision of box office and marketing facilities. Combining 'own promotions' with 'hires' generates new areas of opportunity and of risk that need careful handling in order to protect the integrity of the existing artistic vision and audience base. In this respect, the traditional division of management roles in arts organizations can be a hindrance, with operational staff often disassociated from artistic directors, development, marketing and box office staff. There is a need to effectively track and manage the utilization of space where additional facilities are being promoted and booked. Although dependent on the scale of bookings on offer, the use of computerized systems to manage this can be vital. There are a number of festival and event management systems on the market at present, each possessing particular strengths.

Issues and ethical concerns in ticketing

So far, this chapter has presented a case for an integrated management of the ticketing function and set out some of the key operational issues for a festival manager designing a box office system. In this final section, a number of questions and ethical concerns related to ticketing are introduced.

Privacy and data protection

In an age of increasing concern about the 'surveillance society', members of the public can be sensitive about organizations keeping records of their personal information, spending habits and leisure interests. However, for a successful integrated box office system to work hard for an event organizer, this is precisely the sort of data that should be stored, analysed and used. Therefore, this possible conflict of interest between festival and audience arises which must be managed sensitively and within legal constrictions.

National data protection legislation exists to ensure correct storage and use of personal data and is tending to become more restrictive for organizations or 'data users'. Within the European Community, legislation has tightened in the favour of the individual, so that their express consent must be given for their data to be used for marketing purposes, the 'opt-in principle'. So, for example, it is reasonable for a box office to collect the name and address of a customer in order to send out their ticket, but permission is needed to add them to a mailing list or to share their details with other organizations (including partners in a festival, such as other venues or touring companies). In order to store information on an individual, an organization should be registered under data protection legislation as a data user, and abide by its regulations. To ensure consent from a customer for their data to be used for purposes other than the sale of their ticket, box office staff must be trained to seek consent to put them on a mailing list and software must be capable of recording their preference.

Organizations must consider the ethics of their use of personal data. For example, routine tracking of purchasing and attendance patterns is undertaken to evaluate audience development strategies and to identify loyal audience members who may be potential donors. Some box office software includes a feature to produce lists and tracking information on 'best customers'. Managers must decide if this is an acceptable or appropriate way to treat customers.

Barriers to access

Whether to meet a social agenda or simply to maximize sales revenue, most event organizers seek to reduce barriers to access for their audiences. Barriers can take a number of forms including physical, practical or psychological (Hill *et al.*, 1995). When designing a ticketing system it is important to address this issue and some of the areas that need to be considered are as follows:

- Are people comfortable using your outlets? Are box office staff friendly and welcoming to new bookers or do they use jargon and talk down to people who do not know, for example, where they want to sit? Would your event be more accessible if you used a broader range of outlets such as banks or shops to sell tickets?
- Is your booking system accessible to disabled people, including those with visual or hearing impairments? Is everyone dealing with bookings (including staff at agencies) aware of your disability access policy and the access provision at the venue? Have booking staff had disability awareness training?
- If you use online booking, is the website easy to find, clearly laid out and easy to navigate? Do customers have a choice of seats or ticket types? Is it clear how to use the online booking facility? Do people know exactly at what stage they are making a purchase and that the booking has been processed? Are you able to reassure them about security?
- Is it possible for people without a bank account to book or do customers have to use a credit or debit card, or a cheque?

Staffing

The success of a ticketing system is not simply predicated on the effectiveness of the technology on which it is based or the level to which it is integrated into the strategic management of a festival. It is also dependent upon the way it is used by staff. An effective ticketing system needs well-trained and motivated box office staff to operate it. These staff are usually the first, and sometimes only, point of contact the public will have with a festival or venue. It is essential that this contact is a positive experience for the customer.

However, box office staff can be part-time, on temporary contracts, low paid and poorly trained, often coupled with a low status within the organization. Even worse, in many organizations a box office is uncomfortable and physically separated from the accommodation for the rest of the staff – sometimes even in a different building – leading to a feeling of isolation within an organization (Furber, 2002). But with a motivated, well-briefed staff member in a box office, trained in the use of the ticketing system and confident and happy to talk to members of the public, a ticket purchase can be a memorable and pleasant event for a customer, helping to build their relationship with your venue or festival. Customers recognized and treated as individuals are more satisfied (Tomlinson, 2002). And a box office manager integral to the management team can ensure effective use of the box office.

Staff development opportunities should be available to box office staff. In the UK, the National Vocational Qualification (NVQ) acknowledges skills gained in work and recognizes achievement, helping to build the status and recognition of the role of all staff, including those in practical roles.

Set-up and running costs

As computerized box office systems have become more sophisticated, they have also become cheaper. The cost of computer equipment and specialized software continues to fall, bringing them within the reach of an increasing number of organizations. However, this process has coincided with the almost universal use of computer box office equipment, so that it is now very difficult to set up and run an event without a computerized box office. Despite reductions in cost, it is still an expensive outlay for many organizations and, particularly in the subsidized arts sector, it is not uncommon for organizations to manage with outdated and inefficient technology that can put a strain on staff and their relationship with customers. What could be worse than an overloaded box office computer failing half an hour before an event, with eager potential customers queued out of the door? This is particularly problematic when no manual back-up system exists. Managers must recognize the need to invest in appropriate technology and to budget adequately for the training of staff to use the technology and for its maintenance and upkeep.

Conclusion

In conclusion, ticketing and reservation has developed considerably since the 1980s, so that the choice and range of ticket distribution systems is now much wider than was previously the case. Sophisticated computerized box office systems are now almost universal for festival and event organizers, with increasing use of communications technology to enhance services and improve access. This process has been closely related to the development of computer technology and the concurrent reduction in capital costs associated with it. More powerful processing capacity has allowed the development of software systems that integrate box office functions into a wider operational and marketing environment.

However, the full implication of this capability has yet to be exploited by all event organizers. Whilst the absolute state-of-the-art Information and technology equipment (ICT) is beyond the resources of many cultural providers, and can only be exploited by the most commercially driven sections of the sector, the lack of a full and effective exploitation of technological capabilities may be blamed on the absence of a strategic approach to technology in many organizations. The integration of the box office function into the management structure of an organization and full and appropriate training of staff is essential for the long-term effectiveness of a box office, playing a full role in the running of successful festivals and events.

Bibliography

Allen, J., O'Toole, W. and McDonnell, I. (2002). *Festival and Special Events Management*, 2nd edn. Queensland: John Wiley and Sons.

Bennet, R. (2002). Ticket sales forecasting methods and performance in UK theatre companies. *International Journal of Arts Management*, **5(1)**, 36–49.

Bowdin, G., McDonnell, I., Allen, J. and O'Toole, W. (2001). *Events Management*. Oxford: Butterworth-Heinemann.

Furber, M. (2002). Just the ticket. *Classical Music*, 10 February [JB33].

Hill, E., O'Sullivan, T. and O'Sullivan, C. (1995). *Creative Arts Marketing*. Oxford: Butterworth-Heinemann.

Kotler, P. and Scheff, J. (1997). *Standing Room Only*. Boston: Harvard Business School Press.

Morsman, P. (2002). Get creative with CRM. *Arts Professional*, No. 30, 15 July.

Prochak, M. (1996). *Computers for the Arts*. London: Arts Council of England.

Thamnopoulos, Y. and Gargalianos, D. (2002). Ticketing of large scale events: the case of the Sydney 2000 Olympic Games. *Facilities*, **20(1/2)**, 22–33.

Tomlinson, R. (1993). *Boxing Clever*. London: Arts Council of England.

Tomlinson, R. (2002). The ones that got away. *Arts Professional*, No. 30, 15 July.

Questions

1 You are the manager of a venue considering the introduction of all-in-one inclusive ticket and catering packages. What are the strategic and operational issues that you will need to consider?

2 What are the differences between a postal and a face-to-face ticket sale for the customer and organization? How would your understanding of these differences influence the design of a ticket distribution system?

3 An effective customer relationship management strategy involves the capture, handling and monitoring of potentially sensitive personal data. What might the ethical, operational and legislative considerations be?

13

The potential for revenue management in festivals and events

Una McMahon-Beattie and Ian Yeoman

Introduction

Revenue management (RM) or yield management marries the issues of supply, demand and price, and is considered to be a method of managing capacity profitably. It has gained wide acceptance in many service industries (airlines, hotels, golf, cinemas, car rentals and cruising) and there is substantial evidence that it is effective in improving revenues. This chapter will explore the potential application of RM to within festivals and event venues. It sets out to explain the process of RM and the benefits of adopting a strategic approach for using demand-management mechanisms to manage festivals and events, in particular highlighting the application via the internet.

Stelios Haji-Ioannou (Cox, 2003) has made millions through applying the principles of RM. It is a simple idea, basically to offer lower prices to people who book well in advance and to persuade people to buy on the internet. So could a formula work within a festival and events framework? Why not? If it works in the airline, car hire and hotel industries, there seems to be potential in the arts, festival and events industry.

Revenue management within festivals and arts is of importance, but it has different roles. Edinburgh International Festival (Anon., 2003) has launched a £5 ticket scheme to win new audiences. For the 2003 festival, 50 tickets for every show will be available for £5. The scheme is sponsored by the Royal Bank of Scotland to encourage a younger audience to participate and sample the experience. Yeoman and Leask (2000) argue that RM is fundamental to organizations like Historic Scotland and National Trust for Scotland when planning events. These heritage organizations need to raise revenue in order to deliver their core activity of 'conserving and presenting Scotland's heritage to the nation'. Historic Scotland uses a variable pricing policy to distinguish between different levels of visitor interpretations at castles and venues. Prices are higher for more popular venues and during the summer months. Variable pricing is also used for special historical events that create added value and a live tourism experience. Kolb (1997) investigated the price elasticity of students in attending art venues. Finding that whilst students are concerned about cost, the major barrier is the perception that arts events are boring. It was found that students would purchase tickets for arts events that are perceived as entertaining and allow socialization. However, Schimmelpfenning's (1997) paper on the pricing analysis of the Royal Ballet season identifies the problems of using a commercial pricing model for an artistic event, as the costs of production and pricing policies do not marry. It is this problem, of matching costs and visitors' willingness to pay, that leads to a constant problem of many arts organizations having a dependency on government subsidy. Cox (2003) suggests that arts companies should turn to the practice of RM, as a means to fill theatres and maximize revenue. Hence the purpose of this chapter, in discussing its potential.

Origins and spread of revenue management

Revenue or yield management originated with the deregulation of the US airline industry in the 1970s, when airlines like American, Delta and United used a capacity management strategy in order to compete with the success of People's Express. People's Express was a new, low-cost, no-frills airline, operating out of Newark Airport. The major airlines competed by offering a few seats at even lower prices than People's Express but maintaining higher fares for higher-paying passengers. In this way, they attracted the low-spend passenger who would book flights well in advance from People's Express, but maintained the higher-spend passengers who booked flights one or two days before departure. As a result of this, many People's Express passengers switched back to the major carriers and the company was eventually declared bankrupt. Today, RM is a management technique being utilized by an increasing number of service industries in order to maximize the effective use of their available capacity and ensure financial success. The application of RM can be seen in hotels (Huyton and Peters, 2000), the conference industry (Hartley and Rand, 2000), package holidays (Hoseason and Johns, 1998), rail transport (Hood, 2000), cruising (Hoseason, 2000), football (Barlow, 2000) and theatres (Oberwetter, 2001).

Definition of revenue management

In general terms, RM is the application of information systems and pricing strategies to allocate the right type of capacity or inventory unit to the right type of customer at the right place at the right time so as to maximize yield or 'revenue' (Kimes, 2000; Weatherford and Bodily, 1992). In the airline industry, for example, RM can be considered to be the revenue or yield per passenger mile, with revenue being a function of both the price the airline charges for differentiated service options (pricing) and the number of seats sold at each price (seat inventory control) (Donaghy et al., 1998). In practice, RM has meant setting prices according to predicted demand levels so that price-sensitive customers who are willing to purchase at off-peak times can do so at favourable prices, while price-insensitive customers who want to purchase at peak times will be able to do so. Therefore, the goal of RM is the formulation and profitable alignment of price, product and buyer. As such, RM can be defined in the service industries as a 'revenue maximization technique which aims to increase net revenue through the predicted allocation of available inventory capacity to predetermined market segments at optimum price' (Donaghy et al., 1998). With regard to festival and events revenue, it becomes the 'ability to sell the right experience to the right attendee, for the right price in order to optimise revenue'.

Preconditions of revenue management

Revenue management is applicable in the festival and event context where capacity is relatively fixed, where the demand is unstable and where the market can be segmented. Combining these features with low marginal costs and the ability to sell a perishable product to attendees well in advance of consumption are the key characteristics of sectors that can adopt RM. Developing these ideas further, Kimes (2000) has outlined a number of preconditions for the success of RM.

Relatively fixed capacity

Revenue management is suitable for capacity-constrained services industries. As Kimes (2000) states: 'Firms not constrained by capacity can use inventory as a buffer to deal with fluctuations in demand, but capacity constrained firms must make do with what they have.' Capacity in services cannot be inventoried to deal with fluctuations in demand; however, capacity can be measured in the terms of physical and non-physical units. Physical capacity is about bedrooms, number of theatre seats or number of square metres of exhibition space. Non-physical capacity can also be thought of as time based and reflects the notion of a physical capacity used for certain periods of time (seat-hours of theatre performances, time slots for aeroplane departures and landings etc.). Therefore, time becomes the unit of inventory that is also a constraint on capacity. In the long term, capacity can be changed, for example, by adding a new function suite in a conference centre or reconfiguring the seating in a theatre. However, this usually involves considerable financial investment in terms of plant or equipment.

Predictable demand

This is about managing festival and events attendees who book through reservations and those who simply 'walk-in' to, for example, performances or recitals. Both forms of demand can be managed. It is about predicting what advance bookings will be made at different price levels against walk-in or 'on-demand' situations (otherwise known as demand forecasting). In order to do this, the manager needs to compile information about percentage of reservations, walk-ins, customer time periods and service duration (Kimes, 2000). Collecting information on extraneous variables that can affect demand, such as weather conditions and school holidays, will also assist the festival and events manager to make effective forecasts.

Perishable inventory

As stated earlier, the inventory of a capacity-constrained event should be thought of as unit of time. Theatres, airlines, hotels, package holidays and cruises all have the characteristics of service, or particularly, they are selling an inventory unit of 'a piece of time'. This may be a performance of play, a concert or a day ticket for an event. Since unsold capacity cannot be inventoried, it is lost forever. If the opportunity to sell that experience is lost, the revenue cannot be recovered. The perishability of the capacity-constrained service organization adds to the complexity of finding the optimal revenue (Kimes, 2000).

Appropriate cost and pricing structures

Revenue management is used in service industries that are capital intensive because of the nature of their high fixed costs. In terms of festivals and events, we may think here particularly of theatres, museums, galleries or conference centres. These organizations exhibit extremely high fixed costs. They may need to generate sufficient revenue to cover variable costs and offset at least some fixed costs.

Time-variable demand

The festival and event attendee may vary by the week, day of the week or time of the day. Managers must be able to forecast the uptake of the component parts of the festival or the event. Allocations of available inventory units can be given effective pricing decisions against demand and supply issues. This flexible pricing structure against time-variable demand enables organizations to make decisions against off-peak and peak periods.

Necessary ingredients for a revenue management system

Kimes (2000) has also categorized the ingredients necessary for an RM system: '...a company must possess the ability to segment the market based on willingness to pay, information on historical demand and booking patterns, good knowledge of pricing, a well developed overbooking policy and a good information system' (Kimes, 2000). Each of these ingredients will be discussed in relation to festivals and events.

Market segmentation

Within RM systems an organization can segment its users by degree of revenue. This relates to purpose, time and price sensitivity. Airlines are an excellent example of this: they can predict demand per type of passenger for a given flight (Ingold and Huyton, 2000). Airlines place restrictions on purchase depending on demand and supply, i.e. non-refundable cancellations and advance purchase requirements. They also know, for example, that business travellers are not price sensitive. As such, airlines hold capacity in order to sell to this type of customer rather than selling the capacity in advance to budget travellers who tend to look for low fares. Business travellers are time sensitive and do not mind paying a higher price only a few days before departure. By holding capacity available, airlines risk not selling the capacity but predict that they will sell it to a higher-yielding passenger. Likewise, those that manage festivals and events can segment their customers/attendees by purpose, price and time. It is about balancing these dimensions.

Historical demand and booking patterns

Accurate forecasts are essential to an RM system. As such, appropriate management information systems are required. Managers must be able to predict likely demand by attendees or customer type in advance. Festivals or events that are held on a regular basis will have an obvious advantage over the 'one-off' event. However, even if the event is a 'one-off', the experience and knowledge of the manager at similar events may be useful in estimating demand patterns. The generation of forecasts is based upon extensive information and tracking systems that allow for the development of historical booking patterns per attendee type which assist the festival and events manager to forecast into the future. These forecasting systems develop and mature over time. They act as a self-learning experience. Knowing booking patterns helps manage demand and revenue optimization.

Pricing knowledge

This is about knowledge of situations and how to manage price in different situations. By using multiple rates to optimize revenue, the manager must know when to use price discrimination and how. Typically, when demand is high, no discrimination takes place, but when demand is low, concentration moves to discounting.

Reservations policy

Many RM approaches use an overbooking policy in matching demand and supply. But this may not be appropriate for festivals and arts venues. Alternatively, venue managers should develop a reservations policy that curtails the problems of cancellation and no-shows. By using a reservations and prepayment policy, organizations can overcome this problem without having to overbook.

Information systems and knowledge management

Successful implementation of RM depends on the quality of knowledge the organization holds about its customers/attendees. It is necessary to develop an effective process of holding knowledge about customers through knowledge elicitation, retrieval, coding, storage and dissemination (Sparrow, 1998). It is about manipulating and analysing 'multiple knowledge' which is a management device to integrate different types of knowledge such as hard factual information and personal recounts of experiences within RM systems. The use of artificial intelligence (AI) has enormous potential for handling the complexities of RM because of its abilities in complex problem solving, reasoning, perception, planning and analysis of extensive data. Expert systems (ES) are 'knowledge-based' software packages that reflect the expertise in the area of the application and have extensive capacity in dealing with non-numeric, qualitative data (Russell, 1997).

What is the opportunity?

Returning to easyJet (Barlow, 2000; Cox, 2003), Haji-Ioannou is currently working on a project to open a cinema in London, using the principles of RM. Haji-Ioannou points out that the average cinema screening is only 20% full; the man with the Midas touch believes that by offering 20p tickets to people who book seats a month in advance and charging people who book at the last minute full price, he will attract bigger audiences and make money. So Haji-Ioannou thinks an RM approach could be used as a solution to Scotland's festival and arts funding problem.

I am sure that going to the theatre is as price-elastic as going to the movies ... if you reduce the price, more people will go. Someone should try it with the theatre some day (Cox, 2003).

James Rothney (Cox, 2003), the EasyGroup's Director of Corporate Affairs, states that:

'I would have thought easyTheatre could work ... you'd have to consider the costs of salaries, but then in a cinema you've got the cost of buying a film. The whole easyCinema thing is a bit of a leap of faith. Just because we've succeeded with flights and car hire, there's no guarantee it'll work with cinemas, but we believe it will. The real skill is to use prices and incentives to get people to book more often, and in that way the market grows. There's no reason why you can't get more people to go to the theatre more often using price as an incentive.' Despite this, Rothney admits that whatever success easyCinema has will be down, at least partly, to its association with an already recognisable brand name. In other words, the company doesn't have to spend time and money explaining how it will work to the public because they already understand it (Cox, 2003).

Hamish Glen, Dundee Rep's Director, thinks that what the Scottish theatre, festival and arts need is more money, but the easyJet approach has potential, as an average show at Dundee Rep, for example, often runs at 60% seat occupancy.

I see no inherent reason why EasyJet principles shouldn't be applied to the theatre ... I think the worry would be that those audience members who have traditionally paid £14 or whatever for a ticket would all start buying substantially cheaper tickets and not enough new people would come, so that in effect we would take less money.

Also, the margins are much tighter. We don't have a capital investment that we are able to lose. If any such exercise was attempted and backfired a theatre could go bust in a single season. But I think it is an interesting notion, and if we could somehow make these discount tickets exclusively available to people who would not otherwise come, it could work (Cox, 2003).

How to make it work?

An article in *Marketing Science*, called 'SilverScreener: a modeling approach to movie screens management', showed how an RM model, commonly used by operational researchers, yielded a 37.7% higher cumulative profit for a Manhattan theatre (Swami *et al.*, 1999). So could it work elsewhere?

Oberwetter (2001) highlights the practical application of RM for the movie theatres, which could easily be adapted for festival and live theatre venues. Companies that have adopted RM as part of their corporate culture have seen their revenues increase from 3% to 9% a year, with 80% of that going directly into profits.

But to make it really work, festival and events venues have to maximize the potential of the internet. It is the internet that has revolutionized easyJet's (Barlow, 2000; Cox, 2003) approach to RM. It is the internet that will allow festival and event venues to change their business model to impact on their bottom-line profits. The internet allows venues to operate a reservation and pricing policy based upon social, educational and revenue objectives of the company. Tickets can be reserved for special income groups or educational groups, using mathematical codes and algorithms. An online ticketing system allows the venue manager to track and monitor ticket sales on a daily basis, therefore making pricing and capacity allocation decisions easy. An online ticketing system allows an RM policy to be implemented via a market segmentation process. The potential is enormous, and the first company to do this will gain a significant competitive advantage (Oberwetter, 2001). So how does it work?

Advance sales

Advance sales are the first hurdle for a successful RM programme in fixed-capacity venues. Venues can sell tickets in advance by utilizing online reservation systems. By selling tickets in advance, venues can develop different market segments, increase demand in low-demand areas and greatly increase revenues, all while increasing customer satisfaction.

This way, venues can avoid paying commission to third-party agents who handle ticket sales; rather they should be sold through the internet by credit card. This is the easyJet model of business (Barlow, 2000). An online ticketing system even handles the mailing process, therefore cutting out another expense.

Market segmentation

It is typical for theatres to segment customers to a very minimum. For example, full price, students, families, evening and afternoon tickets etc. Using an RM approach, there are lots of opportunities for market segmentation, in some very creative combinations. An approach just like the airlines could be utilized where there are multiple price segments (Oberwetter, 2001). In addition, specialized multiple ticket market segments could be developed to complement the usual approach.

The airlines represent a great example of what the festival and events venue industry could do with market segmentation. Just as the airlines have multiple flights to the same and different locations throughout the day, venues could adopt a range of prices for each different segment depending upon demand, time of booking and pricing policy, showing the same and different movies at multiple times during the day. Basically, as the time of theatre performance gets nearer, discount-priced market segments would be automatically opened and closed, based upon an analysis of the current demand in relation to the historical sales figures and other factors. An RM approach allows venues to introduce an innovative way to manage and monitor segments, such as:

■ *Multiple pricing:* offering tickets for a range of performances, therefore maximizing yield not just on one show, but on a range of shows and nights.
■ *Two for the price of one:* two tickets for the price of one on shows where demand is low.
■ *Timed tickets:* see as many shows as you like on a specific day.
■ *Low-rate special:* targeting specific groups that are price sensitive rather than time sensitive.
■ *Allocation models:* offering limited free tickets to disadvantaged groups for popular shows.

The number of packages that could be developed is limitless. These multiple ticket market segments would also be utilized in the RM engine along with the individually priced market segments. For example, the system might determine that it is better to forgo a higher-paying customer if it expects to get more revenue by selling that ticket to a repeat-date customer. Additionally, RM systems can be programmed to have a social function, i.e. preference given to disadvantaged groups. Prices also vary according to the type of seat in the theatre; this is based upon the view, comfort and position of the seat in the theatre.

Membership schemes

There is significant opportunity for membership schemes using an online RM system. For example:

- By tracking purchases, members can be offered focused packages. It is always easier to attract customers that have seen a performance than a new customer.
- Membership schemes offer the opportunity for quick e-mail promotions, which saves on postage costs.
- Microprofiles can be built up over time that focus on the individual needs of the customers, building up customer relationship marketing schemes.

Conclusion

For RM to work in festival and events venues, the focus must be on a ticket and reservation system, in order that the right decisions can be made about pricing and capacity allocation. These systems are driven by computer software, based upon RM algorithms. These determine the right prices and restrictions placed on advance reservations. The software builds a forecast based upon historical information and assumptions set by a revenue manager. The forecast is a mathematical formula to determine how much inventory to make available to each market segment and when, driving a reservation system based upon an allocation model. Revenue management for the festival and event sector is all about selling tickets at the right price to the right customer at the right time in order to maximize revenue. There is enormous potential in this application, but it is the internet that makes it possible, with a little bit of help from Stelios Haji-Ioannou and the world of easyJet.

Bibliography

Anon. (2003). Festival offers cheap seats. http://news.bbc.co.uk/1/hi/scotland/2892577.stm.

Barlow, G. (2000). Capacity management in the football industry. In *Yield Management: Strategies for the Service Industries* (A. Ingold, U. McMahon-Beattie and I. Yeoman, eds). London: Continuum Press.

Cox, R. (2003). Welcome to cheap seats. *Scotsman*, 29 January. www.arts.scotsman.com/headlines_specific.cfm?id=675.

Donaghy, K., McMahon-Beattie, U., Yeoman, I. and Ingold, A. (1998). The realism of yield management. *Progress in Tourism and Hospitality Research*, **4(3)**, 187–196.

Hartley, J. and Rand, P. (2000). Conference sector capacity management. In *Yield Management: Strategies for the Service Industries* (A. Ingold, U. McMahon-Beattie and I. Yeoman, eds). London: Continuum Press.

Hood, I.S.A. (2000). Merlin: model to evaluate revenue and loadings for Intercity. In *Yield Management: Strategies for the Service Industries* (A. Ingold, U. McMahon-Beattie and I. Yeoman, eds). London: Continuum Press.

Hoseason, J. (2000). Capacity management in the cruise industry. In *Yield Management: Strategies for the Service Industries* (A. Ingold, U. McMahon-Beattie and I. Yeoman, eds). London: Continuum Press.

Hoseason, J. and Johns, N. (1998). The numbers game: the role of yield management in the tour operations industry. *Progress in Tourism and Hospitality Research*, **4(3)**, 197–206.

Huyton, J. and Peters, S. (2000). Application of yield management to the hotel industry. In *Yield Management: Strategies for the Service Industries* (A. Ingold, U. McMahon-Beattie and I. Yeoman, eds). London: Continuum Press.

Ingold, A. and Huyton, J.R. (2000). Yield management and the airline industry. In *Yield Management: Strategies for the Service Industries* (A. Ingold, U. McMahon-Beattie and I. Yeoman, eds). London: Continuum Press.

Kimes, S. (2000). A strategic approach to yield management. In *Yield Management: Strategies for the Service Industries* (A. Ingold, U. McMahon-Beattie and I. Yeoman, eds). London: Continuum Press.

Kolb, B.M. (1997). Pricing as the key to attracting students to the performing arts. *Journal of Cultural Economics*, **21(2)**, 139–146.

Oberwetter, R. (2001). Building blockbuster business. http://lionhrtpub.com/orms/orms-6-01/oberwetter.html.

Russell, K. (1997). Expert systems. In *Yield Management: Strategies for the Service Industries* (I. Yeoman and A. Ingold, eds). London: Cassell Publications.

Schimmelpfenning, J. (1997). Demand for ballet: a non-parametric analysis of the 1995 Royal Ballet season. *Journal of Cultural Economics*, **21(2)**, 119–127.

Sparrow, J. (1998). *Knowledge in Organisations*. London: Sage.

Swami, S., Eliashberg, J. and Weinberg, C.B. (1999). SilverScreener: a modeling approach to movie screens management. *Marketing Science*, **18(3)**, online.

Weatherford, L.R. and Bodily, S.E. (1992). A taxonomy and research overview of perishable asset management: yield management, overbooking, pricing. *Operations Research*, **10(5)**, 831–844.

Yeoman, I. and Leask, A. (2000). Yield management. In *Heritage Visitor Attractions: An Operations Management Perspective* (A. Leask and I. Yeoman, eds). London: Continuum Press.

Questions

1 Pick a festival or event organization that you are familiar with and discuss how it exhibits Kimes's (2000) preconditions and ingredients.

2 How does the internet allow festival and events organization to manage their revenue more effectively?

3 Again, looking at your chosen festival or events organization, what type of membership schemes currently exist (if any) and what new types might you develop if you had an online ticket and reservation system?

Policies and strategies of art and leisure event management

14

Politics, public policy and the destination

C. Michael Hall and Kristy Rusher

Introduction

The relationship between the hosting of events and public policy is one that has received only relatively limited analysis within tourism studies. Certainly, such analysis has only usually been conducted on the basis of individual case studies and not on a comprehensive examination of the policy settings and structures within which events are conducted (Richter, 1989; Hall, 1994, 2001; Judd and Fainstein, 1999; Gratton and Henry, 2001). At one level such a situation may not be surprising given the typically cursory level of policy analysis within the field of tourism studies (Hall and Jenkins, 1995). However, given the importance of events as components of tourism strategies as well as of wider regional development strategies, it is clear that events are of some policy significance (Roche, 2000; Higham and Hinch, 2003).

This chapter seeks to provide an overview of a number of issues associated with analysing the policy dimensions of events. First, it discusses the nature of policy analysis and identifies approaches that may be used in the study of events. Second, it discusses the means by which events fit into the set of institutional arrangements for government policy making. Third, it provides a case study of the political dimensions of a local event.

The policy dimensions of events

Public policy is the focal point of government activity. Public policy can be studied for three primary reasons (Dye, 1992). First, public policy can be studied for purely academic reasons so as to gain an understanding of the causes and consequences of policy decisions, and to improve our knowledge about society. In this instance, public policy can be viewed as a dependent variable *or* as an independent variable. If policy is viewed as a dependent variable, the critical focus for inquiry becomes 'what socioeconomic or environmental forces and political system characteristics operate to shape the content of policy' (Dye, 1992: 4). If public policy is viewed as an independent variable, then the central question becomes, what impact does public policy have on society (the environment), including the events held within them, and on the political system? Second, public policy can be studied for professional reasons in order to understand the causes and consequences of policy. Thus, we might apply public policy knowledge to the solution of practical problems, and input that knowledge into the political process in order to improve it so as to improve policy and planning outcomes. Third, public policy can be studied for political purposes so as to ensure that a political unit, such as a nation, region or municipality, 'adopts the "right" policies to achieve the "right" goals' (Dye, 1992: 5). This last focus raises the critical issues of defining what is 'right', and identifying by whom 'right' is determined. However, if studies are undertaken for purely political purposes, these issues may not even concern the analyst (Hall and Jenkins, 1995).

The study of the policy dimensions within which events operate offers the opportunity to examine many topics which should be of interest not only to the tourist industry, government agencies and students of tourism, but to researchers working within and on the boundaries of many other social science disciplines. These topics include:

- The political nature of the event policy-making process
- Public participation in the event planning and policy process
- The sources of power in event policy making
- The exercise of choice by public officials in complex policy environments
- Perceptions as to the effectiveness of event policies.

According to Cunningham (1963: 229) 'policy is like the elephant – you recognise it when you see it but cannot easily define it'. For the purpose of this chapter public policy 'is whatever governments choose to do or not to do' (Dye, 1992: 2). This definition covers government action, inaction, decisions and non-decisions as it implies a deliberate choice between alternatives. Such recognition is significant as a number of discussions on tourism policy and government involvement in tourism only focus on the visible element of government decision making, indicating a substantive lack of understanding of the nature of public policy studies as well as the workings of government (e.g. Edgell, 1990; Pearce, 1992). For a policy to be regarded as public policy, it must have been processed by public, i.e. government, agencies (Hogwood and Gunn, 1984). Nevertheless, pressure groups, community leaders, administrators and others working inside and outside the 'rules of the game' established by the state, and more specifically government, influence and perceive public policies in significant and often markedly different ways.

Building on the approach of Dye (1992), Hall and Jenkins (1995) defined tourism public policy as whatever governments choose to do or not to do with respect to tourism. Similarly, we can define event public policy as whatever governments choose to do or not to do with respect to events. Such an approach may at least provide us with a starting point when trying to understand the relationship between events and public policy but it is also rather deceiving in how it may represent the complexity of such issues. For example, we perhaps need to distinguish between event policies and policies for events. The former refers to the policies established to enable events to run effectively and efficiently. It therefore represents a micropolitical approach. In contrast the latter notion refers to the means by which government establishes policies, as well as associated institutional structures, which enable events to be run. The two approaches are related but the macropolitical approach of the latter is more helpful in asking the how, where, and why regarding the hosting of events; particularly if one takes the perspective that public policy is a process, as policies are formulated and implemented in dynamic environments where there is a complex pattern of decisions, actions, interaction, reaction and feedback (Hall and Jenkins, 1995). Such a systems approach to the policy process implies 'that public policy is best understood by considering the operation of a political system in its environment and by examining how such a system maintains itself and changes over time' (Jenkins, 1978: 21).

Events are hosted within the context of a political system. Importantly, in terms of why they are held, it needs to be recognized that attracting visitors is only one justification for the hosting of events; other reasons include: celebration, maintaining or enhancing community pride, employment generation, increased publicity and media coverage, enlivening otherwise quiet areas, maintaining cultural identities, encouraging regeneration and attracting industry and capital (e.g. Roche, 1992, 2000; Hall, 2001). Just as significantly it must be noted that all of the reasons may have a political dimension to them if one regards politics as who gets what, when, where and how (Lasswell, 1936) rather than within the narrow confines of party politics. Decisions affecting the hosting of events; the nature of government involvement in events; the structure of agencies responsible for event bidding, development, management, marketing and promotion; and the involvement of communities in events all emerge from a political process. This process involves the values of actors (individuals, interest groups and public and private organizations) in a struggle for power. As Lindblom (1959: 82) noted, 'One chooses among values and among policies at one and the same time.' Values, power and interests therefore lie at the heart of the event policy process (Simmons *et al.*, 1974). However, the interrelationships of these factors find representation not only in the physical surroundings of the event but also in the administrative and institutional structures which are established.

Given that tourism is only one, albeit often significant, dimension of the hosting of events it therefore means that the policy dimensions of events are therefore also significantly broader than tourism. Such an observation has substantial implications not only for the setting of tourism policies but also for their organizational dimensions. For example, rather than events having a specific policy setting of their own, it is often more likely that events come under a range of policy and regulatory jurisdictions which will often include tourism, but which will also involve public bodies responsible for sports, culture, heritage, the arts, community development, regional development and regeneration depending on the nature of the event. These issues are discussed further in the next section which examines the institutional context for the events–policy relationships.

Institutional arrangements

'Policy making is filtered through a complex institutional framework' (Brooks, 1993: 79). Therefore, event public policy analysis demands some understanding of and reference to the institutional arrangements in which tourism policy is made. Such frameworks vary significantly between countries and between policy sectors within an individual country. The state can be conceptualized as a set of officials with their own preferences and capacities to affect public policy, or in more structural terms as a relatively permanent set of *political institutions* operating in relation to civil society (Nordlinger, 1981). The main institutions of the state include: the elected legislatures, government departments and authorities, the judiciary, enforcement agencies, other levels of government, government–business enterprises, regulatory authorities, and a range of para-state organizations, such as trade unions. The functions of the state will affect tourism policy and development to different degrees. However, the degree to which individual functions are related to particular event-related policies and decisions will depend on the specific objectives of institutions, interest groups and significant individuals relative to the policy process (Hall, 1994).

In the longer run, institutional arrangements, for example the creation of an event bidding agency, 'may themselves be seen as policies, which, by building in to the decision process the need to consult particular groups and follow particular procedures, increase the likelihood of some kinds of decisions and reduce that of others' (Simeon, 1976: 575). New government agencies may be established as part of the growth in the activity and influence of government, particularly as new demands, such as regional economic development concerns, reach a high priority on the political agenda. As Mercer (1979: 107) noted, 'The setting up of entirely new government departments, advisory bodies or sections within the existing administration is a well established strategy on the part of governments for demonstrating loudly and clearly that "something positive is being done" with respect to a given problem.' Such an observation may arguably not only apply to the creation of specific event agencies but also to the infrastructure, such as stadia and sports and event facilities, which they may operate (Baade, 1996; Whitson and Macintosh, 1996; Hall, 2001). In Australia nearly every state has established either an event bidding agency or an event unit within its set of institutional arrangements. In Western Australia, for example, an event bidding agency, Eventscorp, was established in order to assist with tourism promotion and development in the wake of the loss of the America's Cup in 1987. In January 1991, Eventscorp was transferred from the Western Australian Development Corporation to the WA Tourism Commission and the Perth Convention Bureau was absorbed by the Commission as the Perth Convention Unit. The Eventscorp Unit aims to attract major sporting and cultural events to Western Australia, such as the Commonwealth Bank Rally of Australia, the Hopman Cup, the World Swimming Championships and the Whitbread Round-the-World Yacht Race. The Perth Convention Unit has since been renamed the Perth Convention and Incentive Unit and is responsible for attracting conventions and incentive travel to Western Australia. The establishment of such a specialized unit undoubtedly helps show that something specific is being done with respect to the attraction of events. The success of such institutional measures though is difficult to gauge given that every other state has done a similar thing (Hall, 2003). While a short-term competitive edge may have been gained by such institutional innovation, longer-term advantage has not accrued and other factors related to the attraction of events, e.g. subsidies, infrastructure, media rights and accessibility, may prove more important in attracting events.

As noted above the different policy sources for events will derive from different sections of government because of the diverse nature of events themselves. Such an observation is significant because public policy varies across sectors, and even within sectors. Patterns observed in other public policy arenas (e.g. sport or culture) cannot be assumed to be repeated in the tourism public policy process, nor can we assume that those processes are similar between countries and regions. For example, because of different democratic and political traditions, we can expect event policy in the United Kingdom to look different from that of, say, South Africa, and policy will be processed, discussed and perceived differently in those countries as well. Therefore, although there may be some similarities, policies and institutional arrangements will differ within and between countries and there may be little integration among different government organizations with interests in hosting events because they gave different objectives as well as different stakeholders demands to meet. For example, in the case of the South African bid for the 2004 Olympic Games, the bid deliberately targeted the urban poor as a beneficiary of the development process associated with the hosting of any Games bid. Such an approach is substantially different from bids developed in countries such as the United Kingdom and Canada (Hall, 2001; Page and Hall, 2003).

Furthermore, different government levels will also tend to have different policy objectives. Indeed, the study of the tourism public policy process, including that related to events, is made more complex because the aims of the local state may diverge from those of the central state (Williams and Shaw, 1988). Nowhere may this be more apparent than in federal political systems, such as Australia or Canada, where there exist three or even four levels of the state: national, state/provincial, regional and local (Anderson, 1984).

Such concerns have had significant impacts on the hosting of events. For example, while municipalities may have been interested in bidding to host large-scale international events, they are often unable to do so unless they also obtain the support of central government. Similarly, at times some communities may feel that events have been imposed on them by higher levels of government. For example, opposition to the hosting of the Olympic Games or Grand Prix is often termed, in relation to the imposition of events, that although they may have wider national or regional benefits, these are not perceived as such by some members of the directly impacted community (Economists At Large, 1997). Because of the interests and stakeholders that impact upon upper levels of government, local concerns may well be lost in the search for the national or regional good with special legislation often being enacted to minimize disturbance to the hosting of an event.

The short timeframe in which governments and industry have to react to the hosting of events may lead to 'fast track planning', where proposals are pushed through the planning process without the normal economic, social and environmental assessment procedures being applied. For example, in the case of the hosting of the 2000 Summer Olympic Games in Sydney the New South Wales state government passed legislation in 1995 with respect to the Sydney Olympics to assist in the development and regeneration of projects associated with the Games. This was achieved at the cost of the people, of citizens losing their rights of appeal to initiate a court appeal under environment and planning legislation against the proposed Olympic projects (Totaro, 1995). Further legislation passed under the New South Wales Government's *Olympic Coordination Authority Act* allowed, somewhat ironically given the green image which the Games were seeking to present (Sydney Organizing Committee for the Olympic Games (SOCOG), 1996), all projects linked with the Games to be suspended from the usual Environmental Impact Statements requirements (Totaro, 1995). Unfortunately, however, the same reasons which propel cities to stage large-scale tourist events (i.e. redevelopment, dramatic urban development), and also to fast-track the planning process, 'are also some of the very factors which result in an adverse effect on residents in cities in which they are held' (Wilkinson, 1994: 28).

Community involvement in event and policy development

Various authors (e.g. Whitson and Macintosh, 1996; Roche, 2000; Hall, 2001) have criticized the process of event development for often excluding the input of the host community. This exclusion occurs in both formal and informal policy development. Informal development is where policies are made to assist the interpretation or ensure the smooth working of existing laws and regulations. For example, the wording of the statute may be unclear, or it may be necessary to develop guidelines to ensure the statute works in a special set of local circumstances. In contrast, formal policy development informs the process of making legislation or interpreting regulation. In this instance, policy is a precursor to the full development of legislation or a proposed amendment to legislation. Both forms of policy development are part of the 'rules of the game', which surrounds the politics of events. Indeed, in the case of many events, the rules of the game are such that the public rarely gain the opportunity to vote on the hosting of the event.

There are methods for accepting submissions from the community on issues pertaining to the development of policies, which are transformed into laws and regulations. However, because the policy dimensions of event tourism are often broader than the immediate policy boundaries of the event, it is not easy for the host community to identify the implications of proposed regulations in the context of the event. An example of this is the issue of traffic manipulation, where the same legislative sections would govern the event environment as well as other appropriate circumstances such as roadworks. Traffic manipulation during an event has an obvious and significant impact on the host community. The legislation governing powers to divert traffic is contained within transport legislation, and it is difficult for the host community or event organizers to anticipate the implications for themselves and respond appropriately during the submissions stage of the policy development process when the regulations deal with circumstances that are broader than a strict event environment.

This is a failure of the event policy-making process which is most common at a central government level. However, such failings of the policy development process also occur at a local government level. Local governments are largely concerned with the implementation of legislation at a local level. This is the environment where informal policies are developed. The degree of community input is highly dependent on the relationship between local government and the community they act on behalf of. This means that there is a typically large degree of variation between the degree of input that different community groups, lobby groups and influential individuals have in the event environment across higher-level political jurisdictions.

A good example of how community input into the policy-making process has evolved over the lifecycle of an event is the Alexandra Blossom Festival, an annual event held in a rural community in the South Island of New Zealand. The context of the community and a brief outline of the event is important in illustrating how the complex social structures of the community have shaped the political environment and how this in turn has evolved into a relationship with local government that ensures a high degree of community input into policy development.

The Alexandra Blossom Festival

Alexandra is a small town in the Central Otago region, with a population of 4400. Central Otago's economy is predominantly agricultural and focuses on production of stone fruit such as cherries and apricots. Its small population is sparse, with a density of just 1.5 people per kilometre. Each year at the beginning of October, Alexandra hosts the Alexandra Blossom Festival, to celebrate the arrival of spring blossom on the region's fruit trees. As well as being an aesthetic icon, to an experienced orchardist, the volume of tree blossom is the first indication of the size of the fruit harvest and the length of the fruit season. Spring, therefore, is the first opportunity to speculate on the region's prosperity for the subsequent year.

The Alexandra Blossom Festival is a relatively simple community event, which opens with a street parade. The parade audience is then led to the show grounds where they are entertained with craft and art stalls, hotdog stands, live music, fairground rides, bouncy castles and other children's entertainment. The festival is the focal celebration of the year for the rural communities of the Central Otago District and approximately 30% of the 20 000 people who attend the weekend event are from the neighbouring Southland and Otago regions.

The Alexandra Blossom Festival is one of New Zealand's oldest community events. The first festival was organized by the Jaycees Club of Alexandra in 1957 as a means of raising funds to build the region's first swimming pool. The festival was so successful that the money was raised more quickly than expected, allowing the pool construction to be completed early. Following the success of the first event, the festival was held annually in subsequent years, with the money being donated to other community projects and community groups. The community use of the festival proceeds became a tradition that ensured the festival became increasingly popular with sponsors and spectators.

What makes this festival unique is not the festival content, but the evolution of the organizational structure of the event and how the festival has had an important influence in shaping the development of event policy within the region. The high degree of community participation means that the organization of the festival reflects the structure of political relationships within the community. This has been the most significant factor in ensuring that the community has retained a degree of ownership of the event, and it is this degree of ownership which has had the most impact and influence on the development of the region's event policies, particularly as the festival is used as a benchmark for other event activities.

Community ownership has been a dominant facet of the festival since its inception. After the success of the initial festivals, a committee of community leaders was formed to coordinate future festivals. The commitment of these individuals was broad. Often committee members became heavily involved in the operational aspects of the event as staff of the fairground entertainment, and in other roles. As the festival grew in size and complexity, the committee members focused more on the planning and design aspects of the festival, and other tasks were divided amongst community groups such as the Lions Club of Alexandra which staffed the gates, and ran the fairground raffles. The profit of the festival was heavily dependent on the efforts of volunteers to manage the costs, and often volunteers were recruited by co-opting able-bodied relatives and leveraging long-standing friendships. This illustrates the dependence of such community events on the complex community network structures.

The growing festival also required a greater commitment from volunteers with increasingly specialized skills such as stage construction, and crowd control. This signalled to organizers that the festival was becoming a complex event that required more professional management. In particular, the festival needed to secure long-term funding, given the costs involved with underwriting professional musicians and other entertainment. As the festival had become increasingly important to the development and promotion of the region, the Central Otago District Council became the major financial stakeholder in the event, designating it a 'community project', a legal status similar to that used for building recreation facilities. This security of funding enabled the organizing committee to employ a professional event coordinator. It is also significant because it signalled an important shift in local government policy which had previously only recognized projects with a tangible outcome such as a park or other recreational facilities as worthy of council funding. However, the need to seek council funding was also influenced by changes in the community fabric and structure, and over time, this was reflected in the development of the festival.

The festival was highly dependent on volunteer labour. However, volunteers became less available as the community structure changed as a result of the economic reforms of the 1980s that restructured the New Zealand economy and changed the work patterns of the Central Otago residents. For example, orchard owners had to spend more time on their fruit production to comply with new export regulations, and this eroded the time that they had available to volunteer for activities such as the Alexandra Blossom Festival. The region's children also moved to other parts of New Zealand to pursue higher education and other work opportunities, making it difficult to pass on the skills learnt to a new pool of volunteers, and new residents and types of investment altered the community structure. Gradually, the number of paid staff involved in the festival operations grew. Over time, this created the need to charge an entry fee to cover the increased costs. This meant that the emphasis of revenue generation from the show part of the festival became ticket sales rather than cost management. The festival required large crowds, rather than time commitment from individual residents. The shaping of the themes and images of the festival for a large part of the event reflected the organizing committee's need to attract a large audience. Therefore, the design of the festival show became heavily influenced by constructing community values and identities in a manner that provided entertainment to attract a large number of people and media attention, rather than a 'bottom-up' expression of the host community's values and identity. This shift in philosophy for the event also signalled a further change in local government policy which determined not to fund the deficit of the increased costs from ratepayer funds.

On the surface, the function of the Alexandra Blossom Festival Parade appears to be just an entertaining means of opening the festival. In fact, it is a critical element of the festival and the wider community structure. The parade provides a means for the region's community groups to participate in the event, and express their role in the community. It is a means of meeting the interests of various stakeholders as it is an important opportunity for the community groups to raise awareness of their organization's role and the importance of their function, and this assists in the group getting support for their other fundraising efforts throughout the year. The community groups arrange sponsorship of their float by local businesses. The sponsorship money is provided to pay for the costs of decorating the float, and any surplus funds are applied to the group's coffers to contribute to providing services. The community group coordinates their members and other volunteers to construct the float, which must be made with a large number of blossoms. Originally, the floats used genuine flower blossom to construct the float decorations, but the difficulties in ensuring the blossoms did not wilt before the parade meant that hand-made crepe paper blossoms were soon substituted. The float construction also cements the social and hence political relationships between the community groups. Community groups such as the Catholic Women's League members make surplus flowers and give them to other community groups to assist their float construction.

The evolution of the organization of the Alexandra Blossom Festival illustrates the social interdependencies within a rural community and the changes in economic and social structures that they have adapted to over the lifetime of the festival. The festival is an example of how community ownership at the organizational level has changed from exclusive control to being arranged by a professional event organizer guided by a committee comprising residents of the festival's host community. This adaptation has meant that the focus of the festival has become oriented to entertaining an audience rather than just being an expression of the host community's values and identity. The gradual evolution of the festival has also influenced the development of policy at local government level, which has enabled the festival to continue its success as a community event.

While some of the strategic development and management of the festival has left the direct control of the host community, there is still a large level of involvement and community ownership of the festival in terms of the participation in different parts of the festival, such as the Alexandra Blossom Festival Parade. This element of ownership has been the most critical factor in shaping the informal policies developed in relation to the festival, as individuals have leveraged this sense of ownership to lobby local government members and influence the direction of policy in the region. The Alexandra Blossom Festival is therefore more significant than being a simple celebration of seasonal change and is instead a reflection of the community's social and political culture and values, and demonstrates mechanisms for accommodating a variety of interests within an events framework.

Conclusions

The political and policy dimensions of events are inherently complex. As this chapter has argued there is a need to differentiate between event policies and policies for events. The latter perspective assists in grounding the management and hosting of events within the web of values, interests, institutional arrangements and power within which events are situated. Despite their significance there still remains relatively little analysis of the political context of events and the means by which events come to be developed and hosted within communities. Nevertheless, it is argued that an examination of the political dimensions can help give a better indication of how events may fit into a community and who wins and loses from the hosting of events. For this chapter a case study was provided of a festival which sought to be inclusive in terms of its accommodation of interests and values. However, while this may be the case with community level events it must be noted that, generally, the larger the event, the less accommodating they are, as the political interests of government, business and 'boosters' may then come to dominate the policy process because of the financial and political opportunities they may provide.

Bibliography

Anderson, J.E. (1984). *Public Policy Making*, 3rd edn. New York: CBS College Publishing.

Baade, R.A. (1996). Professional sports as catalysts for metropolitan economic development. *Journal of Urban Affairs*, **18**, 1–17.

Brooks, S. (1993). *Public Policy in Canada*. Toronto: McClelland and Stewart.

Cunningham, G. (1963). Policy and practice. *Public Administration*, **41**, 63.

Dye, T. (1992). *Understanding Public Policy*, 7th edn. Englewood Cliffs, NJ: Prentice-Hall.

Economists At Large (1997). *Grand Prixtensions: The Economics of the Magic Pudding*. Prepared for the Save Albert Park Group. Melbourne: Economists At Large.

Edgell, D. (1990). *International Tourism Policy*. New York: Van Nostrand Reinhold.

Gratton, C. and Henry, I.P. (eds) (2001). *Sport in the City: The Role of Sport in Economic and Social Regeneration*. London: Routledge.

Hall, C.M. (1994). *Tourism and Politics: Power, Policy and Place*. London: John Wiley.

Hall, C.M. (2001). Imaging, tourism and sports event fever: the Sydney Olympics and the need for a social charter for mega-events. In *Sport in the City: The Role of Sport in Economic and Social Regeneration* (C. Gratton and I.P. Henry, eds), pp.166–183. London: Routledge.

Hall, C.M. (2003). *Introduction to Tourism*, 4th edn. South Melbourne: Pearson Education.

Hall, C.M. and Jenkins, J.M. (1995). *Tourism and Public Policy*. London: Routledge.

Higham, J. and Hinch, T. (2003). *Sports Tourism Development*. Clevedon: Channelview Publications.

Hogwood, B.W. and Gunn, L.A. (1984). *Policy Analysis for the Real World*. Oxford University Press, Oxford.

Jenkins, W.I. (1978). *Policy Analysis: A Political and Organisational Perspective*. London: Robertson.

Judd, D. and Fainstein, S. (eds) (1999). *The Tourist City*. New Haven: Yale University Press.

Lasswell, H.D. (1936). *Politics: Who Gets What, When, How?* New York: McGraw-Hill.

Lindblom, C.E. (1959). The science of muddling through. *Public Administration Review*, **19**, 79–88.

Mercer, D. (1979). Victoria's Land Conservation Council and the alpine region. *Australian Geographical Studies*, **17(1)**, 107–130.

Nordlinger, E. (1981). *On the Autonomy of the Democratic State*. Cambridge, MA: Harvard University Press.

Page, S. and Hall, C.M. (2003). *Managing Urban Tourism*. Harlow: Prentice-Hall.

Pearce, D.G. (1992). *Tourist Organisations*. Harlow: Longman Scientific and Technical.

Richter, L.K. (1989). *The Politics of Tourism in Asia*. Honolulu: University of Hawaii Press.

Roche, M. (1992). Mega-events and micro-modernization: on the sociology of the new urban tourism. *British Journal of Sociology*, **43(4)**, 563–600.

Roche, M. (2000). *Mega-Events and Modernity: Olympics and Expos in the Growth of Global Culture*. London: Routledge.

Simeon, R. (1976). Studying public policy. *Canadian Journal of Political Science*, **9(4)**, 558–580.

Simmons, R., Davis, B.W., Chapman, R.J.K. and Sager, D.D. (1974). Policy flow analysis: a conceptual model for comparative public policy research. *Western Political Quarterly*, **2(3)**, 457–468.

Sydney Organizing Committee for the Olympic Games (SOCOG) (1996). *Environmental Guidelines*. Sydney: SOCOG.

Totaro, P. (1995). Olympic opponents denied sporting chance. *Sydney Morning Herald*, 16 December, 1.

Whitson, D. and Macintosh, D. (1996). The global circus: international sport, tourism, and the marketing of cities. *Journal of Sport and Social Issues*, **23**, 278–295.

Wilkinson, J. (1994). *The Olympic Games: Past History and Present Expectations*. Sydney: NSW Parliamentary Library.

Williams, A.M. and Shaw, G. (1988). Tourism policies in a changing economic environment. In *Tourism and Economic Development: Western European Experiences* (A.M. Williams and G. Shaw, eds). London: Belhaven Press.

Questions

1 What is event policy and to what extent might it be different from tourism policy?

2 How might values and interests influence the event policy process?

3 What are institutional arrangements and why are they significant for events?

15

Event management for the arts: a New Zealand perspective

Lee Harrison and Fiona McDonald

Introduction

Events management in New Zealand is a relatively young industry; until recently it had more generally been a feature of the hospitality, tourism, marketing and communications industries. In recent years the steady rise in demand for professionally planned and managed events, due in part to increasing consumer expectations concerning the degree of technical support and the quality of delivery of events, has resulted in a market for specialized event management professionals in New Zealand.

While technology is improving the design of the events management industry, it is also changing and developing the way artists work and the ways they exhibit their work. The arts in New Zealand, defined as 'all forms of creative and interpretive expression' (Creative New Zealand, 2001: 5), has evolved from the traditional forms of dance, music, writing, film, visual arts (painting and photography, craft), ceramics and sculpture and traditional Maori craft and performance, to contemporary forms such as urban design, food preparation, ritual design and fashion, each reflecting influences as diverse as culture, ethnicity, heritage, gender and sexuality. The sometimes uneasy alliance between art and technology has reorganized through diversification the way New Zealand artists are profiled and the way they exhibit their work globally. It has eased the isolation of being thousands of miles away from the galleries of New York, the fashion houses of Europe and the theatres of London and provided a forum for New Zealand artists to showcase their work with the best the world has to offer.

The purpose of this chapter is to outline and describe routine processes involved in event management for the arts in New Zealand, with a focus on highlighting the characteristics that make event management within this field a unique experience. The first section will bring together the planning processes, from the initial stages of establishing event purpose and objectives to the investigating issues relating to the why, what, who, when, where and how of event design, then investigating the means of structuring planning to production, by way of organizing committee and the role of the event management professional in this process. The second section discusses the operational management or the logistics of the event. Key focus points in this section are logistics and communication along with a description of typical operational activities event management professionals may perform in preparation for, and during, event production. Following this is an examination of risk management for events, which includes a case study of a New Zealand arts production. The third section examines the financial organization and management of events; it addresses the issues of basic event income and expenditure organization, cashflow management and sponsorship design. This section will draw on the examples of two high-profile New Zealand arts events where diverse and positive sponsorship relationships have been created. A case study of a New Zealand designed and produced multimedia, fashion, design and performance arts production is followed by the conclusion which will review the key points of event management for the arts. Although in this chapter processes are assigned to sections, it is important to be aware that often processes can occur simultaneously, overlap and be executed numerous times throughout the event planning, operational, and general management processes.

Planning: transforming concept to reality

Events for the arts and culture sectors are often designed not simply to exhibit an individual's or organization's latest creation or achievement, whether it is a design or visual arts exhibition, or a fashion or performance production. Often the event concept involves taking the audience on a journey that captivates, entertains, informs, challenges, inspires, educates, showcases, and stimulates the senses, while balancing financial objectives, such as selling products, securing sponsorship, raising funds and building and maintaining clients and contracts. For events management professionals given the task of realizing this, the journey begins months in advance with the planning process, as it is the attention, detail and effort applied during this process which will impact significantly on the outcome of any event.

Establishing event purpose and objectives

The planning process essentially begins with taking the idea or concept and identifying (a) the event purpose (why you are staging the event) and (b) specific and measurable event objectives (what you hope to achieve from staging the event). A simple example is a seasonal fashion launch: the purpose of the event is to showcase the latest collection of clothing; the objectives are to introduce and showcase the latest collection, to receive media coverage in an attempt to raise the profile of the business and brand and to secure new clients and contracts. By identifying the purpose and establishing the objectives of an event, the parameters, which will direct further planning and decision making, have been determined.

Investigating event design

Now that the event purpose and objectives have been determined, the next step is to identify key areas of organization and management. Questions that events management professionals routinely ask themselves relate to the why, what, who, when, where and how of event design. As the following examples illustrate, the questions need to be general enough to gather as much information as possible while being specific to the event purpose and objectives.

■ *Why is the event being held?* This will clarify the purpose of the event and should include an investigation and analysis of the motivation behind the event, the wider societal, developmental and commercial issues directing the event and any possible positive or negative outcomes.

■ *What will be the design of the event?* This explores the event type or style. Determining the right type or style is central to achieving the objectives of the event; for example, if the event objective is to bring together an industry for a forum where knowledge, ideas and experiences can be shared, rather than hold a standard conference with presentations and lectures, a more suitable design would be a series of interactive workshops run by those involved and specialists in the different areas of the industry. Careful selection of event style will not only assist in meeting the event objectives but will enhance the overall event experience.

■ *When is the best time for the event to take place?* It is essential to consider issues relating to the selection of event dates as a poorly informed event date can impact on the success or failure of the event. An important issue to consider is whether or not the date supports meeting and achieving the objectives. If we use the fashion launch as an example, the date selected should be at the beginning of the season in order to secure clients and contracts for the season. It is essential to investigate the intended date for other events, which may be in competition with your own, and check the availability of the venue and product and service providers for the intended date.

■ *Where is the best location/venue for the event?* Make a list of suitable venues and check these against a summary of the facilities and services you require of the venue. If you are using a new venue, during the site inspection ask for references and later check industry websites and venue directories. If you intend using product and service providers the venue does not have an existing relationship with, enquire about their policies and procedures for bringing providers into the venue.

■ *Who will participate in the event?* This question is best addressed on two levels, first selecting those who will be involved in the organization and management of the event along with a list of suitable product and service providers, and second, establishing the intended audience or target market for the event. By evaluating the strengths and weaknesses of possible organizational or managerial candidates, product and service providers and relating these to the objectives of the event, the likelihood of getting the right people and providers in the right role increase significantly. Further, an early indication of the intended or target audience is central to planning. Information gathered about this group will indicate the possible nature and numbers of attendees which will in turn influence the budget, the marketing campaign and the content and structure of the event.

■ *How will it be done?* Creating a checklist of what needs to be done, a timeline and a preliminary budget are all valuable starting points for organizing events. From this the events management professional will begin sourcing quotes, screening and selecting venues and product and service providers, seeking and securing sponsorship, designing and implementing a marketing campaign and designing and coordinating the registration or RSVP process. Crucial to the success of each of these processes is continual evaluation and revision from the start of planning through to the conclusion of the event.

Directing planning to production

Subsequent to the initial stages of planning and organization the scope of the production and management for the event will become evident. This will profile the number and nature of tasks involved in the production and will indicate whether an organizing committee is needed and its appropriate size. An effective way of structuring committees such as this is by designating each member an area or areas of responsibility such as the budget, venue, technical support, sponsorship, advertising, catering and so on. Each area of responsibility involves tasks such as determining the event requirements, procuring and processing quotes, checking provider availability, booking likely providers, negotiating prices and managing any other specific requirements. Each task is ideally given a timeframe, and progress, issues and recommendations are reported on and discussed at regular committee meetings and consensus for future action made. From committee consensus a chronologically ordered event plan will develop; this will detail the tasks and times each section of the event will occur, who will be involved in it and what resources will be used. It is at this point the role of the event management professional becomes one of coordinator and advisor, coordinating the reorganization of planning into a logistical schedule and acting as advisor in negotiating artistic vision with logistical and financial practicality.

Operational management

Logistics and communication

The key to successfully staging an event that is both on time and to budget relies on researched and detailed planning combined with strategic logistical organization. Logistics in the context of event management refers to the distribution and flow of service providers and goods to the venue. The logistics of event management requires a large degree of skilled communication, as it is the task of the event management professional to translate the often-complex conceptual information of the event into clear and specific guidelines and directions, and, as often is the case, to a wide range of product and service providers and contributors both directly and indirectly involved in the set-up, staging and general production of an event.

The operational management process begins months in advance of the event when the event management professional will begin to liaise with the venue, the numerous product and service providers and the organizing committee, if one exists. During this process, bookings and quotes continue to be finalized and confirmed, product and service provisions double-checked and issues relating to the set-up and production of the event researched and unique requirements identified and organized. Important issues to address are whether or not the product and service providers are familiar with the venue, their pack-in and pack-out times, how much space they require and what facilities they need to access. In order for this to be achieved, communications need to be structured so that the correct information is imparted to the correct person according to priority and in clear and specific terms.

Operational activities

Events in the New Zealand arts sector are generally as individual as the artists and the artwork being showcased; as such the production of these events requires a unique and fresh approach from the events management professional. In saying that, there will remain several key aspects of event planning and production which will generate operational activities familiar to the event management professional. Some of the factors which routinely determine such operational activities are (a) the style of events,

(b) the roles and responsibilities negotiated with the client, (c) the capabilities and limitations of the venue and the staff, and (d) the thoroughness of planning and preparation. The following examples present the sorts of operational activities events management professionals typically handle in relation to those factors.

The style of the event will largely determine the nature and number of operational activities the event management professional will undertake. For instance during a conference they will arrive long before any delegates are due and will begin by setting up for registration as well as setting up a conference information desk. They will meet with the venue coordinator to double-check arrangements for the day and will then prepare to welcome delegates and process their registrations. From then they will generally base themselves at the conference information desk, the central point for delegates to make inquiries or seek assistance. The role of the event management professional then becomes one of troubleshooter, information provider, communicator and coordinator.

Often clients negotiate with event management professionals specific roles and responsibilities that match their specialist areas of knowledge and skills. For example the role of an events management professional with specialist technical knowledge can be to supervise and direct the lighting, sound and visual components of a production from the operator's booth. This is usually done in cooperation with the contracted multimedia production company.

Being aware of the capabilities and limitations of factors such as the venue and staff is essential when planning for events. For example, if the events management professional is aware that the venue is limited to providing only two of the five required data projectors, then action can be taken to outsource the supply and installation of a further three data projectors. Likewise, if the event management professional is aware of the capabilities of event staff, they are able to ensure the staff are given jobs which best suit their skills and experience. All of these examples serve to highlight the importance of thorough planning and preparation in managing events efficiently and effectively.

Risk management

As the event plan continues to develop, possible risks to the successful staging of the event will begin to emerge. Each risk has the potential to impact upon the production of the event, but by identifying risks during the planning and operational processes, the event design can be adapted to circumvent any negative impacts. The process of risk management involves identifying the risks, specifying the nature of the risks, assessing the degree to which the risks could impact upon the event and developing contingency plans designed to avoid or minimize the potential impacts. When developing contingency plans, always plan for the worst-case scenario and as many different and disastrous outcomes as possible. Thorough risk management analysis should involve the examination of issues relating to personal safety and emergency procedures, access to and reliability of technical equipment, risks to achieving the artistic and financial objectives, risks of damage to the venue and equipment caused during production along with examination of other logistical risks involved in the transport, delivery, pack-in, construction and pack-out of the event. A common mistake events management professionals make in their risk analysis is to focus primarily on personal safety and emergency procedures. This becomes a problem when the other risk management issues are not analysed carefully. A good example of successful risk management comes from the case study II DIE IV. During the analysis of risks it was identified that the laser machine had to be transported by train from another city with a 10-hour transportation timeframe. Given that the laser machine was the only one in the country available on that night and that the visual presentation needed the laser in order to achieve the artistic objectives of the event, the risk of organizing delivery of the laser for the day of production was assessed as too high. The producers organized the delivery of the laser one-and-a-half days ahead of the event. It was fortunate that this contingency plan was organized, as a scheduling problem occurred with transportation and the laser arrived just hours before the staging of the event. Had the laser not arrived the artistic objectives of the event would not have been met.

Financial management

This section examines the areas of basic event budgeting, income and expenditure organization and sponsorship design. Often events within the arts sector are not designed to create profit; more generally the financial objective is to create enough income to match the costs of the event with an additional and usually modest amount to form a contingency fund. Therefore the primary task when creating a budget is to outline the anticipated costs of producing the event. This can be structured as a schedule of quotes and costs such as those sourced during the planning process. By identifying and documenting the costs involved in the production of the event, the events management professional and/or organizing committee can establish the necessary income and possible sources of income. Typically income for events in the arts sector is a combination of funding and or sponsorship with income from ticket sales. By securing some form of sponsorship or funding the ticket prices can be reduced, which can lead to greater ticket sales. Events often fail financially when income from ticket sales is less than what has been budgeted for.

Managing cashflow

With the costs or expenditure and income of the event outlined, consideration now needs to be directed at the flow of income and expenditure – the cash flow. Often venues and some product and service providers require a percentage of their fees or costs as a deposit at the time of booking. When these bookings are made months in advance of the event and before any regular income has been received, such as income from ticket sales, some expenditure will need to be made. This is where the benefit of sponsorship or funding is highlighted, by having an initial operational fund available for costs such as deposits, as it reduces the strain on future event income. Throughout the planning and preparation of an event, careful attention needs to be given to ensuring that costs and expenses are consistent with the existing budget. It only takes a few small increases in budgeted costs or a few small incidental costs for expenditure to become greater than income, in which case the event may be cancelled or run at a loss. To avoid such financial difficulties the event management professional and/or the organizing committee needs to ensure they are aware of the payment terms of the venue and all product and service providers. They need to ensure they have an initial operational fund with sufficient funds to cover anticipated deposits and establishment costs and a contingency fund available for incidental costs.

New Zealand experiences with sponsorship design

As acknowledged throughout this chapter, events in the arts and culture sectors characteristically rely on some form or amount of funding or sponsorship. In New Zealand funding or sponsorship can come from a range of organizations and agencies. These include central and local government, arts funding and development agencies such as Creative New Zealand and local councils, national corporations and companies, national, regional and local businesses, lottery grants and industry-related training institutions. On the surface this list would suggest that there is a considerable amount of funding and sponsorship available; this is the first mistake an events management professional can make when preparing to secure funding or sponsorship. The actual amount of funds and resources made available through these organizations and agencies is negligible compared to the wealth of artistic, creative and innovative talent that exists in New Zealand today, and the competition to secure these resources is fierce. When approaching organizations for funding and/or sponsorship it is essential to ensure that a match exists between the event's target audience and the sponsor's target market. Research such as a demographic analysis examining the age, profession, socio-economic status and areas of expenditure may be required to ensure that a match exists; the results of this should be included in the proposal as evidence of the event reaching their market.

An apt example of matching an event with a sponsor comes from the L'Oreal New Zealand Fashion Week. Key to the success of this sponsor-ship relationship was the match that existed between the event's target market and the sponsor's target market. Further and more importantly, a match existed between the two organizations with regard to the message they jointly communicated at public relations opportunities and times of media exposure, which was their commitment to professionalizing and raising the profile of the New Zealand fashion industry and design. This cooperative and cohesive approach to the sponsorship relationship was an essential factor in the success of the event. Often organizations use sponsorship and funding of arts and culture events as a way of improving public awareness and perceptions of their organization; proposals should outline the ways involvement with the event will achieve this. Funding and sponsorship proposals need to describe, in clear and specific terms, how the organization will benefit from involvement with the event and what funding or resources are required. A useful way of structuring this is by way of written agreement. The agreement will document the roles and responsibilities of each party and the terms and conditions of the spon-sorship agreement. The agreement can be tailored to include clauses each party requires. Agreements can stipulate ticketing packages and hosting opportunities, advertising and promotional exposure and can address issues such as sponsorship conflict, i.e. sponsors generally will not spon-sor events that their industry competition is involved with. In relation to what the sponsor provides, this can range from initial financial funding to the use of in-house resources such as design teams, financial advice and distribution of advertising and promotional material. Take for example the New Zealand Festival of the Arts. Here is an event that tailors its sponsorship, funding and support agreements to meet the needs of the event while benefiting from the available resources a range of organizations and agencies can provide. The festival has gold sponsors which include a range of public and private corporations and organizations, it receives core funding from a local council, it receives major grants from Creative New Zealand and Industry New Zealand and it works with the support from community trusts. Each agreement is specific and unique between the festival and the supporting organization or agency and makes the most of the funds, resources and support made available.

Sponsorship proposals also need to address the issue of evaluation. With events in the arts and culture sectors it is difficult to quantify what business or growth an event may generate for a sponsor; monitoring sales figures prior to and after the event is too narrow an analysis to assess the impact of sponsoring an event. Evaluation design needs to go further and gather information about who attended the event, what happened at the event, how the event was received, what feedback was received, whether or not the sponsor was represented at photo and media opportunities, the ways the organization was presented to the public, and how this could have raised and impacted on awareness and perceptions of the organization. By collating and analysing this type of information a picture will begin to emerge as to how the sponsorship agreement worked and how it did not.

Case study:
a New Zealand events management experience

II DIE IV: a multimedia fashion, design and performance arts production

Conceived from concern about the distinct lack of large-scale industry forums for established and up-and-coming artists and designers to showcase their talent and creations, II DIE IV was staged to an audience of 1200 in Wellington on 29 June 1996. The purpose of the show was to showcase, through live presentation and video recording, the exceptional cross-section of talent that existed in New Zealand across the art forms of design, dance, fashion, music and visual art. The objectives were to celebrate leading creative artists established in their fields and to open doors of opportunity for young up-and-coming artists. Creator, Director and Executive Producer Derek Elvy intended II DIE IV to become a brand synonymous with his established nationally and internationally recognized hairdressing salon. The event became a cult presentation of cutting-edge design and contemporary visual and performance art aimed at increasing audience awareness and challenging existing perceptions about the then-current social issues of AIDS, drugs and sexuality. The show was structured as a mix of highs and lows, emotional storytelling and performance arrangement realized through a synthesis of art, technology, music and performance. Additional to the performance were the pre-show cocktails and the post-show dance party.

Given the size and complexity of the task, immediately recruited to join Derek on the II DIE IV management team were Producer Lee Harrison, an established event management professional with specialist technical knowledge, and Choreographer Glen Birchall, one of the nation's leading and experienced and innovative contemporary dance practitioners. It was this team whose varying skills, knowledge and experience, contacts and industry awareness sourced, screened, enlisted, employed, managed and brought together the production team of approximately 120 people. This consisted of a mix of contrac-tors, such as set and lighting designers, a set construction team, audio-visual designers and operators, video operators, sound engineers, a laser operator, graphics and visual designers and manipulators, a stage manager, backstage coordinator and model coordinator. Additionally there were a multitude of performers, dancers, fashion designers, models, hairdressers, make-up artists and photographers. Volunteers from the national drama school worked as stagehands, hosts and ushers and unit assistants. Derek, Lee and Glen, each with their specialist areas of knowledge, worked both collaboratively and independently with the contractors, product and service providers and performers to ensure that at no point was the event concept or vision going to be obscured by logistical complication or misunderstanding.

The event date was set and the venue booked a year before the staging of the event. This was crucial to the planning and management of the event as it meant that the workload could be broken down into manage-able steps and distributed amongst the management team throughout the year. It made accessing leading product and service providers and contractors possible and gave the management team the time to oversee and if necessary redesign each aspect of the production from the stage design and construction through to the distribution of tickets. Setting the date a year out also allowed for the development and implementation of an extensive advertising campaign. As the event objectives involved creating a brand and staging a cult production of cutting-edge design, visual and performance art, the advertising and ticketing were designed with a mix of manipulated imagery, dark colours and gothic-style fonts, with the additional use of a haunting soundtrack for cinema and radio advertising. The advertising campaign included regional radio, cinema, billboard and newspaper advertising along with a flood of posters, flyers around town and a sophisticated national magazine campaign. The entire advertising and publicity campaign was underpinned by the objective to create a brand of II DIE IV arts production. Due to the months of detailed and specific planning, the set-up and staging of the production was near perfect with almost all of the objectives being achieved.

Key success factors

The success of the event planning and management of II DIE IV was due mostly to two key factors: a long lead-in time, and a specialist production team. The lead-in time of one year allowed for thorough planning and preparation. It meant that proper consideration could be given to sponsorship, design and procurement. It also meant that possible venues and product and service providers were visited and researched in relation to the specific requirements of the event. The lengthy lead-in time also allowed for a comprehensive risk management programme to be designed and contingencies to be set in case of possible problems. Having a specialist production team allowed for clear communication and collaboration with all those involved in the production of the event, from the stagehands, to the numerous product and service providers, to the artists and performers. It ensured the event would be delivered just as the original concept and vision intended without misunderstanding of production processes.

Conclusion

Event management for the arts sector is a unique experience; it requires from its practitioners skills and qualities as carefully crafted as those of the artists that they work with. Detailed planning with clear connections to event purpose and objectives along with continual evaluation provide structure and links between the planning and production of events. Operational skills such as communication, flexibility and versatility are the tools for dealing with a multitude of operational activities which can range from setting desks and directing operation booths, to booking the supply and installation of equipment. The chapter has illustrated that financial management structures for events do not need to be complex but they do need to clearly outline the flow of income and expenditure, along with outlining the key components to securing and building successful sponsorship relationships. The case study concluded this chapter with an examination and analysis of an actual, albeit brief, event management process in the context of an arts event in New Zealand, serving to highlight the strength of detailed event planning, organization and management. Last words of advice: plan, monitor and manage carefully and thoroughly for positive outcomes and have fun.

Bibliography

Creative New Zealand (2001). *Strategic Plan, Te Mahere Rautaki, 2001–2004.* Wellington: Creative New Zealand.

Questions

1 What unique characteristics are involved in event management for the arts?
2 How do we link event purpose and objectives with event practice and management?
3 How can we manage advertising and ticketing to reflect the tone of the event?

16

The economics and evaluation of festivals and events

Jack Carlsen

Introduction

The economic importance of festivals and events is now widely recognized. Events have an impact on local, state and national economies through investment, employment and income. They also generate increased tourism and media coverage which leads to increased visitation and awareness of the host destination. This chapter will explain the relevant economic principles that apply to events and the economic and evaluation techniques that are used to determine the value of events.

Hallmark and mega-events have major impacts on particular sectors within the economy, including trade, transport and tourism. These sectoral impacts, when combined, can influence the total value of economic activity in a given period (usually one year) as measured using Gross Domestic Product (GDP) or Gross State Product (GSP). It is important to recognize that it is not just the initial expenditure in these sectors that increases economic activity, but also the subsequent flow-on, or multiplier effects that follow an initial injection of new money in the economy. The size of the multiplier effects will be determined by the extent to which the economy can retain the additional event-related expenditure in the local economy and prevent it from flowing out on imported goods and services.

Evaluation approaches

According to Allen *et al.* (2002), '*Event evaluation* is the *process* of *critically observing, measuring and monitoring* the implementation of an event in order to assess its *outcomes* accurately.' There are several key words in this description (in italics), which need further explanation:

- *Event* – involves some form of celebration or occasion which is carefully planned to meet specific social or economic objectives.
- *Evaluation* – is an assignment of some value based on economic and/or social outcomes.
- *Process* – as with all forms of research, event evaluation is process that is either iterative (step by step) or systemic (dynamic), which is undertaken in an ordered, systematic way.
- *Critically* – event evaluations should be a means by which event managers and organizers learn to improve the events or festivals they organize. In order to encourage improvement, the evaluation process must use a critical approach to assessing the event outcomes.
- *Observing, measuring and monitoring* – these terms indicate that there are several approaches to conducting event evaluation. Direct observation and systematic recording during an event can identify any on-site problems such as crowd discomfort, congestion points, sanitation or service failures. Other factors can be measured using social survey techniques and include visitor demographics, satisfaction and behaviour. Monitoring the implementation of event is also an important role of management and helps to control factors such as ticket sales, budgets, security and staging and any other issues that emerge.
- *Outcomes* – most events evaluations focus on outcomes that are measured against desired financial, social or tourism goals. There are other stages of evaluation – in the pre-event period and during the event itself

– but the planning and management of these stages culminates in the outcomes, which are most often the focus of evaluations.

The following sections outline the techniques available to conduct critical and useful event evaluations for the purpose of ensuring that the event outcomes are critically recorded and analysed.

Observation techniques and applications

Participant observation is a form of research in which the researchers take part in the experience being studied as if they were partially (non-participant) or completely involved (participant) in the event. Non-participant observers can be staff members or volunteers that have been instructed to systematically record their observations and activities at the event. Alternatively, participant observation researchers can be recruited specifically to assume the role of an event visitor and be instructed to record all of their impressions during an event in a set of diary notes (see, for example, Box 16.1). Participant observation is a useful technique for recording key elements of an event experience, including:

- *Initial impressions of the event* – the sense of arrival, access and parking, queuing and site entry, information and directions
- *Viewing the event or performance* – sight lines, seating, sound and audiovisual quality
- *Atmosphere and excitement* – sense of anticipation, arousal, action, or aggression
- *Facilities and amenities* – toilets, rubbish bins, special needs of children and disabled people
- *Catering* – quality of food and service, cleanliness and capacity of dining areas, taste and temperature of food and beverages
- *Merchandising* – quality and availability of merchandise
- *Crowding and congestion points* – times and places where crowding or congestion occurs, or discomfort or aggression as a result of crowding
- *Exiting* – problems in exiting the event, flow of pedestrian and vehicular traffic.

According to Seaton (1997) observation can also be used in combination, or triangulated, with other survey techniques to validate:

- Visitor satisfaction
- Hospitality service quality

Box 16.1 Participant observation notes at a surfing event

1. Approach to site

   Signage and access to the parking area was adequate, but there were both vehicles and pedestrians using the same narrow entrance to the car park. This was not only causing delays for vehicles but was also potentially dangerous for pedestrians. There was also a heavy vehicle wetting down the road at 8:30 a.m. and this also caused minor delays.

2. Parking area

   The parking was not in marked bays, but there were attendants to give direction to parking areas. They also maintained a presence there all day, which provided some security for parked vehicles. Leaving the parking area required a steep walk to the site, which some would find arduous.

3. Enter site

   No sense of arrival or welcome statement at the main entrance to the event, which was disappointing. Some banners/signage at the entry point along the road would be appropriate, perhaps with some information handouts and audio commentary.

4. Information search

   No signage on site as to direct access to main viewing, beach or VIP areas. Programmes were available in the VIP area, and an update of the surfing heat winners and progress was displayed on a board *outside* the VIP area. There was no dedicated information centre, but the commentary on each heat was enough to give spectators information on the surfing, provided it was audible.

5. Seating/comfort

   Seating in the viewing area was in short supply, and seats were difficult to find and keep. As soon as one person vacated a seat, someone else would occupy it. This was a problem around meal times, when visitors wanted to sit and eat. Viewing from the seating was inadequate, with people standing along the front of the marquee disrupting the view of those seated behind. The grandstand provided good viewing of the surfing, but seating was uncomfortable and difficult to access when the grandstand was full. There was also the risk of sunburn sitting in the uncovered grandstand – it should be covered in case of rain as well.

6. Food and beverage

   Food service was adequate at most times during the event and food quality was acceptable. Pricing of food was reasonable, but there was some evidence of overpricing of sponsors' products (Coke products, Emu Bitter and Southern Comfort). This impedes enjoyment and discourages consumption of beverages as prices were about double normal bottle shop prices. The range of beverages was also limited to sponsors' products only, so, for example, flavoured milk was not available. This appears to be a monopolistic approach to beverage provision at the event.

7. Viewing competition

   The commentary enhanced viewing, although the commentators did not always know who was competing, and sometimes were a bit 'over the top' with their offhand comments. However, a major problem exists with the lack of a PA system in the VIP area, and there was inadequate commentary in those areas. This was a source of frustration and annoyance – people in these areas were not informed of the progress of heats. Other areas such as the car park and the beach had good, audible PA systems. Binoculars certainly enhanced viewing of the event, and should be available to VIPs or at least recommended to all visitors to the event. People standing along the front of the marquee disrupted viewing of the event in the VIP area.

8. Toilet break

   Toilets were adequate most of the time, although by Sunday afternoon the toilet in the VIP area was wet and smelly, and may not have been cleaned all weekend.

9. Special elements

   The VIP facilities have already been described. There were VVIP areas for sponsors, which seemed like a double standard. There was also an ad hoc VIP area set aside for surfing administrators, using a roll of plastic barricade material. This segregation also seemed unnecessary, and left the VIP area feeling like a VUP (very unimportant persons) area.

10. Depart site/leave area

   Leaving the site and the car park was easy, with parking attendants and police directing traffic on to Caves Road. Traffic along Caves Road was heavier than normal, and combined with the trucks and local traffic to make driving fairly hazardous.

- Audience composition
- Accuracy of visitor counts
- Operating effectiveness.

Many event organizers spend a great deal of time and effort in creating the right 'atmosphere' and festive spirit to encourage 'joyfulness (even revelry), freedom from routine constraints and inversion of normal roles and functions' (Getz, 1997). This is what makes an event 'special' according to Getz (1997) and the management of these events has been described as 'The art and science of celebration' (Goldblatt, 1990). Observation methods can record the extent to which event visitors are in a state of anticipation, arousal, actively involved or experiencing aggravation at an event during different points in the programme or periods of the day. This will help the event manager to organize a venue and programme that creates and maintains the air of celebration and active involvement of the event visitors.

The main advantages of participant and non-participant observation are:

- It is unobtrusive and does not interfere with other event visitors' enjoyment.
- It accurately simulates and records the actual visitor experience of the event.
- Multiple observers can be used to ensure that a variety of event perspectives are covered.
- Observers can be trained to evaluate important dimensions and factors (such as the VIP experience in Box 16.1).
- Observers can record factors that event organizers are too busy to observe, or are unaware of.
- Observation can augment other visitor surveys and enable triangulation of data.

The main disadvantages of participant and non-participant observation are:

- Objectivity of observers must be maintained.
- Observers' own values may influence observations.
- More complex events will require more observers.
- Some events can only be observed from a single point (seated, for example).
- Advance knowledge of the event programme, schedule, management systems and setting is required.

In summary, participant or non-participant observation provides a useful form of evaluation of an event from the visitor's perspective. It can draw the attention of event organizers to the positive and negative aspects of the event experience and provide a means by which to learn the lessons from staging events. This is especially useful for recurring events where continuous improvement in the event visitor's experience is a desirable goal. Observation notes provide the basis of service mapping for events (Getz *et al.*, 2001), in which staff interactions, physical evidence and invisible management processes can be plotted on a diagram that maps the event experience from start to finish in an easy-to-interpret schematic. This form of evaluation contributes a greater level of understanding of the event experience and therefore the success of the event in a qualitative and management sense, particularly when triangulated with visitor surveys and financial data from the event.

Economic impact evaluation

Public funding is an important component of almost all festivals and events and it is a given that many events would not be staged without some form of government subsidy or support. Whilst the tourism and management aspects of festivals and events are widely recognized and studied (Allen *et al.*, 2002; Getz, 1997; Hall, 1992) there is increasing pressure on governments to justify public funding of events in terms of economic returns (Faulkner, 1993; Carlsen *et al.*, 2000; Burgan and Mules, 2000; Mules and Faulkner, 1996).

Increasing public funding of events has led to a focus on the methods and measurement of the economic impact of festivals and events as measured in terms of income, employment and investment in the host region, state or nation. It has also given rise to a tendency for those charged with estimating the economic impacts of events to use techniques and estimation methods that inherently overstate the value of economic benefits whilst disregarding some economic costs. The following sections provide an overview of the advantages and disadvantages of current economic tools used for event evaluation and concludes with a discussion of the factors that need to be considered when thinking about the economic evaluation of events and festivals.

Benefit–cost analysis of events

As an initial step in assessing the economic viability of an event, potential benefits and costs of events should be identified and evaluated. The techniques available to conduct such benefit–cost analysis (BCA) are well established (Mishan, 1975), but their application to some aspects of events are subject to interpretation. Dwyer *et al.* (2000) produced a framework that can be used to forecast and evaluate the tangible and intangible impacts of events (Tables 16.1 and 16.2).

Table 16.1 Tangible benefits and costs of events

Tangible benefits	*Tangible costs*
■ New facilities and venues	■ Capital and construction costs
■ Employment for event employees and entertainers	■ Wages plus other employment costs (workers' compensation, insurance etc.)
■ Increased tourism expenditure before, during and after the event	■ Cost of additional essential services (police, road maintenance, cleaning and sanitation)
■ Positive media coverage and images	■ Long-term maintenance of event facilities

Table 16.2 Intangible benefits and costs of events

Intangible benefits	*Intangible costs*
■ Enhanced community pride	■ Crowding and inconvenience
■ Cultural renewal	■ Noise and visual pollution
■ Increased interest and investment in host destination	■ Personal crime and property damage
■ Enhanced commercial and residential property values	■ Resident exodus and tourist avoidance of event area

Tangible costs and benefits are readily quantifiable and include the value of investment, income and employment generated, the estimated level of tourist expenditure generated and other economic activity that can be attributed to the event. Where these costs and benefits are likely to be incurred at some time in the future (such as maintenance costs of an event venue) an appropriate discount rate (usually based on the government cash rate) is applied. There are also a set of 'intangible' benefits and costs that are harder to evaluate but should also be included in a full benefit–cost study. Intangible costs include the overcrowding or inconvenience to local residents associated with an event, while intangible benefits can include the enhanced image that a destination projects having hosted a successful event. A landmark study of an Australian motor sport event (Burns et al., 1986) attempted to place a dollar value on the intangible costs associated with the event, including traffic congestion and parking problems, crowding and road accidents. Potential long-term benefits were also explored, including increased business confidence and entrepreneurial activity that may lead to increased investment and economic activity in the future. The basic rule of BCA is that net benefits (that is total benefits less total costs) should be positive, in which case the event is economically viable. Tables 16.1 and 16.2 include tangible and intangible costs and benefits that could be included in a BCA of arts, cultural or leisure events.

The main advantages of BCA analysis are:

■ Can include tangible and intangible costs
■ Includes opportunity cost
■ Includes externalities (such as crime and pollution).

The main disadvantages of BCA are:

■ Is data intensive
■ Does not consider distribution of costs and benefits
■ Counts 'costs' as benefits and vice versa (e.g. clean-up costs are counted as employment benefits).

Input–output analysis

Input–output analysis is a method of estimating the total economic impact across a range of industry sectors that flows from an increase in demand for the output of those sectors. It is based on a matrix of coefficients (referred to as multipliers), which estimate the overall effect on the value of the output of each sector of the economy when there is an injection of new money in the form of investment, tourism expenditure or other income into that economy. An injection of new money into an economy through an event will have three main economic effects:

- *Direct effects* from increased sales revenue to firms that cater for event visitors
- *Indirect effects* on the suppliers to firms that cater for event visitors
- *Induced effects* across all sectors of the economy when the owners of these firms and their employees spend their increased incomes.

The derivation of input–output tables is based on historical economic data and models the economic transactions between different sectors in the economy and the way that these sectors respond to increased demand for the goods and services they produce. Sectoral responses involve an increase in output, employment and income that is measured in dollar terms. Thus there is both production and consumption effects associated with an event that results in an injection of new money into an economy. It is these effects that give rise to the output, income and employment multipliers used in event evaluation.

Input–output analysis has been used extensively to evaluate events that have attracted tourists and investment from outside of the host region, state or country. Crompton *et al.* (2001) use input–output analysis to demonstrate how the IMPLAN input–output modelling system can be used to evaluate events. Likewise in Australia, input–output analysis has been used widely by consultants to estimate the indirect and induced economic effects of events. Table 16.3 gives an indication of the range and types of multipliers used for event evaluation in Australian states and raises questions about the application multipliers for estimating the economic impact of events. The following total economic impacts of a hypothetical event that generated $10 million in tourist expenditure (including direct, indirect and induced economic effects) for the host state is estimated using the value-added multipliers (Table 16.3) as:

- $17 million in the Victorian economy
- $11 million in the Western Australian economy
- $4.27 million in the South Australian economy
- $13.3 million in the Queensland economy
- $12 million in the New South Wales economy.

Clearly, these disparities cannot be explained by differences in the economies of the Australian states and must be attributable to other factors. It may be the case that some proportion of the initial direct

Table 16.3   Multipliers used in Australian event evaluation

	Value added	Output	Income
Victoria	1.7	–	–
Western Australia	1.1–1.2	2.06–2.13	2.38–2.45
South Australia	0.427–0.608	–	0.542–0.579
Queensland	1.33	–	–
New South Wales	1.2	–	–

Sources: MacroPlan (2000) and Dwyer *et al.* (2000).

expenditure is 'leaked' from the economy (in the form of imports or immigrant labour from other states) resulting in a lower value-added multiplier than if all of the incremental production associated with the event had taken place within the state. It is also assumed that there is always surplus productive capacity on the economy so that any increased demand for products or services does not cause an increase in the cost of labour or cause price inflation. Thus, for the purposes of input–output analysis, variables such as wage rates, prices, exchange rates and interest rates are all assumed to be constant, which is clearly not the case in a real-world scenario. In fact, mega-events can directly affect the level of wages and prices in the host destination as workers and producers attempt to extract maximum returns from the event.

The main advantages of input–output analysis are:

■ Models of national, state and regional economies are widely available
■ Captures initial and flow-on effects on production and consumption
■ Estimates the value-added, income, output and employment multipliers.

The main disadvantages of input–output analysis are:

■ Based on historical data
■ Does not consider exchange rate, labour market and price effects
■ Unrealistic assumptions about surplus capacity in the economy.

Computable general equilibrium modelling

Computable general equilibrium (CGE) models are a more sophisticated economic tool for understanding the consequences of an event for the level of equilibrium in an economy. CGE models are used widely to assess the effect of 'shocks' in the form of new investment or exchange rate effects in shifting the economy from one level of equilibrium to another. CGE models include more economic variables than input–output analysis and acknowledge that some of the growth effects of events may be offset by contractions in other parts of the economy. This applies particularly to mega-events, which can distort or 'crowd-out' the market for labour, land and capital, having a negative effect on other non-tourism-related sectors in the economy. Events can also have a temporary price-inflationary effect on the cost of tourism products and services that will also have negative connotations for the rest of the economy. There can also be taxation, import and exchange rate effects around events that work against economic growth. The feedback from these economy-wide effects of events, when measured correctly, can produce estimates of economic impact that are much lower than those based on input–output analysis alone. It is important to recognize that input–output and CGE modelling are essentially based on the same approach, but the restrictive and unrealistic assumptions involved in input–output analysis are not used in CGE modelling.

The main advantages of CGE are:

- Can measure multiplier effects
- Can accommodate price, taxation, import and labour market effects
- Can measure 'crowding out' effects in labour, product, land and capital markets.

The main disadvantages of CGE are:

- It is based on a range of different economic scenarios
- Models can lack transparency and general legibility
- Models can be complex and require extensive data manipulation
- Modelling is data intensive and expensive and therefore only suited to major or mega-events.

Conclusion

Event evaluation and the study of event economics are inchoate. There has arisen a range of techniques available to event managers, researchers and government agencies to assess the economic and social benefits and costs of events. The tangible benefits of events can be systematically observed and recorded using a combination of observation and social survey methods. It is essential that researchers and event managers retain their objectivity during the event evaluation process and avoid the tendency to overstate the economic benefits while ignoring the economic and social costs of events.

This chapter has described how all evaluation techniques have their advantages as well as disadvantages, and should all be used with caution when estimating the event outcomes. Regardless of the technique, or combination of techniques, used, the outcomes of the event must always be considered critically in order that continuous improvement in event management is achieved. As our understanding of the economics of events and the techniques used in evaluation is refined, the overall management of events as important social and economic phenomena could also be expected to improve in the future.

Bibliography

Allen, J., O'Toole, W., McDonnell, I. and Harris, R. (2002). *Festival and Special Event Management*, 2nd edn. Brisbane: John Wiley.

Burgan, B. and Mules, T. (2000). Event analysis – understanding the divide between cost benefit and economic impact analysis. In *Events Beyond 2000: Setting the Agenda* (J. Allen, R. Harris, L. Jago and A. Veal, eds). Sydney: Australian Centre for Event Management, University of Technology.

Burns, J., Hatch, J. and Mules, T. (eds) (1986). *The Adelaide Grand Prix: The impact of a special event*. Adelaide: The Centre for South Australian Economic Studies.

Carlsen, J., Getz, D. and Soutar, G. (2000). Event evaluation research. *Event Management*, **6(4)**, 247–257.

Crompton, J., Lee, S. and Shuster, T. (2001). A guide for undertaking economic impact studies: The Springfest Festival. *Journal of Travel Research*, **40(1)**, 78–87.

Dwyer, L., Mellor, R., Mistilis, N. and Mules, T. (2000). A framework for evaluating and forecasting the impacts of special events. In *Events Beyond 2000: Setting the Agenda* (J. Allen, R. Harris, L. Jago and A. Veal, eds). Sydney: Australian Centre for Event Management, University of Technology.

Faulkner, B. (1993). Evaluating the tourism impacts of hallmark events. *Occasional Papers*, Vol. 22. Canberra: Bureau of Tourism Research.

Getz, D. (1997). *Event Management and Event Tourism*. New York: Cognizant Communication Corporation.

Getz, D., O'Neill, M. and Carlsen, J. (2001). Service quality evaluation at events through service mapping. *Journal of Tourism Research*, **39(4)**, 380–390.

Goldblatt, J. (1990). *Special Events: The art and science of celebration.* New York: Van Nostrand Reinhold.

Hall, C.M. (1992). *Hallmark Tourist Events: Impacts, management, and planning.* London: John Wiley.

MacroPlan (2000). Review of event evaluation. EventsCorp, Western Australia, unpublished.

Mishan, E.J. (1975). *Cost-benefit Analysis: An informal introduction.* London: G. Allen and Unwin.

Mules, T. and Faulkner, B. (1996). An economic perspective on special events. *Tourism Economics,* **2(2)**, 107–118.

Seaton, A. (1997). Unobtrusive observational measures as a qualitative extension of visitor surveys at festivals and events: mass observation revisited. *Journal of Travel Research,* **35(4)**, 25–30.

Questions

1 Why is it important to critically evaluate the economic and social outcomes of an event?

2 Explain the main advantages and disadvantages of using observation techniques to evaluate an event.

3 Why do economic models and techniques produce different estimates of the impacts of events?

17

A strategic approach for the use of sponsorship in the events industry: in search of a return on investment

Guy R. Masterman

Introduction

Recent and forecasted growth in the sponsorship market (Mintel, 2000) has key implications for the UK events industry as a whole. The signs are that sport, the largest UK sponsorship sector, is maturing with an increase expected in revenue but with new deals slowing. In the newer markets, such as festivals, music, arts and community sponsorship, there are lessons to be learnt, for whilst they are in growth, in order to remain competitively advantaged they need to draw on the past experiences of the sponsorship market at large. Arts sponsorship investment alone grew 23.5% in one year to 1999 (Mintel, 2000).

With increased spending, sponsors have increased their expectations and for event managers to achieve competitive advantage they need to focus on what those expectations are. Essentially sponsors have objectives that fit into one or more of these areas: to increase product or corporate awareness, to develop product or corporate image, to drive sales, or to develop market position. In other words, they seek a return on their investment. This shows how sponsorship has moved on from the days when sponsorship decisions were more philanthropic than strategic. For a strategic approach therefore, consideration of the aspects that are important for successful event sponsorship is required.

There are four key areas. The first is to consider how events can acquire the right sponsor through target marketing and an understanding of the segmentation process where the contribution of research in order to achieve success cannot be underestimated. An audit of what the event has to offer is required, not just in terms of what benefits package a potential sponsor might gain, but also in relation to which target markets the event is reaching. The aim then is to segment the market of potential sponsors into targets that can benefit from the package because they have the same target markets as the event.

The second area concerns the importance of building relationships. Having identified the target sponsors a process of relationship marketing can begin. By researching each sponsor's needs an event can look to how it can meet those requirements and ensure that the sponsor's objectives can not only be met but also exceeded. For example, Mastercard achieved a change of image via its sponsorship of the Brits and Guinness gained a foothold in new markets through its involvement with the Witnness music festival (Sponsorshiponline, 2002). Whatever the objective, it is the responsibility of the event to identify its sponsor's requirements and deliver its side of what is a mutually agreed partnership. This can be achieved by not only accurate targeting but also through the nurturing of existing clients and contacts and the relationship the event has with them.

Thirdly, the critical importance of exploiting event sponsorship rights with support marketing activities needs to be considered. There used to be broad rules of thumb on how much a sponsor should spend over and above its outlay on the event rights and sponsorship benefits, in order that they achieve their objectives. Indeed it was not that long ago that sports events sponsors bought their rights and nothing more and almost sat back in the hope that they might benefit from their involvement. Now the use of advertising, public relations and other tools from the corporate communications mix are used to ensure that objectives are met and that there is a return on investment. Prior to any involvement, a potential sponsor needs to not only research how its objectives will be delivered by the event, but also consider how supporting activities across the whole business can help achieve its aims. There is also a responsibility for the event to recruit the most appropriate sponsors. In any successful targeting of potential sponsors there is a need for a focus on those organizations that can best support and exploit the sponsorship rights they buy. This is because they will be the sponsors that are most likely to achieve their objectives and will therefore be the happiest to renew their involvement. It is also that they will bring extra exposure and credibility to the event through those supporting activities that of course the event benefits from but does not pay for.

Finally, the importance of evaluation is key to the process. Research into the success of sponsorship can reveal if it has indeed met the objectives that were set for it. More importantly it can help identify how the sponsorship can be developed. It is important then that not only sponsors evaluate their involvement with events but also events evaluate their sponsorship recruitment process and how they meet the requirements of their sponsors.

What follows is a description of the process by which events can acquire and then successfully maintain their sponsorship programmes by focusing on the above key implications for event managers. Using various examples from the events industry it will be shown that it is possible for sponsorship to achieve a return on the investment made by both sponsors and events alike.

A strategic process

There are a number of stages in the development of an event sponsorship programme. With the identification of the events objectives, and no doubt an appropriate budget with optimistic income generation targets, it may become clear that sponsorship can become an effective vehicle for the achievement of those targets. What can then follow is a situational analysis: an audit of the facets of the event that could prove to contribute to the development of a sponsorship programme. This audit could reveal a set of benefits that could be bundled together to form packages that could be sold off-the-shelf to interested parties. Past history shows that the bundling of corporate hospitality, advertising in the programme and logo flashes on promotional materials have been regular occurrences at festivals and events. This process, however, is selling what the event wants to sell and not necessarily what the sponsor wants to buy. It is at this point that careful research can be used to produce more productive sponsorships: sponsorships that can grow in benefits and duration for the event. The key is in regarding sponsorship as a mutual relationship.

Targeting sponsors

A successful event is managed by those that are aware of who their target markets are. Research by managers into the demographics of those that attend their events will not only lead to better marketing decisions and the promotion of the event but will also point the way forward for the development of a sponsorship programme. An event that reaches a target market, in sufficient quantity, becomes an attractive sponsorship proposition for any organization with the same target market. An assessment of which those organizations are is required. There are therefore two steps to this part of the process and both require market research.

The first step is an identification of the types of people that attend the event and a clear understanding of the market segmentation process is required in order to maximize all the opportunities. There are no set ways in which a market should be segmented (Jobber, 1998) and this is where events have the opportunity to be innovative. Using new criteria in creative ways can produce insightful segmentation methods and if event managers are aware of how their audiences may be of use in novel ways they will be able to enhance their prospects in recruiting suitable sponsors. For example, a business centre created for one particular seven-day event at the Royal Albert Hall ensured that Minolta-sponsored secretarial services and equipment were used and admired by the executives who had purchased corporate hospitality box packages.

Audience surveys and collected data are required to determine the nature and characteristics of the event attendees. Simple forms of research would include identifying their demographic, socio-economic and geographic profile. Further information could be behavioural or psychographic in nature, where lifestyle information on the types of products and services they buy and what they seek may be useful. The production of such information can lead to the formulation of comprehensive sponsorship proposals that can be directly tailored to the requirements of potential sponsors (Figure 17.1).

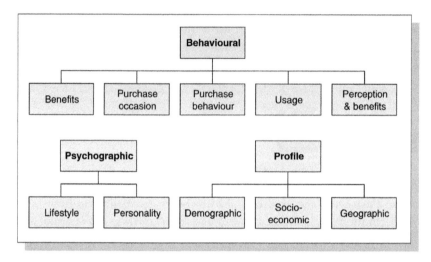

Figure 17.1 Segmenting consumer products. (Adapted from Jobber, 1998.)

The second step involves researching the potential organizations that have target markets that match those of the event. An event can hire a sponsorship agency or consultant to find them such organizations or can help itself by being better aware of the market. Information is being poured into the public domain on a regular basis via company accounts, trade press, marketing media and, of course, events. Therefore, continuous observation and research of other events is important as opposed to only at the times when sponsors are required.

Building the relationship

Having identified appropriate organizations and mutual target markets there is still a great deal more work to be done. The right vehicle has to be developed by the event, together with the potential sponsor, in order that the latter's objectives are entirely met. An off-the-shelf package that has been predetermined without any thought towards the buyer's needs is unlikely to meet the unique requirements that differ from organization to organization. A bespoke approach that considers the individual requirements and objectives of the potential sponsor is therefore more appropriate. This customization requires the building of relationships and applies to new as well as existing sponsors. The building of the relationship for the acquisition of a new sponsor needs to continue throughout the relationship in order that it might grow and that future changes in requirements on both sides may be met.

The requirements sought by sponsors that are considered most prevalent are the development of sales, customer loyalty, brand awareness, new markets, internal communications, business-to-business relationships, new products, community relations, product knowledge, financial sector confidence, post-merger identity, and the revitalization of brand image (International Marketing Reports, 2002). With such an array of requirements there is a need for the careful consideration of the vehicle that will successfully deliver one or more of these and this requires that the event gets as close as possible to its sponsor.

This process involves:

- The mutual determination of the requirements of the sponsorship
- The development of measures by which the requirements will be evaluated
- The development of a series of event rights and benefits for the sponsor that satisfy and meet the requirements of both the sponsor and the event
- The agreed payment and/or provision of services by the sponsor in return for the event rights and benefits.

This process is continuous in that it needs to be applied throughout the relationship in order that changing needs are adequately met and the benefits are maximized for both the event and the sponsor. An initial wooing of the sponsor on behalf of the event will be required in order that the sponsor be brought on board, but this is also needed throughout the duration of the relationship. It may also be that there is a call for the wooing to go beyond the parameters of the agreement to nurture the relationship into growth. For example, a simple allocation of event tickets that are over and above the agreed sponsor's number may well be a wise investment and worth the cost.

One of the key elements of relationship marketing with customers is maintaining sustainability, in other words retaining them over the long term (Piercy, 2000). Varey (2002) would maintain that the key CRM (customer relationship management) guidelines for event managers would lie in the development of mutual trust through effective communication of information. This is of particular importance when considering the complex logistics that emerge in the running of events, the need to ensure that sponsors' needs are met, and to meet the terms of the agreement. However, sponsorship requires more than this. In order to keep sponsors, the quality of the interaction becomes critical and this is where sponsorship innovation can come into its own. The continual development and evaluation of the relationship between the event and the sponsor will help sustain it, but the exceeding of expectations will go further and help it grow. For the event this can mean greater income from an existing sponsor and no costly effort in finding a replacement. The guidelines are that this approach needs frequent and direct contact with a flexibility to accommodate change, and whilst sponsorship agreements and contracts are made for a purpose, the continual reference to existing contractual arrangements and a rigid adherence to such is not going to help a sponsorship grow.

The event cannot work alone in determining the best sponsorship vehicle for a potential sponsor. A mutual audit of event assets supported by a collaborative development of the final vehicle will ensure a more successful relationship and results. Regular rights benefits such as title acknowledgements, use of event insignia, media and print exposure, ticketing and hospitality are benefits that need to be tailored to meet the sponsor's particular requirements, but something else is also required. More often than not these types of benefits will need to be supplemented by some unique element that bonds the relationship together. This could well be the use of the sponsor's products or services at and by the event, but principally it is something that gives the event manager an opportunity to be creative. Orange, the communications organization, for example, is a sponsor at four music festivals, Glastonbury, Reading, Leeds and T in the Park in Scotland, and provides mobile phone recharge stations at each (BDS, 2002). The use of a fleet of Ford courtesy cars at the Royal Albert Hall event mentioned earlier also achieved product exposure for its sponsor, literally on the road and away from the venue. Music festivals not only offer brewer sponsors the opportunity to get products into their customers' hands, they can also drive their sales via sole pouring rights. By getting the product in sight and, even better still, used in the context of the event, the sponsorship may perhaps be perceived as a credible addition to the event and serve to leverage more from the association and the achievement of the sponsor's objectives. Unfortunately, there is very little research into the customer reactions to sponsorship and how sponsorship influences their decisions. What research there is, is predominantly from the sports sector and is concerned with recall and recognition (Lee *et al.*, 1997) where traditionally evaluation has focused on numbers of sightings.

Case study

Capital Expo at the Business Design Centre, London, in 1993 was a lifestyle event that sold a sophisticated sponsorship programme to a diverse range of corporations including Pepsi as title sponsor. The event ran for 14 days and consisted of seven separate entertainment zones for a family-focused target audience. The event owner, Capital Radio Group, used its two London stations, Capital FM and Capital Gold, to promote the event and drive ticket sales. This included live Capital FM broadcasts from the event every day. Lengthy negotiations were held with Pepsi to identify the objectives for their sponsorship and this consisted of pre-event promotional and advertising airtime on both stations, significant branding opportunities at the event and the launch of the Pepsi Network Chart, the weekly Sunday night independent radio show broadcast nationally. The key to the negotiations and the subsequent rights package lay in the mutual target markets of both sponsor and event. The objectives were to increase brand awareness of Pepsi and their new product Pepsi Max to 15–40-year-olds, and Capital could deliver that (researched audiences: Capital FM 15–23 years old, Capital Gold 25–40 years old). The relationship with Pepsi had been established earlier and a mutual identification of requirements and nurturing enabled the greater sponsorship to be created.

Exploitation

The sponsor cannot afford to rely on the event rights alone to achieve the delivery of its objectives. Reaching the target market may well require significant support with other activities that will cost over and above the outlay for those event rights. This appears to be the case the higher the profile and the cost of the event rights, particularly in the sports sector where this kind of exploitation has been more significant. In 1996, Coca-Cola spent over ten times the amount it gave for the rights with the Olympic Games in leveraging its sponsorship (Kolah, 1999). There are cases now where there has been a realization that there is a need for exploitation across all sectors by sponsors in order that they achieve their objectives. This is a key factor for event managers. Such exploitation can bring exposure, promotion and sales for the event even though it is not the event that funds those activities. Therefore, a prospective sponsor that provides beyond their sponsorship fees and services is a very attractive target. Given a choice, the event needs to be able to identify the sponsor that offers the greatest benefit overall to the event.

Case study

In 1999, an event was created for Guinness, and its exploitation of its sponsorship extended over a 12-month period (Witnness, 2002). The event was called Witnness and it was completely different from anything the brewer had been involved with before. The overall objective was to change perceptions of the Guinness brand in Ireland, where 60% of 18–24-year-olds rejected the product, and yet at the same time not alienate existing consumers.

The focus was a music festival in August 2000 but there was an entire lead-up programme that began in the September of the previous year with the inception of an entertainment sub-brand that had been developed having identified the needs of the target market. This brand was to come across as credible, non-corporate and cutting-edge, and therefore innovative exploitation was implemented in order to achieve this. All in all there were three key phases to the event, each with firm objectives:

■ An eight-month teaser period that was to establish and build on the Witnness name and identity, create intrigue and achieve prescribed awareness targets.
■ A four-month period that included a more open message with a media launch and more detail on the festival being imparted into the public domain. The objectives were to drive festival ticket sales, achieve further awareness targets and establish perceived links between the Witnness and Guinness brands.
■ The festival itself was to be the best music event in Ireland, in terms of attendance and quality of the acts, in order to gain maximum media and broadcast exposure and achieve 300% return on media investment.

Over these three phases a number of very creative activities were implemented in order to achieve comprehensive exploitation. These included the following:

■ Police-style incident boards placed at roadsides carrying cryptic messages leading to Witnness.com that in turn led to further online information. They were moved about to keep the message fresh and many were stolen as souvenirs.

- Graffiti posters were created as pieces of art and placed around Ireland.
- Female senior citizens were recruited to visit bars and purposefully give vague information about the festival.
- Video teasers were sent to the media in cryptic police-style evidence bags.
- Contact reports were deliberately left in bars thus revealing information on the bands that were due to play at the festival.
- The use of viral marketing activities to create word-of-mouth information, including the design of the cups that were used to serve Guinness at the festival that looked like they were glasses of the beer from afar, and the making of fake hotel bookings for artists such as Oasis.
- The double 'n' in Witnness titling was used to enhance the perceived links with Guinness whilst at the same time develop a sub-brand.

These activities reached their target audiences via personal interaction but also attracted significant interest from the media, thus reaching greater publics. Witnness is still operating and mid-programme evaluation has revealed a decrease in those that rejected Guinness and an increase in awareness (Marketing Society, 2001).

These exploitation activities were considered to be key to the success of this programme where the sponsor had clear objectives in reaching beyond just the people who attended the event. The event benefited from the sustained pre-event promotion with the result being a 40,000-strong audience.

Evaluation

In order to continually grow the relationship with sponsors there needs to be continuous evaluation of it throughout so that any changes in requirements can be met. There also needs to be an evaluation of the sponsorship against the objectives set for it. Using these prescribed forms of measures, decision making can be improved in order that the return on investment can be maximized.

The evaluation needs to address three key questions:

- *Visibility*. How clear was the sponsorship?
- *Sightings*. Who took notice?
- *Objectivity*. Did it achieve what it was supposed to?

In addressing these questions there are a number of evaluation methods that can be used. These include the commonly used though unreliable media value method; where the amount of brand visibility is quantified as being worth the amount it would cost to buy the equivalent in advertising space. It is unreliable because there is no proof the brand has been seen and rate card prices are used for the calculation when they are seldom actually paid in the buying of media space. Also, whilst logo or product sightings might be cheaper than running advertising, the two are not interchangeable in terms of communication effectiveness (Lainson, 1997). Other methods using media audience measurements include levels of circulation and viewing or listenership figures. The other approach is via the customer, with the identifying of the quality of awareness through focus groups, surveys and interviews. Sponsorship awareness is a difficult area to evaluate accurately and effective evaluation can be expensive, which goes some of the way to explain why so few sponsors and events undertake it. However, combinations of different methods implemented together can produce more reliable information. A detailed list of sponsorship evaluation tools is featured in Figure 17.2.

More recently sales objectives are being applied to sponsorships (Mintel, 2000) and consequently evaluation has shifted more towards sales results (Lainson, 1997). The comparison of sales results before and after an event and over a tracked period is becoming more common. This is as opposed to assessing brand awareness via numbers of sightings in this shift towards measurable rather than intangible evaluation.

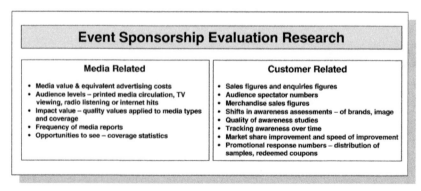

Figure 17.2 Sponsorship evaluation tools.

There is one dominant ethical issue concerning the sponsorship of events and one that is pertinent to the process discussed here – to what extent, if at all, should an event sell itself off into the hands of product or service endorsement. Within the sports sector this appears to have been and gone. It is now not only accepted, it is seen as a financial necessity for events in order to be staged. We have already seen rock musicians resist product overtures for their endorsement where there have been concerns over artistic integrity and who controls artistic content. Now many artists accept tour and festival sponsorship quite readily. The early 1990s saw the Coca-Cola Music Festival feature such rock stalwarts as Neil Young, Bob Dylan and Van Morrison for example. The younger sponsorship markets are perhaps due to progress in the same fashion. Already it can be seen that Bradford's bid to be the 2008 European Capital of Culture is supported by Yorkshire Building Society, First and Yorkshire Television (Bradford Capital of Culture, 2002).

Summary

Ultimately, the sponsor, and therefore the event too, needs to know if sponsorship has made best use of the budget used. Whilst it is evaluation that can determine the extent to which the sponsorship has been successful for both the event and the sponsor, the process must start with clearly defined and measurable objectives that can be evaluated. The process that has been presented here suggests that a successful sponsorship is (a) a relationship that has been nurtured to gain an ongoing mutual understanding of requirements, and (b) a provision of benefits that will require thorough exploitation in order that those requirements are met. Evaluation at the end of the process will help determine the effectiveness and thus determine the return on investment.

Bibliography

BDS (2002). www.sponsorship.co.uk. *European Sponsorship Newsletter*, Issue 20, March. Accessed 1 April 2002.

Bradford Capital of Culture (2002).
www.bradford2008.com/partners/2008sponsorship. Accessed 22 October 2002.

International Marketing Reports (2002). www.im-reports.com/Sample3. Accessed 15 April 2002.

Jobber, D. (1998). *Principles and Practice of Marketing*, 2nd edn, p. 174. London: McGraw-Hill.

Kolah, A. (1999). *Maximizing the Value of Sports Sponsorship*. London: Financial Times Media.

Lainson, S. (1997). www.onlinesports.com/sportstrust/sports13. Accessed 10 October 2002.

Lee, M., Sandler, D. and Shani, D. (1997). Attitudinal constructs towards sponsorship. *International Marketing Review*, **14(3)**, 159–169.

Marketing Society (2001). Guinness Ireland Group and KLP Euro RSCG entry submitted for the Marketing Society Awards 2001: Witnness.

Mintel (2000). Sponsorship report. Mintel.

Piercy, N. (2000). *Market-led Strategic Change: Transforming the Process of Going to Market*, Chapter 6. Oxford: Butterworth-Heinemann.

S.Comm Research UK (2002). www.scomm-research.com. Sponsorship: Maximising return on your investment. Accessed 11 October 2002.

Sponsorshiponline (2002). www.sponsorshiponline.co.uk. Accessed 11 October 2002.

Varey, R. (2002). *Relationship Marketing: Dialogue and Networks in the e-Commerce Era*, Chapter 6. Chichester: John Wiley and Sons.

Witnness (2002). www.witnness.com. Accessed 15 October 2002.

Questions

1 How can the building of a relationship between an event and a sponsor lead to a more successful sponsorship?

2 To what extent is exploitation important for event sponsorship?

3 Analyse the importance of evaluation in the event sponsorship process.

The behavioural aspects of financial management

Razaq Raj

Introduction

Financial management effectively controls growth and should be carried out by event organizations for the protection of creditors and shareholders and generally keeping the company in business. The behavioural aspects of budgeting are a vital part of financial management that is essential in keeping the right balance between markets and the financial activities of organizations with regard to liquidity in terms of credit terms to secure rapid market penetration.

Financial management and budgeting are vital components of event management. It is important for event managers to develop skills and strategies that cultivate and maintain effective control over the income and expenditure of the event, regardless of the size of the event. Budgets must not be used only as a tool to develop the revenue and control the expenditure but also to include the behavioural aspects. Budgeting must also be considered to increase the staff morale in order to achieve the budget's goals set by the event organizer.

This chapter introduces the importance of budgeting within event organizations and it will also provide a general overview of the financial management process. The chapter will outline the most important elements of the budgeting process, particularly the flexible budget and cash budget system for the success of events. It will provide clear-cut accounting terms for event managers enabling them to become familiar with the financial management process.

Purpose of budgeting

Budgeting is about making plans for the future, implementing those plans and monitoring activities. A budget has been defined by the Chartered Institute of Management Accountants (CIMA) as 'A plan expressed in money. It is prepared and approved prior to the budget period and may show income, expenditure and capital employed.' Allen *et al.* (2002) comment that the 'budget of an event is used to compare actual costs and revenues with projected costs and revenues'.

Therefore the budgeting process provides managers with the opportunity to carefully match the goals of the organization with the resources necessary to accomplish those goals. Budget information is used to communicate responsibilities to individuals who are accountable for a particular segment of the organization. Performance measures are carefully selected to motivate individuals or teams to achieve targeted goals.

Behavioural aspects of budgeting

The system of budgetary control can rely heavily upon individuals of an organization to make the system successful (Harris and Hazzard, 1992). The human aspect in the budgetary system can be just as complex as it is essential. All budgetary processes involve relationships between different people within the organization – these can be managers, employees and directors. Chadwick (1993) suggests that 'budgets are in fact designed to affect people's behaviour'.

Another consideration is how involved these managers are when it comes down to the preparation of the budgets. It could be said that the participation from the managers in the budgeting setting process would lead to better performance (Crowther, 1996). This could be because the managers within organizations are able to negotiate how high these budgets should be set for that particular period. It will therefore make them more determined to achieve the targets because they have contributed in some way and they do not want to fail. Sometimes the setting of budgets does not involve the management and therefore the budgets should be set with goals and targets that are fair and attainable.

Budgets can be very tight within some organizations and there can often be a great deal of control from above. Sometimes managers have no say in how the budgets are compiled and they just have to work with the budgets that they are given. Again this illustrates how conflict might arise in events organizations, reinforcing the impact that human behaviour has on budgetary control.

Advantages of a budgeting system

The advantages of having budgets can also make the events manager more aware of what is going on in the business and can be illustrated as follows (Bull et al., 1990):

- Budgets provide a detailed means of controlling all income and expenditure of the business.
- The preparation of budgets focuses management to engage in planning, in looking forwards rather than backwards.
- The responsibilities of each manager have to be clearly identified.
- The management team becomes more 'cost conscious' and this can help to eliminate waste and efficiency.
- The managers throughout the different functions are forced to work together and coordinate their activities.

From this you can see that all the reasons for having budgets will affect the behaviour of the event manager in controlling their business activities and working with the budgets and not against them.

If budgets are set with the individuals who also have to work with them in mind, then this can create a motivated workforce who can manage the budgetary controls more effectively ensuring that all players in the event strive for the same targets.

Moreover, budgetary control is part of the overall system of financial management accounting within an event organization. Budgeting is a system of accounting in which costs and revenues are assessed and measured in accordance with the requirements of the financial management terms. The budgetary control system provides clear and concise feedback to event management who are then able to make corrections to current event operations and activities in order to meet the original targets set.

Budgetary control is not supposed to be used as a device to blame those responsible for budgets when objectives are not achieved. Individuals will inevitably have their own perception of goals which may conflict with company objectives. Behavioural factors cannot be ignored and budget education attempts to enlighten employees as to what the budget is and what it is trying to do.

Budgeting within event organizations

The budget is the most important part of financial management that the event organization will use to make effective decisions. The budget is the key element of each event and for this reason it is important that event managers understand the budgeting process. Event managers often neglect the importance of budgeting, which in return may cause great stress or even destroy good events. Goldblatt (1997) states that 'Knowledge of financial management is essential to the practice of modern Event Management'.

Budgets are designed to carry out a variety of functions: planning, evaluating performance, coordinating activities, implementing plans, communicating, motivating and authorizing actions.

Moreover, event managers often confuse budgets with forecasts. A forecast is a predication of what will happen as a result of a given set of circumstances, but a budget is a planned result, which the organization aims to achieve. It is important for event managers to create and establish a budget for the event. The budget for the event sets clear goals and standards to compare and analyse the actual results with projected resources. The budget is neither mere penny pinching nor a cost-saving activity, but is a positive and integral part of the event's planning and control activities. In addition, budgets provide a formal basis for monitoring the progress of the event as a whole and its component parts towards the targets set by the original objectives and plans.

It is vital for the event organization to produce a budget as a benchmark to provide a guideline for the client. Event managers need to be familiar with the following budgets.

Flexible budget

A budget should recognize the difference between fixed, semifixed and variable costs and be designed to change in relation to the size of event attained. The flexible budget is able to make valid comparisons between actual cost incurred and a realistic budget allowance. The flexible budget approach provides wider scope to event managers to make changes to the event budget. Exhibit 18.1 shows the example of a flexible budget being used by the event manager.

Cash budgets

A cash budget is designed to show the expected cash income and expenses during the specific event or period. The cash budget is the most important tool for any event manager. Cash budgets provide the guide to managers to project income and expenses for the event. A cash budget gives early indication of whether the event is going to make a profit or loss. The cash budget is illustrated in Exhibit 18.2. The following reasons outline why a cash budget is important to the event manager:

- Event managers are given forewarning of any adverse cash situations so that they can take appropriate action.
- Events managers can arrange in advance to cover any cash deficits revealed in the forecast (for example arrange an overdraft, or change stock and credit policies).
- The cash budget is another way to examine the money cycle.
- Cash is the most liquid asset an event organization can hold.
- Cash is constantly coming into and leaving an organization – this is often referred to as cash inflow and outflow.

Cash budgets are also largely a matter of 'timing', and there is usually some degree of slack, which allows control of the final balance by adjustment of the revenue and payment schedules. In addition, budgeting is a successful tool; it provides a general guideline to event managers to produce efficient and effective budgets to gain successful results at the end of each event.

Exhibit 18.1 Leeds Carnival event in the park.

Revenue	Budgeted £	Actual £
Grant from Local Authority	30 000	30 000
Sponsorship	65 000	54 000
Income from food/clothes stands	12 000	17 500
Total revenue	**107 000**	**101 500**
Payments		
Venue hire	4 000	4 800
Advertising cost	3 900	3 200
Printing costs	2 600	1 700
Staff cost	34 700	39 600
Artist fees	12 400	10 200
Stage and lighting	7 800	10 800
Security charges	4 300	3 600
Cleaning cost	6 800	9 300
Total expenses	**76 500**	**83 200**
Surplus	**30 500**	**18 300**

Event managers can use the above two examples to control the activities of the event as closely as possible. The above two budgeting methods illustrate the importance of carrying out a budgeting process to plan and controlling various sections of the event to achieve the desired outcomes.

Exhibit 18.2   Charity dinner.

Income	£
Ticket sales	5 600
Donations	2 200
Total income	**7 800**
Payments	
Venue hire	800
Food/drinks	3 250
Printing costs	425
Staff cost	625
Speaker expenses	275
Total expenses	**5 375**
Surplus	**2 425**

Essential financial management terms

It should be remembered that budgets are intended to influence individuals' behaviour and create individual responses. Moreover, a budgeting system operates within an organization environment to improve the effective decision-making process. Therefore, organizations need to understand the other important elements of financial management. The budgeting process is only one element of the financial management process. In order for events organizations to develop their business performance for the future, they need to understand the following financial management terms. From an international perspective, individual managers should have in-depth knowledge of the financial management process. In addition, it has been suggested that unless the events organization takes into account all the financial management factors, the overall performance will be weakened. Therefore, it is vital to understand the role and concept of the following financial management terms:

- *Assets:* Economic resources owned by the organization that will benefit it in the future. Cash, inventory, supplies and equipment are examples of assets.
- *Liabilities:* Amounts that are owed to suppliers, creditors, employees or the government. If the business receives money in advance of performing a service, they have a liability to perform the service.
- *Owner's equity:* The residual interest or the claims of the owners to the assets of the business. There are four types of transaction that affect the owner's equity:

  □ *Investment:* Assets that are invested in the organization by the owner. These assets can be cash or other assets. Investments increase the owner's equity.
  □ *Withdrawals:* Assets that are taken out of the organization by the owner for personal use. These assets could be cash or any other asset. Bills that are paid by the organization for the owner's personal expenses are also withdrawals. Withdrawals decrease the owner's equity.
  □ *Revenue:* Increases in assets (or decrease in liabilities) and an increase in the owner's equity from operating the organization. It does not have to receive cash to record the revenue, only perform the service. The cash may be received before, during or after performing the service.
  □ *Expenses:* Decreases in assets (or increases in liabilities) and a decrease in the owner's equity as a result of operating the organization. Expenses do not have to be paid at the time the expense is recorded. Purchasing assets is not an expense because the owner's equity has not decreased.

Financial statements

Accounting information is communicated to interested parties through the financial statements. These are the only statements that are available to people outside the company. Companies produce financial accounts at the end of the year to show how the business is performing. By law, limited companies must publish a full annual report containing a wide range of financial information. The two fundamental financial statements are now described.

Profit and loss account

This shows the revenue, expenses and net profit for a period of time. The heading should include the name of the company, the type of statement and the period of time that the statement is covering. Moreover, the profit and loss account includes both cash and credits transactions for a given period and is used as a performance document from which judgements and assumptions about sales, costs, expenses and profits can be made. The profit and loss account also provides a clear picture of the level of net profit a company has made during the year. In addition, managing financial information is a very important part of the decision-making process for business to reflect the performance of any event organization.

Balance sheet

This shows the financial position of the company as at a certain date. The assets, liabilities and owner's equity are shown. The headings include the name of the company, the type of statement and the exact date of the statement. Managing the balance sheet can help avoid running out of cash, which can be an acute problem during periods of rapid growth when financial resources are necessary. Consequently, the balance sheet involves ensuring that cash is flowing into the business and not free-financing someone else's company. Cash is tied up by financing debtors, or when customers are allowed to take excessive amounts of credit, preventing the possibility of short-term investment or the ability to reduce debt financing. Moreover, the prime objective is to generate adequate finance during the year to take advantage of the market and able to compete with rival competitors. Managing the balance sheet effectively is vital for business growth.

Ratio analysis

For many reasons it is important that the performance and financial position of an event should be monitored. Ratio analysis is a technique that compares crucial relationships between numbers in a readily understood form (usually a percentage).

Ratios present an event's performance in ways that allow for easy comparison with other events. It is important for the event companies to produce ratio analyses, because the ratio analyses will provide a clear picture of the areas that need improving in the short and long term. To support this view, Allen *et al.* (2002) state: 'By performing a series of appropriate ratio analyses, an event management company can obtain a clear picture of the viability of the organization and identify areas requiring more stringent control.'

Although ratios may be categorized in many different ways, two of the more important groups of ratios are:

■ Liquidity ratios
■ Profitability ratios.

Some of the more important ratios in each of the above categories are considered below.

Liquidity ratios

These ratios give an indication of the working capital or liquidity position of the business, and they indicate the efficient use of specific working capital items such as creditors, debtors and stock:

■ *Current ratio* = (current assets)/(current liabilities). Gives ratio of current assets to current liabilities.
■ *Quick ratio* = ((current assets) − (closing stock))/(current liabilities). Instead of closing stock, we are using only the current assets that can be converted to cash quickly.

Profitability ratios

The profitability ratios are expressed to show the profit earned on sales, or the profit earned on the capital employed in the business:

■ *Profit margin* = (net income)/(net sales). Gives the percentage of each sales pound that is profit.
■ *Asset turnover* = (net sales)/(total assets). Indicates how well assets are being utilized to create sales.
■ *Return on assets* = (net income)/(total assets). Gives what percentage of the assets is profit.
■ *Return on equity* = (net income)/(total owner's equity). Shows how much the owner's investment is earning.

Cost accounting

Cost accounting is a vital part of any event. Event managers have the responsibility for planning and controlling the resources used. To carry out tasks efficiently they must have accurate and detailed costing information of all goods or services being used in the event. For this reason it is important to have an effective cost accounting system set up by the event organization, which analyses the past, present and future data to assess the final results more accurately. Moreover, cost accounting also provides a basis for managers to take effective action when costs and revenues are being incurred.

The essential elements of costing that events managers need to be familiar with are as follows:

- *Fixed cost* – a cost that remains fixed for a period, and which is unaffected by the increases or decreases in the level of activity. The fixed cost increases with the time span. The most common fixed costs are staff wages, rent, and rates, insurance, and light and heat standing charges. For event organizations to run a very effective and successful business, it is important to keep fixed costs under control. In this way they can enjoy a healthy profit at the end of the year.
- *Variable cost* – a cost that changes with the level of activity. The variable cost is one which is hard to control. Examples of variable costs for the event industry can be cost of advertising, printing, speakers and hiring of venue. The variable cost for event organizations will change with the size and type of event. For example, the advertising cost will be charged for the number of advertising channels used to promote the event. For event managers it is important to understand the role of variable cost, because the pattern of variable cost changes with the level of output.

Conclusion

In this chapter it has been suggested that the budgeting process is a vital tool for event organizers – it helps the organization to plan and control the expenditure of the event regardless of its size. The behavioural aspects of the budgeting process help the event manager to ensure close control of event income and expenditure and closely work with relevant staff to achieve the budget's goals.

The two traditional methods of flexible and cash budgets were illustrated to show how organizations use these methods to control the business activities of an event. These are budgets that analyse each item of the cost and set the standards for the individual managers to plan and control the overall activities in line with set budgets.

It was further suggested that there is another role for financial management besides that of the budgeting system. It is important for the event organization to understand the essential elements of the other financial management process, the behavioural aspects, in order to provide a formal basis for monitoring the progress of the organization as a whole.

Bibliography

Books

Allen, J., Harris, R., McDonnell, I. and O'Toole, W. (2002). *Festival and Special Event Management*, 2nd edn. Milton: John Wiley and Sons Australia.

Bull, R., Lindley, L. and Harvey, D. (1990). *Accounting in Business*. London: Butterworths.

Chadwick, L. (1993). *Management Accounting*. London: Routledge.

Crowther, D. (1996). *Management Accounting for Business*. Cheltenham: Stanley Thornes.

Davies, D. (1997). *The Art of Managing Finance*, 3rd edn. Maidenhead: McGraw-Hill.

Goldblatt, J. (1997). *Special Events Best Practices in Modern Event Management*, 2nd edn. New York: International Thompson Publishing Company.

Harris, P. and Hazzard, P. (1992). *Management Accounting in the Hospitality Industry*, 5th edn. Cheltenham: Stanley Thornes.

Journals

The British Accounting Review: Journal of the British Accounting Association. British Accounting Association. BRI Vol. 27, 1995.

2001 Annual Review. Financial Reporting Council. London: FRC, 2002.

Questions

1 Why is the budgeting system important to an event organization in both the private and public sector?

2 As an event manager for Leeds Students Christmas Ball 2003, prepare a month-by-month cash budget for the months of October, November and December, from the following information:

- Staff costs are £1000 for October, £3400 for November and £6500 for December, paid same month as they are incurred.
- Advertising cost will be £500, paid on 28 October.
- Fixed costs of £2000 per month are paid on the 15th of each month.
- Cost of venue hire is £5000, paid one month before the event.
- 975 tickets have been sold at £35 each, 150 people paid in October, 300 in November and 525 in December.
- Cost of equipment hire is £400, paid in November.
- Security charges are £350 for the event, paid on the day of event.
- Food and drink for 1000 has been ordered at £9 per person, paid in December.
- Cash in bank is £4550 on 30 September 2003.

3 Discuss how ratio analysis can help the event manager assess the company's business activities.

19

Risk and decision making in events management

Phyllis Laybourn

Introduction

In 2002 another milestone in decision making occurred with a Nobel prize being awarded to a psychologist, Daniel Kahneman. His research, published in the early 1980s, shook the foundations of economic theory and its model of the decision maker as a rational, selfish actor. It showed that when making a decision we do not systematically or exhaustively appraise the options but use mental shortcuts or 'heuristics' to arrive at a selection (Kahneman *et al.*, 1982; Tversky and Kahneman, 1974; Kahneman and Tversky, 1996). The debate generated, however, presented a very pessimistic view of the human mind and its decision-making capacities. Essentially, these heuristics were seen to be sources of bias and systematic error in decision making.

This research has since come under criticism (Einhorn and Hogarth, 1981; Lopez, 1991; Gigerenzer, 1991; Gigerenzer *et al.*, 1999). Indeed, just as Kahneman's contribution is achieving widespread recognition in the public domain, so we see fundamental paradigmatic shifts in decision-making research: naturalistic decision making – looking at decision making involving expertise and intuitive processes in real life situations (Klein *et al.*, 1993; Zsambok and Klein, 1997); ecological rationality – evolutionary adaptations, which involve a more positive use of heuristics that allow 'fast and frugal' decision making (Gigerenzer *et al.*, 1999); emotion – guiding and influencing selection (Janis and Mann, 1977; Loewenstein *et al.*, 2001).

What insights can this research provide for planning and operations in special event management? This chapter will provide a critical review of the decision-making literature, introducing fundamental issues and the scope of current thinking. It will also explore risk assessment and factors which may undermine the quality of decisions made. It will do so in the context of decisions made in the events planning cycle.

Event management

A special event is an opportunity for leisure, social or cultural experience outside the normal range of choices or beyond everyday experience (Getz, 1997: 4).

Event management has a long history. However, the basic elements of event management have changed little, only what is possible, what suits the taste of the consuming public and what is morally and ethically acceptable to modern society. There is evidence that market demand for events has risen in the western world and has been attributed to wealth, relative peace (on home soil) and an increasing awareness of tradition leading to 'reinvention' of historical and religious events and rituals (Shone, 2001). Difficult to quantify in revenue terms given the sheer diversity of events it involves (Shone, 2001), it is now a distinctive part of the hospitality and tourism area of the service sector as evidenced from the formation of industry associations, specific training courses and accreditation schemes (Harris and Griffin, 1997, in Allen *et al.*, 2002). Shone (2001) suggests, somewhat cryptically, that events management is 'more art than science'. According to Tarlow (2002), it is the intuitive knowledge built up from first-hand experience of the entire events industry that moves events management from 'pure science to art'. Goldblatt

(2002: 7) states that the event manager is responsible for 'researching, designing, planning, coordinating and evaluating events'. These activities require a balance of creative and logical thinking. Most crucially, for successful management, these thinking processes must culminate in good decision making which spans selection, responsibility and implementation (Mintzberg, 1973; Harrison, 1987).

The pursuit of excellence requires a critical review of the decisions made. In event management this involves completing the event cycle with evaluation and interpretation of the outcomes or legacies of a given event (Shone, 2001; Goldblatt, 2002; Allen *et al.*, 2002). This type of reflective practice is now seen to be fundamental to successful learning organizations (Schon, 1983; Goldblatt, 2002). Greater understanding of decision making enhances this evaluative process through helping the manager to make better decisions and giving greater insight into stakeholder decisions, e.g. commissioning clients, event participants.

Event decisions: an overview of context

Special events, by definition, are non-routine and unique; however, the literature on event management gives a very consistent view that the techniques used to plan, organize and manage them are not unique. Event management has benefited by:

- Viewing events as a service activity. This involves improving understanding by analysing the service characteristics of specific events (uniqueness; perishability; personal interactions; ritual or ceremony; intangibility; timescale; ambience and service; labour intensity) (Shone, 2001).
- Viewing events from an operational perspective, as a project (Shone, 2001). This involves analysis of stages:
  - □ Objectives and getting started
  - □ Planning
  - □ Organizing and preparing the event
  - □ Implementing: running the event
  - □ Divestment/legacies/evaluation.

The characteristics of perishability, uniqueness and diversity make special events potentially labour and resource intensive. Aligning events management with service and operations perspectives allows the manager to limit and organize the type and range of decisions made. The next sections will look more closely at the processes underlying decision making, beginning by analysing different types of event decisions and their associated stages of planning.

Decision making – strategic and operational decisions

Cooke and Slack (1991) use four descriptive dimensions to classify decisions: operational/strategic (how repetitive, novel; scope of impact; short- or long-term concern); structured/unstructured (clarity of definition; degree of ambiguity); distinctiveness (relates to probabilities, uncertainty, risk); dependent/independent (scale of influence; links to past/future decisions; isolated or wide-ranging effects in other areas of the organization). Bowdin et al. (2001) break the event planning process into strategic and operational planning. Strategic planning develops from the setting of a mission and objectives and includes agreeing policies and examining funding culminating in an overall event strategy which will enable the mission to be achieved. Operational planning involves decisions about specific operational procedures and steps needed to undertake the event. It might involve single-use plans for non-recurring events or standing plans for recurring events. Breaking down this complex process into stages and more specific concerns for the decision maker to focus on helps counter a human tendency to avoid decisions. Factors such as memories of past mistakes, group pressures, role confusion and time pressure can all too easily foster a climate of indecision (Hogarth, 1987). The planning cycle, in contrast, generates tasks that must be broached and decisions that have to be made.

In the strategic planning stage the needs of key stakeholders are held in mind whilst there is close scrutiny of the mission and objectives, i.e. whether they meet the qualities of being specific, measurable, achievable, realistic and time based (SMART). Another crucial part of strategy is to analyse the external and internal environments. Environmental scanning involves screening for external factors which might affect the event: political, economic, social/cultural and technological impacts (PEST) and demographic, meteorological and competing organizations and events. Situational analysis or internal scanning may involve screening for strengths, weaknesses, opportunities and threats (SWOT) imposed by the organization running the event. Effective strategic planning involving analysis and screening of risk maximizes the chances of success but minimizes the time and resources spent planning an event strategy which may in the end be deemed not feasible. The event manager must be effective in identifying and predicting the impacts (both positive and negative) of events and managing them so that the outcome is positive (Bowdin et al., 2001).

Schroeder (1993) describes the value of an operations strategy which develops out of and is informed by the corporate strategy. The primary task of an operations strategy is to define a set of operations policies to guide decision making for each of five decisions: quality; process; capacity; inventory; workforce (Figure 19.1).

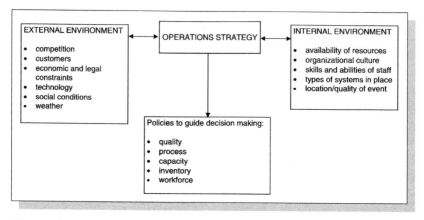

Figure 19.1 Operations strategy, defining policy, guiding decision making.

Examples of decisions under each of the five decision categories are given below.

- *Quality*: Decisions about matching the service to standards set. Involves measurement, informs staffing needs and resource requirements.
- *Process*: Decisions about the process and procedures used to provide the service. Concerns about layout design, purchase and maintenance of physical resources (often involving long-term, high-capital investment).
- *Capacity*: Decisions relating to planning the level of access so that the appropriate number of visitors can attend the event at the suitable time.
- *Inventory*: Relates to the ordering of materials and products needed to run the operation, e.g. food for the catering; information leaflets.

- *Workforce*: Relates to the selection, hiring, training, supervision, even dismissal of staff (this is a particular challenge for event management which is labour intensive over a limited lifespan).

Hallmark events, in particular, require a far more systematic approach involving strategic planning which ensures not only short-term success but encompasses longer-term benefits to the wider community, e.g. a tourism asset. Bramwell (1997) provides an interesting review of different strategic planning perspectives in a review of the Sheffield Student Games. The classical perspective is sequential and formal. It involves rational processes, and operations derive from a clear strategy. Authors such as Getz (1997) and Inskeep (1994) endorse this approach. The 'processional perspective' puts more emphasis on the imperfections and complexities of the human being. It is more pragmatic, where strategy emerges retrospectively through learning and adaptation. Both these perspectives are essentially inward-looking in that success or failure is seen as dependent on management. The final 'systematic' perspective puts emphasis on the social system and political and sociological forces affecting the outcome of the event. It is outward-looking and takes account of external influences. It is clear that event management textbooks incorporate a mixture of these approaches, particularly the classical and systematic perspectives. Increasingly event managers are being urged to plan with external influences very much in the forefront.

Essentially, risk assessment is a major aspect of strategic planning. The following section will examine risk assessment in event management.

Defining and measuring risk

One definition of risk is a decision in which probabilities (the likelihood that something will occur) are involved. Risky decisions vary between situations in which the probabilities of outcome are objectively known, e.g. tossing a coin (risk), to those in which objective probabilities of outcome are unknown and in practice are not easily estimated (risk under uncertainty). In this sense risk relates to probability rather than danger. The greater the influence of external factors, the more uncertainty there is in the event scenario. Meteorological factors are particularly problematic and need to be considered very carefully in large events. For example, the British Grand Prix was moved to April in 2000 from its usual slot in July and due to poor weather resulted in significant loss in revenue (Bowdin *et al.*, 2001).

Slack *et al.* (1998) outline a typology for events in terms of increasing levels of complexity (individual, group, organizational, multi-organizational, national, international) and uncertainty (cost, time schedule, technical requirements). Events with high complexity and high uncertainty involve more decisions of risk under uncertainty, e.g. planning a cross-channel, hot-air balloon race involves many external factors difficult to measure and control. Therefore, decisions of risk under uncertainty are the most intractable, arising when dynamic, changeable and unknowable variables, events or states of the world influence the outcome, e.g. global economy, the weather (Cooke and Slack, 1991).

The more commonly used definition of risk associates it with hazard or the possibility of an adverse outcome and uncertainty surrounding the likelihood, timing or magnitude of that adverse outcome (Warner, 1992). In event management, risk has been defined as the likelihood of the special event or festival not fulfilling its objectives (Allen *et al.*, 2002) but is more often associated with the assessment and management of potential hazards. An event crisis may vary from a visitor who does not receive his or her 'paid for reality' (Sternberg, 1999) to loss of life (Tarlow, 2002). Risk assessment and management should be effective and efficient but not paralysing. It includes three elements of control: the setting of goals, whether explicitly or implicitly; the gathering and interpretation of information; action to influence human behaviour and physical resources (Hood *et al.*, 1992).

Risk categories for event management include (Shone, 2001):

- Staff and others
- Health and safety
- Catering
- Crowd management
- Security
- Transport.

Risks have to be identified, problems pre-empted and ways to manage them fully integrated into the planning of the event. This often involves contingency plans having necessary resources on standby should they be needed, e.g. celebrations on Australia Day, 1998, involving the Tall Ship Fleet, involved a collision of a ship and the wharf. Contingency plans involving tugs etc. allowed swift resolution of this problem and the event to carry on successfully (Allen *et al.*, 2002). How far should event managers go in developing costly contingency plans? In 1999 a bomb scare at the Aintree racecourse resulted in the evacuation of 60 000 race-goers;

20 000 cars and hundreds of coaches were trapped in the grounds. Finding overnight accommodation for those stranded required the help of the Merseyside Emergency Committee (Henderson and Chapman, 1997). With increasing threats from global terrorism, what is the responsibility of event managers in handling a large-scale emergency? How do you estimate the probabilities of this occurring?

Risk management involves the estimation and use of probabilities, possibly the greatest challenge to any decision maker. Risk perception is a human and social phenomenon not easily measured, described and predicted. Inevitably, the literature on risk perception, its influences and consequences, is extensive (Pidgeon *et al.*, 1992). An excellent resource for assisting risk assessment in events is the *Event Safety Guide* (Health and Safety Executive, 1999).

Tarlow (2002) applies the principles of 'Gemba Kaizen' (Imai, 1997) to risk management. Originally devised for risk assessment in production situations, the eight steps and the underlying ethos have considerable worth in the events setting. Key factors are the centrality of the event manager and the gathering and analysis of reliable, useful data. Gemba Kaizen advocates that the manager must maintain meaningful contact with the operational side of the event in order to track potential sources of risk. The next section will look more closely at the processes involved when a decision is made. It will also look at factors that influence the process and circumstances where error may occur. An overriding question here is, how rational are we when we make decisions?

Rationality and decision making

Rational theories of decision making (Von Neumann and Morgenstern, 1944) rest on the assumption that decision makers ought to follow a rational procedure for making decisions, i.e. selecting the option that will produce the best possible outcome. This has much intuitive appeal for the manager (Cooke and Slack, 1991). The decision is broken down into component parts and mathematical equations used to model the decision-making process. Decision makers are assumed to have perfect knowledge and to use perfect judgement. These theories were not originally intended to describe how people do behave but how the ideal hypothetical decision maker should behave.

Models have been produced for riskless decision making, e.g. multiattribute decision making (Keeney and Raiffa, 1976), and for risky decision making, e.g. subjective expected utility theory (Savage, 1954; Edwards, 1954). (See Wright, 1984 for an introduction to rational theories.)

Decision support techniques range from simple descriptive modelling, e.g. using a decision tree, to complex mathematical modelling of the decision situation, usually with the help of a specialist management science consultant. This modelling process is used for different purposes: to help represent or 'capture' the essence of the decision maker's judgement policy; to make comparative judgements of the quality of decisions made; to 'bootstrap' or replace the decision maker (Dawes and Corrigan, 1974). The quantitative, specialist decision models come under the area of 'operations research' or 'management science' (Buffa and Dyer, 1978). Leigh (1983) reports that one-third of the top 500 American firms use some form of decision analysis at board level.

Many of the tools and techniques recommended in the event management literature, designed to minimize error, are reminiscent of these formal, rational approaches. There are clear benefits. It promotes a systematic approach to decision making. It also helps to simplify the decision-making process and exposes the decision maker's interpretation of the salient aspects of the decision. This may promote understanding and critical analysis (Cooke and Slack, 1991). The cost of more complex management support solutions is likely to be prohibitive in many event management contexts.

Research has shown that many managers find these techniques time consuming, cumbersome or difficult to understand. Beach and Lipshitz (1993) state: 'Even when they have been trained to use classical decision theory (and even when they have decision aids to help them apply it) managers rarely use it.' Isenberg (1984, 1985) further adds that they seldom implement decisions prescribed by these procedures if they conflict with their own subjective intuitions.

How many event managers rigorously complete the steps in the event planning cycle? According to Bramwell (1997), even in mega-events there is little evidence of the rigorous application of the full planning cycle being applied. The reality of decision making is somewhat more messy than the rational models would suggest.

The focus of criticism of 'rational' theories has centred around the assumptions of 'perfect knowledge' and 'perfect judgement' (Kahneman et al., 1982; Simon, 1956; Wright, 1984). There is a large and ever-growing body of research which indicates that decision makers are not naturally rational in their approach (Plous, 1993; Hardman and Harries, 2002). They apply shortcuts and make-do strategies which abbreviate the process of selection. What are these shortcuts and how will they impact on event management?

Heuristics and bias

Kahneman and Tversky conducted the pioneering work which revealed simplifying shortcuts or heuristics which provide quicker routes to a decision by reducing the complexity – but in so doing introduce severe and systematic biases (Kahneman *et al.*, 1982). For example, judgements are strongly influenced by an initially observed value. This is termed anchoring and adjustment. An initial value seems to act as a reference point which influences the decision maker's future estimates and judgements. 'Anchoring' has been demonstrated in a wide range of different decision scenarios, e.g. estate agents' estimates of property value being influenced by the seller's asking price (Northcraft and Neale, 1987). Great care must be taken in data collection in event management, since anchoring could affect both participant responses (to badly structured questionnaires) and manager's interpretations. Early estimates, for example, may lead to inaccurate anchoring for future decisions.

Another heuristic or bias is termed 'availability'. Instances or examples which are readily brought to mind bias our estimation or judgement of the likelihood of an event. This shows the importance of managing media coverage to protect the legacy of an event for attracting future participants. For example, the Roskilde Music Festival, in spite of being one of the longest-running, large-scale festivals in Europe, with a reputation for safety, gained an unfortunate notoriety in the press following a crushing incident in the 'moshpit' (the area close to the stage) in adverse weather. Widely reported attributions of equipment failure and drug abuse were all later found to be wrong. However, the damage in reputation had been done (Shone, 2001).

Outcomes which are easier to imagine (Sherman *et al.*, 1985) and those which are more often mentally rehearsed (Gregory *et al.*, 1982) are more likely to be selected. Thus less optimistic managers who dwell on the difficulties or drawbacks of a new-style event or innovation may be less likely to embark on it. The 'availability' bias has been linked to errors in disaster forecasting and perception (Slovic *et al.*, 1977). In forecasting future disasters, people are strongly conditioned by their immediate past. If someone has never experienced a flood they are unlikely to be able to conceptualize it, therefore they will play down the likelihood of its occurrence. Another common decision bias is a tendency to underestimate the likelihood of negative events (Plous, 1993). These have serious implications for risk assessment. The problems which occurred on the opening night of the Millennium Dome, on New Year's Eve, 1999, have been attributed to poor management and planning. A number of factors contributed to 4000 guests being stranded at Stratford underground awaiting transport to the Dome. The management clearly failed to perceive that a crisis was looming when less than half the participants had not received tickets just a few days prior to the event. Further systematic underestimations related to the time taken to undertake security checks on 4000 guests arriving at roughly the same time with only one security gate working. The cost of these errors was high – within a month the chief executive had been replaced (Shone, 2001). As Tarlow (2002) suggests, it is significantly less expensive to manage risk prior to the event than deal with the crisis after it has occurred.

Another significant contribution relates to the perception of 'value' or 'utility'. Kahneman and Tversky (1979) have shown that people apply different decision-making strategies when faced with potential losses or gains. When people stand to gain they tend to be more cautious in their decision strategy. They will select the sure bet, avoid long odds. If they stand to lose they will be more daring in an attempt to avoid a loss (Kuhberger, 1998). (See also Connolly et al., 2000, and Maule and Hodgkinson, 2002, for reviews.)

This might explain the prominence given to any negative experience by event participants. It is an unfortunate truism that 'everyone notices when something goes wrong, but few people notice the tremendous effort involved in getting even a simple event right' (Shone, 2001).

The 'investment trap' shows that current decisions are strongly influenced by previous decisions made. Previous financial investment, costs of withdrawal, fear of failure and losing face all contribute to a potentially disastrous sequence of entrapment leading to risky decisions in favour of a losing course of action (Drummond, 1991; Staw and Ross, 1987; Bazerman, 1994; Staw, 1997). Mega-events with significant social and political objectives may proceed regardless of large escalation of costs, e.g. the Millennium Dome, Greenwich.

To date, more than two-dozen 'biases' have been identified. This research has gained considerable prominence in the field and applies to a variety of decisions including strategic decisions (Maule and Hodgkinson, 2002). It has also been used to suggest methods of improving decision making, e.g. Kahneman and Tversky (1982) describe a simple set of procedures to help overcome 'bias'; Russo and Schoemaker (1989), in a 'cult classic', devote an entire book to describing and avoiding ten 'decision traps'. In a similar vein, Tarlow (2002) discusses the importance of the risk manager increasing their awareness of the assumptions they make and the potential biases that may influence their decisions.

There has been a growing tide of research criticizing the 'heuristics and biases' research for being too negative. Gigerenzer *et al.* (1999) argue that heuristics confer a distinct evolutionary advantage. Terms such as 'fast and frugal' are used rather than 'errors and biases' and suggest that in most circumstances, our mental shortcuts serve us well.

Information and perception

In an ideal scenario, the decision maker is interested, has time, has the ability to plan, comprehend and interpret information, is aware of the goals and has the experience and skills to implement a decision once made – rarely are these fully realized in real life (Drummond, 1991). Event management does not always successfully complete the evaluation stage of the planning cycle. Information collected may be somewhat patchy due to a variety of reasons: lack of expertise; effort required; cost; resources being shifted to focus on the next event. Thorough analysis of feedback of an event can take up to three years. Potential sources of information include both qualitative and quantitative data, e.g. ticket sales; attendance figures; written survey; the use of participant observers giving ongoing written and verbal feedback; survey after the event (telephone or mail); pre- and post-event survey (Goldblatt, 2002). Interpreted information could (a) determine how well the event met the objectives and (b) aid future event planning (Shone, 2001). However, some regard the detailed analysis of event information as 'yesterday's news'. In predicting future outcomes, 'Research mostly looks down the hill and gives an idea where you are' (Griffin, 1994) rather than where you would like to be.

A particularly important influence on information gathering and appraisal is the process of perception. Perception is active, selective and interpretative. It often involves adding in, missing out or amending data (Gregory, 1974; Neisser, 1967, 1976). It is influenced and guided by the personal characteristics of the perceiver, e.g. attitudes, motivation, past experience, personality, mood. For example, decision makers tend to be overconfident of the accuracy of their judgements, particularly in situations where subjective estimates are called for (Oskamp, 1965; Lichtenstein and Fischoff, 1977; Janis, 1982). They also fall into the trap of seeking out or selectively emphasizing evidence which supports or endorses their own decisions (Plous, 1993). A very subjective process, perception influences problem diagnosis (Pfeffer, 1978), selection of alternatives (Plous, 1993) and interpretation of evidence (Tarlow, 2002).

Expertise and decision making

Recent research into decision making in real-life settings draws attention to the development of expertise in decision making. Klein *et al.*'s (1993) and Klein's (1998) recognition-primed decision model (RPD) shows that in expert decision making, a perceptual process, situation assessment, begins the process of fast, effective decision making. Previous experience has built a battery of intuitive knowledge to enable the decision maker to classify a situation as typical or novel and to generate a potential course of action. Before implementation, however, experts report mentally simulating the outcome (imagining the course of events if the option is selected). Only if the simulation proves to have few flaws will the outcome move on to implementation. This method is fast and effective, originally applied to time-pressure decisions, but has since been explored in a wide variety of settings, including service contexts (Gore, 1995; Yeoman and Ingold, 1997; Klein, 1998).

Klein's work reveals the value of developing expertise in a specific context or situation. Whereas the novice seems to engage in a more laborious evaluation process comparing several options, experts will only fall back on this when they find their experience is inadequate. Klein presents a convincing view of expert decision making and also a critique of rational approaches, saying that they are unrealistic: you rarely have all the data; you are often unclear about the methods; weightings, attributes and probabilities and time and resources are limited. 'Optimising is hard and it takes a long time, "satisficing" is more efficient' (Klein, 1998: 20). Thus, Klein links his ideas to the Nobel prize-winning work of Herbert Simon (1956, 1957) by suggesting the decision maker operates 'bounded rationality' by choosing the option that is good enough, i.e. will 'satisfice'.

This echoes Tarlow (2002: 37) who suggests that there never can be a manager who has complete information to assess options: '... no-one can observe everything, no-one can collect all the data needed ... the need to create an internal, professional database is one principal reason [event] risk managers should try to gather first hand knowledge of the entire events management industry ... this produces the base from which professional intuition grows'.

Both Klein and Tarlow clearly show the importance of the person most experienced in any event being managed being close enough to the event itself to be able to recognize potentially problematic cues in a situation and to engage the appropriate actions. Klein is sceptical of courses teaching formal methods of decision making, since they teach methods people rarely use. He further argues that we run the risk of slowing the development of skills. The aim of training should be improvement of situation recognition with the use of scenarios. Another important lesson for training is the use of 'mental simulation' to review the quality of a potential course of action. This would be particularly important in crisis decision making, while an event is going on.

Decision making – the broader context

Personal factors

So far, the cognitive processes involved in decision making have been explored. However, meaningful analysis must extend beyond this to examine other personal, social, organizational and external factors which affect the process. Figure 19.2 summarizes the range of factors influencing the decision maker.

Firstly, all those involved in the decision making are affected by psychological characteristics and processes, e.g. personality, motivation, mood, attitudes, ethics and values. There is a recent increasing interest in the role emotion plays in decision making and risk assessment (Janis and Mann, 1977; Loewenstein et al., 2001). Traditional, rational theories regard decision making as a cognitive activity. Feelings triggered by the decision situation are regarded as not integral to the decision-making process. However, some early researchers did look at emotion and the choice process. Bell (1982) and Loomes and Sugden (1982) looked at

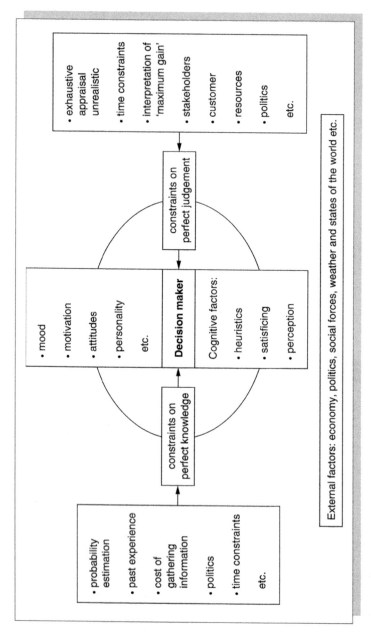

Figure 19.2 Constraints on the decision maker.

disappointment or regret which are imagined or projected later reactions. Other research looked at the general effects of mood, e.g. happy decision makers are more optimistic (Isen and Patrick, 1983) and less willing to gamble. Other research showed that 'stress' and high levels of negative emotion have negative influences on decision making, e.g. lowered attention span, conflicting thoughts, level of clarity.

Newer work (Damasio, 1994; Loewenstein et al., 2001) highlights emotions as sources of information assisting decision making. Affective reactions are noted to be more rapid and basic than cognitive evaluations. This gives people a fast but crude assessment of the situation and the options available. Emotion can also redirect limited cognitive processes where they are most needed (De Becker, 1997). Loewenstein et al. (2001) suggest that decisions made in risky situations are directly influenced by 'gut feelings': worry, fear, dread, anxiety. These feed directly into the cognitive evaluations and action sequences or intentions to act.

Clearly, a new research direction is opening up and suggests that it should be routine to collect information on emotional reactions in risk and decision making. Moreover, observations of gender differences suggest that emotion might explain differences in decision strategy, e.g. males tend to be more risk averse and experience emotion less intensely, particularly nervousness and fear.

Social factors

An organization consists of a collection of people with their own needs, wants and interests. They are internal stakeholders in the event business. The concept of a decision aiming to achieve the maximum gain is, therefore, a logical impossibility. Decisions will be good for some, not for others. Politics arising out of, among other things, unequal distribution of resources leads to the further development of 'interests'. A 'systematic' strategic perspective involves exploring politics and interest groups in the planning process. There are numerous ways in which this influence will be manifested, e.g. information flow. People may conceal problems, implement information-gathering methods differently, provide selective interpretations of data, selectively release information, control the setting of agendas, constrain the diagnosis of a problem, or hold back the implementation of a decision (Drummond, 1991).

The presence of other people has a profound influence on decision making (Asch, 1956; Stoner, 1968) even when there is no direct physical presence of others (Kelman, 1958). The majority of research has been directed towards illuminating group decision making. 'Groupthink' involves an involuntary withholding of critical faculties and can result in superficial problem analysis, biased and selective search and appraisal of information, limited discussion of alternatives and overconfidence and feelings of invulnerability (Janis, 1982). The Delphi technique has been used to circumvent the problems of group processes (Department of Trade and Industry, 1973; Harris, 1989). Tetlock (1991) has examined the social and institutional variables that moderate decision making. He concludes that what might be viewed as 'errors or biases' from one perspective might be rational judgement from a wider, social perspective which considers things such as: people may seek to protect or enhance their social image; they may also choose the option which seems most likely to be accepted by others.

External factors

A whole range of external factors completes the broader context in which decision making occurs. As has been stated earlier, external dependencies vary from event to event. Drastic changes in the broader environment will necessitate fundamental strategic and operational change. These external, environmental factors are the most difficult to predict and control. Managing risky situations well has a positive side with potential high payoffs or opportunities associated with taking risk. One reason an event is 'special' is because of risk – it has not been done before! Amongst the theoretical perspectives surrounding risk, conflict theory suggested that there can only ever be winners and losers, that in a sense, events management is a zero-sum game with competing players and participants. However, the event manager who can perceive the opportunities in times of external change is the one who will thrive and outwit the less inspired, less creative competitors. For 'without risk, there can be no competitive advantage' (Allen et al., 2002).

Summary and conclusion

Event management involves making many types of decisions. Decision making can be related to the event management planning cycle and can focus on strategic and operational concerns and risk management.

Rational theories focus on the cognitive processes in decision making and describe how decisions ought to be made. Many of the planning tools of event management are reminiscent of this approach. They promote a systematic approach, using frameworks or models to break down and analyse decisions. They may also help communication about decision making and the documentation supporting bids.

The rational premises of perfect knowledge and perfect judgement are rarely fully sustained in real-life decision making. Behavioural decision research reveals a complex interplay of influences on decision making: within the decision maker; the internal environment; the external environment.

Recent research on decision making has focused on heuristics, perception, expertise, skill development and emotion. These are important factors for event management.

The event manager who understands decision making is well placed to manage, develop professionally and understand interest groups involved in the event business.

Bibliography

Allen, J., O'Toole, W., McDonnell, I. and Harris, R. (2002). *Festival and Special Event Management*, 2nd edn. Sydney, Australia: John Wiley.

Asch, S.E. (1956). Studies of independence and conformity: a minority of one against a unanimous majority. *Psychological Monographs*, **70**, 6.

Bazerman, M. (1994). *Judgement in Managerial Decision Making*, 3rd edn. New York: John Wiley.

Beach, L.R. and Lipshitz, R. (1993). Why classical decision theory is an inappropriate standard for evaluating and aiding most human decision making. In *Decision Making in Action: Models and Methods* (G.A. Klein, J. Orasanu, R. Calderwood and C.E. Zsambok, eds). Norwood, NJ: Ablex.

Beach, L.R. and Mitchell, T.R. (1990). Image theory: a behavioural theory of decisions in organisations. In *Research in Organisational Behaviour* (B.M. Staw and L.L. Cummings, eds), p. 12. Greenwich: JAI Press.

Bell, D.E. (1982). Regret in decision under uncertainty. *Operations Research*, **33**, 961–981.

Bowdin, G., McDonnell, I., Allen, J. and O'Toole, W. (2001). *Events Management*. Oxford: Butterworth-Heinemann.

Bramwell, B. (1997). Strategic planning before and after a mega-event. *Tourism Management*, **18(3)**, 167–176.

Buffa, E. and Dyer, J.S. (1978). *Essentials of Management Science/Operations Research*. Santa Barbara: John Wiley.

Connolly, T., Arkes, H.R. and Hammond, K.R. (eds) (2000). *Judgment and Decision Making: An Interdisciplinary Reader*, 2nd edn. Cambridge: Cambridge University Press.

Cooke, S. and Slack, N. (1991). *Making Management Decisions*, 2nd edn. Hemel Hempstead: Prentice-Hall.

Damasio, A.R. (1994). *Descartes' Error: Emotion, Reason, and the Human Brain*. New York: Putnam.

Dawes, R.M. and Corrigan, B. (1974). Linear models in decision making. *Psychological Bulletin*, **81**, 95–106.

De Becker, G. (1997). *The Gift of Fear: Survival Signals That Protect Us from Violence*. Boston: Little, Brown and Company.

Department of Trade and Industry (1973). Delphi forecasting. *Technolink*, 1312.

Drummond, H. (1991). *Effective Decision Making*. London: Kogan Page.

Edwards, W. (1954). The theory of decision making. *Psychological Bulletin*, **51**, 380–417.

Einhorn, H.J. and Hogarth, R.M. (1981). Behavioural decision theory: processes of judgment and choice. *Annual Review of Psychology*, **32**, 53–88.

Getz, D. (1997). *Event Management and Event Tourism*. New York: Cognizant.

Gigerenzer, G. (1991). How to make cognitive illusions disappear: beyond 'heuristics and biases'. *European Review of Social Psychology*, **2**, 83–115.

Gigerenzer, G., Todd, P.M. and the ABC Research Group (1999). *Simple Heuristics That Make Us Smart*. Oxford: Oxford University Press.

Goldblatt, J. (2002). *Special Events*, 3rd edn. New York: John Wiley.

Gore, J. (1995). Hotel manager's decision making: can psychology help? *International Journal of Contemporary Hospitality Management*, **7(213)**, 19–23.

Gregory, R.L. (1974). Perception as hypothesis. In *Philosophy of Psychology* (S.C. Brown, ed.). London: Macmillan.

Gregory, W.L., Cialdini, R.B. and Carpenter, K.B. (1982). Self reliant scenarios as mediators of likelihood and compliance: does imagining make it so? *Journal of Personality and Social Psychology*, **43**, 89–99.

Griffin, J. (1994). Strategic linkages and networks. In *Manual of Heritage Management* (R. Harrison, ed.). Oxford: Butterworth-Heinemann.

Hardman, D. and Harries, C. (2002). How rational are we? *The Psychologist*, **15(2)**, 76–79.

Harris, N.D. (1989). *Service Operations Management: Management Techniques for the Service Sector*. London: Cassell.

Harris, R. and Griffen, T. (1997). Tourism events training audit, prepared for Tourism New South Wales Events Unit, Sydney.

Harrison, E.F. (1987). *The Managerial Decision Making Process*, 3rd edn. Boston: Houghton Mifflin.

Health and Safety Executive (HSE) (1999). *The Event Safety Guide*. Norwich: HSE Books.

Henderson, P. and Chapman, A. (1997). Thousands are left stranded. *Mail on Sunday*, 6 April, 2–3.

Hogarth, R.M. (1987). *Judgement and Choice*, 2nd edn. New York: John Wiley.

Hood, C.C., Jones, D.K.C., Pidgeon, N.F., Turner, B.A., Gibson, R., *et al.* (1992). Risk management. In *Risk Analysis, Perception, Management*, report of a Royal Society Study Group. London: The Royal Society.

Imai, M. (1997). *Gemba Kaizen*. New York: McGraw-Hill.

Inskeep, F. (1994). *National and Regional Tourism Planning: Methodologies and Case Studies*. London: World Tourism Organization. Routledge series.

Isen, A.M. and Patrick, R. (1983). The effect of positive feelings on decision making: when the chips are down. *Organizational Behaviour and Human Performance*, **31**, 194–202.

Isenberg, D.J. (1984). How senior managers think. *Harvard Business Review*, Nov.–Dec., 81–90.

Isenberg, D.J. (1985). Some hows and whats of managerial thinking: implications for future army leaders. In *Military Leadership in the Future Battlefield* (J.G. Hunt and J. Blain, eds). New York: Pergamon Press.

Janis, I.L. (1982). *Groupthink: Psychological Studies of Policy Decisions and Fiascoes*, 2nd edn. Boston: Houghton Mifflin.

Janis, I.L. and Mann, L. (1977). *Decision Making: A Psychological Analysis of Conflict, Choice and Commitment*. New York: Free Press.

Kahneman, D. and Tversky, A. (1979). Prospect theory: an analysis of decision under risk. *Econometrica*, **47**, 263–291.

Kahneman, D. and Tversky, A. (1996). On the reality of cognitive illusions. *Psychological Review*, **103(3)**, 582–591.

Kahneman, D., Slovic, D. and Tversky, A. (1982). *Judgement under Uncertainty*. Cambridge: Cambridge University Press.

Keeney, R.L. and Raiffa, H. (1976). *Decisions with Multiple Objectives and Value Trade-offs*. New York: John Wiley.

Kelman, H.C. (1958). Compliance, identification and internalisation, three processes of attitude change. *Journal of Conflict Resolution*, **11(1)**, 51–60.

Klein, G.A. (1998). *Sources of Power: How People Make Decisions*. Cambridge, MA: MIT Press.

Klein, G.A., Orasanu, J., Calderwood, R. and Zsambok, C.E. (1993). *Decision Making in Action: Models and Methods*. Norwood, NJ: Ablex.

Kuhberger, A. (1998). The influence of framing on risky decisions: a meta analysis. *Organisational Behaviour and Human Decision Processes*, **75**, 23–55.

Leigh, A. (1983). *Decisions, Decisions! A Practical Management Guide to Problem Solving and Decision Making*. London: IPM.

305

Lichtenstein, S. and Fischoff, B. (1977). Do those who know more also know more about how much they know? *Organisational Behaviour and Human Performance*, **26**, 149–171.

Loomes, G. and Sugden, R. (1982). Regret theory: an alternative theory of rational choice under uncertainty. *Economic Journal*, **92**, 805–824.

Lopez, L.L. (1991). The rhetoric of irrationality. *Theory and Psychology*, **1(1)**, 65–82.

Loewenstein, G.F., Weber, E.U., Hsee, C.K. and Welch, N. (2001). Risk as feelings. *Psychological Bulletin*, **127(2)**, 267–286.

Maule, J.A. and Hodgkinson, G.P. (2002). Heuristics, biases and human decision making. *The Psychologist*, **15(2)**, 68–71.

Mintzberg, H.A. (1973). *The Nature of Managerial Work*. New York, London: Harper and Row.

Neisser, U. (1967). *Cognitive Psychology*. New York: Appleton-Century-Crofts.

Neisser, U. (1976). *Cognition and Reality*. San Francisco: W.H. Freeman.

Northcraft, G.B. and Neale, M.A. (1987). Experts, amateurs and real estate. An anchoring and adjustment perspective on property pricing decisions. *Organisational Behaviour and Human Decision Processes*, **39**, 84–97.

Oskamp, S. (1965). Overconfidence in case study judgements. *Journal of Consulting Psychology*, **29**, 261–265.

Pfeffer, J. (1978). *Organisational Design*. Illinois: AHM.

Pidgeon, N., Hood, C., Jones, D. *et al.* (1992). Risk perception. In *Risk Analysis, Perception, Management*, report of a Royal Society Study Group. London: The Royal Society.

Plous, S. (1993). *The Psychology of Judgement and Decision Making*. New York: McGraw-Hill.

Russo, J.E. and Schoemaker, P.J.H. (1989). *Decision Traps: Ten Barriers to Brilliant Decision Making and How to Overcome Them*. New York: Fireside.

Savage, L.J. (1954). *The Foundations of Statistics*. New York: John Wiley.

Schon, D.A. (1983). *The Reflective Practitioner: How Professionals Think in Action*. New York: Basic Books.

Schroeder, R.G. (1993). *Operations Management: Decision Making in the Operations Function*. New York: McGraw-Hill.

Sherman, S.J., Cialdini, R.B., Schwartzman, D.F. and Reynolds, K.D. (1985). Imagining can heighten or lower perceived likelihood of contracting a disease: the mediating effect of imagery. *Personality and Social Psychology Bulletin*, **11**, 118–127.

Shone, A. (with Parry, B.) (2001). *Successful Event Management: A Practical Handbook*. London: Continuum.

Simon, H.A. (1956). Rational choice and the structure of the environment. *Psychological Review*, **63**, 129–138.

Simon, H.A. (1957). *Models of Man*. New York: John Wiley.

Slack, N., Chambers, S., Harrison, A. and Harland, C. (1998). *Operations Management*. London: Pitman.

Slovic, P., Fischoff, B. and Lichtenstein, S. (1977). Cognitive processes and societal risk taking. In *Decision Making and Change in Human Affairs* (H. Jungermann and G. De Zeeuw, eds). Dordrecht: D. Reidel.

Staw, B.M. (1997). The escalation of commitment: an update and appraisal. In *Organizational Decision Making* (Z. Shapira, ed.). Cambridge: Cambridge University Press.

Staw, B.M. and Ross, J. (1987). Behaviour in escalation situations: antecedents, prototypes and solutions. *Research in Organisational Behaviour*, **9**, 39–78.

Sternberg, E. (1999). *The Economy of Icons: How Business Manufactures Meaning*. Westport, CT: Praeger.

Stoner, J. (1968). Risky and cautious shifts in group decision: the influence of widely held beliefs. *Journal of Experimental Social Psychology*, **4**, 442–459.

Tarlow, P.E. (2002). *Event Risk Management and Safety*. New York: John Wiley.

Tetlock, P.E. (1991). An alternative metaphor in the study of judgment and choice: people as politicians. *Theory and Psychology*, **1(4)**, 451–475.

Tversky, A. and Kahneman, D. (1974). Judgement under uncertainty: heuristics and biases. *Science*, **185**, 1124–1131.

Von Neumann, J. and Morgenstern, O. (1944). *Theory of Games and Economic Behaviour*. Princeton, NJ: Princeton University Press.

Warner, F. (1992). Introduction. In *Risk analysis, Perception, Management*, report of a Royal Society Study Group. London: The Royal Society.

Wright, G. (1984). *Behavioural Decision Theory*. Harmondsworth: Penguin.

Yeoman, J. and Ingold, T. (1997). *Yield Management Strategies for the Service Industries*. London: Cassell.

Zsambok, C.E. and Klein, G. (1997). *Naturalistic Decision Making*. Mahwah, NJ: Erlbaum.

Questions

1 Outline the key decisions in the event planning cycle and tools or methods used to assist the process.

2 Define risk and discuss approaches to its assessment and management.

3 Explain why an understanding of decision making is useful for event managers and should extend beyond an explanation of decision making as a rational process focused on the point of selection. Use examples from the event management context to clarify your answer.

Case studies and
contemporary issues of arts
and leisure festivals and
events

Attitudes of visitors and residents to the impacts of the 2001 Sidmouth International Festival

Peter Mason and John Beaumont-Kerridge

Introduction

This chapter is based on research investigating the attitudes of visitors and residents to the impacts of the 2001 Sidmouth International Festival. According to the organizers, the Festival is the largest folklore festival of its kind in Europe (S. Heap, pers. comm., 2001). The Festival takes place during the second week of August, and in excess of 60 000 domestic and international visitors come to the small coastal resort in Devon, in South West England, which has a resident population of only 12 000 (S. Heap, pers. comm., 2001). The Festival has been held annually since 1955, but in its early days was small scale and locally oriented in terms of performers and audience. However, by the late 1960s it was a major folk festival in the UK and, since the mid-1970s, has provided visitors with an opportunity to watch internationally renowned folk singers and musicians. Traditional dance troupes from the UK, Europe, Africa, Asia and the Pacific Region have helped give the Festival its international dimension. Unlike many similar events, the Festival is dispersed around Sidmouth itself, in a wide variety of venues, including cinemas, theatres, clubs, public houses and church halls as well as in specially erected marquees. Originally organized by the English Folk Dance and Song Society (EFDSS), by the 1990s it was run by an organization that specializes in music events called Mrs Casey's Music. Although the Festival has been in existence for almost half a century, no research relating to tourism themes has been published.

The research discussed here took place in August 2001 during the Festival itself and later in October 2001. At the Festival, a questionnaire survey was distributed to 490 visitors and, using closed, Likert-scale, and also open-ended questions, gathered demographic data and asked views on the impacts of the Festival. A total of 411 returned questionnaires were usable (representing a response rate of 84%). Focus group interviews were conducted with Sidmouth residents during the Festival and in October and these investigated local views on the Festival.

Research on the impacts of festivals

Economic impacts

The majority of research in tourism, in general, has been concerned with impacts and most of this has focused on economic impacts (Pearce, 1989; Mason, 1995). In terms of research into festivals, assessing economic impact has been a very significant element of all research in the field (Getz, 1997). Hall (1992) argued that, in fact, this has been the single most researched area in event tourism. Economic impact research at festivals has investigated such aspects as the amount of money injected into the local economy, examined various economic multipliers and considered the extent and nature of job creation (Getz, 1997; Hall, 1992).

Nevertheless, Getz (1997) and Crompton and McKay (1994) have indicated that there are problems with these approaches, particularly when calculating multipliers. A key issue is attempting to assess the direct contribution of the event or festival and separating this effect from others in a particular location. Daily spend on accommodation, food and drink and entertainment can be measured in an attempt to ascertain the contribution to the local economy and this approach can help overcome the limitations of the more traditional approach of trying to determine tourism multipliers within aggregated data (Getz, 1997).

Festival impact research has often been driven by the need to discern the economic gain to the venue hosting the event (Getz, 1997). Such research may be an attempt to lend support to existing policy statements on tourism development or to assist in the creation of new policy. As Hall (1992) indicated, events tend to be seen positively by government and industry, not only because of their perceived economic impacts, but also because of their commercial and promotional benefits.

Largely as a result of the perception that they bring economic gain to the hosting venue, festivals and events are often viewed in a positive light by governments and other bodies (Hall, 1992). Festivals and events are also seen as beneficial because they are viewed as adding to the status of the location in which they take place (Select Committee on Culture, Media and Sport, 1999; Getz, 1997). There is certainly some research evidence to support both the contention that events bring economic benefits and can enhance the status of the hosting location (Bowdin et al., 2001; Lilley and DeFranco, 1999; Policy Studies Institute, 1992).

Reference to the concept of 'positive impacts' indicates that it is customary to subdivide tourism impacts under two headings: positive and negative (Bowdin et al., 2001; Mathieson and Wall, 1982; Mason, 1995). In relation to events, Bowdin et al. (2001) grouped positive and negative impacts into subgroups with the following subheadings: social and cultural, physical, political and economic. Hall (1992) provides a similar classification of the impacts of events. Bowdin et al.'s (2001) classification of the impacts of events is shown in Table 20.1.

Although much research into festivals has investigated supposed economic gain, it is not clear that festivals and events bring the major benefits that are desired (Hall, 1992; Crompton and McKay, 1994) and the intended economic gain may not be as large as expected. One significant reason is that locals often make up a significant proportion of a festival audience (Crompton and McKay, 1994; Getz, 1997). Events also have costs (Wang and Gitelson, 1988) and these are likely to include, for example, pre-event promotion and marketing, as well as policing during the festival and clearing up afterwards.

Table 20.1 The impacts of events

Sphere of event	Positive impacts	Negative impacts
Social and cultural	Shared experience	Community alienation
	Revitalizing traditions	Manipulation of community
	Building community pride	Negative community image
	Validation of community groups	Bad behaviour
	Increased community participation	Substance abuse
	Introducing new and challenging ideas	Social dislocation
	Expanding cultural perspectives	Loss of amenity
Physical and environmental	Showcasing the environment	Environmental damage
	Providing models for best practice	Pollution
	Increasing environmental awareness	Destruction for heritage
	Infrastructure legacy	Noise distribution
	Improved transport and communications	Traffic congestion
	Urban transformation and renewal	
Political	International prestige	Risk of even failure
	Improved profile	Misallocation of funds
	Promotion of investment	Lack of accountability
	Social cohesion	Propagandizing
	Development of administrative skills	Loss of community ownership and control
		Legitimation of ideology
Tourism and economic	Destinational promotion and increased tourist visits	Community resistance to tourism
	Extended length of stay	Loss of authenticity
	Higher yield	Damage of reputation
	Increased tax revenue	Exploitation
	Job creation	Inflated prices
		Opportunity costs

Source: adapted from Hall, 1989 (Bowdin *et al.*, 2001).

Crompton and McKay (1994) indicated that there is such a strong belief that festivals bring economic benefits, they felt the need to challenge this conventional wisdom. They discussed what they regard as a number of myths about festival impacts and particularly the economic impacts. They suggested that of the seven myths they propose, three of these are concerned with the supposed economic benefits and another is about employment creation. They argued that an important myth is that festivals create economic benefits. Although this may be partially true, Crompton and McKay claimed that as local people make up a relatively large proportion of any festival visitors, the impact on the local economy is proportionally smaller than if all visitors were non-local. Crompton and McKay's second economic myth relates to the fact that, often, festival organizers derive a good deal of their funding from sponsors. In their efforts to obtain financial support from the sponsors, organizers tend to inadvertently overestimate the economic value of the impacts of the festival. A third myth, Crompton and McKay argued, refers to the issue that such is the pressure on festival organizers that they may deliberately insist that the festival makes money when it does not. Organizers also may claim that the event creates jobs in the local economy, but as Crompton and McKay argued, many of these jobs will be given to those from beyond the local area.

Sociocultural impacts

Although there is some doubt about the supposed economic gain, most research focusing on events until very recently has concentrated almost exclusively on economic impacts (Hall, 1992). Hence, the majority of festival research has tended to ignore or at least play down the other impacts that can be classified under the headings of environmental, sociocultural or political (see Table 20.1). This may be the result of the research being commissioned by festival organizers or councils and requiring a particular focus on economic aspects. Sociocultural impacts are also less easy to quantify than economic impacts (Mason and Cheyne, 2000). It is also likely that research concerned with sociocultural effects may produce results that are less politically palatable than research on economic aspects. This may be true, particularly if what might be regarded as negative consequences, such as increases in crime or conflict between locals and visitors, are seen to outweigh the perceived economic gains. However, as Craik (1988) argued, it is the social effects of events and not the economic that are probably more important. Craik made this claim when referring specifically to the need for local community members to take a positive

315

view of the festival or event in their locale. Without this, she contended, the festival was likely to be unsuccessful. Hall (1992) also claimed that the relationship between the host community and the event is vital for the event to be a success and this point is discussed in more detail below.

A major reason that sociocultural impacts of festivals have tended not to be the focus of research is that they have been regarded as an undesirable by-product of an event (Hall, 1992). This is very much the case when the event leads to poor behaviour and even crime. There is evidence of an increase in crime at a number of large-scale events. For example, Hall and Selwood (1989) noted an increase in both petty crime and vandalism in Fremantle, Australia, during the 1987 America's Cup Yacht Race, and Wall and Guzzi (1987) reported similar findings at the 1980 Lake Placid Winter Olympics. Most of this crime was committed by spectators, and the victims were predominantly other spectators. In extreme cases, events can be the target of terrorism, as was the Munich Olympic Games of 1976.

An important sociocultural issue, particularly at sporting events, but also some arts and music festivals, is crowd behaviour. 'Rowdyism' at sporting events has usually been accompanied by excessive consumption of alcohol (Bowdin et al., 2001). Crowd behaviour was one of the concerns at the 2002 World Soccer Finals. However, bad behaviour did not manifest itself, largely because of careful planning and management, but also because the great majority of spectators appeared uninterested in becoming involved in this form of activity. In fact, the 2002 Soccer World Cup would seem to be much more in line with Bowdin et al.'s (2001) view that events can have positive sociocultural impacts through the sharing of an entertainment experience.

Environmental impacts

What are referred to in Table 20.1 as physical impacts can be regarded as mainly impacts of events on the environment. As stated above, festivals may have unintended or unplanned effects. A number of these may impact on the local environment. They may include increased traffic congestion, more litter, greater noise levels and undesirable behaviour such as drunkenness and vandalism. As stated above, sociocultural impacts are often difficult to accurately measure and this can also be the case with environmental impacts. In addition, environmental impacts such as increased litter and traffic congestion are clearly negative consequences that are likely to be played down by festival organizers, promoters and pro-event local politicians. However, most festivals and events do indeed cause increases in waste, and litter is often the most visible environmental impact. Litter is not only unsightly but may pose a health hazard to both visitors and locals. Consequently, waste disposal is often a major cost for festival organizers (Bowdin et al., 2001). In addition, events frequently lead to increases in traffic and congestion close to the event site and parking problems are often associated with this increased traffic.

Residents of festival venues may also report increases in other forms of environmental pollution. Those living close to music festivals, in particular, may report noise pollution, and this can be a major environmental nuisance at festivals (Hall, 1992). Other forms of environmental pollution at festivals may include aesthetic changes, such as an, albeit temporary, erection of unsightly campsites and other short-term structures.

However, events may have important dimensions that contribute to positively highlighting environmental factors. For example, a festival held in a seminatural location, where the landscape provides an appropriate setting and adds value to the overall experience, is likely to be beneficial to the event itself and may contribute to greater environmental awareness and appreciation.

Political impacts: festivals and local communities

Whether impacts are classified as 'positive' or 'negative', it is clear that they will be largely borne by the local community in the festival location and are likely to have a marked impact on the community. Hence, resident communities in festival venues have an important role, and for the event to be successful it needs at least the tacit support of the community, or possibly their direct involvement.

Literature on the social effects of tourism frequently emphasizes visitor interaction with residents and discusses ways in which the visitors may disrupt activities and behaviour patterns of the local residents (Doxey, 1975; Krippendorf, 1987; Haralmbopolous and Pigram, 1996). However, there is also some evidence that events provide an opportunity, or an excuse, for locals to behave differently from the norms of their society. For example, Hall (1992) reported on what are termed 'hoons' in Australia. These are young males, predominantly, who drive recklessly. It is reported that Australian 'hoons' have been inspired by major motoring events such as the Melbourne Grand Prix (Hall, 1992). In other contexts, local youths, in particular, may use a major event to act irresponsibly by, for example, getting excessively drunk or engaging in acts of vandalism. Such behaviour would appear partly a product of the excitement generated by the event. It may also be a more cynical attempt to use the event as a 'cover' for behaviour that is known by the perpetrators as unacceptable, but it is hoped will be blamed on the visitors to the event.

Hence, festivals and events can have significant dislocating effects on local communities. This may be relatively small scale and short term, such as impacts on those living near a football stadium in the UK, who may feel the need to protect their homes from vandalism and find alternative street parking on match days. However, in extreme cases local residents may leave their home in a festival venue because of their concerns about the impacts of an influx of visitors and the perceived disruption caused to their 'normal' way of life.

In terms of the political impacts, loss of community control of an event is an important issue (Bowdin *et al.*, 2001; Hall, 1992). A badly managed event can have significant effects on the social life and structure of communities (Bowdin *et al.*, 2001). It follows that communities should have a major role to play in festival planning and management (Bowdin *et al.*, 2001). However, as Hall (1989: 32) indicated, in general, important decisions about festivals are taken 'outside the public arena, behind the closed doors of a private office or city hall ... and ... public participation usually becomes a form of placation'. Under these circumstances public participation within the planning process is reactive, not proactive, and will have an effect in only an incremental fashion and then only at the margins (Hall, 1989). Hence the public will not be able to discuss the advantages and disadvantages of staging an event, but merely legitimate governments' and organizer's decisions regarding the means by which an event should be held. On the other hand, a successful, well-organized and well-run festival that helps put a place 'on the map' regionally or indeed nationally can help generate or maintain a sense of community pride and wellbeing. This community pride can be an important tool in the hands of local politicians and members of the business community and indicates that a festival may have a significant local, regional or even a national political dimension.

Methodology

Four hundred and ninety copies of the questionnaire survey were distributed during the Festival week, 3–10 August. These were distributed at nine sites over six days of the Festival (Saturday 3rd to Thursday 8th).

Following the technique used by Raybould et al. (1999), every fourth person passing a particular point at each of the nine sites was selected and given a copy of the questionnaire to be completed on the spot. Research took place at selected times between midday and 9 p.m. and researchers spent approximately one hour at each of the nine sites. A total of 420 completed questionnaires were returned, of which 411 were usable. A variety of question types was employed including open-ended, closed (e.g. 'Yes/No' type) and Likert-scale (e.g. respondents give their views on a statement using a scale from 1 to 5 in which '1' is 'Strongly Agree', '5' is 'Strongly Disagree' and '3', the midpoint, is 'Don't Know'). The statements used in the Likert-scale questions were generated from media and the organizer's comments and their design was informed by the research conducted by Raybould et al. (1999) and attitudinal survey research suggested by Ryan (1995) and Mason and Cheyne (2000).

Given the importance of the involvement, or at least the tacit support, of the local community with regard to a festival (see Hall, 1989, 1992) acquiring the views of members of the Sidmouth community was regarded as desirable. Local media and the organizer (S. Heap, pers. comm., 2001) suggested that locals made up a significant proportion of the Festival audience. As the Festival takes place in several venues in Sidmouth, it was assumed that a number of impacts, particularly eco-nomic, but also social and environmental, would occur and residents would be aware of, and have views on, these. The organizer indicated that some locals would have direct economic involvement in the Festival (S. Heap, pers. comm., 2001). In addition, it was clear that many Sidmouth residents did not have any economic stake in the Festival. Hence it was decided to run two focus groups, one involving local traders with an economic involvement in the Festival, and the other comprising residents with no direct Festival involvement. For each of the two focus groups, selection of those to participate was made by East Devon District Council staff. Each of the focus groups followed a semistructured format with the same questions asked, although the sequence was not identical in each. On each occasion, responses were recorded on audiotape, with the permission of respondents having been obtained.

In summary, the main research instruments in relation to the Festival were as follows:

- a questionnaire survey used with Festival visitors
- a focus group involving a sample of Sidmouth residents
- a focus group involving a sample of Festival traders.

The questionnaire survey was conducted during the Festival week; one focus group was held during the Festival and the second with 'traders' in October 2001.

Results from the questionnaire survey

Demographic data from the questionnaire survey indicated that just over half (54%) of those questioned in the questionnaire survey were female and just under half (46%) were male. In terms of age, over 70% of Festival visitors were over 40 years old (including 18% over 60 years old). Only 16% were under 30 years old. Festival visitors were generally well educated, with just over half the respondents (52%) having at least an undergraduate degree, including over one-fifth (22%) with a postgraduate qualification. Different types of visitor groups attended the Festival. Approximately one-third comprised 'traditional couples', another third were couples without children and approximately a quarter were 'solo' without children. Approximately 10% were single parents. The majority of visitors were relatively well-off. The household income of 44% of respondents was in excess of £30 000 per annum. (The average annual income in late 2001 was £23 600.) In relation to place of residence, just under a quarter of visitors (24%) were from Devon including 14% from the East Devon and Exeter region and approximately one-fifth (18%) were from elsewhere in the South West. However, at least two in every five (41%) came from a region encompassing the Midlands, South-East England and East Anglia. This indicates that at least in terms of visitors, the Festival is of national importance. A small proportion of the sample (3%) came from continental EU countries and another 3% from other overseas countries.

Three-quarters of respondents had visited the Festival before (with a third visiting more than five times before). However, just under a quarter (23%) were making their first visit. The Festival is important in terms of the tourism sector 'Visiting Friends and Relatives'. Over half of respondents (54%) attended with family members and/or friends. Approximately half the visitors (53%) had season tickets and just under half (47%) were day visitors. In terms of transport to the Festival, over 90% of respondents used a car. In addition, as approximately 4% of visitors indicated that they used a camper-van, almost nineteen out of twenty Festival visitors arrived in a private motor vehicle. Most of the small number who travelled by train were overseas visitors. Festival visitors used a wide range of accommodation. One-fifth of respondents were camping at a Festival site, another 14% were camping elsewhere and 7% stayed in caravans. Approximately 11% stayed in bed-and-breakfast accommodation, 9% were in self-catering accommodation and 8% in hotels. Approximately 12% stayed with friends and relatives. However, approximately one-fifth (19%) were visiting the Festival from home.

Impacts

Visitors were asked to indicate how much they spent per day on various items at the Festival. The question did not involve a scale, but was open-ended and respondents completed using a figure of their choice. The great majority of responses in each of the categories 'Food and Drink', Live Entertainment' and 'Accommodation' were in the range £10–25. Respondents spent, on average, £17 per day on food and drink, £16 per day on live entertainment and £19 per day on accommodation. Respondents were asked what proportion of their daily spend actually took place at the Festival. Just under half (45%) of respondents indicated that they spent more than 60% of their daily amount at the Festival, although just over a quarter (28%) indicated they spent less than 20% of their daily amount at the Festival.

Questionnaire respondents were also asked to give their views on statements concerned with impacts of the Festival. The views were expressed using a five-point Likert-scale in relation to ten statements. Figure 20.1 indicates the mean scores for each of the ten statements.

This question revealed largely positive views on the Festival, with high proportions responding positively to the following statements: 'The Festival crowd is generally well behaved', 'The Festival makes a major contribution to the Sidmouth economy', 'Sidmouth's atmosphere is enhanced by the Festival' and 'Sidmouth locals are generally welcoming to visitors', although views were not quite as positive in relation to the statement 'The Festival contributes to greater international understanding'. Questionnaire respondents to this Likert-scale question suggested that parking was a significant problem during the Festival. However, they did not believe that 'drunkenness', 'noise', 'overcrowding' or 'litter' were major problems.

Respondents were asked two closed (Yes/No) questions about the impacts of the Festival. In relation to each of these questions they had the opportunity to provide reasons for their responses. Visitors were

Sidmouth's atmosphere is enhanced by the Festival	4.4
Local people are generally friendly and welcoming during the Festival	4.1
The level of noise is excessive during the Festival	2.1
Litter is a problem during the Festival	2.6
The Festival makes a major contribution to the Sidmouth economy	4.4
Parking in Sidmouth is a problem during the Festival	3.9
The Festival crowd is generally well-behaved	4.6
The Festival makes an important contribution to international understanding	3.9
Drunkenness is a significant problem during the Festival	2.3
There are too many people in the streets during the Festival	2.1

Figure 20.1 Mean scores for Likert-scale question on visitor attitudes to the Sidmouth International Festival ('5' is 'Strongly Agree', '4' 'Agree', '3' 'Don't Know', '2' 'Disagree' and '1' 'Strongly Disagree').

almost unanimous in their view that the Festival was a positive experience for them, suggesting that the atmosphere, quality of folk music, the entertainment factor and cultural dimensions were particularly important. In response to the second of these closed questions, visitors also believed that Sidmouth residents viewed the Festival in a largely positive way, with the contribution to the local economy, the enhancement of Sidmouth's atmosphere and cultural aspects important contributory factors.

Results from the focus groups

The focus group research revealed a wide range of views on the impacts of the Festival. There was a unanimous view in each focus group that the Festival was a considerable asset to Sidmouth and should continue. However, several of those involved believed there was a good deal of opposition to the Festival within Sidmouth itself.

In the focus group that was conducted during the Festival week itself (involving those with no economic stake in the Festival) concern was expressed about a perceived local, vocal minority who opposed the Festival. This focus group also suggested that the local media tended to portray a negative image of the Festival. However, they claimed that the Festival was a considerable asset to Sidmouth. This group believed that the Festival had lost some of its original ethos, particularly the cultural and international aspects. They suggested that, to some extent, a commercial spirit now prevailed, but they accepted that this was probably due to a different organization in charge of the Festival, compared with EFDSS. Hence, it was almost inevitable that such an organization would need to make the Festival more commercial to enable it to survive, they believed. A minority view in the group was that the Festival was too large and too commercial and contributed to congestion and parking problems. A member of a local church suggested that recently the Festival had lost much of its international dimension and the positive cultural aspects that this had brought in the past were no longer significant. Others accepted that the Festival had grown, but had not yet reached a threshold level.

In the focus group involving traders, there was disagreement amongst the hoteliers present on the economic importance of the Festival. Some indicated that their trade was little affected by the Festival, while others suggested that a very high proportion of their income was made during the Festival. However, a representative from a local sports club indicated the economic importance of the Festival when suggesting that almost all of the club's annual income was derived from allowing its field to be used for car parking during the Festival.

Discussion

The demographic information collected indicates that a large number of visitors were in a relatively high-income bracket. Data on daily spend on 'entertainment' and 'food and drink' would seem to provide support for the notion of relatively wealthy visitors. If these figures are accepted as reliable (average daily 'food and drink' spend £17, and that on 'entertainment' £16), with 60 000 visitors during the Festival week, this should lead to an injection of £1.02 million on 'food and drink' and £0.96 million on 'entertainment', respectively, into the local economy. However, results indicating that approximately 60% of visitors spent less than half their full daily amount on these items at the Festival itself should be noted here. Also of particular importance here is the percentage of Festival visitors who were local (see Crompton and McKay, 1994) and would be spending their money in the local area anyway. In relation to the Festival research, approximately one-fifth were local, hence the extra money injected into the local economy spent on 'food and drink' and 'entertainment' would be one-fifth below that calculated above.

The results indicate that Festival visitors used a wide range of accommodation. Respondents indicated that they spend on average £19 per day on accommodation. With 60 000 visitors this would yield £1.14 million. However, not only is the point made previously, that one-fifth of the visitors are local, relevant when calculating the amount generated through accommodation, but also the survey results indicate that as many as 14% of visitors stayed with friends and relatives. When considering the importance of the Festival for conventional accommodation providers (hotels/ bed and breakfast), it should be noted that one-fifth of visitors stayed at the Festival campsite. Also of importance when assessing the benefit to local accommodation providers is that almost half the respondents were day visitors, and although three-quarters of these were staying in local accommodation, some were staying with friends and relatives in the area, and others were staying/living non-locally.

In summary, even when calculating the impact of daily spend, and as Getz (1997) claimed, this is a preferable method to the use of multipliers, care needs to be taken, as it appears very easy, as Crompton and McKay (1994) argued, to overestimate the economic gain from a festival.

However, the questionnaire survey results indicate a very high percentage of Festival visitors are 'regulars'. This provides some evidence that the Festival will have continued economic viability. Responses to the Likert-scale questions indicating that the visitors believe the Festival makes a major contribution to the local economy adds some support to this view. Nevertheless, despite the Festival attracting a wide range of visitor groups, in particular couples and families, the preponderance of an older age range indicates that the Festival's long-term economic sustainability must be in question. However, comments, made on some questionnaires and statements during focus groups, reveal that three generations of some families now regularly attend the Festival and this may help to ensure its longevity.

Sociocultural and environmental impacts are often linked at festivals and events. For example, conflict between locals and visitors may be limited to noisy behaviour, but in more extreme cases can take the form of theft, vandalism, serious damage to property and disruption to local services (Bowdin et al., 2001). For almost 50 years, the Sidmouth Festival has been marketed as an international event and its history has been one in which cultural awareness and appreciation has been promoted (S. Heap, pers. comm., 2001). Under these conditions, it could be assumed the understanding and tolerance will be a feature of crowd behaviour (Bowdin *et al.*, 2001). The research generally confirms this to be the case. A number of factors may contribute to a largely well-behaved crowd. The Festival is dispersed around the town in venues of different sizes, so there is no single, continuous spatial and temporal focal point for disruptive activity to occur. The visitors are a mixture of ages and visitor type, which means one potentially disruptive group does not predominate. It is likely that the generally older age range also means lower policing problems. Many of the audience are return visitors to the Festival, which means, it can be assumed, that they know what to expect. With approximately one-fifth of visitors from the local area, this may also contribute to the general lack of conflict between visitors and the host community.

In terms of the local political dimension, although the Festival has lost some of its international dimensions and has probably become more commercialized, in general it appears supported by the local community (see Hall, 1992). However, there is a perception, particularly in the focus groups, that a vocal minority opposes it. The local media may also over-represent the views of this supposed anti-Festival group. Statements in the focus groups indicated, however, that some local youths use the Festival for an excuse to get drunk and indulge in rowdy behaviour (see Bowdin *et al.*, 2001). However, this has not, as yet, reached the level of the 'hoon' behaviour reported on by Hall (1989). Nevertheless, a number of residents as well as sections of the local media portray this activity as caused by Festival visitors.

In relation to specific environmental considerations, both the questionnaire survey and focus group results suggest that Sidmouth is viewed largely as an excellent venue for this type of Festival and the environmental context enhances it (see Bowdin *et al.*, 2001). In the focus group conducted during the Festival, several of those present indicated that the Festival 'put Sidmouth on the map'. One of the focus group members indicated that the most familiar image of Sidmouth was of a very conservative coastal resort that traditionally catered for upmarket hotel-based visitors. The Festival helped to counter this image, she contended. This not only helped promote an alternative image, but, she argued, helped her and at least some other residents feel more part of and even proud of the town. However, she also stated that she knew not everyone felt this way, and referred to some residents who actually left Sidmouth to escape during the Festival.

Festival and Events Management

With as many as five times the resident population present during the Festival, a number of pressures are placed on local services. Clearly, there is a great increase in litter. Local contractors maintain a daily waste collection service during the Festival and there is a major clean-up in Sidmouth after the Festival. This may explain why, both during and after the event, litter is not perceived as a major issue.

It could be expected that this large influx of visitors would contribute to a perception of an increase in noise or crowding. The results from the questionnaire survey do not support this, however. It would appear that the Festival, spread spatially and temporally in the town, contributes to a feeling of a shared positive experience both within the crowd and between locals and visitors (Bowdin et al., 2001).

However, the major environmental issue at the Festival relates to car usage. The questionnaire survey results, in terms of visitor origins, indicate the Festival is of national importance as a large number of visitors are from other parts of Britain. A very high percentage of visitors use cars to get to the Festival. Car parking and related congestion problems appear to be the major negative environmental impact of the Festival and arguably the single most important issue of concern to locals and visitors. The Council response to date has been to increase car parking provision but also put up charges during the Festival. However, the Council also hire extra car park attendants and require more traffic wardens and police during the Festival. It was not possible to ascertain (and appears unclear to the Council) whether the extra revenue from car parking charges exceeds, or is indeed exceeded by, the extra traffic related cost incurred and should form the focus of any future Sidmouth International Festival related research.

Conclusions

It is clear that the Festival leads to benefits for the Sidmouth economy. However, the questionnaire results indicate that it is easy to overemphasize this economic gain, particularly as a significant minority of visitors are from the local area.

The presence of a significant proportion of locals at the Festival appears beneficial in relation to sociocultural and environmental effects, in that it probably helps to reduce the potential for visitor/host conflict.

The Festival crowd seems well behaved and there is, largely, local support for the Festival. Nevertheless, there appears to be a small, local minority who are vocal in their opposition to the Festival. Continued community support for the Festival will be vital for its long-term survival.

In terms of environmental factors, Sidmouth is regarded as a very good setting for the Festival, but car parking problems and traffic congestion are the most important negative impacts of the Festival.

Bibliography

Bowdin, G., McDonnell, I., Allen, J. and O'Toole, W. (2001). *Events Management*. Oxford: Butterworth-Heinemann.

Craik, J. (1988). The social impacts of tourism. In *Frontiers in Australian Tourism: The Search for New Perspectives in Policy Development and Research* (B. Faulkner and M. Fagence, eds), pp. 17–31.Canberra: Bureau of Tourism Research.

Crompton, J. and McKay, S. (1994). Measuring the economic impact of festivals and events. Some myths, misapplications and ethical dilemmas. *Festival Management and Event Tourism*, **2(1)**, 33–43.

Doxey, G. (1975). A causation theory of visitor-resident irritants, methodology and research inferences. *Conference Proceedings: Sixth Annual Conference of Travel Research Association*, San Diego, pp. 195–198.

Getz, D. (1997). *Event Management and Event Tourism*. New York: Cognizant Communications Corporation.

Hall, C.M. (1989). Hallmark events and the planning process. In *The Planning and Evaluation of Hallmark Events* (G. Syme, B. Shaw, D. Fenton and W. Mueller, eds), pp. 20–39. Aldershot: Avebury.

Hall, C.M. (1992). *Hallmark Tourist Events*. London: Belhaven Press.

Hall, C.M. and Selwood, H. (1989). America's cup lost, Paradise retained? The dynamics of hallmark events. In *The Planning and Evaluation of Hallmark Events* (G. Syme, B. Shaw, D. Fenton and W. Mueller, eds), pp. 103–118. Aldershot: Avebury.

Haralmbopolous, N. and Pigram, A. (1996). Perceived impacts of tourism: the case of Samos. *Annals of Tourism Research*, **23**, 503–526.

Krippendorf, J. (1987). *The Holidaymakers*. London: Heinemann.

Lilley, W. and DeFranco, L.J. (1999). *The Economic Impact of the European Grand Prix*. Washington DC: InContext Inc.

Mason, P. (1995). *Tourism: Environmental and Development Perspectives*. Godalming: World Wide Fund for Nature.

Mason, P. and Cheyne, J. (2000). Resident attitudes to a tourism development. *Annals of Tourism Research*, **27(2)**, 391–411.

Mathieson, A. and Wall, G. (1982). *Tourism: Economic, Social and Environmental Impacts*. London: Longman.

Pearce, D. (1989). *Tourist Development*. London: Longman.

Policy Studies Institute (1992). Arts festivals. *Cultural Trends*, 15. London: Policy Studies Institute.

Raybould, M., Digance, J. and McCullough, C. (1999). Fire and Festival: authenticity and visitor motivation at an Australian Folk Festival, *Pacific Tourism Review*, **3**, 201–212.

Ryan, C. (1995). *Researching Tourist Satisfaction*. London, Routledge.

Select Committee on Culture, Media and Sport (1999). *Staging International Sporting Events: Fourth Report*. London: The Stationery Office.

Wall, G. and Guzzi, J. (1987). *Socio-economic Analyses of the 1980 and 1988 Winter Olympics*. Waterloo, Canada: University of Waterloo.

Wang, P. and Gitelson, R. (1988). Economic limitations of festivals and other hallmark events. *Leisure Industry Report*, **4(5)**, 14–25.

Acknowledgement

The authors would like to thank East Devon District Council (EDDC) for their financial and technical support for the research conducted at the 2001 Sidmouth Festival. In particular, the authors would like to acknowledge the work of Claire Stein, Arts Development Officer, EDDC and her team. The authors would also like to thank Steve Heap, the Festival Organiser, for his help with, and support for, the research.

Questions

1 What reasons would you give for the majority of Sidmouth residents being supportive of the Festival?

2 Under what conditions could there be conflict between locals and visitors to the Festival?

3 How could parking problems at the Festival be alleviated and what could be the consequences of this?

Wine tourism events: Apulia, Italy

Marina Novelli

Introduction

This chapter examines empirical research conducted in the Apulia region of Italy, followed by an evaluation of the role of festivals and events in wine tourism development. Particular attention will be given to certain events, such as the *Cantine Aperte* (Open Cellars), the *Calici di Stelle* (Chalices of Stars), the *Benvenuta Vendemmia* (Welcome Wine Harvest) and the *sagre* (local festivals) taking place throughout the year. The chapter also includes considerations on the importance of implementing a general tourism strategy, aiming to identify a balanced tourism portfolio in harmony with the environment, meeting the interests of the local community, and providing adequate opportunities to the tourists.

Background

Since the Second World War, the relationship between the rural environment and free-time activities has changed remarkably. Recreation and tourism have become dominant agents in the transformation and control of the landscape and of local communities, determining strong consequences on their cultural, political, economical and natural environment. Since the early 1980s, rural areas have been affected either by a declining agricultural production or by a change to less labour-intensive farming methods, followed by a growing flow of people abandoning the countryside in search of better economic opportunities. As a consequence, rural communities have had to look for new ways to address problems of their declining economy and peripheral status.

In this context, government planners looked at tourism as a possible tool for agricultural diversification and job creation. Since the mid-1980s, tourism has demonstrated itself as a popular avenue for economic revitalization (Bramwell and Lane, 1993) and a key component in the regeneration process of affected regions.

In Italy, the rediscovery of the countryside started at the beginning of the 1970s. First in Trentino and Valle d'Aosta, then in Tuscany, rural tourism developed mainly because of certain favourable conditions to its growth. The increasing interest of tourists in the natural environment and sport activities such as skiing and trekking, and the presence of numerous mountain cottages and farms, were some of the key factors.

The Apulia region has seen the rise of this phenomenon since the beginning of the 1980s, due to the increasing interest in the countryside lifestyle by certain citizens in search of a better quality of life. On the other hand, the growing abandonment of agricultural areas by local communities became a matter of concern for government at the municipality level. Rural tourism appeared as the most appropriate form of economic diversification for the region.

On 22 May 1985, Apulia was the first region in Italy to implement a law on agrotourism called *Interventi a favore dell'Agriturismo*. This was followed by a national version called *Disciplina dell'Agriturismo* on 5 December 1985.

In the context of growing rural decline, the EU implemented a set of programmes to face the countryside crisis and support tourism. A set of criteria was established to identify EU regions in need of economic and social development. According to this, the EU Structural Funds offered the opportunity to certain regions to diversify their economy also through rural tourism.

The Apulian Government implemented numerous initiatives aimed at the agricultural diversification of the region and to the development of an established rural tourism sector. Relevant financial help was given by the EU Structural Funds, which were implemented in the form of a programme named *Programma Operativo Plurifondo* (two phases: P.O.P.1991/93 and P.O.P.1994/99) (Regione Puglia, 1999).

The LEADER programme (*Liaisons Entre Actions pour la Développement des Economies Rurales* – LEADER I, LEADER II, LEADER+) has been operating under the umbrella of Agricultural Policy and Rural Development for the advancement of disadvantaged rural areas of the EU. It was realized to encourage private and community-based initiatives and rural development. In Apulia, they have been adopted to support private projects and to guide and order the fragmented and often 'independent' set of rules implemented by local operators.

Agenda 2000, in the form of an initiative named *Programma Operativo Regionale* (P.O.R.2000/2006), is the most recent programme adopted by the local government to stimulate rural development and specifically rural tourism in the region (Presidenza Giunta Regionale, 2000).

In Apulia, as in many other Italian regions, the increase in demand for cultural and environmental holidays has stimulated the establishment of a variety of special-interest activities, such as trekking, horse riding, cycling and food and wine tasting. Traditional events, such as religious festivals and the *sagre* (celebrations usually related to local craft and food products), have become a form of recreation for locals and tourists. From a wider tourism perspective, this is a great opportunity for the Apulia region to develop a balanced tourism portfolio, which would include a variety of niche tourism products as well as the more traditional heritage and coastal tourism.

Wine tourism and the Apulia region of Italy

Wine tourism is emerging as one of the most interesting and potentially vibrant forms of niche tourism. A synergy of traditional activities such as agriculture, viticulture and the hospitality sector has emerged to develop a relatively new rural tourism product. This consists of visits to vineyards, wineries, traditional wine cellars, festivals and events related to the wine harvest, usually involving product tasting (Hall *et al.*, 2000; Getz, 1998). In growing regions, like those in Australia, New Zealand and California, the presence of extended agricultural areas has given the opportunity to plan the creation of vineyards as visitor attractions. In Germany the 'wine routes' along the Rhine and the Moselle rivers have been active since the early 1980s. In the summer season, wine cellars become recreational spaces for residents and tourists. Wine tasting is one of the key activities, together with the purchase of other local craft and food products. Since the early 1980s, such events have been revitalized by a growth in wine consumption as part of a shifting pattern of consumer culture in many tourism-generating regions.

Italy is the world's largest producer of wine, with Apulia being one of its biggest and traditionally oldest regions involved in viticulture. However, wine tourism is a relatively recent phenomenon, which is often recognized as synonymous with rural tourism in regions like Tuscany.

Apulia is one of the most extended regions of Italy, consisting of almost 20 000 km^2 with a long coastline of 800 km. Its nature is varied from a morphological and sociocultural point of view. The region is characterized by harmonious geographical traits: a lack of mountains, a diffusion of plains and hills, a scarcity of surface moisture, extended contacts with the sea and a Mediterranean climate. Within these, there are perceptible differences between certain zones. In fact, the region is divided into subregions: the Subappennino Dauno; the Gargano; the Tavoliere; the Cimosa Litoranea; the Murgia; and the Salento (Figure 21.1).

The coast and the climate guarantee a long summer season. The natural and the built environment, as for example the Foresta Umbra and the Murgia dei Trulli, together with the arts, the craft, the rural traditions and the cuisine, make Apulia rich with potential tourism attractions.

Tourism plays an important role in the Apulian economy. Since the mid-1990s, an increase in the demand of rural areas for recreational purposes has determined the creation of services responding to the demanding market. On the other hand, the presence of a variety of typical products like wine and food have stimulated initiatives aiming to the development of *eno-gastronomic tourism* (translated from the Italian *turismo eno-gastronomico*, meaning 'wine and food tourism'). This process started in 1994, when the second phase of EU Structural

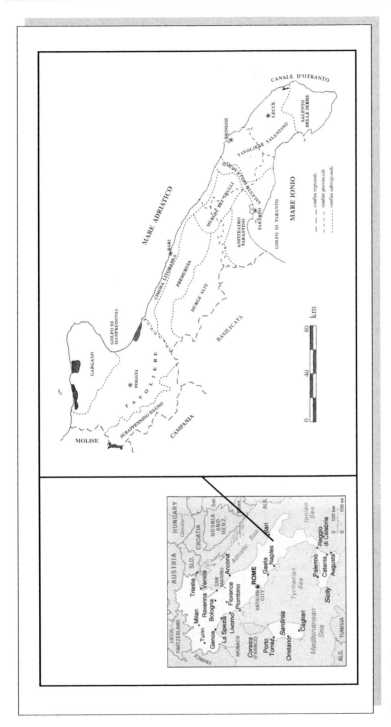

Figure 21.1 Subregions of Apulia.

Funds, implemented in Apulia by the P.O.P.1994/1999, encouraged the generation of projects aimed at the economic development of rural areas through tourism. One of the most relevant was focused on the 'elevation and promotion of quality agricultural products of the region' (measure 4.3.2). Part of the EU funds were assigned for the establishment of 'wine and olive oil routes' and for the refurbishment of museums, cellars and wine factories with a potentially valuable heritage character.

Wine tourism initiatives had to be conceived within a set of guidelines focusing on the realization of 'suggested wine itineraries', called *Strade del Vino*, related to the typical wine produced in the area. The nine recognized routes shown in Table 21.1 develop through the territory of the twenty-five regional DOC (*Denominazione di Origine Controllata*) wines.

The quality of products and the presence of wine cellars and cooperative wineries were to facilitate the development of the rural tourism sector, which needed the support of promotional initiatives aiming to the elevation of such characteristics. The realization of theme events to attract tourists to the area was also in the plan (Regione Puglia, 1999).

The need for a recognized image of the local agricultural productions has only recently stimulated the promotional activity implemented by the Regional Government. This process seems to have started with the participation in major international events such as the 'Vinitaly' in Verona, the 'Salone del Vino' in Turin, the 'Anuga' and 'Vinexpo' in Bordeaux, the 'Nuremberg Expo', the 'Fancy Food' in Chicago, as well as other sector meetings in Boston and New York (Regione Puglia, 2001).

Wine festivals and events in Apulia

Apulia has a rich and long tradition of both secular and religious festivals and events. They represent aspects of the cultures, tastes, religion and traditions of the region, and have always been a form of entertainment for large numbers of people.

A number of *wine* and *wine and food* festivals have emerged around the world, becoming a very interesting form of recreation and tourist attraction. In Italy, such events are usually associated with the internationally known Chianti territory in Tuscany, where the wine routes run through visually magnificent wine-growing areas which, apart from the obvious vineyards and wineries, offer an integrated tourist package of cultural,

Table 21.1 Wine routes and Apulia DOC wines

Province	Wine route no.	Name	DOC wines
Foggia	1	Strada dei vini DOC del Tavoliere, San Severo e Cacc'èmmitte	San Severo Cacc'èmmitte
Foggia e Bari	2	Strada degli Antich Vini Rossi	Ortanova Rosso di Cerignola Rosso Canosa Rosso Barletta Moscato di Trani
Bari	3	Strada del vino DOC Castel del Monte	Castel del Monte
Bari	4	Strada dei vini DOC Murgia Carsica	Gioia del Colle Gravina bianco
Bari e Taranto	5	Strada dei vini DOC Locorotondo e Martina Franca	Locorotondo Martina Franca
Taranto	6	Strada dei vini DOC Primitivo di Manduria e Lizzano	Primitivo di Manduria Lizzano
Brindisi	7	Strada dei vini DOC Ostuni e Brindisi	Ostuni Brindisi
Lecce	8	Strada del vino Vigna del Sole	Salice Salentino Leverano Squinzano Copertino
Lecce	9	Strada dei vini DOC Salento	Martino Nardò Alezio Galatina

Adapted from Regione Puglia (2001)

historical and natural attractions. These trails are also a means of fostering rural development and promoting the so-called *eno-tourism* (Regione Toscana, 2002).

In Italy, wine tourism attracts 3.5 million visitors, is worth 2.5 billion euros and has registered growth trends in both income generated (about 10%) and visitor numbers (about 8%) between 2001 and 2002. Since 1993, in many parts of Italy, various initiatives have been launched by an association called *Movimento Turismo del Vino* (Wine Tourism Movement) to stimulate rural development through wine tourism. Since the early 1990s this movement has managed to develop wine itineraries and to organize wine-related events and festivals, such as the earlier-mentioned *Cantine Aperte* (Open Cellars), the *Calici di Stelle* (Chalices of Stars) and the *Benvenuta Vendemmia* (Welcome Wine Harvest).

The *Cantine Aperte* is one of the most important events, taking place in various regions of Italy, and involving wine producers and local communities. This event has taken place in certain selected cellars every last Sunday of May, since 1993. This event consists of opening wine cellars to the public, showing the production sites and giving details of the wining process to the visitors, who are also encouraged to taste and buy the wine. The Apulian 2002 event saw 37 of the 41 wine cellars (members of the 'movement') taking an active part in this wine tourism initiative. Since the very first event in 1993, *Cantine Aperte* has had an exponential growth in numbers of visitors (up to 1 million in Italy in the 2002 event) and has demonstrated to be itself a key wine tourism attraction, which could be promoted overseas.

The *Calici di Stelle* is a national event organized every 10 August in the squares of chosen wine towns, consisting of festivals, dance, poetry, music and wine and food tasting. The Apulian 2002 event saw 23 cellars open to about 12 000 visitors. Lucera, in the Foggia province, has been the protagonist of this wine celebration, together with other wine towns, such as Locorotondo, Noci, Ruvo di Puglia, Fasano, Cerignola, Monteroni di Lecce and Manduria. It has been also an occasion for charity fund-raising in favour of the Italian Multiple Sclerosis Association.

The *Benvenuta Vendemmia* is another national event organized on the last Sunday of September, aiming to celebrate one of the most important moments prior to wining: the *wine harvest*. Like the *Cantine Aperte*, this is an occasion to open the wine factories and cellars to the public and encourage quality wine consumption. Cycling from one cellar to the next, walking in the vineyards and tasting the wine and the food are the core activities of the event. The 2002 Apulian event was characterized by a charity fund-raising event named *Bicchiere per la vita* (Glass for Life) and by a variety of activities in the land of Primitivo, Castel del Monte and Grifo wines. This event attracted about 10 000 visitors (Movimento Turismo del Vino, 2002).

From a wine tourism perspective, the presence of such events could give the opportunity to the Apulia region to have a status equal to other Italian wine regions.

In addition, there are over one hundred Apulian local festivals (*sagre*), which take place every year celebrating the traditions and the history of places. These events are the result of the perseverance of the *Pro Loco* organizations (committees working for the safeguard and promotion of the local heritage), which review each year's edition to improve their quality.

A typical example of these local festivals would be the *Sagra delle Contrade* (Hamlets Festival). It consists of a rural festival taking place every year in the months of July, August and September and involving a variety of *contrade* set in the landscape of the Valle d'Itria (the area within the provinces of Bari and Brindisi). This area is characterized by a countryside marked by the unique *trulli* (houses with whitewashed dry-stone walls), the *masserie* (farm cottages) and the bounding dry-stone walls dividing the fields. The wine plays its key role, being a unique local product, and barbecues are set at every corner. Fireworks, folk music, dance and plays animate the *contrade* and the *piazze* of historical towns like Cisternino, Martina Franca and the UNESCO Site of Alberobello.

Much more could be mentioned about the *sagre*. However, the most important aspect to be addressed at this point is the way these events can play a role in the promotion of Apulia as a wine tourism region.

Rural and wine tourism events, image building and product development

Festivals and special events can play an important role in rural tourism and economic development. They keep alive certain traditions and can play a relevant role in the diversification process of those rural areas in search of alternative forms of income, for their socio-economic wellbeing. In Apulia, many local farmers have kept their traditional activity and have found in rural tourism a way to diversify their business, letting visitors into their farm and offering them the fruits of their production. In the case of wine tourism, the ritual and mechanics of wine making have become a tourist attraction, together with wine events and festivals. These are inevitably elements influencing the increase of demand for tourism services in rural areas. The supply of accommodation, transport and recreational activities, responding to the visitors' needs, have in many cases proved to be the input stimulating the rural regeneration process of the area.

Although Apulia has about 200 dwellings for agrotourism accommodation and a variety of recreational activities like walking, horse riding, cycling and the *sagre*, there is a problem with the tourism marketing process. The region has a limited profile in the international context and needs to engage in image building in order to foster tourists' interest. While marketing rural Apulia as tourist destination involves more than promoting local resources and typical products, festivals and events offer an extremely good tool to attract attention, send positive messages and encourage good word-of-mouth communication (Getz, 2000). Although the Regional Government has started working on the image of the local agricultural resources through the participation in major international events, it is recognized that a tourist-oriented marketing strategy with a fair vision of what has to be achieved is the most urgent action. A clear idea of the position covered by the region in the marketplace is required and a situation analysis is needed before undertaking any further stage in the realization of its strategic marketing plan.

Table 21.2 highlights certain SWOT elements of interest to the development of the regional tourism sector. Although the presence of *strengths* and *opportunities* is encouraging for the future of Apulia rural areas, rural and wine tourism remain in need of a distinct and accurate product development plan, as much as the other forms of tourism present in the region. On the other hand, the *weaknesses* need to be faced in order to enable the tourism sector to be competitive. It is also a matter of stimulating awareness and interest, facilitating the access to information, monitoring the competitors and promoting the tourism experience through key images.

Within the international marketing of wine tourism, a key role would be played by a recognized wine brand, as happens in the case of Tuscany with the well-known Chianti wine. However, this is not the case for

Table 21.2 The SWOT key elements of Apulia

Strengths	*Weaknesses*
■ Competitive advantage related to the regional unique environmental features ■ The quality of eno-gastronomic products (e.g. DOC wines, DOP olive oils, etc.) ■ The presence of UNESCO sites and the existence of a growing rural hospitality sector (e.g. agrotourism)	■ Poor image of the region in the international context ■ Vague performance standards both in areas of operations and marketing ■ Lack of integrated tourism plans ■ Rural operators' individualism ■ Poor and/or not existing public transport networks
Opportunities	*Threats*
■ Presence of a variety of events and festivals ■ 'Made in Italy' highly requested on the international markets ■ Potential varied tourism portfolio (3S, cultural, rural and wine tourism) ■ Sustainability through rural diversification and regeneration ■ Affirmation of local identity	■ Competitors' activity (e.g. other Italian wine tourism regions and New World wine tourism destinations) ■ Lack of sustainability

Apulia and although the local production includes a variety of high-quality wines, the *image building* and *brand development* remain key requirements.

The destination's image provides one of the reasons for visiting it and often its tourism success depends on the development of an appropriate 'product positioning strategy' (Cai, 2002; Font, 1997; Grumo and Novelli, 2001). It involves creating an attractive image in the mind of the tourists, which can be stimulated through advertising, event marketing and 'theming' (Getz, 2000). It is believed that event marketing and 'theming' can be the key elements in the promotion of a tourist destination, mainly because they pursue a dynamic image of the place.

The previously mentioned events organized by the Movimento Turismo del Vino can be valid contributors to the image building of

Apulian wine tourism overseas. However, all the initiatives in this sector are targeted mainly to the Italian market and an internationalization process is essential in order to attract a larger number of tourists. In the international context, a relevant example would be the Napa Valley wine region in California. Here, a combination of natural resources, quality wines, appropriate marketing, large numbers of nearby potential customers and a sophisticated image with 'theming' (e.g. fine dining, arts and charity events) gave the right mix for wine tourism success (Getz, 2000; Hall *et al.*, 2000) and international recognition.

Wine tourism can be a great tool for local and regional regeneration. As indicated in Figure 21.2, the regeneration process could be a direct result of a growing 'wine tourism flow'. The financial support of public investments together with private initiatives would encourage the establishment of a regional 'wine tourism reputation'. An implemented international marketing strategy would attract visitors from a larger market and further development would materialize in the form of new employment opportunities and consecutive economic welfare.

Consideration: a strategy for rural Apulia

Considering the competitiveness of the European tourism sector, an essential requirement for the success of a destination is the presence of quality tourist attractions, responding to the demand of the market. The identification of target market segments is possibly the first step. They can be based on age, family structure, income, lifestyle, behaviour, interests, home location and mobility. In Table 21.3, it is possible to recognize some existing broad segments of visitors of the Apulian rural areas, which should be considered in the planning process.

As previously suggested, Apulian tourism is in need of a *tourism image*, which could possibly be built on the reputation of those destinations having a recognized role (e.g. the World Heritage Sites of Alberobello and of Castel del Monte in the Bari province). Newspapers and television coverage, the presence in established travel guides and the creation of websites can all be tools for the promotion of a quality image, to be supported by *branding* supported by the creation of a logo and/or a slogan.

The provision of *reservation services* is a need that cannot be ignored, as the small nature of rural businesses, generally family run, can make it hard for potential visitors to make a reservation. A solution to this

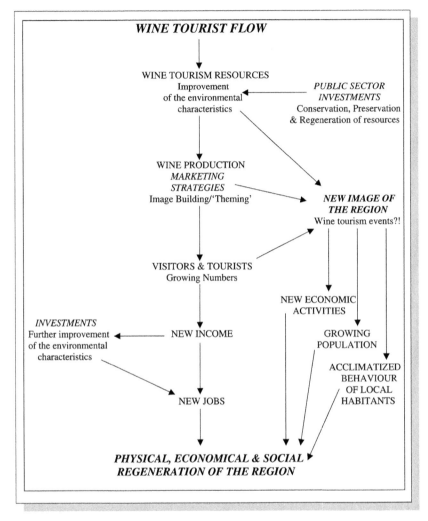

Figure 21.2 Regeneration process of a region through wine tourism.

problem could be the realization of a computerized and centralized reservation system for small rural enterprises able to provide regularly updated information about accommodation in the countryside.

Once the tourism experience has taken place, it should be kept alive through regular contacts consisting of communication of new festivals and events and holiday offers made by the hosting rural business. This would constitute an encouragement to the tourist to return to the area.

Table 21.3 Typology of visitors to the Apulian rural areas

Segment	Description
Visitors on day trips from home	A fast-growing segment mainly from the nearby provinces of Bari, Brindisi and Taranto
Short-holiday takers	Due to the length of their break they require: better access to rural area; a higher quality of services
Special-interest groups	Wine and food tasting; sport activities such as walking, cycling and riding horses; visiting local festivals and events
Educational visits	Understanding the local 'folklore'; study and taste of local products; learning about particular flora and fauna species, farming, conservation and heritage
Senior tourists	Tourists enjoying the traditions and tranquillity of the countryside
People with disabilities	Tourists requiring the provision of: accessible rural environment to them and their carers; adequate services

The creation of *packages* inclusive of accommodation, transport, visits to heritage sites and small attractions, participation in festivals, exhibitions and events, such as the mentioned wine festivals and events, could be another option.

The journey to the destination is part of the visitor experience. The peripheral location of Apulia influences the *accessibility* to the area, which relies on the use of expensive air links and private transportation. The presence of two airports (Bari and Brindisi) and their expected elevation to international status constitutes a great opportunity. A wider range of airlines would offer more competitive options to visit the area. This would possibly include the opportunity to benefit from 'no-frills' airlines, which have demonstrated to be a valid way of developing the target markets of many minor destinations in Europe. An important and challenging task is the improvement of the local public transport network, a typical weakness in all rural areas.

Much can be achieved at municipal level to improve, protect and promote the environment and its resources. The local governing bodies are under an obligation to develop and implement a strategic tourism plan. Since the early 1980s, the Apulia region's major problems have been lack of cooperation between the different local governing bodies and 'red tape', discouraging most private initiatives and leaving areas like tourism, environment, heritage and culture all governed independently and not as a synergetic system.

Apulia tourism planning strategy should focus on a clear set of actions to be undertaken. It should be about setting objectives, working together, understanding visitors, setting standards, obtaining visitors' reactions, making improvements, and checking impacts. Wine tourism, festivals and events would be a foundation for future tourism development. A useful step would be the punctual collection and publication of statistical data related to the area such as the tourist supply and demand and its impact on the various businesses. The *Assessorato al Turismo* (Local Tourism Authority) has been involved in such a task only since 1998 with the implementation of the *Decreto Legge 6/9/1989 n.322* on the collection and elaboration of tourism statistical data. The lack of reports is because the Apulian Regional Government became computerized only in 1998 and the collection of data by tourism authorities became compulsory only in 1996 (ISTAT-circular n.45-16/12/96).

The objectives of a *regional tourism strategy* should be clearly stated and the local communities informed and directly involved in its development and implementation. A constant monitoring of quality should be established.

The participation at international exhibitions and events could be a successful method to gain presence on the international scene. The typical sun, sea and sand holiday will, no doubt, continue to be popular, but could be diversified to include a rural option, consisting in activities such as festivals, events and wine itineraries.

Attention should be given to the alleviation of *seasonality*, which could be faced encouraging the organization of the *business tourism sector* (e.g. meetings, exhibitions and fairs, conferences and conventions and incentive travel), through the use of the numerous refurbished *masserie* (farms) and castles distributed throughout rural areas.

Conclusion

Any tourism strategy undertaken today should incorporate a *sustainability philosophy*, which often remains the result of subjective interpretation. In the case of Apulian tourism, the preservation of cultural heritage and rural communities' wellbeing is as important as the conservation of environmental resources. A stronger effort should be made to promote the region's landscape and folklore, the local productions and hospitality facilities together with the presence of valuable local festivals and events. Any strategy should look into tourists' preferences in order to keep the standards high as well as the number of visitors.

The contribution that tourism can make to the Apulian rural environment goes beyond the benefits to the countryside's wellbeing, in fact it involves the entire regional economic system. This may suggest that any forthcoming tourism development projects should be approached and managed with a more caring and prompt attitude, aiming to a systematic improvement and development of the regional economy.

Acknowledgements

I am grateful to Professor Peter Burns for his helpful advice in reading and commenting on earlier drafts and to Claire Weeden for her useful opinion on the marketing aspects of this chapter.

Bibliography

Bissanti, A.A. (1991). *Puglia. Geografia attiva*. Bari: Adda.

Bramwell, B. and Lane, B. (eds) (1993). *Rural Tourism and Sustainable Rural Development*. University College Galway, Conference Proceedings.

Cai, L.A. (2002). Cooperative branding for rural destinations. *Annals of Tourism Research*, **29(3)**, 720–742.

Font, X. (1997). Managing the tourist destination's image. *Journal of Vacation Marketing*, **3(2)**, 123–130.

Getz, D. (1998). Wine tourism: Global overview and perspectives on its development. *Wine Tourism–Perfect Partners: Proceedings of the First Australian Wine Tourism Conference*. Canberra: Bureau of Tourism Research.

Getz, D. (2000). *Explore Wine Tourism: Management, development and destinations*. New York: Cognizant Communication.

Grumo, R. and Novelli, M. (2001). *Progetto RIN.TUR – Rapporto Finale*. Lecce: Università di Lecce, Italy.

Hall, C.M., Sharples, L., Cambourne, B. and Macionis, N. (eds) (2000). *Wine Tourism around the World: Development, management and markets*. Oxford: Butterworth-Heinemann.

Movimento Turismo del Vino (2002). *Wine News – Movimento Turismo del Vino*. Downloaded on 25 September 2002 from www.movimentoturismovino.it.

Presidenza Giunta Regionale (2000). *Programma Operativo Regionale 2000–2006*. Bari: Area di Coordinamento delle Politiche Comunitarie – Informazione e Comunicaione.

Regione Puglia (1998). *Programma Operativo Regionale 2000–2006 – Allegato A*. Bari: Assessorato Programmazione Politiche Comunitarie.

Regione Puglia (1999). *Documentazione d'ausilio per la costituzione delle strade del vino e dell'olio d'oliva*. Bari: Assessorato Agricoltura, Foresta Caccia e Pesca.

Regione Puglia (2001). *Puglia: Civiltà del bere*. Bari: Assessorato Agricoltura, Foresta Caccia e Pesca.

Regione Puglia (2002). *Lista degli esercizi agrituristici in Puglia*. Bari: Informazione e Comunicaione.

Regione Toscana (2002). *Wine Trails in Tuscany*. Downloaded on 24 September 2002 from http://www.terreditoscana.regione.toscana.it/stradedelvino/.

Questions

1 What does wine tourism involve and what role does it play in events?
2 What are the five Ps of wine tourism event marketing?
3 What are the benefits to the Apulia region of active event involvement?

Edinburgh's Winter Festival

Kenneth MacMillan Wardrop and Martin Robertson

Introduction

While the City of Edinburgh plays host to some twenty festivals each year and an increasing number of one-off events, this case study will focus on the Winter Festival, comprising *Edinburgh's Capital Christmas* and *Edinburgh's Hogmanay*. This case study considers from a practitioner rather than an academic perspective the Winter Festival and associated events in relation to the key theme of 'ensuring a balance between entrepreneurial activity and long-term public sector development strategy'. The following areas will be addressed:

- A history of the Winter Festival events
- The evolution of the Winter Festival events in relation to the marketplace

■ Funding of the Winter Festival and the challenges of commercial viability and sustainability.

This chapter should be read in conjunction with Chapter 8.

Background to Edinburgh's Winter Festival

Scotland has always celebrated the passing of the old year and the emergence of the new with both heartfelt passion and, for a great many of the younger generations, barely contained revelry. Such is the significance of this event for Scotland that it has its own name, *Hogmanay*. A derivation of a seventeenth-century Norman French term meaning 'New Year's Eve gift', the name reflects the celebratory significance of the event. This significance is known throughout the western world, and increasingly around the globe. The emergence in 1993 of Edinburgh's Hogmanay festival has been followed by a meteoric rise in importance. So while Germany, Austria and Holland do have a history of holding winter festivals and markets, the Edinburgh Winter Festival can now claim to be one of the biggest winter festivals in Europe as well as one of the leading events of its type in the world. The fruition of the Christmas programme in 2000, a programme set to complement the existing Hogmanay festival, with the declared intention of developing a five-week programme of winter festival activities to rival any in Europe, the Winter Festival's resultant world media coverage, the international make-up of visitors, and the scale of the street party which lies at the heart of the Hogmanay celebrations have together ensured its high standing in the world.

The event has as its base the long-standing tradition of public gathering outside the Tron Kirk on the High Street (The Royal Mile) to bring in and celebrate on New Year's Eve (Hogmanay). By the early 1990s, up to 20 000 people would gather each year around the Tron Kirk for this event with the only management influence being the presence of the police force. The contemporary *Edinburgh's Hogmanay* event emerged from the Edinburgh Tourism Review in the early 1990s which identified the need to develop the tourism product in the city in a way that would enable the expansion of tourism beyond the shoulder months.

In 1992 the city played host to the European Council of Ministers. The associated programme of events in the city centre on 31 December (New Year's Eve/Hogmanay) offered the opportunity to dry-run the concept of a large-scale, organized Hogmanay event. In December the following year, a specially formed project team contracted *Unique Events*, an Edinburgh-based specialist events organizer, to launch the first three-day Hogmanay programme. The project team sprang from the Edinburgh Tourism Review and involved the local authorities, Edinburgh and Lothians area tourist board, and the local enterprise company and, latterly, the police.

The stated objectives for the three-day programme were:

■ To attract visitors to the city during a historically off-season period and to maximize the value added by visitors at this time of the year
■ To raise Edinburgh's profile as a European capital at a UK and international level (subsequently extended with the addition of 'as a year-round destination')
■ To provide a high-quality event for the enjoyment of participants, including Edinburgh residents.

The management structure

The management structures for Edinburgh's Capital Christmas and Hogmanay, respectively, are considered best practice models. In these the organizational structure comprises a *Strategic Project Advisory Group* with a *Safety Group* and *PR and Marketing Group* reporting to it. In addition, the Hogmanay Festival has a working group, the *Street Party Review Group*, created as a consequence of the concerns of public safety arising from the 1996/1997 event. The remit of this group is the control of participant numbers for the Hogmanay Street Party. Core tools for achieving this include cordoning off the central event area of Edinburgh and the issuing of street passes.

It should be highlighted here that the Safety Group plays a vitally important role given the need to ensure public safety for events such as the *Hogmanay Street Party* and the *Grand Fantastical Christmas Parade*, in which these free street-based events attract circa 100 000 participants and 150 000 spectators, respectively. As the street party is central to the success of Edinburgh's Hogmanay, safety issues are a critical factor.

The creative and artistic programming of both Edinburgh's Capital Christmas and Hogmanay are contracted out through a process of competitive tendering. For the period 1999/2000 to 2002/2003 both these contracts were won independently by the Edinburgh-based events company Unique Events Ltd. Given the scale of the Hogmanay contract –

typically £1.6 million – this contractual process has to comply with European Union procurement legislation. Not surprisingly, then, this is a long involved procedure.

The various project groups for both Edinburgh's Hogmanay and Capital Christmas are made up of representatives from organizations such as the City of Edinburgh Council, Scottish Enterprise Edinburgh and Lothians, Edinburgh and Lothians Tourist Board, Lothian and Borders Police and the Edinburgh City Centre Management Company. Neither Edinburgh's Hogmanay nor Capital Christmas have full-time dedicated staff working on the events, rather they are supported by full-time officers applying part of their working time on the organization of the events on a year-round basis. Currently there is a move to create a dedicated team of staff to work on festivals year-round. In particular there has been recognition of the need for a commercial manager to create the commercial partnerships and sponsorship deals necessary for an increasingly sophisticated event. Considering the financial commitment and the accumulated and potential paybacks as social and economic dividends for the city as a whole, the part-time nature of the management for the two events will undoubtedly need to change. The maturity of the event product (see Chapter 8) will soon demand a further dedicated human resources commitment.

Nevertheless, it is the way in which the management of Edinburgh's Hogmanay integrates the activities of its steering group with those of the public safety planning group and the marketing and public relations group which has precipitated many event operators across the world to emulate the model. Furthermore, this management model has been followed in Edinburgh's *Capital Christmas* and there is increasing thought that this model be followed in the creation of a single Winter Festival management structure.

The marketplace evolution of the Winter Festival

Edinburgh's Capital Christmas was championed at the outset by the Leader of the Council who assisted in securing Council resources in support of the event. The lead for the delivery of the management of the event was assigned to Economic Development within the Council's City Development Department. The development of the Winter Festival from its original platform as an additional product for the Hogmanay events to its current five-week portfolio of events clearly reflects that marketplace evolution has been a key driver in shaping delivery. Critically, this evolution is not just directed at an expanding domestic UK or international market but also the host population.

In relation to the Winter Festival there has been a recognition of the need to broaden the market reach beyond the traditional predominance of heritage-focused visitors, i.e. a move away from the 'grey' profile (older and more affluent visitors). Correspondingly there are two clear strategic actions to affect the market profile: one displayed in changes to the Hogmanay event, the other being changes and additions to the Christmas festival programme. In the first of these, there had been a push to widen the visitor profile to capture a younger market of 18–35-year-olds typical of other contemporary cultural destinations. Edinburgh's Capital Christmas, on the other hand, emerged in 2000 aiming at three distinct markets: short-break visitors, leisure retail day visitors and local residents. These were in reaction, consecutively, to the evident spare capacity through December in Edinburgh's hotel stock and to the increasing competitive nature of the Christmas retail market enlivened by retail centres throughout Scotland and the North of England. Correspondingly the creation of *Eventful Edinburgh* (see Chapter 8) as an online promotional and positioning tool has sought to facilitate the positioning and packaging of the Edinburgh event product in many subtle and ongoing ways to these target markets. However, before moving onto the product evolution of the Edinburgh winter festival, it is important to reflect that recognition of the need for a festival or large event product to evolve is not the same as actually ensuring success in it doing so. The combined issues of the event lifecycle, the destination lifecycle and brand image need to be considered first. Further attention to these factors as they relate to Edinburgh's Festival is given in Chapter 8.

Funding and product evolution

Since 1993, under the management of a partnership of agencies led and core funded by the City of Edinburgh Council, other funding has been drawn from various public agencies, commercial sponsorship and additional income-generating endeavours. The Millennium Hogmanay festival of 2000 represented an upward shift of financial support through Millennium Lottery funding. This brought with it a concomitant change in emphasis, whereby the local residents were defined as an important target audience. That year Edinburgh's Christmas programme was also established with an initial investment of £180 000 from the Council with the target of raising funding from sponsorship and other income generation to create a programme to the value of circa £360 000.

From the outset the project was ambitious in aiming to generate a month-long programme of activity, commencing in late November and running through until Christmas Eve. Under the marketing banner of *Edinburgh's Capital Christmas* the programme has aimed to combine a financially supported core of new events, targeted at different age groups and, crucially, families. These included the extension of the Edinburgh central arena area and the development or enlargement of the following products: *The Grand Fantastical Christmas Parade*; an international street theatre weekend; the *Christmas Lights Night*; carol concerts; *The Traditional German Christmas Market*, and the addition of other specialist interest markets; and *The Edinburgh Wheel* (a giant Ferris wheel strikingly placed and lit in Princes Street in the centre of the city). Concomitantly, encouragement was given to enliven the entrepreneurial activities of existing providers. As well as accommodating lighting programmes in traditional retail areas, support was also given in promoting, packaging and enhancing the planned visitor activities in these areas. Everything was done to encourage private industry involvement.

This privately initiated and operated entrepreneurial spirit is exemplified in: the *Winter Wonderland*, comprising an outdoor skating rink – again placed strategically and strikingly in the centre of the city, in East Princes Street Gardens; a series of Christmas events provided by the visitor attraction operators around Edinburgh Castle in the shape of the *Castlehill Christmas* programme and lighting scheme; and *Edinburgh's Capital Christmas Ice Hockey Tournament*. Importantly, these offered added value to the Edinburgh Winter Festival product whilst the core products themselves served to direct their quality – clearly vital to ensure overall customer satisfaction and market success.

Other entrepreneurial activity is focused on the development of short-break visits to the city around the Winter Festival events so that the accommodation sector benefits from and dovetails with the active marketing of these events. This is aided by marketing actions of the Edinburgh and Lothian Tourist Board under the banner in 2002 of the *Eventful Edinburgh Campaign*, and further enabled by the launch in January 2003 of the online animated guide to Eventful Edinburgh, *Eventful Ed*. These are covered more fully in Chapter 8.

Economic impacts and future projections

In 2000 an estimated 288 000 attendees participated in Edinburgh's Capital Christmas programme, 20% of whom were from outwith the Edinburgh and Lothians area. That year the economic impact assessment of the programme identified an economic benefit accruing to the city of £10 million in additional expenditure. Moreover, positive media coverage was generated for the city, with a value of circa £500 000 through UK national coverage (*source:* The City of Edinburgh Council).

In 2001 as a 'taking stock' exercise of the development of the event, a business plan for the period 2002–2005 was drafted for Edinburgh's Capital Christmas (RGA Ltd, 2002). The targets and outcomes identified were to:

- Achieve an incremental increase of 10 000 visitors each year to Edinburgh's Capital Christmas
- Increase the number of day visitors from 23% (68 654 in 2000) to 26% by 2005 (85 280)
- Increase the number of UK tourists from 5% (14 400 in 2000) to 12% by 2005 (39 360)
- Increase the number of overseas tourists from 5% (14 400) in 2000 to 7% by 2005 (22 960)
- Increase the average daily spend of visitors by 3% (in present values) year on year by 2005
- Maintain the very varied age profile of Edinburgh's Capital Christmas
- Maintain current levels of public funding but increase levels of funding from other sources (including private sponsorship)
- Measure the visitor perceptions of 'traditional spirit of goodwill', 'value for money', 'world class quality standards', 'positive community involvement', and achieve improvements year on year.

Ensuring the economic sustainability of the Winter Festival

Synergy between the Capital Christmas and Hogmanay programmes in terms of organizational and public safety logistics, staff resourcing and tasks, and PR and marketing activity is vital – as it must be for all major events. Accordingly, though the market segments to which the two Edinburgh winter events are targeted are distinctly different, the City Council is of a view that the creation of a Winter Festival brand with sub-brands will be advantageous. This would mirror the six main summer festivals with the segmented brands of the Jazz, Book, Fringe, International, Film and TV (see Chapter 8).

The identical and sometimes overlapping management and organizational structures for the two events, the cross-representation of key individuals from the partner organizations, the commonality of funding sources including approaches to corporate sponsors, the similarities in marketing approach, and the sharing of a common creative/artistic input from *Unique Events* has increasingly pointed to management, organizational and cost benefits from the full integration of the two events. The funding profile of Edinburgh's Hogmanay over the years since its inception in 1993 is presented in Table 22.1.

Table 22.1   Edinburgh's Hogmanay development

Year	Attendance (Street Party)	Attendance (all events)	Cost (£)	Economic impact (£)
1993/94	50 000	90 000	237 000	N/A
1994/95	150 000	250 000	438 000	N/A
1995/96	200 000	325 000	600 000	23 000 000
1996/97	350 000	425 000	934 000	29 000 000
1997/98	180 000	450 000	1 300 000	29 000 000
1998/99	180 000	500 000	1 400 000	30 000 000
1999/00	180 000	565 000	2 700 000	31 000 000
2000/01	100 000	500 000	1 600 000	30 000 000
2001/02	100 000	500 000	1 600 000	36 500 000

Source: The City of Edinburgh Council (2002).

In 1993 the cost of the Hogmanay event was £237 000, growing to a peak of £2 700 000 in the Millennium year and falling back to around £1 600 000 in 2001/2002. Comparable expenditure figures for Capital Christmas are shown in Table 22.2.

The issue of sustainability of the funding for both Hogmanay and Capital Christmas is a consistent source of debate and challenge for all partners involved. The case for sustaining high levels of public support continues to be based on the arguments around the wider economic benefit or return which accrues to the city and the wider promotion of

Table 22.2   Edinburgh's Hogmanay and Capital Christmas 2001/2002

Event	Total expenditure	CEC core funding		CEC funding including underwriting		Commercial income and sponsorship/ contribution	
	(£)	(£)	(%)	(£)	(%)	(£)	(%)
Edinburgh's Hogmanay	1 582 000	343 000	22	768 000	48	632 500	40
Edinburgh's Capital Christmas	350 000	185 000	52	–	–	165 000	48

Source: The City of Edinburgh Council (2002).

the Edinburgh brand gained from the direct and indirect media coverage of the Winter Festival. This wider economic benefit argument has been increasingly hard fought in the internal City Council funding decision-making processes. However, there is increasing scrutiny made of the 'in-kind' costs of the festival, such as the policing costs and organizational support from Council staff. This sum was estimated to be in the region of £550 000 (*source:* The City of Edinburgh Council), and thus represents an additional real cost of at least half again on top of the actual cash contributions made by the Council. Accordingly, with the backdrop of a decline in contributions from the other public sector funding partners, the volatility of commercial sponsorship, and the difficulties of generating commercial income from events staged as free events in public open space, the question 'Is the current position of funding sustainable?' has become increasingly audible.

Both Hogmanay and Christmas have at their cores large set-piece street-based events: the *Hogmanay Street Party* and the *Grand Fantastical Christmas Parade*, both of which absorb disproportionate shares of the total budgets and last only a few hours. Both create a 'wow' factor, memorable moments, but equally both are highly resource intensive. However, market research suggests that 80% of people (*source:* The City of Edinburgh Council Hogmanay Visitor Survey, City of Edinburgh Council, 2002) would be willing to pay for the Hogmanay Street Party. This would create both a new source of income for the event and a considerable change in the philosophy of the event. This change would also bring with it – and potentially arouse – significant political sensitivities. At the time of writing, the debate on whether to retain the Street Party in its present form, as the core element of the current Hogmanay celebration, and whether to make it a charged rather than a free event, is a very live issue for the City Council.

Conclusions

Following the success of the first two years of Edinburgh's Capital Christmas programme (2000 and 2001) political aspirations to extend the programme have grown. The success of the event is witnessed by the fact that Edinburgh's principal hotels achieved their highest occupancy rate ever for the month of December in 2001 at 63% (*source:* Edinburgh Principal Hotel Association members survey, January 2002). This is all the more impressive when one thinks that these occupancy rates have been achieved in the face of the lingering impacts on visitors consequent to the outbreak of foot-and-mouth disease in Britain, and the repercussions of the international war on terrorism following the attacks of 11 September 2001. Moreover, the Hogmanay festival has fulfilled the original objectives set for it, having:

- Positioned Edinburgh in the top league internationally as a New Year destination
- Ensured Edinburgh's Hogmanay achieves a widespread and positive profile in the UK and international media
- Generated substantial economic benefit for the Edinburgh and Scottish economy, estimated in 2000 at £36.5 million per annum
- Generated high satisfaction ratings, typically 9 out of 10.

(*Source:* The City of Edinburgh Council Visitor Survey and Impact Assessment 2000.)

The use of the Winter Festival as a marketing vehicle for the city continues to be an important rationale behind the City Council's ongoing financial commitment. The City Council remains convinced of the advantages of creating 'home grown' events targeted at defined market segments for the city and at times of the year when there is spare tourism infrastructure capacity. The alternative approach of courting peripatetic events, which often have their own preferred timing and target audience, is currently seen as a greater challenge in terms of ensuring a match to the desired market profile of the city (see Chapter 8).

Taking a long perspective in the approach to the development of the Winter Festival is considered essential. It has taken a decade to build Hogmanay into a truly international event achieving a global profile and reach with the desired target markets for the city. The brand profile, visitor numbers achieved, and economic impact are taken to be clear evidence of success. The 2002–2005 business plan for Edinburgh's Capital Christmas aims to mature this event product over time in the same way, with clear targets to increase the percentage of UK and international overnight visitors. Aspirations are high for the Winter Festival to maintain world leadership and to mirror the success of Edinburgh's summer festivals. The challenge at this time is to continue to secure the optimum level of finance to sustain the Winter Festival through commercial income generation based on core public funding under pinning. In addition every effort is being made to engage fully with the private sector partners in the retail, accommodation, visitor attraction and transport sectors in the financial support, packaging and marketing of the Winter Festival product. This is considered as vital to ensure that the shared aspirations for the Edinburgh product and brand are maximized, achieving the greatest possible economic impact and return to the city.

Bibliography

City of Edinburgh Council (2002). *Events in Edinburgh*, April.

Edinburgh Tourism Action Group (2000). *Edinburgh Tourism Action Plan*, October.

RGA Ltd (2002). *Capital Christmas Review and Business Plan 2002–2005*, proposed by RGA Limited on behalf of the City of Edinburgh Council.

Questions

1 The case study refers to the management structure for both Edinburgh's Capital Christmas and Hogmanay as being models of best practice.

  ■ What are the core attributes and dynamics indicated as the reason for this?

  ■ What are the potential weaknesses of the management structure and how can these be eradicated?

2 The funding for large-scale events is a vital component of its management.

- Who are the core funding bodies in the case of Edinburgh's Winter Festival and how – and why – has this changed over time?
- What do you believe are the likely problems in getting finance from the private sector and what advantage do you think the City of Edinburgh Council has over other cities in trying to ensure this?

3 The economic sustainability of the Edinburgh Winter Festival is governed by two main factors: the maintenance of funding, and the changing needs of the market. How can these two factors come into conflict?

Sponsorship, funding and strategic function: Carling Festival and V-Festival

Paul Walters and Razaq Raj

Introduction

The purpose of this chapter is to introduce two annual outdoor festivals that operate under the Miscellaneous Provision Act 1982. One of the many purposes of this act is to cover licensed entertainment with singing or dancing, prerecorded or live music. This chapter will outline the significant importance of obtaining and maintaining an occasional public entertainment licence for outdoor festivals, along with the economic impact to local communities and the necessity to fully consider their opinions within the planning and application process. The chapter will also outline how principal sponsors add to the dynamic nature and long-term sustainability of outdoor festivals.

Two case studies, V-festival and Carling Festival, will be presented to illustrate and discuss the issues presented in this chapter. Furthermore, the two case studies will attempt to demonstrate how sponsorship can enhance the event profile, increase revenue and brand identity.

The principal reason for presenting these two events is located in the licence obtained under the Miscellaneous Provision Act 1982, along with a dual-sited arrangement and a major principal sponsor for each event.

Leeds Carling Festival, England

The Leeds Carling Festival is an annual event held at Temple Newsam Park since 1999. The organizer, Mean Fiddler, extended the Reading Festival to create the first three-day dual-site festival in the UK. The event is held on the August Bank Holiday weekend from Friday to Sunday, under the banner of the Carling Weekend, and attracts around 30 000 attendees each day.

The Carling Festival primarily attracts those between the ages of 15 and 35. The festival is an event where children are not catered for. It is mainly a music festival for young people to enjoy a weekend of live and prerecorded music; there are beer tents and other peripheral activities for the revellers. It is a music festival first and foremost, and there is a phenomenal choice of music throughout the three days for the customers to enjoy.

Despite its commercial success, the media and many local residents have criticized the event regarding the clean-up operation, crowd behaviour and subsequent damage. Such physical and environmental issues instigated discussion by local councillors, in October 2001, regarding the termination of Mean Fiddler's contract. Thus, it has become apparent that, despite the economic benefits that large events may have on the city, many communities who experience the physical impact are unhappy with the event.

McDonnell *et al.* (1999: 20) believe that it is the task of the event manager to identify, predict and manage the range of impacts, 'so that in the balance the overall impact of the event is positive'.

An aftermath of concern, upset and complaints can contribute to a sense of hostility toward the event and its organizing bodies, which may ultimately impact upon its future. Therefore, it is an important issue for both event managers and local councils to establish the overall impacts of hosting such events. Therefore, within the planning process it is of paramount importance to canvass opinions from the immediate community and incorporate those opinions in conditions of the licence to alleviate any future situations that could arise. The conditions directly associated with the licence agreement will determine to what degree an event should carry out the rule of management within the licence agreement.

In 2002, Leeds City Council refused to grant a full licence, due to residents complaining on issues of noise and environmental damage. Mean Fiddler went through an appeal procedure on those issues that had blighted the event over the previous years. Mean Fiddler successfully won the appeal procedure and the event went ahead as scheduled. However, the impact of publicity on the event, surrounding the issues raised in the appeal procedure for the licence over the previous years, must have a positive or negative effect on the sponsorship that is attached to the event.

Sponsorship of the Carling Festival

Bass Brewery manages the leading brand Carling Lager. Carling is Britain's biggest selling beer and has held this position since 1971. In 1997, Carling was the first to reach 2 million barrels in sales and the first and only beer to reach 3 million barrels. In 2001, it achieved sales of 4 million barrels in one year. Carling has an annual marketing and sponsorship budget of 33 million. Carling, as a brand leader, has moved into many areas of promotion over the years, with the brand direct association with Carling Weekend Reading and Leeds Festival. This festival is the largest dual-sited music festival in the world. In 2001 there were over 110 000 visitors and 200 music performers, drinking 1600 barrels of beer.

The partnership arrangement drawn up between outdoor festivals and sponsor through sponsorship product identification has continued to increase sales and market share regardless of the external issues that emanate around a particular event. Through documented research over a number of years in local newspapers, publicity attracted to Carling by activities undertaken at the festival complements the hard edge nature of the advertising campaign presented by Carling for the product over the previous years. Therefore customers can relate and respond to the product. As with any product association where there is a potential for 'danger', the event can no longer retain its identity and becomes known as the product, which in turn can have a drastic effect on the sustainability of the product as an independent entity within the wider marketplace. To ascertain if the partnership that has developed between Mean Fiddler and the Carling brand can be mutually beneficial in the short to long term will be tested primarily in the continued submission and approval of an occasional public entertainment licence. The major sponsor must be aware of the ethos and ideology of the event and its customer base. This will add to product identification and product loyalty, and ultimately increase sales. The customer base for the majority of outdoor festivals stems from the performers, who have been the main focal point at the event since its inception, along with external product identification with performances throughout the year. Longevity is now sustainable as can be seen from the continued partnership agreement, but the partnership deal must have a definable lifecycle, reviewed and renegotiated with both major stakeholders at the end of the event. From this position, it will allow the event to attach itself to another product/service, if required, without interrupting the ethos or ideology. It also encourages the product to acquire new markets and stand alone as a single entity.

Venue background

Temple Newsam is a stately home in the LS15 district of Leeds, four miles from Leeds City centre, in a national park that includes 1200 acres of parkland and a working Rare Breed Centre.

Previously, Temple Newsam Park has played host to a variety of concerts and music festivals including Breeze, a week-long youth festival, V festivals of similar nature to the Leeds Carling Festival, and Party in The Park, which brought an audience of over 50 000. Leeds City Council, owner of the site since 1922, has played a major role in the hosting of this event over the years. It also provides the licence and opportunity for the festival to take place in the National Park.

Event background

The Carling Weekend: Leeds Festival was born in 1999, allowing festival-goers in the North of England to enjoy the stunning and often exclusive line-ups that its older brother Reading secured. Both festivals make up The Carling Weekend, the UK's only simultaneously occurring 3-day festival, with the line-ups rotating between the two sites. Unlike the more urban setting of Reading, Leeds takes place in the smaller, but far more picturesque setting of Temple Newsam Park (http://www.virtual-festivals.com/festivals/festival.cfm?festivalid=7).

The festival itself comprises music of a hard-rock genre. The headline acts have included Eminem, the Manic Street Preachers and Travis. Dance stages, comedy tents, bars and stalls are amongst other attractions of the festival. Ten unsigned local acts had the opportunity to display their performance after a competition with the *Yorkshire Evening Post*. (See Appendix to this chapter for the full festival programme for 2002.)

Benefits

Economic growth is promoted by an increase in the quality or quantity of inputs into an economy (Tribe, 1999: 299).

Getz (1991) claims that spending on local facilities, induced by an event, has a much wider economic impact than money spent at the event site, thus increasing the quality of inputs. Events that stimulate overnight visits lead to greater economic benefits, hence increasing the 'quantity' of inputs (Getz, 1991; McDonnell *et al.*, 1999), although Bull (1995) asserts that limits of disposable time, set by work and public holiday allowances etc., can constrain the effects of expenditure. On balance, however, it can be seen that the greater the duration of the event, the greater the economic benefit.

In order to portray a realistic view of economic benefits, only expenditure that represents 'new money', generated specifically from event tourists originating from outside the destination, should be included in the economic impact assessment. Getz (1991), Hall (1992) and Erkilla (2000) agree that locals' expenditure should be viewed only as transfer expenditure reassigned from local permanent businesses, to the event site. Studies may, as Getz (1991) observes, include a percentage of resident spending on the assumption that the events retained money that would otherwise be spent elsewhere, or generated resident spending over and above normal levels. Hall (1992) and others claim that deductions should be made for those who would have visited the area anyway, regardless of the event. In addition to this disagreement of analysis, both Getz (1997) and Erkilla (2000) point out that measurement of these factors is complex, causing significant analytical problems.

The council receives the capital sum of £250 000 to lease the site and pay for clean-up costs. Therefore, this is a major economic benefit for the Leeds City Council to host the event. The economic benefit is also profited by the planning, environmental health, building control, West Yorkshire Metropolitan Ambulance Service (WYMAS) and police costs, which is all paid by Mean Fiddler.

The retail sector of the local economy is likely to be the largest benefactor, because over the three days over 90 000 people attend the Carling Festival. Besides that, local transport and hotels are also cited as important sectors, as buses to the site are provided by the event and facilitated by local transport companies.

Moreover, the event attracts significant publicity for the city of Leeds. The festival attracts international artists to a city without an arena that would otherwise be unable to attract stars of the calibre of Eminem, for example. Live links through TV and radio generate publicity for the event but also brand the Leeds logo to a vast audience. This national and international recognition generates greater publicity for the local area and attracts greater tourism to the city of Leeds. Three major subcontractors and suppliers to the event based locally are the porta-cabin, signage and medical/first aid providers, who operate for a financial profit.

Conversely, Leeds City Council considers that the event also promotes the social side of Leeds attracting repeat visitation to bars and clubs. The economic benefit from the event can overshadow the negative side of the event. The event helps the local businesses to benefit from the event attendees.

The event has proven to generate financial benefits to certain sectors, namely in retail provision, of the local economy. Most sectors observed a substantial increase of trade in the short term of more than 50%.

The impact

The impact of a festival on a region/local area can be discussed from various points of view and each view ultimately will have an overall effect on the event and the locality. The economic impact of an event within a particular geographical area can be assessed from the revenue generated by expenditure from customers over a period of time while attending the festival. Retail outlets, general services, contractual arrangements and temporary employment are some of the indicators for calculating direct economic impact. Apart from the economic impact, not directly associated with the occasional public entertainment licence agreement, there is also the environmental impact before, during and after the event. It is this particular area that is of most concern to the local community and the condition attached to the licence agreement. Every outdoor festival should stipulate within their licence condition measures by which to deal with environmental issues that may influence the local area in the short to long term. Waste management at festivals carries an enormous responsibility to the organizer from sanitary provision, clean water supply and clean-up after the event. Within the condition of the licence agreement, waste and the management of waste must have adequate management systems and procedures to ensure that previous situations that have contributed to abuse of the provisions at the event do not affect any future management systems and service delivery.

The impact can also refer to the government revenue generated through event expenditure less associated government expenditure (Dwyer et al., 2000). Mean Fiddler pays a substantial fee to Leeds City Council for the use of land. Further sources of income may come in the form of licence fees and tax revenues, thus 'Governments benefit from increased tax revenue, and research has found that grants to events can have significant, positive returns to government coffers' (Getz, 1991: 38).

The publicity that the event attracts is not always for the right reasons, as the event has received substantial negative press, particularly regionally, due to the violence and burning of toilet blocks at the event, which has occurred for two years running. Negative publicity is believed by local people to have an effect on the customer and potential customer. In addition, Friends of Temple Newsam Park believe that camping has too much of a detrimental effect and that the irresponsibility of attendees also raises concerns. Both the Friends of Temple Newsam Park and local councillors believe that the site is unsuitable for a three-day event of this nature. They believe that although other events held on the site also have a detrimental impact on the park, the damage is more limited and recovers quickly.

The host community: impact of complaints

In any location, harmony must be sought between the needs of the visitor, the place and the host community (English Heritage, 2000: 29).

As has been demonstrated throughout this chapter, the impacts of events can greatly affect the quality of life of the local residents.

Resident perceptions provide an important non-economic dimension for gauging how events benefit or impinge on the host community (Jeong and Faulkner, 1996; Hall, 1992). Gursoy *et al.* (2001) assert that residents become a threat to a tourism project when it is planned and constructed without the knowledge and support of the host population.

Negative impacts can determine the public's perception and willingness to support the event as discussed above. Awareness and understanding of resident concerns and attitudes, it is suggested, can help planners to reduce disruption to community life (Delemere, 2001; Williams and Lawson, 2001). This, Delemere (2001) believes, will encourage a balance between social and economic development forces within the community.

The view of the host community may also help to refine the analytical framework used by planners and policy makers, helping the industry to be sustainable in the long term (Jeong and Faulkner, 1996; Williams and Lawson, 2001).

The Friends of Temple Newsam Park originated from residential concerns raised resulting from the 'V-festivals' held on site before the Carling Weekend where there was no consultation with the local community. These concerns of noise, access to property, congestion and litter instigated the Temple Gate Neighbourhood Watch, with the assistance and finance from local Councillor Benson, to form a more specific 'Friends' group. The Friends currently represent 205 households from across the region.

Over the years, the Friends have become more actively involved at a consultation level with the organizers and Leeds Leisure Services. Such meetings have been set in place to reduce negative impacts upon both the community and the park.

The camping areas were resited away from residential housing, although there are still complaints. The camping created noise disturbance to the residents as, although the bands stop playing, the party carried over to the campsites. The stage has been resited over the years to minimize noise impacts. Closure of the streets meant parking restrictions throughout the event, with only residents receiving passes.

Friends are also concerned about the lack of access to the park and diminished enjoyment of it for the duration surrounding the event.

V-festival, Weston Park, Staffordshire, England

Management structure and history

V-festival has a history that dates back to 1997. The event was held at Temple Newsam in Leeds under the auspices of Roseclaim between 1997 and 1998. From 1999 to 2002, the event became based at Weston Park, Staffordshire. Additionally, from 1996, Maztec Ltd has continually managed and promoted the event at Hylands Park, Chelmsford. This dual-sited arrangement is similar in concept to Leeds and Reading Carling Festival. Some artists are shared between the two sites over the duration of the event. It should be stated that V-festival's artist line-up for the event duration has a different customer base in relation to Carling Festival and other festivals held in the UK.

The management and operation of V-festival was born out of a consortium group of companies who specialize within the field of artist management, club promotion, venue management and live music promotion. The four-core management structure was based around Metropolis Music, London; SJM Concerts, Manchester; MCD, Dublin; and DF Concerts, Glasgow.

To oversee the operation, financial and logistical control of the event, the consortium has introduced Maztec Ltd and Roseclaim Ltd. These two companies were incorporated to oversee and take full liability for V-festival.

This form of overall management and operation is a common business management concept within the events and entertainment industry, whereby the parent company or group of companies will incorporate a limited company that will take sole responsibility for financial management, project management artist booking, subcontracting and event operation etc. throughout the preplanning and on-site delivery.

For the purpose of this case study, we shall concentrate on Weston Park, Staffordshire. The site is located 10 miles east of Telford town. The main route to the site is along the A5 from Stafford on the A449. The nearest village to the site is Weston under Lizard. V2002 applied for and obtained from Staffordshire council an occasional public entertainment licence under the Local Government (Miscellaneous Provisions) Act 1982. This licence held and ran between Friday 16 August 2002 and 19 August 2002. The purpose of this licence is to allow mass gathering with singing and dancing over a period of three days. To accompany this licence are the conditions by which the event is legally regulated and managed. The responsibility rests with the licensee and deputy to manage the event under specific conditions outlined in the licence agreement.

Sponsorship branding and product identification

V-festival as an event has a sponsorship arrangement with the Virgin group. This relationship has been in operation since 1997. Over the period that Virgin has collaborated with this event, they have introduced different brands to the event, starting with Virgin Coke and Virgin Radio, the two brands promoted in 1997 throughout all promotional and communication literature. From 1999, Virgin Mobile has been the chosen brand from the 200 companies that exist within the Virgin group. With the proliferation of the communication market from online subscribers to the mainstream networks and its continual year-on-year growth, Virgin Mobile entered the mobile communication market in 1999; that same year the single brand Virgin Mobile aligned itself to the festival and the introduction of the new site. The event now viewed by its customer base is synonymously known as the 'V-festival'. Product identification and association has proliferated the customer base and the nature of the event. Through marketing and promotion in all significant areas of communication, the Virgin brand has stamped its presence on a product that has a large, fixed target audience for a three-day duration. In October 2002, Virgin Mobile announced a figure of 2 million customers subscribed to their network. This accumulation of customers over a three-year period is a significant amount considering that the mobile communication market in the UK was nearing saturation point.

Impact

Issues related to the impact from a social, environmental or economic principle have differing effects. The impact on the local community from an economic perspective is not as significant, principally due to locality and appropriate amenities for the customer base. Environmental issues are a concern to the landowner and local council; however, public access prior to and after the event is not a major community activity. This does not negate the responsibility of the organizer to implement and carry out under the licence agreement appropriate measures to return the site to its former state.

Conclusion

Case studies have been presented of two outdoor festivals, which take place on an annual basis under the Miscellaneous Provision Act 1982. Both have a dual-sited arrangement; artists are also shared between both sites throughout the duration of the event. Attendance at these festivals fluctuates between 55 000 and 90 000 over a three-day period. Each event also has a major principal sponsorship arrangement, which in turn has redefined the customer perception and product identification to the point that each event is synonymously known as the product. However, there are distinct differences with the management and operation of each festival. First and foremost we have Leeds Carling Festival located within a metropolitan city perimeter with a high-density residential population. The residents' acceptance of the event over the period of time has become a major bone of contention, to the point that objection to the occasional public entertainment licence has become a contentious issue for the council, local community and the city at large. The event organizers find themselves in a landmark position in regard to this particular festival. Is it necessary to accumulate further consultation with the local community to allay their fears and concerns regarding the future of the festival on this particular site? Or can the event sustain continued disturbance at the festival and community condemnation? These particular questions are enshrined within the public entertainment licence and in part related to outdoor events; therefore, if these questions are not addressed to the satisfaction of the organizer, local council or the community the future for many outdoor festivals will be regulated heavily to achieve the stated objectives.

V-festival, as indicated earlier, has a number of similarities, but what is distinct to V-festival is its location. The Staffordshire site has a number of advantages which have enabled 'V' to sustain itself over a number of years without major concerns from the local community. Consultation with the immediate village was taken on board and planned for within the planning process and application for an occasional public entertainment licence. Satisfying local community concerns are major issues; objections brought by community representatives or a legal representative can have a major impact on securing and maintaining a licence.

Bibliography

BBC Leeds (2002). http://www.bbc.co.uk/leeds/news. Accessed on 4 July 2002.

Bond, C. (2001). Violence brings call for event move. *Yorkshire Post*, 16 October. http://www.ypn.co.uk/scripts/editorial2_search.cgi. Accessed on 7 Nov. 2001.

British Tourist Authority (BTA) (2001). http://www.visitbritain.com. Accessed on 20 Nov. 2001.

Buller, A. (2001a). 'Ban pop festival from city' call by councillor. *Yorkshire Post*, 28 August. http://www.ypn.co.uk/scripts/editorial2_search.cgi. Accessed on 7 Nov. 2001.

Buller, A. (2001b). Rubbish blights historic park a week after trouble-hit festival. *Yorkshire Post*, 31 August. http://www.ypn.co.uk/scripts/editorial2_search.cgi. Accessed on 7 Nov. 2001.

Council for the Protection of Rural England (1990). *Tourism Towards the Year 2000*. London: CPRE.

Department for Culture, Media and Sport (DCMS) (2001). http://www.culture.gov.uk. Accessed on 20 Nov. 2001.

Dwyer, L., Mellor, R., Mistilis, N. and Mules, T. (2000). A framework for assessing 'tangible' and 'intangible' impacts of events and conventions. *Event Management*, **6**, 175–189.

English Heritage (2000). *Tourism Facts 2001*. Swindon: English Heritage.

English Tourist Board (1991). *Tourism and the Environment: Maintaining the Balance*. English Tourist Board.

Erkilla, D. (2000). Trends in tourism economic impact estimation methods. In Gartner, W. and Lime, D., *Trends in Outdoor Recreation*, Leisure and Tourism Oxon, CABI Publishing pp. 235–244.

Getz, D. (1997). *Event Management and Event Tourism*. New York: Cognizant Communication Corporation.

Hall, C. M. (1992). *Hallmark Tourist Events – Impacts, Management and Planning*. London: Belhaven Press.

Jeong, G. and Faulkner, B. (1996). Resident perceptions of mega-event impacts: the Taejon International Exposition case. *Festival Management and Event Tourism*, **4**, 3–11.

Leeds City Council (2001). *Temple Newsam*. http://www.leeds.gov.uk/. Accessed on 14 October 2001.

The Leeds Festival (2001). http://www.leedsmusicfestival.co.uk/. Accessed on 30 October 2001.

McDonnell, I., Allen, J. and O'Toole, W. (1999). *Festival and Special Event Management*. Brisbane: John Wiley and Sons.

Mean Fiddler (2001). *Carling Weekend*. http://www.meanfiddler.com. Accessed on 30 October 2001.

Tribe, J. (1999). *The Economics of Leisure and Tourism*, 2nd Ed. Oxford: Butterworth-Heinemann.

UK Sport (1997a). Major events: a blueprint for success. In *'Major events – a blueprint for success', 'Major events – the economics', 'A UK policy', 'A UK strategy'*. London: UK Sport.

UK Sport (1997b). *Major Events: the economics: measuring success*. London: UK Sport.

Williams, J. and Lawson, R. (2001). Community issues and resident opinions of tourism. *Annals of Tourism Research*, **28(2)**, 269–290.

Questions

1 During the final stages of the planning process for an outdoor event that involves the three emergency services, a multiagency meeting is organized; at this point essential individuals from the emergency services should be present. Outline the reasons why the three main emergency services should be present and indicate their roles and responsibilities at a multiagency meeting.

2 Describe three products within the Virgin portfolio (apart from Virgin Mobile) that could bring marketing and promotional benefits to an outdoor festival.

3 Describe what legal representation and intervention local communities can use to delay/interrupt the application process for an occasional public entertainment licence under the Local Government Miscellaneous Provision Act 1982.

Appendix: Carling Festival Programme 2002

Friday	Saturday	Sunday
Main Stage	**Main Stage**	**Main Stage**
Guns 'N' Roses	The Strokes	Foo Fighters
Prodigy	Pulp	Muse
The Offspring	Jane's Addiction	Ash
Slipknot	Weezer	Sum 41
Incubus	The White Stripes	The Hives
NOFX	The Dandy Warhols	A
Puddle Of Mudd	Mercury Rev	Less Than Jake
Hundred Reasons	Soundtrack Of Our Lives	Andrew WK
Amen **(new)**		Vex Red **(new)**
The Dillinger Escape Plan	**Evening Session Stage**	Sahara Hotnights
	Soulwax/Too Many DJs	
Evening Session Stage	**(new)**	**Evening Session Stage**
Spiritualized	Feeder	Black Rebel Motorcycle Club
And You Will Know Us	The Breeders	Jimmy Eat World
By The Trail Of Dead	The Electric Soft Parade	Jon Spencer Blues Explosion
(new)	New Found Glory	The Cooper Temple Clause
Cornershop **(new)**	The Vines	Rival Schools
Haven	Guided By Voices	Alec Empire
Six By Seven **(new)**	Fenix TX	The Yeah Yeah Yeahs
Reel Big Fish **(new)**	The BellRays	The Icarus Line
The Shining	The Von Bondies	Goldfinger
Sparta	Finch **(new)**	Midtown
Capdown		The Libertines
Hoggboy	**Carling Stage**	
Death Cab For Cutie	Fu Manchu **(new)**	**Carling Stage**
	Bobby Conn **(new)**	Ikara Colt **(new)**
Carling Stage		The Parkinsons **(new)**
The Music **(new)**	**Dance Stage**	International Noise
Alpine Stars **(new)**	Aphex Twin	Conspiracy
Easy World **(new)**	Lo-Fidelity Allstars	
	U.N.K.L.E	**Concrete Jungle Stage**
Dance Stage	Sound Decks 'N' Effects	Sick Of It All
The Streets	**(new)**	Alkaline Trio
The Herbaliser	Ladytron **(new)**	Saves The Day
Anti Pop Consortium	Peaches	Face To Face
Blade	Luke Vibert	The Get Up Kids **(new)**
People Under The Stairs	Freq Nasty **(new)**	No Use For A Name
(new)		Bouncing Souls
Blak Twang **(new)**		Dashboard Confessional
		Thursday
		The Anniversary **(new)**
		Hot Rod Circuit
		Lightyear
		Jesse James

Webpage and words © JFM 2002

The Anglesey Sea Symposium, UK

Lester D. Matthews

Introduction

This chapter introduces both an international event as it is now and its genesis, with the intention that readers may see parallels with events that they may either wish to start, or enhance/extend. Content focuses upon the development of the event's format and 'flavour'. Atmosphere and the underpinning values of events can be difficult to either define or to convey in written form, but an attempt is made to do so here. The event interfaces with 'systems' and loose-knit organizations that are independent, but mutually supportive, and those relationships are described only in part. This is due to both restrictions of space and the realization that the relatively specialist nature of this event makes detailed explanation irrelevant to most readers of this book. Readers wanting more detail, say on the

British Canoe Union and their courses, can find such information via their website.

It is the author's contention that the generation of events, or their extension, can and should be based upon careful and complete 'audits' of both similar and dissimilar events. Although no explicit use of the author's own auditing tools are apparent, it is hoped that serious students will find these for themselves.

Arrival

It was with some difficulty that he fought his way to the bar. They had arrived much later than planned; the car park and verges were full of cars with kayaks on their roof-racks, and big commercial trailers, laden with new sea kayaks still wrapped in plastic, lined the road leading to the bar.

He spotted a familiar face which smiled and he heard an American accent; ah yes, Stan Chaldek from the USA, with two of his countrymen. Next to him was a towering man with dark hair who turned and nodded. He was describing his last trip to a group, '... the tidal overfalls were interesting ... six hours in the kayak ... beautiful beach ... sunset and red wine'. A familiar group of two other men with an attractive lady tried to speak over the hubbub. He couldn't hear them; were they Dutch or German? He remembered that they had all kayaked to one of the small islands off Anglesey, the previous year. Behind him the bar door opened again and someone else walked in. They shouted, 'Daj!'; yes, they were Dutch! Two girls, one a sea coach and the other a freelance camera-woman, were discussing their plan to circumnavigate Wales by its sea-coast and inland canals; they just managed to let him squeeze by.

Nigel Dennis, proprietor of Anglesey Sea and Surf Centre (ASSC), came into view, surrounded by Adventure Tourism students and his own staff. They shook hands. At last he was at the bar. As a pint of best bitter was being poured, a bearded pipe-smoker turned and made a small space. The bearded man struck up a conversation about the journey to ASSC. His accent and stare were strangely familiar. 'Where are you from originally?', 'Middlesbrough', 'Me too, what part?', 'Acklam', 'Me too, were you in the Scouts?', 'Yes, are you Paul?', 'Yes! Are you Lester?!'

Two old friends, who had not met since their early teens, were now reunited after over 20 years. Both had become British Canoe Union (BCU) Sea Kayak Coaches and were there to teach on that year's

ASSC/Nordkapp Trust Sea Symposium – by no means a unique occasion at this event!

The genesis of the symposium

This annual event is the most regular and long-lived sea kayak 'meet' of its kind in the UK. Held every year since 1985, it was originally called the 'Nordkapp Meet', the brainchild of Nigel Dennis of ASSC, Frank Goodman of Valley Canoes (designer of the world-renowned 'Nordkapp' sea kayak) and John Ramwell, all internationally respected sea kayakers. In the same era the 'Nordkapp Trust' was also formed to (quoting from the 2001 Brochure) 'Promote safe and sociable sea kayaking'. The annual sea symposium event has since developed and grown into its present form, under the careful direction of Nigel Dennis. Nigel says:

> In 1985 it wasn't a true symposium ... it was free to Nordkapp owners and everyone else had to pay a nominal fee ... it was a simple weekend meet with one key lecture each evening, so it was up in the morning, by half past ten everyone had gone for different paddles [trips] and then came back for the evening lecture. When we started in the old centre, there were probably 25–30 people usually on the Nordkapp Meet. It changed really as the demand grew, to be able to support the present style of symposium ... what we've tried to do is a blend of both because every year there's a number of people who come, go for a paddle, do their own thing, but do not take part in the symposium.

The format of the symposium

The event is held every Mayday Bank Holiday weekend and approximately 30% of the people stay on for the following week to do either expedition training or BCU Star Awards and/or BCU Coaching Scheme training and assessments. The BCU administers an internationally respected (and quite comprehensive, if complex) system of skills and coaching awards. It is possible to undertake those awards as 'stand-alone' courses, or to combine them with appropriate trips and expeditions.

There are a wide variety of options for both symposium days, which start with an early (prebreakfast) indoor-pool session for those wanting either to learn to 'Eskimo-roll', or to improve on their technique (Exhibits 24.1 and 24.2).

ANGLESEY SEA SYMPOSIUM 2001

**B.C.U.
COACHING
COURSES**

A.S.S.C.*M*

PERSONAL SKILL/ LEADERSHIP

The following courses will be run all week

3 Star (1 day)

4 Star Training (1 day)

4 Star Assessment (1 day)

5 Star Training (3 days)

5 Star Assessment (2 days)
(Weather dependant)

COACHING AWARDS:

Level 1 Coach course	7 – 11th May
Level 2 Coach Training	8th / 9th May
Level 2 Coach Assessment	8 May
Level 3 Coach Training	10th / 11th May
Level 3 Coach Assessment	10th / 11th May
Coaching Processes Course	12th / 13th May
Injury prevention in Paddlesport	7th May
Assessor Training Day	8th May

NOTE: Existing coaches may help working on any of the coaching courses in order to gain signatures towards their assessor qualifications. If this is your intention then please contact us before arrival so you can be scheduled onto the appropriate course.

The course fees are at a special reduced rate and are payable at the time of your course. Please also note that for assessment courses a fee is also payable to the BCU.

The Nordkapp Trust

There will be day expeditions on request during the week in addition to the Coaching courses.

PLEASE NOTE: NO C1 – NO COURSE

Exhibit 24.1(a) BCU Coaching Courses information.

BCU COURSES
APPLICATION FORM

Name: _____

Address: _____

_____

_____**Postcode**_____

Tel: _____ **E mail:** _____

BCU No: (if any) _____

Existing qualifications (if any): _____

_____

If taking part in any of the Coaching awards, are you in possession of a stamped C1
form: **YES / NO** (please delete as appropriate)

I would like to participate in the following courses:
(please list ALL the courses you want to do and we will try to schedule you in for
them)

_____

_____

_____

_____

_____

Exhibit 24.1(b) BCU Coaching Courses application form.

Exhibit 24.2   Anglesey Sea Symposium information.

2002 Expeditions

The ASSC is currently planning to run a number of sea-kayaking expeditions during the year 2002. Further information can be obtained from our website www.assc.org.uk. The centre also offers the hiring of equipment/guides for Expeditions to any location.

2002 Courses

The ASSC run a number of BCU approved courses as well as specialist sea kayak courses all throughout the year. We have full information regarding these courses on our website. Alternatively you can phone or email to request one of our new brochures.
info@assc.org.uk

Exhibit 24.2 (continued)

Every level of kayaker is catered for at the symposium, from complete beginner to advanced. Some sessions are completely 'dry', utilizing one of the three teaching rooms at the centre; some combine theory with practical; and some are very wet indeed! Nearby 'overfalls' (places where the sea bed is so close to the surface that, at certain times of the tide, extensive 'standing waves' form), and other features similar to those found on wide rivers, give exciting and challenging places to practise various paddling techniques, including rescues.

How does Nigel himself define the event?

What I'm trying to do, because of our position geographically, I think that it is important that we make use of the facilities that we've got, the natural facilities such as tidal races, the overfalls, so what I'm conscious of doing is to have an action-oriented symposium, as opposed to a lecture/coaching symposium.

In the early days people wouldn't pay for a symposium, that's why we didn't have one; they'd turn up in their rusty car and camp, instead of paying for accommodation, and a lot of them actually would make their own equipment. Unfortunately in this country, it's always been a bit of a poor man's sport, whereas in the States we get the same percentage of people sea kayaking as we do sailing in this country ... but in the last 10 years we've got a growing amount of people that turn up with a Mercedes with a kayak on the roof rack ... they want en-suite accommodation ... now we can charge a better rate.

Sea kayaking is noticeably a 25 to 55 age group ... it always has been a more mature person's sport. I don't think the average age has dropped, but there are more youngsters in it now and there's a lot more people in it generally.

I'd say we get around 150 people now at the symposium [see Table 24.1]. In the key lectures in the last two years, there's been 90 to 100 people sat in the lectures. Not everyone goes to the lectures and there's always people having barbeques with kids and things like that ... some people just come and pay their camp fees and pay their entrance fee for the lectures and don't participate in the actual symposium.

Accessibility

Anglesey Sea and Surf Centre is located on the island of Anglesey, less than two miles from Holyhead, one of the major ports serving Ireland

Table 24.1   Symposium attendance figures

Year	Approx. number attending	Overseas attendees (%)
1998	90	15
1999	95	15
2000	135	20
2001	150	30
2002	150	30

from the UK (Exhibit 24.3). Road and rail links are good and the nearest international airport is Liverpool.

As an island between the UK and Ireland, Anglesey is subject to strong tidal streams along some of its coastline, which is a major attraction to both UK and overseas sea kayakers. The coastline is varied, from sheltered sandy beaches with weak tides, to cliffs where a landing is not a possibility and tides run at over 5 knots. There are a number of small islands and isolated rocks around Anglesey, including 'The Skerries' with its unmanned lighthouse, bird sanctuary and historic wreck, which make for interesting day trips by sea kayak. At times of severe weather, challenging conditions are used to deliver the highest awards of the BCU and to prepare for long and arduous sea journeys. When the weather is fine, beginners and recreational paddlers enjoy an outstanding coastline and environment.

Amenities and their relevance

For an event to be successful, the nature of the venue is usually very significant, perhaps having unusual features, unique location, or a purpose-designed environment, if not all three! The original ASSC had been a converted school in nearby Treardurr Bay:

> That original venue worked well; we moved because we needed more space and it only had big dormitories ... now we've got two or three en-suites, twins and small dorms. Ideally, we could probably do with another six en-suite rooms. It just reflects ... the type of people who have come through the sport.

Anglesey Sea & Surf Centre

Within the grounds of the Centre are the following facilities

- Full board accommodation
- Self catering accommodation
- B&B accommodation
- Fully licensed bar
- Shop - selling specialist kayak clothing & equipment
- Demo boats for Hire
- Scuba diving shop/lecture room & compressor facility
- Mouseloft Sails – The sail makers

How to find us

- Follow the A55/A5 towards Holyhead. After crossing onto Anglesey travel for approximately 36km and turn off at the Trearddur Bay Junction.
- Cross onto Holy Island and continue into Trearddur Bay itself.
- Turn left opposite the Petrol station.
- Follow the coastal road for approx. 3 km, keeping the sea on your left-hand side.
- Turn right into Lon Porthdafarch (by telephone kiosk), ASSC is the second turning on the right hand side.

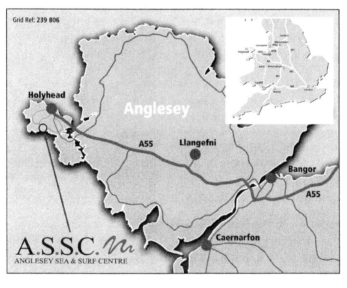

Exhibit 24.3 Anglesey Sea and Surf Centre.

381

The beauty about this location is that we've got fourteen-and-a-half acres, people can camp, and people can do what they want. We've got a bar on-site which has also made a big difference. Trying to run the other place, with people drifting off to pubs, gave us a few problems and we don't get any of those problems now . . . it would be nice not to have the bar at all, but you just have all sorts of problems if you don't.

The new Centre buildings were purpose designed by Nigel (who originally qualified as an architect) and camping around the Centre is on open, undulating ground. It is possible to be less than 60 yards from the main door and not to be able to see the Centre at all! A private, semi-wilderness, camping experience is achievable on-site. Family attendance is a feature of the event and most fine evenings, the smell of campsite barbeques wafts over the site. Tents of every size, plus caravans and mobile homes, are found all over the campsite. The nearest hotels and bed-and-breakfast providers are over a mile away, but as yet, these have not been utilized during the symposium. Even the campers make use of the options to enjoy meals in the Centre's dining room and every option from fully catered to half-board is available. The on-site bar has also recently become a provider of hot and cold bar meals and snacks.

The main Centre building has three levels. On the ground floor is a 'bunkhouse', with its own kitchen. A large drying room (an essential amenity!) is also at ground floor level.

Between the Centre and the on-site bar is a shop selling Nigel's own designs of sea kayaks (five in all) plus other clothing and equipment. Two miles away, a factory unit owned by Nigel builds those sea kayaks, mostly for export to the USA.

Porthdafarch Bay and Trearrdurr Bay are, respectively, one and five minutes' drive away, and both are excellent start points for both easy and challenging sea conditions. Treardurr Bay is a relatively large seaside resort for the island, with hotels and shops, restaurants and pubs, etc. At Porthdafarch Bay during the summer season, travelling traders provide hot and cold drinks, ice creams and fast food, and there are also public toilets.

Within 10 minutes' drive of the Centre is the 'inland sea'. This useful resource is effectively 'flat water' and easy canoeing of over a mile in length, yet is still subject to tidal influence, providing powerful moving water features at 'Four Mile Bridge' and 'Stanley Embankment'. The inland sea itself and the tidal river flowing southwards are a haven for beginners learning new skills. Nearby Holyhead Harbour is also used as a training venue for things such as night-navigation, utilizing illuminated buoyage and the other navigational lights of the port.

The symposium includes large 'key' evening lectures that are held in the Ulcheldre Centre, a community arts and performance centre housed in a converted church, in nearby Holyhead. A chartered double-decker bus takes those who do not wish to drive from the ASSC. Over 150 people can be comfortably seated; displays of artwork (some of which are for sale), gift shop and a bar are added attractions.

Significant attractions

Sea symposiums, generally speaking, often provide a very wide range of lectures, workshops, and clinics. The 1994 May Bank Holiday Jersey Sea Symposium Brochure (Exhibit 24.4) listed 23 lectures (including four travelogues) and 15 different practical sessions!

Had there been a change in the popularity of these kinds of elements, as an attraction at the Anglesey Symposium?

I think that people are keen to learn and the reason for this is partly because of the type of life that people lead. You get two types of people. You get somebody that doesn't earn much money and has a lot of time and their life is there to enjoy and money's secondary. The other class of people are from the cities, who are 'high-flyers' and they've got a short period of time in which to paddle. So it's those people who actually want the lessons and want the lectures because they're keen to short-cut the learning process ... it's been fairly standard through the years. Navigation is a 'black art' to a lot of people and so has always been popular. In the last few years survival training has become popular ... what they can catch and what they can eat off the foreshore ... I don't think that things have really changed over the years, because it's the same set of skills that you need to paddle now, as you always have done.

One of the major perceived advantages of attending a symposium is the opportunity not merely to see and talk about the different kayak designs available, but to actually try them on the sea with a view to an eventual purchase. Nigel has his own kayaks available for demonstration and trial, plus those of other manufacturers, who bring a range of their

---

PROVISIONAL PROGRAMME

SATURDAY 28 MAY – BANK HOLIDAY MONDAY 30 MAY

LECTURES

Navigation Coastal & Crossings	Basic Chart Work
Tides	History of Sea Kayaking
Expedition Planning	Night Navigation
Weather	Shipping Forecasts
Corsica	Greenland
Channel Islands	Natural History
Local Maritime History	France
Astronomy	First Aid
Planning a trip	Open Crossings
Kayak photography	Campfire cookery
Electronics in sea kayaking	Safety at sea
Dolphins	

PRACTICAL SESSIONS

Sea Kayaking Skills, Level 1,2,3	Performance sea kayaking
Rescues	On Water Navigation
Touring	Doubles
Fishing	Try a boat
Sea Prof	Tidal race session
Time trial	Rolling
Stoves & cooking	
3 x ½ day paddles	3 x 1 day paddles

TUESDAY 31 MAY

Mass paddle to the Ecrehous (weather permitting)

WEDNESDAY 1 JUNE – THURSDAY 2 JUNE

Inter-Island paddle (weather permitting)
Coastal trips
Surfing

FRIDAY 3 JUNE

Barbeque at Egypt

Exhibit 24.4 Provisional programme.

own equipment. The quantities and range of kayaks and equipment 'on show' has varied over the years. Valley Canoe products are the only ones that have been consistently present, but even they in recent years have had to come with a reduced range of ancillary equipment and clothing, due to the practicalities of running a 'mobile shop'.

I think that the biggest problem is that you don't sell a lot, at symposiums, you're never quite sure where the sales come from. If you actually cost it out ... then you wouldn't make it pay ... from the sales that you'd generated but you wouldn't know where they come from for the rest of the year, or the year after.

We get lots of requests to try demo boats ... also they're always questioning what paddle they should use. Design, length, feather, stiffness, because that's becoming a 'black art' in itself, apart from that, most people don't come to buy kit; even if they do see stuff, a lot of them are fairly loyal to their local shops.

The Saturday and Sunday 'key' lecture nights have been a major part of each year's programme. Nigel was asked about this and whether there were ways of extending this attraction:

Symposiums are a blend of learning and entertainment; a nice slide show to music, an interesting chat. I think it must be attractive because otherwise there wouldn't be so many people in the lectures. It's important to get key speakers for sure. We used to do two key speakers each evening, but we've dropped that down to one; it's quite important not to go beyond two hours.

Sometimes we've booked bands for after the lectures, back on the main site in the bar. We didn't have a band last year, or this year. When we have a band we definitely have to have two bars, because there are a percentage of people who just want to sit down and talk and there are others that want to enjoy the band.

One of the regular volunteer BCU Coaches, a musician, suggested that at the 1998 event, a 'music afloat' session might be of interest. So after the evening lectures, back at the Centre lounge and dining area, small instruments that could be taken in kayaks on trips were demonstrated in a seminar/'try-it-yourself' format. The next year the same thing happened and has since developed into a regular but informal, one-man folk/blues/country and popular music show in the lounge, supported by a bottle-bar in the kitchen. Occasionally other musicians and singers join in.

Integrated marketing of event and Centre

Nigel commented on the event as a factor in the Centre's long-term success:

> It's not a major factor, but what it does do, it puts us on the map. I suppose it could be regarded as a marketing tool, because people come, they see what we've got, they tell other people who then come back on courses.
>
> It makes for a very interesting symposium in that we do get people from all over the world. The main reason is that where we have access to tide races and overfalls. Probably 10 years ago, the majority of the Dutch people that were actually coaching had come through the ASSC Centre and then they formed the NKB in Holland, which is the equivalent of the BCU ... as for the States, people come across because we sell a lot of boats in the States, so we attract people that way. I think it's probably one of the symposium's strong points ... whereas a lot of the other symposia are just basically British.
>
> Marketing, for someone our size, is always the problem. If we were part of a bigger set-up and we had a dedicated marketing department I think that our occupancy would definitely be higher ... the demand is there, it's just the means that we have to get the word out and get the people in.
>
> Everything that we do adds a little bit more substance to the kayaks [sales]. We're doing a promotional video at the moment and I've been commissioned to write a book and some articles for some magazines, so all of that helps and that is the kind of marketing that we can afford. It's hard work and you have to spend a lot of time on it, but you're not putting your hand in your pocket all the time.

The British Canoe Union and its influence upon the event

Nigel is a Level 5 Coach of the BCU. As such he is one of a small number of UK Coaches who can run the very highest levels of BCU kayak coaching courses. Level 3 Coaches and above are trained to deliver defined levels of expedition experience. These courses form an integral part of the symposium's activities, so just how important an element is that?

> You could run an event without there being a BCU element to it, but there are a lot of people that appreciate the opportunity of picking up

the BCU qualifications. The BCU courses actually extend the symposium. So we have the three days where the actual symposium is run ... and then we go on into a five-day coaching block, with coaching courses, the Star Awards, and I suppose 30% of the people just paddle, but the bulk of the people who come for the rest of the week actually come for the coaching courses. About 30% of the symposium people stay on for the rest of the week.

I think that it'll remain important as long as the industry demands that they [Coaches] need a qualification. The demand is changing ... 10 years ago, everyone would do the old 'Advanced Proficiency', as a way of extending their learning. Now the only people who do the new 'Five Star' [which is the equivalent] are people who are actually in the industry and *need* the award. We get next to no people coming through now who are doing the Five Star at assessment level for their own benefit.

Things are changing because there are more people coming into the sport and they'll probably go to two or three symposiums and then they'll be off doing their own thing.

Staffing of the event and the issue of volunteers

Long-term contracts with educational institutions, such as the Birmingham College of Food, Tourism and Creative Studies, to deliver the practical elements of degree-level adventure tourism management courses, could have produced benefits through providing regular 'volunteer staff' for the event. Most symposiums, it seems, rely to a large extent on 'volunteer' coaches and guides. Nigel was asked how he viewed this.

We're probably one of the only symposiums that have next to no-one who does that. There's maybe two or three out of the symposium staff who actually come on that basis and that's because we've got a strong, permanent paddling staff [Exhibit 24.5]. The people who don't get paid are usually those who are assisting in order to get signatures in their log-books, in order to gain BCU Coaching Awards.

The people that we pull in, the Five Star paddlers like Fiona, Roland, Peter Bray, those people we actually pay. We pay the BCU rate, the rate that's in the handbook. We could actually run the event without the helpers and personally I think that is the best way of running. I'd say that at 90% of the other symposiums, people don't get paid.

387

SYMPOSIUM STAFF

ALL STAFF WILL HAVE SYMPOSIUM SHIRTS. THEY WILL BE ABLE TO HELP IF YOU NEED FURTHER INFORMATION.

PETER BRAY Key speaker Saturday	**THE FIRST TRANS ATLANTIC CROSSING BY SEA KAYAK.** (Paddle only) **NDK Expedition Kayaker.**
LEO HOARE Key speaker Sunday	**GREENLAND 2001**

JUSTINE CURGENVEN	Circumnavigated Wales 2001 Films documentaries and expeditions.
RICK CARRICK-SMITH	**Transport co-ordinator**
NIGEL DENNIS	1st Circumnavigation Great Britain 1980 & more. NDK Expedition Kayaker. Director NDK.
DAVE FENTON	**Director of Knoydart. VCP Demo Kayaks.**
ROBIN GOODLIFFE	**Director Valley Canoe Products.**
TIM GUNN	Survival expert. Spitsberg – South Georgia & more.
PETER JONES	Greenland & more NDK Expedition Kayaker.
GRANT MITCHELL	Overseeing NDK hire & demo Kayaks.
TRYS MORRIS	UK-Greece 2000 & more. NDK Expedition Kayaker.
RICHARD TOWNSEND	BCU COACH 4
NIGEL TIMMINS	BCU Coaching Development Officer North.
FIONA WHITEHEAD	Circumnavigation Wales 2001 & more NDK Expedition Kayaker.
ALED WILLIAMS	Cape Horne 1992 & more NDK Expedition Kayaker.
ROWLAND WOOLVREN	Vancouver Island, Irish sea crossings & more. NDK Expedition Kayaker.
DAVE WILLIAMS	**NDK manufacturing enquiries and retail.**
ANDY STAMP	
KEIRRON TASTAGH	Anglesey-Isle of Man 2001. Overseeing **Swimming pool sessions.**
SNOW	ASSC House manager. **Catering.**
LEAH THIJS	ASSC Assistant manager. **SYMPOSIUM CO-ORDINATOR.**

Telephone Nunbers:

H.M.COASTGUARD	01407762051
ASSC	01407762525
Nigel Dennis mobile	07773787220 SYMPOSIUM TROUBLE SHOOTER.
Holyhead Sports Centre	01407764111
Ucheldre Centre	01407763361

Exhibit 24.5 Symposium staff.

In the early days we did rely on volunteers and people's attitude was also different … it's turned now from hobby to an industry … we are a symposium now and do a lot of advanced stuff … the 'Nordkapp Meet' was a low-budget thing and people decided what they wanted to do and just went off paddling to different venues. That didn't really require high-calibre [qualified] staff.

As long as someone is an employee, or on my say-so, they're covered under our insurance policy. In the early years I used to have to fill out a form and get everyone approved by the insurance company, but after being in business for so many years, they're quite happy to take my say-so as to who is a suitable person and who isn't.

Profitability and critical elements affecting the event

The event could be almost be described in marketing terms as being a 'loss-leader'. The Centre would earn up to 30% more profit on a comparable week of school courses, or similar. Nigel has to take into account the extra fees paid to additional BCU Coaches hired-in for the event. Current BCU rates (in 2002) are £85 per day for a Level 5 Coach.

When asked, 'What are the most important elements in regard to keeping this event running? Is there something of overwhelming importance?', Nigel identified three major factors.

The weather! Traditionally we've been very lucky and we've had good weather on Mayday Bank Holiday.

I think for the event to grow ... it is important to have a date in the calendar that is the same every year and I also think that it is important to do an annual event rather than a biannual event. Most other events have been biannual, the Scottish Symposium, Jersey. The Scottish one runs one year and then it doesn't. In Jersey, they've talked about stopping. I don't really know if that's because they're running out of people to run it, or whether demand isn't there.

Because of changes in the BCU system, it's far harder to find courses that are going to run. We now have to have minimum numbers of students and a higher staffing ratio, so there's a far greater proportion of courses that are actually being cancelled. The good thing about our symposium is that there's so many people around, that the majority of the courses advertised actually run ... that's quite a big advantage.

Nigel was quite definite that he would continue to run the event. Questions remain, however, as to its evolving format and relevance within the wider scope of canoe sport. How can such an event change, reflecting developments within the contexts of both the sport itself and wider external influences, yet somehow retain the same attractive elements that have ensured its survival to date?

Conclusion

Nigel has identified three key factors, as he sees them, in the latter part of this chapter, that can be taken to be major elements of both this event and also (when the technical elements of other events are substituted) to be relevant generally to events planning. Accessibility, amenities and attractions remain as the core focus of such events and it is the combination of these, as found 'naturally' on Anglesey, plus those specifically designed provisions of services and products, that have ensured the expansion and survival of this particular event.

Even though the event itself is small compared to others covered in this book, processes and lessons learned will be found to be common. Attention to detail, staying close to the customer, sophisticated understanding of a dynamic environment, provision of both appropriate and unexpected benefits, and a strong focus upon quality, are those elements that must be provided for any event to survive. Add fun, adventure, achievement and entertainment and success is assured!

Questions

1 If you were asked to design a similar event at a location of your own choice, what are the major criteria that would have to be satisfied with regard to accessibility, amenities and attractions?

2 What are the advantages and disadvantages of a very wide range of optional courses, within a symposium of this type?

3 What forms of media best suit this kind of event and why are others impractical?

A critical examination of Sydney's 2000 Olympic Games

Gordon Waitt

Introduction

The Sydney 2000 Olympic Games are explored in this chapter as an urban propaganda exercise. Such a strategy is not new. The Olympic Games have been used to showcase imperialism, fascism, communism as well as capitalism (Araud and Riordan, 1998). However, the economic and political contexts of Sydney at the end of the twentieth century make the spectacle associated with the twenty-seventh Olympiad unique. The chapter starts by examining the role of Olympics in repositioning Sydney and Australia within the global economy. For Sydney, born of mercantile capitalism, the Olympics provided a mechanism to assist the city reposition itself centre-stage in the world economy. Cities and nations fashioned within the symbolism of the Olympic rhetoric become winning locations for international business. Next, the bidding and organizing of Sydney's Olympics is examined in a political context where predominance was given to entrepreneurial activity over the welfare state. Particular attention is given to the marginalization of Sydney residents within the decision-making processes over the soil remediation at the Olympic site and the silencing of any opposition to the Games as 'un-Australian'. The final section explores the social impacts within the arguments of 'civic-boosterists', who claim that, operating at the level of feeling, the socially disadvantaged would be swept along in the euphoria of the event, entertained by sporting spectacle. In Sydney's case it would appear that the emotional response to the Games was not necessarily associated with occupational status but instead with age, family status and ethnic identity. Apparently, the party atmosphere sustained by the sporting spectacle generated a sense of patriotism and belonging.

The 2000 Olympic Games and integrating Sydney into a global economy

Sydney, founded as a colonial metropolis, had always occupied a marginal location in a European or North American centred capitalist world economy. Sydney, as a remote South Pacific port supplying raw materials predominantly to Britain, was almost inconsequential in global terms. Sydney was positioned on the fringe of the world capitalist economic stage. Sydney, in many overseas public imaginaries throughout the twentieth century, if known at all, remained a colonial outpost, a gateway to the Australian frontier.

However, a series of opportunities were to challenge this marginal position in the world economy at the close of the twentieth century. Massive deindustrialization throughout all the older industrial countries and the realignment of economies along demands of global capitalism provided circumstances for Sydney to reposition itself as a 'world city'. Following the political-economic crisis of the 1970s and 1980s, a new economic 'fix' was required for a Sydney profoundly affected and reshaped by massive deindustrialization and the new demands of global capitalism (Murphy and Watson, 1990; Lepani et al., 1995; O'Connor and Stimson, 1995; Bounds and Morris, 2001). In this context, the federal and state bureaucracy, entrepreneurs and property developers seized the opportunity to restructure Sydney into the orbit of global capitalism through making provisions for international banking (Daly, 1982) and facilities catering for emerging service industries including 'high-tech' and 'creative' industries (Watson, 1990). In short, Sydney was to become a regional-financial headquarters within the Asia-Pacific. In addition, a new economic base was to be derived from the 'cultural economy' including music, software, web design, film and television and 'design-related activities' such as fashion, advertising or architectural services (Scott, 1997: 323; Connell and Gibson, 2002).

Infrastructure improvements alone do not explain the repositioning of Sydney within the world economy. As elsewhere, place marketing was an integral part of a well-documented process of refashioning and includes event-led planning, gentrification and the growth of theme parks, malls and heritage sites. Each emphasized the city as a site of spectacle and the processes of aestheticization (Jacobs, 1999). Place marketing for an international event such as an Olympics allowed a whole city to be refashioned (Figure 25.1). As Ward and Gold expressed, the stakes are high for global sporting events: 'the victors not only earn success in one specific contest but also enhance their promotional curricula vitae compared to their rivals' (1994: 1). The differentiation provided by hosting an Olympics arguably increases, as capital becomes increasingly mobile, and competition intensifies between cities in 'place wars' for their 'market share' of internationally mobile jobs and investment (Kotler *et al.*, 1993). Success attracts not only the spending of large international audiences but is also believed to help foster positive images for potential corporate investors (Bonnemaison, 1990). As spatial boundaries diminish in an increasingly global economy, what different world locations actually or appear to contain are argued to become more rather than less important (Harvey, 1989). Even if the Olympics itself runs at financial loss, the act of hosting the Games is believed to attract other investment forms. In short, hosting the Games arguably enabled Sydney an enhanced world-market profile.

The 2000 Olympic Games and refashioning Sydney as a world city

In Sydney's case the bid themes of 'winning' facilities, multicultural society and pristine environment were critical to repackaging Sydney as a 'world city' that lives by the Olympic Movement's charter of interna-

Figure 25.1 Sydney fashioned as a winning place during the Olympics. *Top:* Sydney's Central Business District and Darling Harbour. *Bottom:* Sydney Harbour Bridge.

tional goodwill. The marketing language reconfigured Sydney's airport, transport and sports facilities and services in a similar fashion to an Olympic athlete's body with its emphasis on precision and winning by being the strongest, fastest, or most efficient (Bale and Sang, 1996). The bid portrayed Sydney's multicultural character as personifying the very essence of a world city because of its alleged tolerance of ethnic diversity. According to the Sydney Olympic Bid Limited (SOBL), 'In Sydney, attitudes, language, religion and food mix easily in friendliness and fairness. The result is a rich cultural community, a city of 140 cultures and over 180 languages' (SOBL, 1993). The SOBL utilized the dominant public discourse of Australia's successful multiculturalism to promote Sydney as a city without inequality. The bid left unchallenged questions of divergent wealth and employment opportunities (sociospatial polarization) and the continuing discrimination against Sydney's ethnic minorities and urban-indigenous peoples.

The bid represented Sydney as a world city that had successfully embraced ecological sustainable development by employing signifiers of both 'paradise' and 'wilderness', for example sunshine, sunsets, dolphins, beaches, palm trees and luxuriant tropical vegetation (Waitt, 1999). Apparently, Sydney's 4 million residents live in an extraordinarily pristine environment. The everyday problems of soil, air and water pollution are noticeable by their absence. In the SOBL's Sydney, suburbia disappears and Sydney Harbour is portrayed as if surrounded by tropical rainforests. Not surprisingly, the society portrayed through the process of refashioning Sydney as a world city to host an Olympics matches exactly the values envisaged by the founder of the modern Olympics, Barron Peirre de Coubertine.

The Sydney 2000 Olympics and urban entrepreneurialism

Since the 1970s, Australia's urban governance, as elsewhere in the older capitalist economies, has been informed by 'entrepreneurial' rather than the previous 'managerial' approach to addressing the widespread economic erosion and fiscal crisis of large cities (McGuirk et al., 1996). Urban entrepreneurialism informed by the 'New Right' agenda includes the virtues of individualism, self-help, public–private partnerships and private property. Within urban entrepreneurialism, obstacles to attaining economic growth include planning regulation, public participation and social equity considerations. Privatization of social services and the emergence of entrepreneurial public–private partnerships for redevelopment and revitalization of city ventures signalled both the severe constraints on public finance and disillusionment with a political ideology of state intervention. Not surprisingly, given the direct participation of private capital in planning ventures, city agencies are behaving like private real-estate developers. A blurring has thus occurred of the distinction between public provision for social goals and private production for economic opportunity and individual profit. Rather than policies of welfare provision, the 'business' of urban development increasingly uses the promotion strategies and tactics of the profit-making sector to increase its share of the capital investment from entrepreneurs, tourists or local consumers

(Roche, 1994). Entrepreneurial urban governance was manifested in the planning of the Sydney 2000 Olympics (Owen, 2002). Dunn and McGuirk (1999: 21) identified at least four problematic outcomes of the entrepreneurial elected and non-elected governing authorities: subsidizing private sector interests at the cost of public concerns; the dilution of local planning powers; the limitation of public participation; and the homogenization of community opinion. Examples of the problematic outcomes of urban entrepreneurialism are explored in the context of the state-owned Olympic site, Homebush.

The dilution of local planning powers and public participation

A number of non-elected governing authorities have been responsible for managing the Olympic site, including the NSW Property Service Group, Homebush Bay Development Corporation and the Sydney Organizing Committee for the Olympic Games (SOCOG). In 1991, the state effectively gave itself *carte blanche* over the land remediation processes at Homebush when the NSW Department of Planning exempted all earth works from the mandatory requirement to prepare an Environmental Impact Statement (EIS), extending in 1992 to all 'designated' or 'significant' Olympic developments. One key objective of an EIS is to alert the decision maker, members of the public and the government to the consequences of a project and to explore alternatives. Effectively under the new legislation the state government became accountable only to itself. Without an EIS the NSW Minister for Planning had full authority to give consent for development of Olympic facilities. Jeff Angel (1993), the director of the Total Environment Centre, noted that without an EIS the government became 'a law unto itself'. Justification by the NSW Minister for Planning for such exemption was to facilitate the Olympic projects within budgetary, time and performance constraints (North and Cook, 1993).

Consequently, without an EIS, results from a series of environmental reports on levels of contamination at Homebush, completed for the NSW Property Service Group, were never made public. An environmentalist, Sharon Beder, secured access to these documents through the Freedom of Information Act. The environmental scientists' reports suggested that a number of contamination problems afflicted the site, particularly heavy metals (arsenic, chromium, copper, iron, magnesium, zinc) and organic chemicals including dioxins and pesticides (Property Services Group, 1992). Beder's own attempts to publish these findings in *New Scientist* were also restrained by the Homebush Bay Development Corporation

(Beder, 2000). The editors of *New Scientist* feared that without articles on the environmental credentials of competing cities, the magazine would be blamed if Sydney lost the bid. Apparently, through ceding the games to urban entrepreneurialism a veil of secrecy was to be drawn over the toxins at the site.

Without the transparency of an EIS, concerned residents and some environmentalists continuously raised questions over the social and environmental 'costs' of such 'fast-tracking' practices (Dunn and McGuirk, 1999). In 1992, within this diluted planning environment, workshops involving contractors and local residents replaced an EIS as the NSW Property Service Group prepared Homebush's remediation strategy. The Group allegedly considered various options including segregating and treating the wastes, sealing up and walling in the wastes in a secure landfill, and a containment landfill (capping the toxic materials and collecting the leachates as they percolate into the underlying groundwater). At Homebush the third option was pursued for the majority of the site after the expense of the secure landfill trial at the Olympic swimming facility. Interestingly, this containment strategy contradicted the Australian and New Zealand Environment and Conservation Council (ANZECC) and the National Health and Medical Research Council (NHMRC) published guidelines for contaminated sites, which prefers *treatment* of the soil either on- or off-site over containment (ANZECC/ NHMRC, 1992). In the absence of an EIS, the planning process exemplifies a series of mechanisms employed by the entrepreneurial state that arguably fast-tracked development in private sector interests.

The role of the local media in the homogenization of 'community' opinion

The local media cannot be overlooked in the homogenizing of Sydneysiders' opinions. Media executives Kerry Packer (owner of Consolidated PressHoldings), Ken Cowley (chief executive of Murdoch's News Ltd), and John Alexander (then editor-in-chief of the *Sydney Morning Herald* (*SMH*)) all accepted invitations to sit on the SOBL committee. In addition, a number of radio stations and all three commercial television channels were either direct sponsors of the bid or members of the SOBL (Darcy and Veal, 1994). Self-censorship is certainly implied in the remark by *SMH* journalist Mark Coultan: 'Journalists who write stories which might be seen as critical are reminded of their boss's support and told that their stories would be used against Sydney by other cities' (quoted in Bacon, 1993: 4). The *SMH* environmental reporter Murray Hogarth (1997: 101) voiced the opinion when reflecting on reporting during the period that to Sydney's Olympic authorities 'the Games has had the status of a sacred cow ... to publish ill of the Olympics was sacrilege, if not outright treason'. Consequently, in 1992 when the levels of toxic waste at Homebush were reported, the *SMH* captured only the dismissive comments of Phil Cox, the site design team leader, who reputedly said, 'It's not though we have Chernobyl on our hands here – they are toxins from household garbage'. Rod McGeogh, chief executive of SOBL, added that 'toxins on Olympic sites are not new. Barcelona, Atlanta, Munich and even Melbourne had to deal with toxins on their sites' (Hawley, 1992). Apparently, given that toxins were not new, they were also not of public concern. Instead, Sydney's 'green' environmental credentials were sustained through the media. The extent of toxic contamination was also arguably effectively silenced by media self-censorship throughout Sydney's bid.

At times during the bid when media vigilance became more apparent, the various Sydney Olympic authorities resorted to verbal threats and condemnation of 'un-Australian' criticism (Bacon, 1993: 2). Such threats drew their jurisdiction from the role sport occupies in the mythology of Australian nationalism. Sport, in the absence of a defining national war of independence, can bestow victory in its pseudo-warlike role. Traits apparently demonstrated on sporting fields have been appropriated as desirable, unique Australian characteristics, including persistence, stoicism, determination and resilience (Kell, 2000: 26). Labelling reproaches as 'anti-' or 'un-Australian' the Games authorities positioned any criticism as contrary to the legitimate national interest. Compliance of the individual was called for in demonstrating loyalty to the nation. For example, when the *SMH* ran the article 'We'd win a gold medal for burying heads in the smog' (Kennedy, 1992), Rod McGeoch, the chief executive of the SOBL, deemed the media unpatriotic. John Valder, corporate chairperson of SOBL, on the Australian Broadcasting Corporation Radio programme 'AM', scathingly spoke of the 'double-ABC'. This, he explained, was the 'Anti-Australian Broadcasting Corporation', which the ABC had become because of its 'constant negative putting down of this country' (reported in Hickie, 1993: 12). In the case of the Four Corners investigation into the bidding process, to be aired in July 1993, Bruce Baird, the then NSW Minister for the Games, asserted that 'anyone who threatens Sydney's Olympic bid better watch out' (PM Australian Broadcasting Commission Radio, 16 July 1993; quoted in Booth and Tatz, 1996: 10). Those reporters who were more critical of the land remediation process allegedly received verbal threats from a former state Minister (Hogarth, 1997). Such threats suggested that anyone who voiced opposition to the Games spoke against the national interest.

The critical role Sydney's media played in creating a favourable climate for hosting the Games and kindling euphoria is also acknowledged by bid chief Rod McGeoch (McGeoch, 1994). Indeed it was Australia's media that tagged Sydney 2000 Games unofficially as the 'Green Games' to help differentiate the bid, almost masking the official labels of the 'Athlete's Games' and 'Millennium Games'. Therefore, Richard Palfreyman's (1997: 98) suggestion that the media were 'extremely enthusiastic about the Games' must be placed within the Games' broader political economy. Australian media self-censorship during the bidding process guaranteed that opposing portrayals would not be circulated, helping to homogenize public opinion.

The Sydney 2000 Olympics and civic boosterism

According to the civic boosterism school, successfully hosting a major sporting event enables the political and urban managerial elite to re-fashion collective feeling, identity, emotion and consciousness (Cox and Wood, 1994). Theoretical explanations for why such a refashioning of collective emotion is necessary at the turn of a new millennium revolve around the alienating nature of contemporary society and social polarization with the emergence of world cities in the transition to global capitalism (see Baudrillard, 1988; Lash, 1990). For Sydney, whilst debates exist over such matters as appropriate measures (Walmsley and Weinand, 1997), attention to geographical scale (Baum, 1997), boundaries (Withers et al., 1995), models (Badcock, 1997) and representations (Mee, 1994; Hodge, 1996), many researchers generally agree that social polarization is present. In terms of real income the greatest divergence has occurred between Sydney's western and lower north shore suburbs.

According to a Marxian political economy perspective, major sports events are propaganda exercises undertaken by various actors dependent on the success of a local economy – capitalist firms and politicians (Cox and Mair, 1988). Such propaganda exercises are not new (Jarvis, 1994); however, they have gained additional status with the emergence of global capitalism. The spectacle of global sporting events, as urban promotion projects, helps to dispel the culture of nihilism allegedly generated by globalization. Events become a mechanism by which the centralized structures of economic power prevent social unrest between the high- and low-income strata by controlling and providing the public with appropriate sites, signs and symbols. Brantlinger (1983) and Harvey (1989) invoked the Roman formulae of 'bread and circuses' to explain the redemptive significance of hallmark events. Winning an Olympic Games bid and the following spectacle is argued to distract those who have taken their place at the bottom of a restructured social stratification ladder as a consequence of the processes of social polarization.

The refashioning of residents' collective emotion is evoked, excited and sustained by the spectacle of the event, rekindling a sense of pride in place and community identity (Boyle, 1997; Cox and Mair, 1988; Jonas, 1991; Wood, 1993). Theoretically, citizens develop a sense of pride and self-esteem from the event, expressed in a feeling of 'we can do it' (Mueller and Fenton, 1989: 275) and a belief that the event will ensure securing the city a prominent and prosperous place in the global economy. Successfully hosting a major hallmark event can be expected to generate feelings of national, city and community pride (Ley and Olds, 1988). People forget their oppressions and class and ethnic differences under the weight of the entertainment provided by the event – in Hiller's (1995) terms the 'showcase effect'. This restyling of civic identity Boyle (1997: 1976) termed the 'redemptive ideology of locality' (Figure 25.2).

In this reading of events, they function to legitimize political projects that function primarily in the interests of business and political elite, whilst creating and sustaining a local and/or national collective identity that undermines internal social divides along class or ethnic lines. Events, such as the Olympics, are argued to generate a euphoric mass consciousness through the excitement, civic achievement and party syndrome associated with the occasion (Brantlinger, 1983; Harvey, 1989a) [JB58]. According to arguments presented by the civic boosterism school, local residents do not contest such 'urban propaganda projects'.

Sydney, Australia: a winning city in a sporting nation

Surveys designed to measure the affect of Sydney's Games suggest that, from 1998 to 2000, respondents held very positive attitudes (Waitt, 2001; 2003). The level of feelings during the Olympic period for the majority of respondents is perhaps best described as 'euphoric'. During the Games, a sense of belonging to a national and Sydney 'community' was the most commonly expressed reward from hosting the Olympics. These two

Figure 25.2 Sydney Olympics and restyling civic identity. *Top left:* Crowds gather in the CBD to watch free large television screens. *Top right:* Vantage points on Sydney Harbour became popular sites to watch sailing events. *Bottom left:* Sydney streets are transformed into elite sportscapes. *Bottom right:* Spectators 'share the spirit' on the Olympic Boulevard, Homebush.

themes are expressed in the words of three Sydneysiders as follows: 'The Olympics have inspired pride in the country', '... everyone who went to the Olympics was on a natural high, I have never seen such enthusiasm and pride in Australia', and, 'The community spirit is amazing. Just being in Sydney was amazing even if you didn't go to The Games.' Therefore, for many Sydneysiders, in a city and nation where sports are already integral to the formation of local and national identities, the Olympics confirmed an actual sense of belonging to these communities.

Many respondents also envisaged the Olympics as a mechanism that might help dismiss widely circulating popular cultural myths of an Australia informed by its distinctive marsupials rather than its human achievements. These views were expressed in the comment that 'The Olympics raised consciousness of the entire world to Australia [pause] its beauty [pause] not a backward nation with kangaroos in the street that is often the overseas view. You know, we managed to host an Olympics without stuff-ups, apart from the torch.' Many Sydneysiders also responded that 'international promotion' was another substantial reward, stemming from the belief that, after the Olympics, Australia would no longer be an unknown destination, a nowhere place. As one respondent remarked, 'Australia would be put on top of the world; many nations have not known Australia's advantages.' An important psychological reward for many Sydneysiders from hosting the Olympics included the belief that the place where they lived, Australia more generally and Sydney in particular, had now achieved a greater international profile, standing and recognition.

The Olympics understood as a force for social equality

Interestingly, Sydney's Olympics, from the period of anticipation to actualization, regardless of place of residence, income or occupation, always held greatest appeal for younger adults, families with children and migrants from non-English-speaking backgrounds. Despite a legacy of discrimination and oppression, several parents spoke of how, in their experience, the Olympics helped in various ways to dissipate perceived differences between people and to illustrate to their offspring the principles of global citizenship, social equity and respect for cultural difference. Two parents articulated this opinion as follows: 'The Olympics is such a worthwhile event to put on [pause] uniting a city and the world [pause] upholding many ideals' and 'The Games are special, each person is counted as equal.' Apparently, amongst the audience who were most enthusiastic about the Olympics the event's rhetoric of social equality still takes precedence over athletes' experiences of discrimination sustained by the nationalism, heterosexism and elitism of the Games.

Similarly, amongst many Sydneysiders with non-Anglo-Celtic ethnicities, the Olympics inspired feelings of inclusiveness in a Sydney-based community. This was expressed in a number of ways including: 'I will always remember walking down the Olympic Boulevards with crowds, it was such a buzz to be part of something this big', 'the friendliness of everyone to everybody, total strangers would just roll up and start a conversation', and, 'it doesn't matter where you go in Sydney you can sense a camaraderie and friendliness'. These Sydneysiders often spoke of the Olympics as sustaining experiences of inclusion and togetherness. Such rewards perhaps confirm optimistic arguments that global sporting events are able to provide a mechanism by which its audience members, especially those who personally identify with minority groups, can also form a stronger identity with a particular city or nation.

Conclusions

International sports events are themselves not new. However, they have acquired a renewed significance in the context of globalization. In economic terms the collapse of spatial boundaries has increased the sensitivity of capital to differences between places. Consequently, intensified competition occurs between places in the global market to attract potential investors, employers and tourists. The successful bidding and hosting of a prestige hallmark event over other cities enables the host city to promote, market, differentiate and image itself as a winning location. In Sydney therefore nothing was left to chance. Illustrating the philosophy of entrepreneurial urban governance a special company was created to bid for the games, SOBL, that had a multimillion-dollar budget and employed professional marketing companies to sell Sydney. By hosting the 2000 Olympic Games it was realized that Sydney would become 'home' to a global television audience for 16 days, providing an opportunity to refashion Sydney from an unknown colonial outpost to a cosmopolitan world city.

Refashioning of the Olympic site itself also must be considered in the context of an urban redevelopment programme conceived in an era of entrepreneurial planning. The authoritative voices of organizations established by New Right policies always positioned the redevelopment of the site unequivocally as an international showpiece of 'green' design and technology. However, the voices of some environmental activists and local residents regarded the 'green' Games as an alibi. Arguably, these voices have been marginalized through the operation of powers given to the entrepreneurial partnerships of the New Right planning policies that minimized local participation and exercised control over the media (Beder, 2000). Certain members of Sydney's Olympic authorities clearly used their privileged position in government or business to cast any criticism as un-Australian. Australia's frequently discussed obsession with sport was capitalized upon to ensure censure.

As theorized by the civic boosterism school's 'bread and circuses' argument, a euphoric mass consciousness was generated amongst Sydneysiders before and during the Games. Unquestionably, a significant psychological reward for many respondents was that of the imagined bond that underpins national identity and a Sydney community that became a lived reality for many respondents over the 16 days of the Games. Furthermore, it was those living in Sydney's most socio-economically disadvantaged suburbs that became most enthusiastic. However, it would appear that age, ethnicity and family structure differentiated respondents in their psychological response, rather than class as theorized within the civic boosterism school.

Whilst the euphoria surrounding the Games has passed, the NSW state government's most recent urban development corporation, Sydney Olympic Park, still calls upon the golden memories of an Olympic-inspired sense of social cohesion and affinity in its most recent 'community' events and development plans for Homebush. Sydney Olympic Park's 'special' events programme has harnessed the public euphoria surrounding 16 days in September 2000 to try and ensure that Sydney's Olympic venues do not become 'white elephants'. Memories of shared fun, enjoyment, family, happiness, laughter, friendships, nationalism and pride are used to fuel interest in attending a range of sports and arts events hosted at Homebush. Future development proposals to create a business and residential node around the sports complex remain closely linked to the Olympics, signifying the coming of age of Sydney in a global economy. How urban planning intersects in the future with the symbolic meanings of the site generated by hosting the 2000 Olympics makes Homebush an interesting space to watch. Interest is only heightened by the controversies that exist over the land remediation programme.

Bibliography

Angel, J. (1993). Sydney's Olympic bid fails key environmental test. *Total Environment Centre Media Release*, 17 June.

Araud, P. and Riordan, P. (1998). *Sport and International Politics: The Impact of Fascism and Communism on Sport*. New York: Routledge.

Australian and New Zealand Environment and Conservation Council and the National Health and Medical Research Council (ANZECC/NHMRC) (1992). *Australian and New Zealand Guidelines for the Assessment and Management of Contaminated Sites*. Melbourne: ANZECC/NHMRC.

Bacon, W. (1993). Watchdog's bark muffled. *Reportage*, September, 3–5.

Badcock, B. (1997). Recently observed polarizing tendencies and Australian cities. *Australian Geographical Studies*, **35(3)**, 243–259.

Bale, J. and Sang, J. (1996). *Kenyan Running. Movement Culture, Geography and Global Change*. London: Frank Cass.

Baudrillard, J. (1988). *America*. London: Verso.

Baum, S. (1997). Sydney, Australia: a global city? Testing the social polarization thesis. *Urban Studies*, **34(11)**, 1881–1903.

Beder, S. (2000). *Global Spin: The Corporate Assault on Environmentalism*. Revised edition. Melbourne: Scribe Publications.

Bonnemaison, S. (1990). City policies and cyclical events. *Design Quarterly*, **147**, 24–32.

Booth, D. and Tatz, C. (1993–94). Sydney 2000: the games people play, *Current Affairs Bulletin*, **70**, 4–11.

Bounds, M. and Morris, A. (2001). Economic restructuring and gentrification in the inner city. A case study of Pyrmont Ultimo. *Australian Planner*, **38(3)**, 128–132.

Boyle, M. (1997). Civic boosterism in the politics of local economic development – 'institutional positions' and 'strategic orientations' in the consumption of hallmark events. *Environment and Planning A*, **29**, 1975–1997.

Brantlinger, P. (1983). *Bread and Circuses: Theories of Mass Culture as Social Decay*. Ithaca, NY: Cornell University Press.

Connell, J. and Gibson, C. (2002). *Sound Tracks: Popular Music, Identity and Place*. London and New York: Routledge.

Cox, K. and Mair, A. (1988). Locality and community in the politics of local economic development. *Annals of the Association of American Geographers*, **78**, 307–325.

Cox, K. and Wood, A. (1994). Local government and local economic development in the United States. *Regional Studies*, **28**, 640–645.

Daly, M.T. (1982). *Sydney Boom, Sydney Bust*. Sydney: Allen and Unwin.

Darcy, S. and Veal, A.J. (1994). The Sydney 2000 Olympic Games: the story so far. *Leisure Options: Australian Journal of Leisure and Recreation*, **4(1)**, 5–14.

Dunn, K.M. and McGuirk, P.M. (1999). Hallmark events. In *Staging the Olympics: the event and its impact* (R. Cashman and A. Hughes, eds). Sydney: University of New South Wales Press, pp. 18–34.

Harvey, D. (1989). *The Condition of Postmodernity: An Enquiry into the Origins of Cultural Change*. Oxford: Blackwell.

Hawley, J. (1992). An Olympian brawl over quay west. *Sydney Morning Herald*, 25 January, 38.

Hickie, J.D. (1993). 'Editorial: Un-Australian Olympic Games. *Sydney Morning Herald*, 13 August, 12.

Hiller, H.H. (1995). Conventions as mega-events. *Tourism Management*, **16(5)**, 375–379.

Hodge, S. (1996). Disadvantage and 'otherness' in Western Sydney. *Australian Geographical Studies*, **34**, 32–44.

Hogarth, M. (1997). The media, the community and the green games publicity. In *The Green Games: A Golden Opportunity* (R. Cashman and A. Hughes, eds), pp. 101–102. Proceedings of a conference organized by the Centre for Olympic Studies, The University of New South Wales, 12 September.

Jacobs, J.M. (1999). Staging difference: aestheticization and the politics of difference in contemporary cities. In *Cities of Difference* (R. Fincher and J.M. Jacobs, eds), pp. 252–278. London: The Guildford Press.

Jarvis, B. (1994). Transitory topographies: places, events, promotions and propaganda. In *Place Promotion, the Use of Publicity and Marketing to Sell Towns and Regions* (J.R. Gold and S.V. Ward, eds), pp. 181–194. Chichester: John Wiley and Sons.

Jonas, A. (1991). A place for politics in urban theory: the organization and strategies of urban coalitions. *Urban Geography*, **13**, 280–290.

Kell, P. (2000). *Good Sports: Australian Sport and the Myth of the Fair Go.* Sydney: Pluto Press.

Kennedy, A. (1992). We'd win gold for burying head in the smog. *Sydney Morning Herald*, 5 June, 15.

Kotler, P., Haidder, D.H. and Rein, I. (1993). *Marketing Places: Attracting Investment and Tourism to Cities, States and Nations.* New York: Free Press.

Lash, S. (1990). *The Sociology of Postmodernism.* London: Routledge.

Lepani, B., Freed, G., Murphy, P. and McGillivray, A. (1995). *The Economic Role of Cities: Australia in the Global Economy.* Commonwealth Department of Housing and Regional Development. Canberra: Australian Government Publishing Service (AGPS).

Ley, D. and Olds, K. (1988). Landscape as spectacle, world's fairs and the culture of heroic consumption. *Environment and Planning D: Society and Space*, **6**, 191–212.

McGeoch, R. (1994). *Bid: How Australia Won the 2000 Games.* Port Melbourne: Heinemann.

McGuirk, P.M., Winchester, H.P.M. and Dunn, K.M. (1996). Entrepreneurial approaches to urban decline: the Honeysuckle redevelopment in inner Newcastle, New South Wales. *Environment and Planning A*, **28**, 1815–1841.

Mee, K. (1994). Dressing-up the suburbs: representations of Western Sydney. In *Metropolis Now: Planning and the Urban in Contemporary Australia* (K. Gibson and S. Watson, eds), pp. 60–77. Sydney: Pluto Press.

Mueller, W.S. and Fenton, D.M. (1989). Psychological and community issues. In *The Planning and Evaluation of Hallmark Events* (G.J. Syme, B.J. Shaw, D.M. Fenton and W.S. Mueller), pp. 250–262. Aldershot: Avebury.

Murphy, P. and Watson, S. (1990). Restructuring of Sydney's Central Industrial Area: process and local impacts. *Australian Geographical Studies*, **28**, 78–87.

North, S. and Cook, D. (1993). 'Immediate' benefits if Games come. *Sydney Morning Herald*, 17 June, 7.

O'Connor, K. and Stimson, R. (1995). *The Economic Role of Cities: Economic Change and City Development, Australia, 1971–1991.* Commonwealth

Department of Housing and Regional Development, Urban Futures Research Progam. Canberra: AGPS.

Owen, K.A. (2002). The Sydney 2000 Olympics and urban entrepreneurialism: local variations in urban governance. *Australian Geographical Studies*, **40**, 323–336.

Palfreyman, R. (1997). The media, the community and the green games publicity. In *The Green Games: A Golden Opportunity* (R. Cashman and A. Hughes, eds), pp. 97–100. Proceedings of a conference organized by the Centre for Olympic Studies, The University of New South Wales, 12 September.

Property Services Group (1992). *Briefing Documents on Site Remediation and Environmental Investigations at Homebush Bay*, March 1992. Sydney: NSW Property Service Group.

Roche, M. (1994). Mega-events and urban policy. *Annals of Tourism Research*, **21**, 1–19.

Scott, A.G. (1997). The cultural economy of cities. *International Journal of Regional Research*, **21**, 323–339.

Sydney Olympic Bid Limited (SOBL) (1993). *Sydney 2000 Olympics Bid, Bid Documents*. Sydney: Sydney Olympics 2000 Bid Limited.

Waitt, G. (1999). Playing games with Sydney: marketing Sydney for the 2000 Olympics. *Urban Studies*, **36(7)**, 1055–1077.

Waitt, G. (2001). The Olympic spirit and civic boosterism: the Sydney 2000 Olympics. *Tourism Geographies*, **3(3)**, 249–278.

Waitt, G. (2003). Social impacts of the Sydney Olympics. *Annals of Tourism Research*, **30(1)**, 194–215.

Walmsley, D.J. and Weinand, H.C. (1997). Fiscal federalism and social well-being in Australia. *Australian Geographical Studies*, **28**, 260–270.

Ward, S.V. and Gold, J.R. (1994). Introduction. In: *Place Promotion: The Use of Publicity and Marketing to Sell Towns and Regions* (J.R. Gold and S.V. Ward), pp. 1–18. Chichester: John Wiley and Sons.

Watson, S. (1990). Gilding the smokestacks: the new symbolic representations of deindustrialized regions. *Environment and Planning D: Society and Space*, **9**, 59–70.

Withers, G., Clarke, R. and Johnston, K. (1995). *Income Distribution in Australia: Recent Trends and Research*. Canberra: AGPS.

Wood, A. (1993). Organizing for local economic development: local economic development networks and prospecting for industry. *Environment and Planning A*, **25**, 1649–1661.

Questions

1 Why have international sporting events, such as the Olympics, become highly sought after by national, state and city bureaucracies?

2 What potential problems arise from organizing an international sport event within an urban managerial policy context of urban entrepreneurialism?

3 Why have the social impacts of hosting an international sport event been conceptualized with the theory of 'bread and circuses'?

Index